The House
THE
BERRYS BUILT

The House
THE
BERRYS BUILT

Duff Hart-Davis

Hodder & Stoughton
LONDON SYDNEY AUCKLAND TORONTO

British Library Cataloguing in Publication Data

Hart-Davis, Duff
  The house the Berrys built.
   1. Newspapers with London imprints. Daily Telegraph &
  Sunday Telegraph, history.
  I. Title
  072.1

ISBN 0-340-52526-6

First published in Great Britain 1990

Published by Hodder and Stoughton,
a division of Hodder and Stoughton Ltd,
Mill Road, Dunton Green, Sevenoaks, Kent TN13 2YA.
Editorial Office: 47 Bedford Square, London WC1B 3DP.

Photoset by Rowland Phototypesetting Ltd
Bury St Edmunds, Suffolk

Printed in Great Britain by
St Edmundsbury Press Ltd Bury St Edmunds, Suffolk
and bound by Hartnolls Ltd, Bodmin, Cornwall

CONTENTS

ILLUSTRATIONS

All photographs are from the *Telegraph* Photograph Archive, unless otherwise credited.

Between pages 240 and 241

The new building at South Quay.
The new print works at West Ferry Road.
Lord Hartwell presiding over a board meeting, December 1985.[4]
Directors of the *Telegraph*, 1988.
Conrad Black.
Andrew Knight.

[1] Royal Commission on the Historical Monuments of England.
[2] *Country Life* magazine.
[3] Desmond O'Neill Features
[4] Press Association Photos.

For all my friends who toiled and wrought and thought with me at No. 135 Fleet Street.

1 THE BERRYS OF MERTHYR TYDFIL

Late in the 1950s the actress Elizabeth Taylor flew to London for a holiday. Then at the height of her beauty, if not yet at the peak of her notoriety, she had come to recuperate after an illness, and at Heathrow Airport she was besieged by reporters firing questions. 'How are you?' they cried. 'How are you doing?' To which she replied, 'I'm feeling like a million dollars.'

Next morning, in dozens of different newspapers, the remark was published the length and breadth of Great Britain. Only *The Daily Telegraph* saw fit to render it as 'I'm feeling like a million dollars (£357,000)'. Only *The Daily Telegraph*, in slavish devotion to its house rules, could have published anything so absurd. No other national newspaper could have made itself so ridiculous without noticing.

On another occasion, not long before that, the paper sent one of its foreign correspondents to report the Suez crisis. Finding himself in difficulties with the Egyptian authorities, he included in one despatch the word 'heliotrope': one of several code-words used to convey hidden meanings, it warned that his reports were being censored. The sub-editors, however, failed to take the hint and printed his despatch verbatim – with the result that the *Telegraph* carried a ludicrous passage about heliotrope sunsets over the Nile.

How could a great newspaper have become so hidebound, so much the victim of its own grey formulas? To answer this question, one must travel back nearly a hundred years to the industrial town of Merthyr Tydfil, in the mountains of South Wales, where the Berry family flourished; and in particular, one must study the careers of two members of that family – William Berry, first Viscount Camrose, and his son Michael Berry, later Lord Hartwell – who between them ran *The Daily Telegraph* for fifty-seven years with a single-minded devotion unique among Fleet Street proprietors.

The Berrys came to Merthyr from the far west of Wales, and the extraordinary feature of the family was that all three boys of one generation rose from humble beginnings to make good in the most spectacular fashion. Seymour, William and Gomer – the sons of Alderman John Mathias Berry, JP – all became lords and millionaires, reaching great heights of achievement and renown entirely by their own exertions.

John Mathias Berry was born in Haverfordwest, Pembrokeshire, on 2 May 1847. He lived for some time in the village of Camrose, then in the nearby hamlet of Wolfsdale, and on 24 May 1870 married Mary Anne Rowe, a girl from Pembroke Dock. He was tall and slim, a good, kind man who wore a beard that turned white in later life; both he and his wife were strict Nonconformists, and allowed no carousing of any kind on the Sabbath. Mary, too, was a strong character who inspired immense affection: her sons remained devoted to her throughout her life, wrote to her frequently about their progress and, when she died, put together a small book about her so that their own children might learn of her remarkable qualities.

It is not clear what J. M. Berry did for a living in Pembrokeshire; but local tradition says that he worked as a clerk on the railway, and that when he took his family to live in the iron and coal town of Merthyr Tydfil, some time in the 1870s, he became station-master at Taff Vale railway station, and as a sideline sold packets of tea around the town. Then he began to amass some money, and set up in business as an estate agent and auctioneer. So well did his firm thrive, and such was the strength of his personality, that he became a leading figure in local affairs, a justice of the peace, an alderman of Merthyr, and in 1912 Mayor of the town.

During the late nineteenth century Merthyr was in a state of frenetic activity and expansion: not just the largest town in Wales, it was the biggest iron and coal town in the world. One of its assets was the canal, along which exports could be shipped down the valley to the sea at Cardiff; but in scrabbling wealth from the flanks of the mountains, man had wrought terrible destruction upon a landscape once lovely. From its centre on the level floor of the valley, where the Rivers Taff Fawr and Taff Fechan (Big and Little Taff) flow together, the town had expanded to climb the hillsides in street after street of small terraced houses. All round the dwellings, high above them, towered the gaunt skeletons of colliery workings and the vast, pale-grey slag heaps spewed out by mining for iron-ore. Above the district known as Dowlais, on the eastern side of the valley, rose the White Tip, the biggest slag heap of all – a hill in itself, resembling Table Mountain at Cape Town, composed entirely of ash and reject scraps of iron. At all times of day the town rocked to the boom of blasting explosions; at night clouds were lit up by the ruddy glow of blast-furnaces, and high over the rooftops ran a cable lift carrying buckets of hot ash, flaming and smoking against the sky.

The men laboured in the mines, their women in the brickworks turning out the lurid orange bricks with which most of the houses, and the town's municipal buildings, were built. Life was hard and dangerous. Many people were killed or maimed in the pits and foundries; whenever a fatal accident took place, the hooters would sound, all work would stop, and the men would trudge home singing a dirge. On duty, halfway through the shift, wives and daughters would bring their menfolk huge flagons of beer to slake the dust from their throats, and even teetotallers would drink with the rest, for at work consumption of alcohol did not count against them. Off duty, men drank prodigiously: during the second half of the nineteenth century the Dowlais district alone boasted 171 inns, hotels and public houses. Fights were common – the most famous ones went on for several days – and boxing was the most popular local sport, with the result that over the years, right up to the present, the town has produced many famous boxers, among them Jimmy Wilde, Dai Dower, Howard Winston and Eddie Thomas.

According to the historian Richard Morgan,

> All the worst aspects of the Industrial Revolution were to be found in Merthyr – long hours of work, low wages, child labour, overcrowding, insanitary housing, disease and child mortality. Three-quarters of deaths were under the age of five. Life-expectancy among the working class was about twenty-two years. The workers were completely at the mercy of economic factors beyond their control.*

In spite of these hazards, people poured into Merthyr from all over Wales – mainly from Glamorgan, but also from the far west and north – lured by the prospect of employment and money; and no doubt J. M. Berry came up from Pembrokeshire for the same reasons: in the 1870s Merthyr was Wales's answer to the Klondike, an irresistible magnet. It was also a particularly good place in which to set up an estate agency, for people were constantly coming and going, and houses changed hands all the time. Not only did fortune-hunters flock in: malcontents left Merthyr in large numbers, emigrating to America, Canada, Australia and Venezuela.

Many of the newcomers, especially those from rural areas, spoke

---

* The sources of quoted passages – each identified by a few words – are given at the end of the book.

Welsh as their first language. Chapel Welsh – like *Hochdeutsch* – was the pure form, but *gegin*, or kitchen Welsh, was also common, and parents whose children spoke only English would slip into it whenever they wanted to discuss something privately. One effect of the immigrants' arrival was to strengthen the Nonconformist character of the town, and Merthyr's numerous chapels became flourishing centres as much of social activity as of religion. But perhaps the feature most characteristic of Merthyr was its energy. A sense of urgency and enterprise pulsated through its narrow streets. In so volatile and electric an atmosphere, there was tremendous encouragement for anybody who wanted to do well.

One such was J. M. Berry, who was generous with time and money, and contributed staunchly to the development of Merthyr during a period of great social difficulty. For many years he acted as political agent for D. A. Thomas, the coal-owner and radical Liberal Member of Parliament for Merthyr from 1888 to 1910, who later became Viscount Rhondda. It was said that no political event of any importance could occur in South Wales without J. M. Berry hearing about it.

His sons proved to be of much the same ilk; less inclined to political involvement, but clever, industrious, brave, and driven by a tremendous will to win, they all succeeded far beyond any dreams their father may have had for them. Seymour was born in 1877, William in 1879, Gomer in 1883, and their sister Elizabeth, or Beta, in 1885. By then the family lived in Gwaelodygarth, the most fashionable area of the town, on the hillside that forms the north-east side of the valley. Later biographical summaries record that the two elder boys were educated privately. Gomer, however, was one of the first pupils at the Merthyr Intermediate School, which opened in 1896.

All the boys would certainly have had a good grounding in essential subjects; even though the normal school-leaving age was fourteen, education in Merthyr, so far as it went, was excellent. They must also have learnt much at the Congregational Church in Market Square, where Pew No. 47 became the family's traditional perch, and where preachers in full flight surely fired the Berry children's imagination with the magic of words, and probably also, with their strict moral code, implanted the seeds of a powerful sense of responsibility.

For all its dark, Satanic mills, Merthyr had one feature of special delight to boys. Immediately beyond the mine-workings and furnaces lay wild, open country. Steep slopes of grass and bracken rose invitingly within easy walking distance of the houses; there were rocks and trees to climb, caves to hide in, pools in the rivers which held fish and in which one could swim. It may have been this natural mountain playground that made the two elder Berry boys, at least, such keen walkers.

The career of Seymour Berry is not of central importance to this narrative; yet it was so spectacular that a brief sketch of it must be included. After an uncertain start, in which he trained as a teacher, he joined his father at the estate agency and auctioneers in Victoria Street, which became known as J. M. Berry & Son. He made a good auctioneer, with the true Welsh gift of the gab, and he was said to have run one sale with such panache that he finished up selling a drift-mine to himself. When his father retired, he took the business over. Then, in 1915, he offered his services as secretary to his father's friend D. A. Thomas, and was soon running his financial affairs so efficiently that he freed Thomas to concentrate on his essential work as Food Controller in the Cabinet. Finally Seymour launched out on his own and started to build up holdings in coal – for which demand was particularly strong during the First World War – iron, steel, transport, shipping, printing and many other fields. Since most of his businesses were private, it is impossible, now, to compute his wealth; but some indication of the multiplicity of his interests is given by the fact that he became a director of over seventy-five companies and held more directorships than anyone else in Britain. One of his biggest coups came in September 1919 when he took over – for £5 million* – the huge iron and steel firm John Lysaght Ltd, which had plants in Bristol, Newport and Wolverhampton.

In some spheres outside Merthyr Seymour acquired a slightly dubious reputation, for he was a sharp financial operator and a compulsive gambler on the Stock Exchange. He always used to walk to work, up the hill to Dowlais, and he would say to his neighbour W. J. Cole, who had worked with his brother on the *Merthyr Times* when they were boys, that until he arrived at his office on a Monday morning he never knew whether he was a millionaire or a pauper. Yet in the town he became a hero, for there were two outstandingly attractive features of his character and career: first, he was exceptionally generous, giving away very substantial sums to deserving causes and people; second, he remained a devoted son of Merthyr, and over the years bestowed innumerable benefactions upon the place of his birth.

These started in 1917, soon after his father had died and he had

* About £100 million in present-day values.

sold the family estate agency. In July of that year he gave £10,000 for the establishment of a badly needed Technical and Mining Institute, which became known as the J. M. Berry Institute in memory of Seymour's father. The following year he presented £1,000 to the Memorial College, Brecon, again in his father's memory; and in 1919, for £1,125, he bought the Carlton Workmen's Hotel in Merthyr and gave it to the ex-servicemen of the town for a club, with the stipulation that it should be open to all except those with Bolshevist tendencies. That same winter he made one of his most important and lasting benefactions – the gift of ten acres of land and £10,000 for the building of a new hospital, which he and his brothers supported for many years. And so it went on: he gave to the Dowlais Male Voice Choir, to the Maesteg and District Hospital, to the Brecon County Infirmary, to the University College of South Wales and Monmouthshire (in Cardiff), to the Merthyr Football Club, to schools, to women's organisations, to the YMCA, to the poor. He built Merthyr a new indoor swimming pool at a cost of £8,000 and gave money anonymously to children in distress, often absolving the organisers from any need to account for what they spent; and in addition to all these acts of personal generosity, he incited local industry to match his own initiatives, goading firms like Guest, Keen & Nettlefold (of which he became Chairman) to make handsome charitable donations.

Although a capitalist to his boots, he had a deep-seated sense of responsibility towards his workers, and made enlightened efforts to increase the security of their employment. During the great slump of the 1920s he and his brothers spent thousands of pounds of their own money in attempts to keep Merthyr's industry alive – and their importance in the community was later neatly summed up by Iorwerth Thomas, Member of Parliament for the Rhondda, with the remark: 'Merthyr had the Berrys. We had nothing.'

A natural Conservative, Seymour resisted overtures to stand as an Independent candidate for Merthyr in the parliamentary elections of 1922, saying that he could serve the town better in his commercial capacity; but he did turn out to make rousing speeches in support of the Conservative candidate, Sir Richard Mathias, that autumn. One morning in March 1924 the socialist Prime Minister Ramsay MacDonald visited Cardiff, and on emerging from the University College found himself ushered into a waiting car. This, as it happened, belonged to Seymour, who, when he arrived to find that his vehicle had been commandeered by the premier, remarked, 'This is Labour policy in practice – confiscation of private property!'

As a result of all his good works and formidable energy, Seymour acquired the reputation of having done more than any other man to steer Merthyr through the social and economic difficulties of the early 1920s. On 6 July 1923, at a ceremony in the Miners' Hall, he was created the third – and only living – Freeman of the town (his two predecessors being Lords Merthyr and Rhondda): seventy-eight schools were closed for the day, 19,000 children tucked into a blow-out tea at his expense, Lloyd George sent a congratulatory telegram, and a colossal banquet in his honour was held in the evening.

Just as he went from one financial success to another, so he rose steadily up the social scale. In 1907, at the age of thirty, he married Gwladys Sandbrook, daughter of a local alderman, whose family was also well known in the town. (After the marriage ceremony at the Zoar Congregational Church, the *Merthyr Express* reported, the couple drove off to the Sandbrooks' home, The Hawthorns, 'where a *recherché* breakfast was served'.)

In due course Gwladys bore Seymour five daughters. While his father was still alive, he bought Gwaelodygarth House, a handsome, early-nineteenth century building made of stone, high on the hillside in the district of its name, backing on to Cyfarthfa Park, then, as now, a lovely open area full of trees and lakes.* In 1919 he bought Gurnos Farm, and then, in 1922, he acquired the Buckland Estate at Bwlch, near Brecon.

This was a splendid property. The sandstone house was no beauty, having been built in mock-Elizabethan style only twenty years earlier, after its predecessor had been destroyed by fire; but it stood on a magnificent site, looking out over the River Usk to mountains, and it was grand enough to suit any fresh-minted millionaire. The main hall was seventy feet long, and the staircase, branching in two at the landing, led up to a gallery which ran the length of the front. There were thirteen main bedrooms, thirteen bathrooms, ten secondary bedrooms, a billiard-room, a music-room and nursery suites. Outside, the amenities included an Italian garden, an American garden, a herb garden with 150 plots, a sunken rose garden, a maze modelled on that of Hampton Court, six tennis courts, a fish hatchery, a lake, and woodlands planted by a previous owner to represent the disposition of the troops at the battle of Waterloo. Enfolding the house and park were 3,000

---

* Today the house is owned by the local health authority and used as a day centre for psychiatric patients; a ghostly harpsichord is sometimes heard to play in it.

acres of land; there were also four miles of first-class salmon fishing in the Usk, and excellent shooting (pheasants, grouse and duck), besides numerous cottages, a licensed inn and the lordships – or reputed lordships – of several manors.

In these sylvan surroundings, the family took to field sports with enthusiasm. Seymour became a keen fisherman, catching numerous salmon in his beat of the Usk, several of them monsters of over forty pounds; he also rode with energy, and his daughter Eileen became Master of the Gelligaer and Talybont hounds at the age of thirteen.

Such was the style in which Seymour Berry established himself; and when in July 1926 – in the middle of the eight-month miners' strike – he was created a baron 'for public, political and philanthropic services', it was natural that he should take the title Baron Buckland of Bwlch, in the county of Brecon. His philanthropy was demonstrated in no uncertain fashion that November, when Hill's Plymouth collieries at Merthyr fell into the hands of the receiver, bankrupted by debts and unpaid rates. After two urgent appeals from a specially formed committee, the new Lord Buckland stepped in and, with a few friends, bought the collieries for £60,000, thereby saving the jobs of more than 1,500 men. As he himself remarked, he had been enabled 'to present Merthyr with a new lease of life'.

By then his fame had spread far beyond the Welsh valleys: he had dined with the Prince of Wales and lent him his car, and at his own palatial house he entertained the highest in the land, among them the Prime Minister, Stanley Baldwin, who was a close friend and in 1927 came to stay for the wedding of Seymour's nephew. Less than a year after moving to Breconshire, he was elected the county's High Sheriff.

Yet he never gave himself airs, never stopped working, never ceased to hand out money or dispense good cheer among working-class people. Every Christmas he stood the forty or fifty children on the estate a special treat – often a trip to the Electric Cinema in Brecon, with tea and presents afterwards. Each year at Buckland he threw a household dance, to which upper-servants were allowed to invite two guests, under-servants one. In 1925 some 130 people, entertained by a six-piece band, got through twenty-seven bottles of port, seventeen bottles of whisky, and gallons of beer and cider.

Even though he had moved a few miles up-country, Merthyr remained his spiritual home to the end of his days. As he said in one of his speeches, 'I felt I had a duty to the town in which I was born.'

*　　*　　*

Seymour's younger brother Bill, though endowed with many of the same admirable qualities, took an entirely different path in life. One of the central figures in this story, he was born on 23 June 1879. In a slightly inaccurate tribute to that great Liberal William Ewart Gladstone, his parents christened him William Ewert. Like all the boys in Merthyr, he went to work at fourteen; but through his brains and initiative he escaped the fate that awaited most of them: employment in the mines or the ironworks.

Tradition has it that Bill went in for an essay competition, in which he was asked to make a précis of a lecture and, although much the youngest entrant, won first prize. On his paper the Editor of the *Merthyr Times*, W. W. Hadley, scribbled, 'This entrant should take up journalism as a career.' In later years Hadley jokingly claimed credit for having made possible the recovery of the *Sunday Times* and *The Daily Telegraph*, both of which, in due course, his young protégé rescued from obscurity; and Berry himself more than once paid tribute to what he called Hadley's 'prescience' in spotting his talent.

In any event, the lad did as Hadley suggested and, in 1894, at the age of fourteen and a half, took a job as an apprentice reporter on the *Merthyr Times*, which had its offices in John Street, near the town centre. The *Merthyr Times* was then an excellent paper – a weekly, usually of eight pages, which came out on Fridays. It was a large broadsheet, with seven wide columns on each page, very well printed, and, in its mix of local news and advertisements, clearly reflected the vigour of community life in the valleys. Under its mast-head a string of lesser titles precisely defined its area of circulation: *The Dowlais Times, and Aberdare, Pontypridd, Rhondda Valley, Rhymney, Tredegar, Brynmawr and Western Valleys Echo*. Among the advertisements crowding its front page, that of the Royal Temperance Hotel jostled for position with that of the definitely non-Temperance Three Salmons Inn. David Jones of Dowlais offered 'Butter Fresh as a Rose, pure as the Driven Snow, and of Exquisite Quality'. J. E. George, Chemist of Hirwaun, offered patent medicines of every description, among them 'Gomer's Balm – the surprising healer'. Drapers, tailors, undertakers, grocers, photographers all cried their wares or services among announcements of pantomimes, children's fancy-dress balls, concerts, performances of the *Messiah* – and in between were reports of local events, episodes from a long-running serial (generally of a religious character), and several columns in Welsh, usually including some poetry.

W. W. Hadley, though instrumental in bringing young Bill Berry on to the paper, was no longer there by the time the boy arrived.

At the start of 1894 a new editor and 'part proprietor' had taken over – David Davies, who had been Acting Editor of the *Western Mail* in Cardiff, and who brought new sparkle to the *Merthyr Times*. Judging from his own articles (the only ones allowed a by-line), and from the lively way in which local news was presented, he was an admirable editor, and must have been an ideal mentor for a boy starting his first job. Under him, besides running errands, Bill Berry began to learn the basic skills of journalism, visiting the court, police station, hospital and other centres of information. The lack of by-lines makes it impossible to identify his contributions, but one can easily imagine him covering such stories as that about an epidemic of scarlet fever ('This malady is prevalent in the outskirts of the town') or the item headed A MERTHYR HORSE DRINKS BEER, about a pony called Tom who called at the Blue Bell for a pint every night. For a boy of Bill's sober, industrious, responsible nature, it was curiously appropriate that the motto of the paper should have been a quotation from Cicero – *Salus populi suprema lex* – the good of the people is the highest law.

Quickly he realised that, at his first attempt, he had hit on a career that fascinated him completely. For the whole of his life thereafter he was a compulsive journalist; and it is amusing to reflect that in entering the essay competition he had in effect made his first effort at sub-editing – an activity which he always loved, and at which he modestly thought himself rather expert.

It can safely be said that one of his assets was a sense of curiosity and wonder: though adequately taught, he now, as he sped about Merthyr and the surrounding valleys, began to learn something of the complexity of human life. It is also clear that he had very little money, for once, when he and his friend W. J. Cole broke a plate-glass window, he was unable to raise the half-crown that the owner demanded for repairs.

Bill grew into a tall young man of six feet one, with his father's dark good looks accentuated to an arresting degree: he became extraordinarily handsome, with features regular enough, in another age, to have made him a film star. And then in 1898, at the age of nineteen, he took a momentous decision – to leave Wales and seek his fortune in London. Five years of local journalism had scarcely equipped him for such a step: he was driven, rather, by the same determination and spirit of enterprise that were evident in his brother Seymour, and also (as he himself later admitted) by his ambition to become a great newspaper proprietor, no less.

In the metropolis he worked first on the *Investors' Guardian*, at a salary of thirty-five shillings a week, and on the *Country Gentle-*

man, both of which belonged to the same proprietor; but then he was sacked after 'a difference of opinion', and spent the next four months out of work – a fact which he managed to conceal from his parents. He did not, it seems, try all that hard to find another job, but used most of his time to read, in an attempt to give himself some sort of a university education.

He then became a reporter for the Commercial Press Association; but his real start as a proprietor came in 1901 when, with some prescience, he foresaw the importance of advertising and launched a new weekly, *Advertising World*, designed to promote the subject and educate British people about it. For capital, he had only £100, borrowed from Seymour. It is said that he wrote and edited every word of the first issue himself, working up to sixteen hours a day in a shared office on the third floor in Fleet Street, living on air, and walking the distance between there and his lodgings in Forest Gate, partly to save money, partly because he enjoyed keeping fit.

Within a few weeks Berry saw that his idea was a winner, and summoned Gomer (who was four years his junior) to join him in London. Gomer had worked for a while as a floor-walker at Manchester House, the main department store in Merthyr, opposite the town hall – a fact which he later took pains to conceal – and had also done a spell on the *Merthyr Times*, but he was always more of a businessman than a journalist – the opposite of his brother. Between them the two formed a rare partnership, William in charge of editorial, Gomer of finances and advertising. In the words of the fourth Lord Burnham, later Managing Director of *The Daily Telegraph*, 'they were the most perfect double turn that ever appeared on any stage'. So close was their mutual trust and understanding that for the next thirty-five years they ran a joint bank account, on which either might draw without consulting the other, and they even managed amicably to share a bachelor flat in Arundel Street, off the Strand, within a couple of minutes' walk of their work.

In 1905, at the age of twenty-six, Bill Berry made one of the best moves of his life, when he married Mary Corns (always called Molly) whose family he had happened to meet in Cornwall the year before. This remarkable young woman had been denied formal schooling by her parents, and, except for one year spent at Orléans, had been educated by governesses; but when she came of age, she seized the opportunity presented by a small legacy from a godmother and, in the face of bitter parental opposition, sent herself to university in America. Travelling with an American girl and her mother, she took a year's course at Radcliffe, the women's college attached to Harvard, and lived in lodgings in Cambridge, a suburb of Boston.

Back in England, she met Bill Berry again in her father's London house, and fell for him. After their marriage she became his closest adviser. Her son-in-law, the second Earl of Birkenhead, referred to her 'character full of independence', 'sometimes unconventional strength' and 'very clear integrity'. He wrote of the marriage that there was something 'almost telepathic' in the understanding between husband and wife; and that Bill 'never took an important decision in his professional career without seeking her advice, on the shrewdness of which he placed implicit reliance ... People meeting her for the first time quickly recognised an altogether exceptional woman.'

With this powerful new ally behind him, Berry continued his upward progress. As the circulation of *Advertising World* grew, he and his brothers started their own publishing company – Ewart, Seymour & Co., Ltd – and launched several new titles, notably *Boxing*, which was a reflection of one of their own interests gained in Merthyr, and which achieved a circulation of 250,000 by the outbreak of the First World War. They also bought the *Penny Illustrated Paper*, *Health and Strength*, and other small journals. By 1909 *Advertising World* was so securely established that they were able to sell it for £11,000 – their first substantial lump of capital.

All this time, Bill Berry was going up in the world, in every sense of the phrase. It would be fascinating to know when, and by how deliberate an effort, he shed his native Welsh accent: by the time he reached middle-age, his voice was that of an English gentleman, except that in moments of excitement a slight Welsh lilt crept back into it (just as Lancastrian elements always lingered in the patrician accent of Gladstone). When Molly began to bear children – Mary in 1906, Seymour in 1909, Michael in 1911 – they took on a nanny, Ellen Grocock, the daughter of a Leicestershire farmer. She proved an admirable choice, and stayed with the family for forty years, one of her few foibles being the fact that she refused to be addressed as 'Nanny' because the name reminded her of goats. Altogether the marriage produced four sons and four daughters, and William put the boys down for Eton as if the family had been members of the aristocracy for generations.

The size of their growing brood forced the Berrys to move house several times. In London, for a while, William shared a large flat in Whitehall Court with Seymour and his friends the David Llewellyns; but then, as space ran short, he bought a house at 2 Seamore Place, off Curzon Street. From 1920 the family's main home was Barrow Hills – like Buckland, a huge, pseudo-Elizabethan mansion set in elaborate and exotic gardens, with a home farm and good stables – but near Chertsey, in Surrey, rather than in the wilds of Wales.

Like Seymour, William was by nature a Conservative and an upholder of authority, but reluctant to become directly involved in political activity. He preferred to pursue his own bent on the fringes of politics, and to exercise influence through friendship with leading politicians. The most famous of these was Winston Churchill, who became a lifelong friend and confidant, and got Berry elected to The Other Club – the society formed in retaliation by Churchill and F. E. Smith in 1911 after they had been rejected by, or at least discouraged from joining, an older body known as The Club. The Other Club dined in the Pinafore Room at the Savoy, and Berry became one of its most regular attenders.

It was William's fascination with boxing which led to his association with James White – and so, indirectly, to his acquisition of the *Sunday Times*. White was 'a jovial, red-faced villain with a bowler hat, a clipped moustache and a strong north-country accent' who had begun life as a bricklayer's lad in Rochdale, but had later sought his fortune in London. There, among other ventures, he tried to promote a fight between the first black heavyweight champion Jack Johnson and the British heavyweight Bombardier Billy Wells. Finding himself desperately short of cash, he had requested a loan from Bill Berry, who lent him £500 (which he repaid). One day in 1915 Berry met White for lunch at the National Liberal Club in Whitehall Place. At the end of the meal West de Wend Fenton, who was also in newspapers, came over to their table and announced that he had an option to buy the *Sunday Times*. Was Berry interested?

He certainly was – and after protracted and skilful negotiations, he and Gomer managed to secure the paper, beating off several competitors. The price was £80,000, most of which the Berrys had to borrow, and they landed themselves with a tremendous challenge, for the paper was wallowing in the doldrums: with a circulation of scarcely 30,000, it had been left far behind by its rival the *Observer*, whose eccentric but brilliant editor, J. L. Garvin, had built his sales up to 200,000 copies and established a high reputation for his coverage of politics and literature. (Garvin had joined the staff of *The Daily Telegraph* in 1899; but, in the words of the anonymous historian of that newspaper, 'he was a voluminous writer, whose ideas demanded room for development, and it was soon evident that in the *Telegraph* there was not enough liberty for the expansion he desired'.)

Quite suddenly, at the age of thirty-six, Berry found his true *métier*. So far he had tried his hand, with no small success, at all forms of journalistic activity – reporting, writing features, sub-editing, laying out pages; but now, as Chairman and Managing Editor of the *Sunday Times*, he became in effect the Editor of a national newspaper, for although he kept on Leonard Rees, who had already held the editor's chair for over ten years, he himself took close personal control. Thus he launched himself on a career which continued unbroken until his death almost forty years later. Not for him ownership from a distance or leaving the work to subordinates: staying on into the early hours of Sunday morning, Berry took a passionate interest in every part of the paper, paying the closest attention to detail and concentrating on news. No chance of improvement was too small for him to miss. One morning, walking home along the Strand at about 5.00 am, he heard a Zeppelin raid beginning – whereupon he rushed back to the office and brought out a special extra edition.

Under his energetic direction, the paper quickly began to improve and to attract new attention as it went in pursuit of the *Observer*. Berry himself wrote leaders, but very few signed articles. He was never much of a stylist, and aimed to express himself with simplicity rather than with elegance. His own great hunger was always for facts, for news; and his first concern was to pass on to his readers, in the clearest possible form, all the information that he and his staff had been able to assemble. Neither at this stage of his career, nor later when he had the newspaper world at his feet, did he ever indulge in the exhibitionism which disfigured rivals like Beaverbrook: he preferred to efface himself and let the facts tell the story. Yet when he did allow himself a major assignment – as on his visit to the battlefields of the Somme in 1917 – the report which he wrote was hailed as a brilliant *tour de force*.

Contemporaries spoke of Bill Berry in glowing terms. One remembered that when he bought the *Sunday Times* he still had 'a somewhat rough exterior', but that this gradually wore off. Later he was always calm, friendly and polite, with a glint of amusement often visible in his eyes. 'Imperturbable' was a word constantly used about him. Unlike Gomer, who could be extremely impetuous, William never rushed into a decision, even though he usually acted on instinct. Some people were disconcerted by his reserve and thought him aloof, finding it strange that a man so decisive, who had made a fortune, could yet harbour a streak of intense shyness. When things were going well, he said very little, and only when some folly had been committed did he suddenly open verbal fire.

By any standards he was a predator, constantly on the lookout for good titles into which he might fasten his claws; but fate, instead of making him nakedly combative, had cloaked his aggression in unaffected civility and good manners. His size, fine looks and erect posture combined to give him a commanding presence. As one man who knew him wrote, 'He looked the man of mark that he was. He had the distinction and force of one accustomed to overcome any obstacle in his path.' And just as his physical stature was very upright, so too were his financial dealings: he never double-crossed people or let them down. Furthermore, he made himself expert in a variety of fields – advertising, finance, investment, as well as journalism. In the words of his grandson Nicholas Berry, 'he mastered an unusual combination of subjects, at each of which he was unusually proficient. He was like a competitor in the Pentathlon, able to do five or six things supremely well.' In private he was excellent company, full of jokes and high spirits, and he liked nothing better than a good-tempered argument, in which he would make points with bantering obstinacy.

On top of all this, he had, like Seymour, an extraordinary flair for making money: once their presses were rolling, he and Gomer acquired new businesses at an astonishing rate. In 1919 they bought the *Financial Times*, the splendidly named *Financier and Bullionist*, and the St Clement's Press. In 1920 they acquired the *Bystander*, the weekly magazine *Graphic*, and the *Daily Graphic*, the first daily picture paper. They also took control of the lucrative Kelly's Directories and bought the old publishing house of Cassell, which produced some of the most popular magazines of the day and had branches in the United States, Canada and Australia. Yet another major purchase was of the premises of W. H. Smith & Son, in the Strand: after extensive alterations, these became the centre of the Berrys' operations, including luxurious offices for the directors and accommodation for 5,000 staff.

By 1919 the Berry brothers had begun to attract widespread attention. In a memorandum of 14 December William Sutherland, press officer of the Prime Minister, Lloyd George, noted that they had 'considerable newspaper ambitions, and intend, if they can, to rival Northcliffe'. He rated them as 'men to be reckoned with seriously', but told his chief that 'with a little effort, I am sure we can keep them substantially in hand'. The easiest way of doing this was by the dispensation of a title or two – and sure enough, in the Birthday Honours of 1921 William was created a baronet. Now Sir William Berry, he continued to forge ahead. In 1922 he brought the enterprises of Iliffe and Sons into his group, and the genial Sir Edward Iliffe became a partner. Then, in 1924, came a really big acquisition.

A year earlier the Berry brothers had opened negotiations to buy the Hulton group of publications, in Manchester and London, from its owner, Sir Edward Hulton, whose health was failing; but in October their hopes were dashed by the sudden intervention of Lord Beaverbrook, who bought Hultons over their heads on behalf of the rival press giant, Lord Rothermere, whose family trusts owned the *Daily Mail*. In 1924, however, Rothermere sold all the Hulton papers back to the Berrys, except for the London *Evening Standard* (half of which Beaverbrook had retained for himself), the *Daily Sketch* and the *Illustrated Sunday Herald*.

To handle this huge volume of extra business, the Berrys set up a new company, Allied Newspapers Ltd, in which Iliffe joined them as a partner. Over the next three years they acquired eight further provincial papers in Glasgow, Sheffield, Newcastle and Middlesbrough, and also bought in the *Daily Sketch* and the *Illustrated Sunday Herald* from the *Daily Mail* Trust. Later, Bill Berry was at pains to emphasise that he did not solicit any of these provincial properties, and that all of them were offered him by their owners. 'Further ... in no case had Allied Newspapers any previous interest in the towns in which they circulated, nor had we any intention, expressed or otherwise, of establishing rival journals in their territories. It is perhaps needless to say that the politics of each of the papers acquired remained as before.'

Such bland statements, true though they might be, did nothing to calm Lord Rothermere, who belatedly woke up to the fact that the Berrys had become an exceedingly powerful force in the newspaper world, with an empire as large as – if not larger than – his own. The discovery threw him into a frenzy of retaliation, which will be described in the next chapter. Meanwhile, in another major acquisition, the Berrys bought from the executors of Lord Northcliffe the group known as Amalgamated Press, which published over a hundred weekly magazines, from *Woman's Journal* to children's comics, and included a strong encyclopedia and book section, besides two printing works and the Imperial Paper Mills at Gravesend. In 1927 yet another paper-mill came into the Berrys' hands – Edward Lloyd Ltd. – one of the biggest in the world.

Such spectacular expansion naturally drew snide comments, most often from the communist *Daily Worker* which several times claimed that Sir William Berry was able to buy so many newspapers simply because he had extorted a fortune from coal and steel. The allegations annoyed him, but for many years he did nothing to refute them; only in 1947, with the publication of his book *British Newspapers and their Controllers*, did he come into the open and dismiss

24

the claims as nonsense. At one time, he agreed, he had been a director of several public companies, mainly in steel and coal, but only as an associate of his elder brother, Lord Buckland; and although the steel companies had made some profit, those in coal had generally lost money. Indeed, during the slump of the 1920s the Berry brothers had invested large sums to keep the pits around Merthyr in business. William's position in the newspaper world had been established before he had any business connections in other fields. He was always proud of the fact that he had started from nothing, and had been through nearly every branch of newspaper production.

During the 1920s all three brothers remained very close, with many of their business interests intertwined; and although William and Gomer were in London, physically separated from their home town, their hearts remained as securely rooted in Merthyr as did that of Seymour, who was still living in Wales. His own benefactions continued to pour out: in January 1927 he announced that he would give £35,000 over seven years towards the cost of a new East Wing for the National Museum of Wales in Cardiff; and in October he laid the foundation-stone of the War Memorial Hospital at Scunthorpe in Lincolnshire, for which he had given 1,000 guineas.

By the end of 1927 the Berry family had achieved extraordinary power and affluence. All three brothers were millionaires. One was a baron, one a baronet (and Gomer was also knighted in the New Year Honours of January 1928). All three had large families – Seymour five children, William eight and Gomer seven. The first two had vast country houses. Gomer was almost as splendidly ensconced at Farnham Chase in Buckinghamshire (and he soon bought yet another immense, pseudo-Elizabethan pile: Wyfold Court, near Reading – a gothic horror built of hideous orange brick). Bill Berry had developed a taste for old silver, books, relics of Napoleon and above all for pictures: in 1928 at Christie's he bought Van Dyck's portrait of the Abbé Scaglia for 30,000 guineas. All three brothers had reached their positions through sheer industry, flair and courage. Yet on the journalistic front, one element was conspicuously lacking: powerful though the Berry group now was, it contained no national daily newspaper. Popular papers like the *Daily Mail* or the *Daily Express* were of no interest to William: what he wanted, and had been seeking for some time, was a serious paper of quality – so when he heard that the ailing *Daily Telegraph* might be on the market, he jumped at the chance to buy it.

Daily Telegraph & Courier.

No. 1.] LONDON, FRIDAY, JUNE 29, 1855. [TWOPENCE.

2 THE BURNHAM ERA, 1855–1928

The Daily Telegraph had been through many vicissitudes since its foundation, in a fit of pique, by a recently retired and slightly crazed army officer during the Crimean War. Why Colonel Arthur Burroughes Sleigh was so incensed, history no longer relates; but it was apparently in pursuit of a vendetta against the Duke of Cambridge that he launched his four-page *Daily Telegraph & Courier* on Friday, 29 June 1855. Taking advantage of the removal of stamp duty from newspapers six weeks earlier, Sleigh published at the recklessly low price of twopence (the *Times* then cost sevenpence, and other leading journals such as the *Morning Post* fivepence), and one of his earliest leading articles was a vicious attack on the Duke, who later became Commander-in-Chief of the Army.*

The front page of the first number – four columns of advertisements and two of 'Late Despatches from the Seat of War' – makes a stimulating read today. Lord Raglan's official reports sent from 'Before Sevastopol' on 14 and 16 June are dull, but the advertisers' announcements offer excellent value. Underwood's First Class Tea House, for instance, burst into rhyme to salute the paper's birth:

> The 'Telegraph and Courier',
>   While kept in active mood,
> Is just the kind of messenger
>   To work for Underwood.
>
> For where a Courier can run,
>   A Telegraph will be;
> And thus all nations 'neath the sun
>   Will hear of First Class Tea.

---

* The account that follows in this chapter is based partly on information supplied by the Lawson family, partly on Lord Burnham's history of the paper, *Peterborough Court*, published in 1955, and partly on an anonymous history of *The Daily Telegraph*, unpublished but evidently compiled by a member of the staff. It is clear that Burnham drew heavily on this, without (for some reason) acknowledging the fact. By a dire mischance – especially severe for a man who spent much of his life dealing with words – in some copies the last fourteen pages of Burnham's book were printed twice, just in front of the index.

Alas, such optimism was premature. The paper did not keep in active mood, and from the start the Colonel was in trouble with his printers. One firm had refused to handle the paper at all, so shaky were his finances. The next – Aird & Turnstall of Exeter Street, off the Strand – printed the first few numbers, but threatened to foreclose if Sleigh did not pay his bills. The infant paper was on the point of expiry when Sleigh happened to meet Joseph Moses Levy, a printer and publisher who had recently acquired the *Sunday Times* and had premises near the bottom of Shoe Lane, where that narrow alleyway runs out into Fleet Street. Levy agreed to print and publish *The Daily Telegraph & Courier*, but only on condition that, if bills remained unpaid beyond a certain period, the paper, its copyright and everything concerning it would pass to him in default.

Earlier accounts have suggested that this happened after only a few weeks; but a document which came to light when the paper vacated 135 Fleet Street, in 1986, shows that Levy made Sleigh a payment of £2,000 on 17 February 1857. Even so, it seems that Levy, with the able help of his son Edward, took over direction of the paper in the very early days. Fate came some of the way towards rescuing them when the fall of Sevastopol on 12 September 1855 provided news which lightened everybody's spirits; but the Levys quickly realised that drastic action was needed to resuscitate their moribund acquisition, and on 14 September, less than a week after assuming control, they printed a bold announcement:

On and from Monday next, the 17th inst., the *Daily Telegraph*, same size and quantity of matter as at present, will be published at the price of *One Penny*.

Intrigued by such a departure, people flocked to buy it – and they found it a good bargain. One major innovation was that the paper carried no fewer than four leading articles, of which the last was humorous; and in the first leader the proprietors gave some account of their aspirations:

There is no reason why a Daily newspaper, conducted with a high tone, should not be produced at a price which would place it within the means of every class of the community. The extension of the circulation of such a journal must prove beneficial to the public at large. If Artisan and Peer can alike peruse daily the same wholesome literary matter, produced by first-class writers, the general tone of society must benefit.

A promise was given that, as soon as public support built up, the journal would be 'the Largest, Best and Cheapest newspaper in the world'. Within a week the publishers were claiming sales higher than any other London paper except the *Times*, and by January 1856 the circulation had reached 27,000 copies a day. Finding that the new baby took up all his time, Levy sold the *Sunday Times*, after only a few months' ownership, to E. T. Smith, the impresario and lessee of the Drury Lane Theatre.

JML, as Levy's family knew him, was no ordinary printer. He had a wide knowledge of music, theatre and books: his friends included many writers and actors, among them Bram Stoker, author of *Dracula*, and Sir Henry Irving; and for the first few years of the *Telegraph*'s life he acted as its music critic. He also had the admirable (but then outlandish) idea that journalism should be lively: a dull paragraph would cause him to groan, 'That sort of stuff is enough to sink the ship.' As his success increased, he took to holding weekly receptions at his London houses, where he gathered literary and musical celebrities in his drawing-room.

In 1856, to finance the expansion of his new property, he approached his brother Lionel, who, for business reasons, had adopted the surname Lawson, and by then was a successful financier and speculator in theatrical properties (among other achievements, he built the Gaiety Theatre in the Strand, and owned a lucrative ink factory in France). Lionel came in with a hefty sum; and, in a move which caused hideous complications later, JML proceeded to set up a partnership divided into sixty-four shares: sixteen of these he kept himself, eight went to his son Edward, and thirty-two to Lionel. A series of interlinked trusts was created, and matters were so arranged that no member of the firm could dispose of his interest in the paper without the consent of all. (In 1879, under the will of his uncle, Edward also assumed the name of Lawson, by royal licence.)

Finance thus posed no great problem. More difficult for the proprietors was the task of finding writers of the calibre needed to produce the lively, amusing and instructive paper they were aiming for. The Levys had one such already, in the form of Thornton Hunt – son of the critic and poet Leigh Hunt – whom they had taken on with the title, and now they set about recruiting others.

Whether by luck or good judgement, the Levy-Lawsons hit on a formula which carried the *Telegraph* to great heights: that of giving value for money – providing maximum information, at minimum expense, to a public whose appetite for facts was constantly being increased by the spread of education. In a far-sighted memorandum to the proprietors, Thornton Hunt pointed out that the country was at 'the beginning of a new era in science', which was soon 'to be taught in every school'. The paper should therefore 'report all striking events in science', as well as new inventions and new methods of conducting business: 'A paper of high authority should always have at command such men as can write with correctness, certainty, distinct force and authority on military, on naval affairs, on law.'

In other words, the aim should be to extend news coverage to a much wider geographical area, and a far greater range of subjects, than had been attempted by other journals so far. In 1856 the paper set up its first office in Paris, and by the end of 1857 was publishing a weekly letter from Toronto. The earliest book reviews appeared in 1855, the first drama criticism two years later. At the same time, however, the intention was to produce something distinctively different from other papers, which presumed that their readers were interested in little else but politics. 'What we want is a human note,' JML told his bright young recruits. He and Edward soon realised that the title of the paper was too cumbersome: they therefore put the words '& Courier' into such small type as to render them almost invisible, and on 28 October 1856 dropped them entirely.*

The paper won its early reputation through radical criticism of established views, customs and people. Tennyson – Poet Laureate from 1850 – took a terrible pasting: his *Idylls of the King* was dismissed as a pot-boiler, 'jingling without music, obsolete and not antique in diction . . .' A scathing editorial suggested that he 'should produce something better for the public money. Let it be hot, Mr Tennyson, or not at all.' Bishops, the Pre-Raphaelites, Tractarians – all found themselves ferociously attacked; but no organisation excited the paper's indignation more furiously than the House of Lords: 'the chartered lords of misrule ogling in the ancient face of bigotry'.

Gradually, however, the *Telegraph* swung round: having lashed

---

* Since then there have been innumerable changes of mind about whether the paper should be called *The Daily Telegraph* or the *Daily Telegraph*. When *The Sunday Telegraph* was launched in 1961, the same confusion and indecision prevailed, the title on the masthead often being different from the version given inside. Generally, the full title has been used for both papers, presumably on the grounds that it seems more imposing; and until recently every opportunity was taken to belittle rivals by printing their names, if at all, without the definite article; the *Times* rather than *The Times*. In this narrative, to avoid a cumbersome amount of italic type, various abbreviations have been used.

out in all directions for a while, it went through a period of Palmerstonian Liberalism, then one of Gladstonian Liberalism, before settling firmly in support of Disraeli and the Conservatives. The Lawsons, being new to public affairs, at first had no strong political views, and, as their descendant the fourth Lord Burnham put it, 'In the early years the proprietorial dog was wagged by the leader-writer tail'. Yet although the paper's first Editor was nominally Thornton Hunt, in practice it was Edward Lawson who ran the show.

Though only twenty-one when his father acquired the paper, Edward proved a journalist of exceptional talent. He had been educated at University College School in Hampstead and, when he left, became Drama Critic of the *Sunday Times*. Even then, as he toiled in what he himself called 'the back office on the ground floor at the corner of Bridge Street', he had visions of a glorious future. To equip himself for it, he went through every department of the newspaper, learning to set type, make up pages and edit copy, as well as to write scathing leaders. He was extremely quick, with an excellent nose for news and the imagination to pioneer new methods, among them the use of foreign correspondents: he always held that overseas news sent in by letter was much better than news which came by telegram, since the inevitable compression eliminated all the gossip and often led to mistakes. Another departure was his predilection for background articles, written in a lively, descriptive style, of the kind now known as 'features'. His aim was to produce not only a newspaper, but also a daily magazine of fresh matter, containing at least one article which everyone who did not read it, but heard about it later, would be sorry to have missed.

Within six years the *Telegraph*'s circulation had risen to 141,000, and was almost equal to that of all the other London papers put together. Under Lawson's forceful direction, a campaign for the removal of paper duty was rewarded by its abolition in 1860 – a change which saved the *Telegraph* £12,000 a year and meant that the proprietors could be altogether more ambitious in their plans for expansion. This, in turn, meant finding new accommodation, for they had quickly outgrown their original premises at 253 the Strand, on the north side between St Clement Dane's Church and Temple Bar; and now they took over No. 135 Fleet Street, whose buildings surrounded and partly covered the small yard known as Peterborough Court, where the Abbots and Bishops of Peterborough had kept their London hostel until the area became too insalubrious to support episcopal dignity. No doubt the site was chosen because it was right next door to the family's printing works in Shoe Lane. After extensive alterations had been made to the building, the publishing operation was moved into it on 22 September 1862. Thereafter, the name Peterborough Court became synonymous with the paper: it was Matthew Arnold who was supposed to have called *The Daily Telegraph*'s florid and exuberant style 'the roaring of the young lions of Peterborough Court'.

It takes some effort of imagination to see a newspaper office with no telephones, teleprinters or typewriters, let alone any computers. But that Edward Lawson ran a tight ship is evident from a copy of the paper's 'Rules and Regulations', apparently from the 1860s:

> No person will be permitted to leave his employment to talk to friends or visitors. All communications with those engaged in every department must be made by letter. The Porter cannot carry messages or transmit notes . . . Except on business of the Office, no Gentleman employed on the 'Daily Telegraph' can be seen in Peterborough Court, or at 135 Fleet Street . . . The Editor cannot be seen by anyone; all communication with him must be by means of letter, to which no answer can be guaranteed . . . By Nine o'clock in the morning all the Offices must be prepared, and all necessary fires lighted . . . No tobacco is to be smoked on the Establishment . . . For the accurate receipt of paper, according to the delivery note, the Chief Wetter shall be responsible . . . Members of the Newsvendors' trade will be prevented from loitering about the Court and Publishing Office by the Porter, and order preserved during the hours of publication.

Lawson soon realised how well the paper could do if special efforts were made whenever events demanded them. Just such an occasion came in 1863, with the wedding of Edward, Prince of Wales, to Princess Alexandra of Denmark. Public enthusiasm was immense, and after suitable trailing articles in the days before the marriage, the *Telegraph* threw everything it had into reports of the ceremony itself. One edition after another kept selling out, and, in attempts to meet the demand for copies, the presses turned all day, until forced to stop by the need to prepare the next day's paper. The result was an all-time record sale of 207,000 – a figure unprecedented in this or any other country at the time.

It was not long before the paper began to grow notorious for its extensive – not to say excessive – coverage of scandalous court cases, and found itself accused of 'dilating on the vices of the aristocracy'. Yet that, in the view of traditional journalists, was only one of the deplorably low tricks to which the newspaper resorted. Another was Edward Lawson's habit of making personal calls on successive Prime Ministers – Gladstone, Derby, Beacons-field – which, though clearly an admirable way of picking up news in days before the existence of Political or Diplomatic Correspondents, struck jealous contemporaries as outrageous.

Lawson's relationship with Gladstone was curious; at first he backed the Prime Minister and his policies, but then in the 1870s fell out with him over the atrocities allegedly committed by the Turks against Christians in Bulgaria, and transferred his allegiance to the Conservatives under the Earl of Beaconsfield (Disraeli). Gladstone evidently much regretted the loss of Lawson's support. On 22 November 1875 he wrote: 'I fear you and I are diverging rather widely . . . on a great matter recently brought into the public view; but you have probably at least the advantage of having about 999 of every thousand on your side'; and then, in 1878, he called in person at 135 Fleet Street for an interview with Lawson and his senior editorial colleagues. Again he failed to convert them to his view, and afterwards reported, 'I do not mean to say that they received me with the least discourtesy, but I saw there was a firmly set purpose in their minds.'

The chagrin felt by more conventional newspaper operators burst out in assaults on Lawson – mainly verbal, but one physical – made by the rival journalist and politician, Henry Labouchere, who was only two years his senior but, in terms of outlook, of an earlier generation. In 1876 he founded *Truth*, with himself as Editor, and used it to launch a series of personal attacks which a century later would certainly have landed him with a six-figure bill for libel. Nakedly anti-Semitic, wildly exaggerated, Labouchere's broadsides sought to pillory Lawson for becoming a Christian when he married out of his Jewish faith, compared him with Judas for his betrayal of Gladstone, and sought to establish that almost every news story printed in the *Telegraph* was either plain wrong or distorted by malice. In due course Lawson sued for libel, but the jury found themselves unable to agree, and the inconclusive exchanges in court led to a brief bout of fisticuffs outside the Beefsteak Club, from which, for the time being, both combatants were expelled.

In Lord Burnham's words, 'Labouchere could not understand, or if he could understand could not stomach, that *The Daily Telegraph* was for a wide and entirely new public who had seldom or never read newspapers before . . . [Its] fault was that it set out to be a popular newspaper.'

Rant as Labouchere might, the upstart went romping ahead: even with regular issues of eight pages, and occasional two-page supplements, the proprietors were often obliged to turn prospective advertisers away. Revenue poured in. The paper established itself as having the best news service of any, both at home and abroad, and appealed not so much to the 'hamlet and the palace' (in Lawson's prediction) as to the rapidly expanding middle-classes: it became, in a famous phrase, 'the paper of the man on the knifeboard of the Clapham omnibus'. By the time it reached the age of twenty-one, in 1876, it was able to carry the daily announcement:

LARGEST CIRCULATION IN THE WORLD
The sales of *The Daily Telegraph* amount to an average which, if tested, will show an excess of half a million copies weekly over any other morning paper.

There were plenty of people who shared Labouchere's hatred of the *Telegraph*, of course. One evening in the 1870s Lawson himself spotted smoke as he left the building, and, rushing back, found three separate fires burning inside. Luckily he arrived soon enough for the blazes to be extinguished, and a man was afterwards convicted of arson. Later, in 1883, when the Irish-American extremists known as the Fenians set off a series of bombs in London, and the *Telegraph* condemned them vigorously, the paper's tough attitude provoked a stream of letters threatening to blow up the new offices. One such, on notepaper headed with a hand-drawn skull-and-crossbones, ran: 'The *Daily Telegraph* office will be blown to atoms this very week. We intend to buy a new dodge that will answer perfectly.'

The proprietors, though not exactly frightened, took certain precautions, among them that of calling for volunteers from the staff to sleep in the office on Saturday nights, when the building was normally deserted. The watchman's duties were scarcely exacting: he was allowed to bring in a friend, and the management provided an excellent dinner for two, with champagne, and supper to follow. With hospitality so lavish, it was perhaps just as well that no disturbance was ever reported; even so, the proprietors decided to insure themselves by setting up a separate office and printing works, which would be able to take over production at an hour's notice if Peterborough Court ever went sky-high. To this end they bought a site in Tudor Street and there built a duplicate office, fully equipped with printing machinery. For years it stood ready, fortunately unneeded; then it was let to the *Daily Express*, before eventually being sold to a printing firm.

Of the writers who carried the *Telegraph* to great heights in the late nineteenth century, none is remembered now – a salutary warning on the ephemeral nature of journalistic fame. In their day, however, they were giants, and none came larger than George Augustus Sala, a flamboyant, hard-drinking Bohemian egoist with a shrill and piercing voice, whose bulbous red nose had been permanently disfigured by a blow from a rival's diamond ring, and who wore a clean white waistcoat every morning, without fail. Sala's energy and facility with the pen were equally prodigious: he took pleasure in describing how once, in the course of twenty-four hours, he produced two leaders, went to the Private View at the Royal Academy, wrote a piece about it, saw and wrote about the Talking Fish exhibited at the Egyptian Hall, and in the evening attended the annual dinner of the Royal Literary Fund and a charity ball, also writing accounts of both events. As a Special Commissioner (his own description) he travelled widely – to Russia, to the Civil War in America, to the War of Liberation in Italy, as well as to France, Spain and Greece. 'GO ODESSA SEE MOB GO CONSTANTINOPLE' sufficed as a briefing when the paper wanted to move him from Warsaw in 1876, so well did he and his proprietor understand each other; and on another celebrated occasion he received a message: 'Please write a leader on Billingsgate and the price of fish and start for St Petersburg this evening.' The effervescent self-confidence with which he tackled any subject won him a huge public.

The industry of Sala and his colleagues was phenomenal. Clement Scott, Drama Critic from 1871 to 1898, thought nothing of writing reviews three or four thousand words long. Edwin Arnold, who joined as a leader-writer in 1862, was a scholar-poet who could turn his pen to any subject and rarely failed to produce articles both stimulating and informative. Winner of the Newdigate poetry prize at Oxford, he began his career as a schoolmaster and spent five years in India as Principal of the Deccan College at Poona. Back in England on holiday, he saw an advertisement for a leader-writer on a popular paper, answered it, and soon found himself being interviewed by Edward Lawson, who later described the meeting:

I asked him if he had ever been inside a newspaper office. He said, 'No.'

'Have you ever written a leading article?'

'No, but I've written some poetry.'

'Do you think you could do a leading article?'

'I think so. But at any rate, if you like, I'll try.'

'Very well. Go into the next room and write me something about the threatened war between Denmark and Prussia.'

He did so. I read his article, shook his hand, and told him he was now on the staff of *The Daily Telegraph*.

In later life Arnold looked (according to Lord Burnham) 'a rugged, rather ugly old man in a black velvet skull cap'. A lifelong Orientalist, he always carried in his pocket a small, leather-bound book in Arabic or Sanskrit, and when he had nothing else to do, turned some lines into English verse. People said that parts of his own epic poem 'The Light of Asia' were written on the Underground as he travelled between Fleet Street and his home in South Kensington.

Less exotic, but of astonishing durability, was John Merry le Sage, who joined the staff in 1863 and remained on it, with one short break caused by ill-health, for sixty years. At first, as Edward Lawson's personal assistant, he was effectively News Editor, and during that period himself carried out many special assignments. By no means the least important was the one on which he travelled to Marseilles to meet the explorer H. M. Stanley as he returned from his rescue of Livingstone, for out of their encounter came Stanley's great journey right across Africa, financed by *The Daily Telegraph* and the *New York Herald*. Le Sage was always more of an organiser than a writer, and for many years was Editor of the paper – although for exactly how many, it is difficult to say, as the organisation was then so loosely structured.

As his newspaper's fortunes rose, so did the personal stature of Edward Lawson, who was soon known by everyone in the firm as 'The Guv'nor'. For a while he lived in Doughty Street, in Bloomsbury, but then he bought a house at 51 Grosvenor Street, and later progressed to 12 Berkeley Square. His move to Mayfair was matched by the acquisition of large houses in the country: first Bridlesmere, near Newmarket, which he had built, and then Hall Barn, near Beaconsfield, in the Buckinghamshire Chilterns, which he bought with 3,200 acres in 1882. In London he became a founder-member of the Beefsteak Club and a trustee of the Garrick: a good trencherman, by no means a teetotaller, convivial and lively in conversation, he was eagerly welcomed at all levels of society.

When he replaced the old structure of 135 Fleet Street with a splendid new building, the official opening on 28 June 1882 was graced by no less distinguished a visitor than the Prince of Wales. According to the *Illustrated London News*, the grand, pillared hall which occupied the whole of the ground floor 'was tastefully decorated for the opening conversazione', and the proprietor 'had the honour of showing the premises, with the printing machinery and other improved appliances', to his royal guests, who included the Prince's younger brother, the Duke of Albany. A sketch showed the royal brothers sitting at a table in the hall, with Lawson – who by then had grown plump and bald – standing opposite with his wife, both looking a little strained. Nearly seven hundred people were present on this, the first occasion in history on which members of a royal family had openly associated themselves with a newspaper. For years the new offices were regarded as the most modern in existence, and were visited by journalists from all over the world.

The opening of the building heralded two decades of unprecedented success, in which the *Telegraph* reached its first zenith. By the mid-1880s sales had climbed to 240,000, and the proprietors could claim the largest circulation in the world. The *Times*, which was perceived as the main rival, had been left far behind. The flow of advertising seemed unstoppable. Most issues were of eight pages, with up to four supplements of two or four extra pages every week. Old J. M. Levy liked to see what he called a 'black' paper – by which he meant with page after page packed by small advertisements: usually sixty-eight columns appeared every day, and often another sixty or seventy columns had to be held over for lack of space, obliged to wait their turn. All this meant handsome profits for the partners. In his will, published in 1878, Lionel (JML's brother) left nearly £1 million: an immense sum by today's standards.

By the late 1880s the *Telegraph* was securely established as a journal of the highest prestige; and in 1887 it naturally played a leading part in organising the celebrations for Queen Victoria's Jubilee. One element in these was the demonstration by, and entertainment of, 30,000 schoolchildren at a colossal tea-party in Hyde Park – an idea put up and followed through by Edward Lawson, who became secretary and treasurer of the committee set up to raise funds. But although outside contributors in the end produced £6,000, Lawson himself led off with a gift of 1,000 guineas, and it seems certain that he spent a great deal more than that – of his own or the *Telegraph*'s money – on the event. Luckily the day chosen for it – 22 June – was brilliantly fine: the Queen, the Prince and Princess of Wales all came, together with other members of the Royal Family and a great gaggle of the nobility;

Lawson's daughter presented the Queen with a bouquet, and he himself was presented to Her Majesty. It is hard to know who enjoyed the day most – the newspaper proprietor or the swarm of children whom he was entertaining. Next day the *Telegraph* devoted nine whole columns to its description of the mighty blow-out.

The paper was now in full flight; and if the next year, 1888, was marred by the death of its founding father, J. M. Levy, that sad event could not impede its progress. In 1892 Edward Lawson was made a baronet: writing to announce the Queen's intention, the Prime Minister, Lord Salisbury, complimented him on the important services which he and his paper had rendered to the Unionist party.

In 1903 when, at the age of seventy, Edward Lawson handed over active control to his son Harry, he was made a baron, the first Lord Burnham of Hall Barn. 'I have ceased to be a journalist,' he told friends in the office, 'and am now going in for farming.' His descendants accepted that his peerage was a reward for many public benefactions, the most spectacular of which had been the tea-party in Hyde Park. In later years his style of running the paper had grown increasingly patrician: he liked to regard all his staff as members of a huge family, and although this attitude produced a mellow atmosphere in the office, it did not make for efficient management, as the proprietor naturally felt reluctant to dispense with any employee, no matter how old or useless, whom he regarded as part of the household. The corollary was that the staff at 135 Fleet Street gradually developed a subservient, sycophantic attitude towards their employer, as though they really were family retainers, and he a feudal chief – a frame of mind which grew into a tradition in the building and led to disastrous consequences a hundred years later.

In the country Lawson set himself up in the greatest style. Hall Barn had once been a country house of reasonable proportions, built of red brick in 1680 by the poet Edmund Waller; but during the nineteenth century another owner had added a whole wing of rooms thirty feet square; and by the time Lawson himself had built on a white-and-gold ballroom to celebrate the coming-of-age of his son Harry in 1884, the house had become a monster, with some thirty-five bedrooms. The estate also grew steadily as Lawson bought in more land, and by the beginning of the First World War it extended to nearly 4,500 acres.

Like many businessmen who had made a great deal of money – Sir Ernest Cassel was another – Lawson wanted to entertain his grand friends; and in the 1880s there was no more fashionable way of doing this than by inviting them to shoot, especially if one of them happened to be the Prince of Wales. The introduction of breech-loading guns had recently revolutionised game-shooting: now that it was possible to load and fire much faster than before, driven pheasants – and enormous bags – were all the rage. At Hall Barn Lawson built up the shoot with the enthusiasm and skill that he had applied to his newspaper, and soon it was one of the most famous of all. Far better naturally endowed than either Sandringham or Holkham – for its beechwoods high on the flanks of the Chiltern Hills formed more effective pheasant-launching platforms than the gentle slopes of Norfolk – Hall Barn became a regular haunt of the Prince of Wales who, from 1892, came to shoot there every year, both before and after his accession to the throne in 1901 as Edward VII. Photographs show the monarch, swathed in acres of cloak, conferring with his tubby little host, and riding from one drive to the next on a pony whose girth pretty well matched his own.

It is good to know that Lord Burnham's country-house parties were not given entirely for the benefit of bloodthirsty philistines: carrying on his father's tradition of entertaining musicians, artists and writers, he always invited some intellectuals – the actor Sir Henry Irving among them – to leaven the lump of men whose minds were focused on the next day's battue.

In sporting terms, Hall Barn's greatest year proved to be 1913, when a special two-day shoot was arranged to mark Lord Burnham's eightieth birthday. He himself did not take part – except as observer and adviser – but his principal guests were the highest in the land: King George V, who used his obsolete but beloved hammer guns, and his son, the new Prince of Wales. Two weeks before the grand shoot, the gamekeeper, E. R. Dadley, caught and broke the necks of eighty pheasants to provide lunch for the guns and their supporters. On 17 December the party of seven guns shot 1,705 pheasants in Egypt and Dorney Woods, and then on 18 December, in a massacre never likely to be surpassed, the all-time record for England of 3,937 pheasants in a single day. At one stand alone, Parson's Underwood, more than a thousand birds were killed. The King was said to have remarked afterwards that he thought Lord Burnham had 'overdone it a bit', but the royal marksman himself had not made much effort to minimise the slaughter. As the Hall Barn estate agent afterwards breathlessly reported, 'I watched the King and kept count. He brought down thirty-nine birds with thirty-nine consecutive cartridges and only with the fortieth did he miss.'

Nor did the staff of *The Daily Telegraph* escape the consequences of these fearful battues. At Christmas 1912, 2,198 of the birds killed in another royal shoot had been sent to the office in Fleet Street, and altogether nearly 6,000 birds were handed out to members of the staff during that winter.

A year later, thrilled or appalled as they may have been by such largesse, a strong delegation of senior staff went down to Hall Barn, in their dark suits and overcoats, to convey the paper's loyal congratulations to Lord Burnham on the occasion of his eightieth birthday, which fell on 28 December 1913. For everyone concerned, it was a day to remember. Telegrams came from the King and Queen, and in the afternoon Prince and Princess Christian arrived to visit the venerable squire. Felicitations poured in — from the Garrick Club, the Drury Lane Lodge of Freemasons, the Beaconsfield Urban District Council. The men from No. 135 Fleet Street were photographed as a group outside the house, with Burnham himself, elegantly dressed in tweed plus-fours and spats, seated on a bench in their midst, standing out like a gaudy partridge perched among a gaggle of rooks; and even he, used as he was to respect and flattery, must surely have squirmed when he heard the grossly obsequious and adulatory phrases of the Loyal Address with which he was presented, signed by every member of the paper's staff:

> We, the undersigned, your loyal comrades and fellow workers, who have been proud to serve under you as the staff of *The Daily Telegraph*, desire to take the opportunity of your eightieth birthday to offer you our sincere and respectful congratulations . . . It is not for us to lay stress on the splendid institution with which your name has been for many years identified, nor to recall the many glowing episodes which your wise counsels and far-sighted enterprise have initiated and inspired . . . Others, who can look at your work from the outside, may give it the meed of their well-deserved praise . . . Ours is a different privilege. We belong, if it may be permitted to say so, to a more intimate circle, the family, as it were, of Peterborough Court . . . Many proud moments of personal happiness . . . your unvarying kindness and sympathy . . . We approach you with gratitude and loyalty in our hearts.

A second address in similarly glowing terms, signed by 250 leading figures of the world's Press, was presented by the rival magnate Lord Northcliffe, who paid his host the most handsome compliments. 'You have never stood still, in former ways, however successful,' he said, 'but by signal strokes of promptitude and courage have shown how journalism may re-adapt itself to the changing circumstances both of its own technical conditions, and of the world which it reflects.' The occasion set a seal on Burnham's reputation as the doyen of British journalism.

Alas, the birthday effusions, well-deserved though they were, did not reflect what was happening in Fleet Street. By 1913 the *Telegraph* had gone into a decline, brought on by a combination of factors. One of the most damaging blows had fallen in 1896 with Alfred Harmsworth's launch of the *Daily Mail*, described as 'a penny newspaper for one half-penny' and the first of the popular papers, whose explosive success took Lawson by surprise. The *Mail* immediately won a circulation of 170,000, and in two years hit 400,000, creating for itself a whole new readership, precisely as the Lawsons had done forty years earlier. In 1908, also under Harmsworth (now Lord Northcliffe), the *Times* had been revived. The result was erosion of the *Telegraph*'s circulation at both the top and bottom ends of the social scale.

On 9 April 1899, as an experiment, Lawson broke new ground by launching a *Sunday Daily Telegraph*. Demand for Sunday newspapers had been increasing, and no doubt he hoped he could make money, not least by spreading his printing costs to the seventh day of the week. He also wanted to report the Boer War as fully as possible. In the words of the anonymous historian, the first number was 'a very mild production' and 'nothing likely to cause a ripple of sensation in Fleet Street or anywhere else, except in the most rigid Sabbatarian circles'. There, however, it created havoc:

> The ire and indignation of that class of people surpassed far the apathy of others. The old and silly cry of 'desecration of the Sabbath' was howled from the house-tops, and the anti-Sunday newspaper big drum was beaten with unparalleled vigour. Moreover, the Sabbatarians appealed to large advertisers to stop their custom to the *Telegraph* during the week, and threatened all manner of other torts . . .

Lawson continued his experiment for seven weeks, but since, at the end of that time, the outcry was if anything louder, he gave up the struggle.* On the daily newspaper front, he saw three possible ways of retaliating against the *Mail* and the *Times*. One was to

---

* The *Daily Mail* launched a similar paper, which failed for the same reasons.

Sunday Daily Telegraph.

No. 1.] LONDON, SUNDAY, APRIL 9, 1899. [SIXTEEN PAGES, ONE PENNY.

BIRTHS, MARRIAGES, & DEATHS.

BIRTHS.

MARRIAGES.

SILVER WEDDING.

DEATHS.

IN MEMORIAM.

HOSPITALS and INSTITUTIONS.

BANKS, INSURANCE, &c.

AMUSEMENTS.

EDUCATIONAL.

SHIPPING AND MAILS.

RAILWAYS.

MIDLAND RAILWAY.

LONDON & COUNTRY HOTELS AND RESTAURANTS.

PERSONAL, LOST AND FOUND.

SALES BY AUCTION.

HORSES AND CARRIAGES.

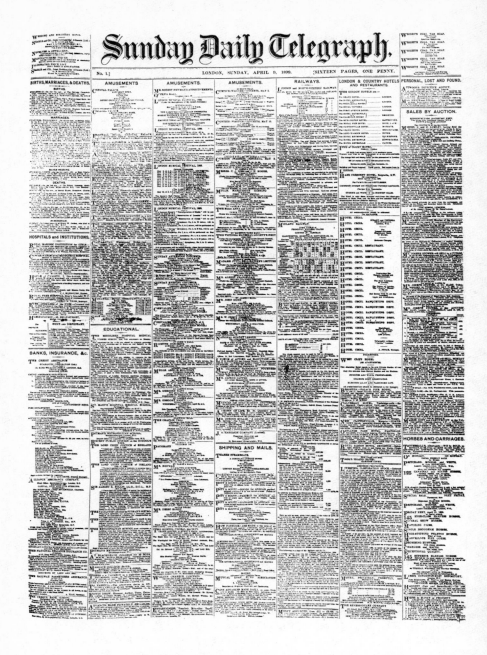

reduce the price of the *Telegraph* to a halfpenny (something which he could well have afforded); another, to aim down, editorially speaking, and fight the *Mail* on its own terms for lowbrow readers; the third, to make the most of his own strong position on the middle ground, between the *Mail* and the *Times*, and keep on as before. This was the course he chose; and it is clear that by then he was too set in his ways to bring about vigorous innovations. Years of success, easy profits and sheer age had made him reluctant to change, and he would not face the fact that his enterprise was going rapidly downhill.

Nor would his son Harry. The second Lord Burnham, who succeeded to the title on his father's death in 1916, and was made a viscount three years later in recognition of his many public services, was an admirable man, whose praises were widely sung: intelligent, hard-working, generous and friendly. But at heart he was a politician, not a journalist, and although he took on the running of the paper from 1903, he never brought to it the sharp, eager, competitive edge that had enabled his father to carve a great swathe through the opposition half a century earlier.

Having startled the university authorities by getting married while still at Oxford – a rare step for an undergraduate in those days – Harry went into politics the moment he came down, elected Liberal Member for West St Pancras in 1885, the baby of the House of Commons at the age of twenty-two. Thereafter he was several times in and out of Parliament, always heavily involved in local government, and, because of his industry and skill as a chairman, repeatedly invited to take charge of official committees, inquiries or commissions. One of his best-known contributions to society was the creation of the Burnham Scale, for teachers' pay, in the early 1920s; but such was his repute by then that he was appointed to a series of international positions – President of the first International Labour Conferences at the League of Nations held in Geneva in 1921 and 1922; Chairman of the Public Health Conference at Bordeaux in 1924; and President of the International Press Conference at Geneva in 1927.

As a result of these public commitments, although nominally in control of the *Telegraph*, Burnham could never give it the single-minded energy which it needed, and sales continued to decline. He made a damaging mistake in 1922, when, to improve the paper's appearance and legibility, he installed new printing presses at enormous cost, but insisted – against the advice of everyone else concerned – on keeping to the old, out-of-date shape of the pages, which were three inches longer than those of any other London paper. The result was that *The Daily Telegraph* remained clumsy and difficult to handle. The final straw came in 1927, when he was appointed to the Simon Commission, which went out to India to report on the Montagu-Chelmsford constitution and to suggest further steps along the path towards self-government. By then sales had dwindled to 84,000, and even with the price at twopence – to which it had been pushed by rising costs during the First World War – it was clear that a powerful new initiative, as well as an infusion of capital, would be needed to start a renaissance. Burnham was by then too old, at sixty-four, and too preoccupied with high-level political tasks to face the effort. Nor had he a son who could take over, his only child being one daughter. So it was that, with infinite regret, and to the great anger and disappointment of his nephew, Lt. Col. Edward Lawson, who was working on the editorial side of the paper, in the autumn of 1927 he made an approach to Sir William Berry and asked if he would buy the *Telegraph*.

Edward – always known as Fred – was then thirty-seven, and full of fight: after Eton and Oxford he had joined the *Telegraph* as a reporter, and during the First World War had commanded the Middlesex Yeomanry with distinction, winning the DSO, MC and three mentions in despatches. In 1927 he felt strongly that, given the chance, he could have raised the necessary funds through friends and given the paper new life himself. *The Daily Telegraph* had belonged to his family for seventy-two years. His great-uncle, who had built it up, had proved himself one of the outstanding journalistic innovators of all time. The paper had never ceased to make money. Yet now, the liveliest young member of the family was not consulted, and after no more than a couple of brief meetings between Lord Burnham and the Berry brothers, the change of ownership went through.

3 THE BERRYS TAKE OVER, 1928–30

On Friday, 23 December 1927, the 22,659th issue of *The Daily Telegraph* carried a small but momentous announcement in a panel on its main news page. Under the heading CHANGE OF OWNERSHIP there appeared the news that the proprietors had made arrangements for disposing of the paper to Sir William Berry, Mr Gomer Berry and Sir Edward Iliffe, who would assume control on 9 January 1928. 'No change in the political policy is involved,' the announcement continued. 'Lord Burnham is confident that the traditions and standards of the journal, which has belonged to his family for three generations, will be fully maintained by its new Proprietors.' The contract for the sale was signed on 18 January, the new proprietors agreeing to pay £1,200,000.

As with any newspaper sale, the impending takeover sent rumours flying among the staff, who had heard the news before the official announcement and were not too sure about this ambitious Welshman, Sir William Berry. They knew that he owned several other newspapers, including the *Sunday Times*, but not why he wanted to buy out the Burnhams. Sensing their anxiety, and fearing that some of them might drift off to rival organs, the Editor of the *Telegraph*, Arthur Watson, went to see Berry at his office in Arundel Street and asked what he might expect in the way of changes. The answer was reassuring: the new owner had no intention of dismissing any of the staff or of making radical innovations. His aim, rather, was to expand and improve the paper gradually.

Rumours spread outside the building as well – among them a claim that the vendors had hawked their title around various possible buyers before finding someone prepared to take it on. This Berry firmly denied. The truth was that Lord Burnham, who knew him anyway, and had heard that Berry was anxious to try his hand at running a serious daily, had made the first approach. After an exchange of letters, the two men met for discussions at the Oxford and Cambridge Club; but because Burnham forgot to reserve a private room, they were obliged to hold their most important meeting in the billiard-room, and a deal was concluded with the minimum of formality.

The paper which Berry and his two partners bought was thoroughly run-down. Its premises were decrepit, its presses out-of-date, its staff old and eccentric, its readers both elderly and dwindling in numbers. Of the 84,000 copies it was selling a day, at a price of twopence, about 10,000 were bought for only one penny by schoolmasters, clergymen, civil servants and others, for whom there existed a special dispensation, granted also by the *Times*.

Leonard Russell, who had recently joined the editorial staff as a junior, left a vivid glimpse of the general decay, and of the characters who drifted around the old building:

> Men in green baize aprons who wandered about with no apparent duties, wizened creatures in cloth caps who would creep up from the bowels and disappear again as if they feared the light of day, seemingly pensioners who had no other home.

For Russell, no one epitomised the old days more strongly than Harry Gellatley, the Librarian: an ancient hunchback with a blotched red face, who would emerge from a corner when other people had gone home, to dry his handkerchief before the coal fire, and then hobble off 'to some secret recess' to make a pot of tea. 'Tea, snuff and dried handkerchiefs were the sweeteners of his existence', and although he was of a crusty nature, he would sometimes open up to his young listener about the legendary characters of the past, telling, for instance, how that drunken Bohemian George Augustus Sala would storm into Sir Edward Lawson's room, already well oiled, and cry out, 'You bladdy Jew, give me some money!'

The handover to the new regime proved easy and good-natured, marred by none of the recrimination which often sours such occasions. Appointing himself Editor-in-Chief, Berry at once took close personal control, and a few days before the official transfer of power held a meeting for all members of staff at the Memorial Hall in Farringdon Street. Emotions ran high. As Berry himself recorded, 'Lord and Lady Burnham were both in tears . . . and a number of the staff were in the same condition. To many of them the future seemed black, as they had no knowledge of what violent changes the new proprietors might have in mind.'

Soothing anxieties, Berry assured them that every one of the old

46

guard might feel as secure under his ownership as they had under the Burnhams', provided they all pulled their weight. Anyone who received this news with scepticism was soon confounded, for the speaker lived up to his word. In April the Institute of Journalists held a farewell lunch for Lord Burnham; five hundred people attended, and the guest of honour's health was proposed by the Prime Minister, Stanley Baldwin, who either did not know about, or prudently concealed, the differences of opinion which had split the Lawsons over the sale, and spoke of the family as a shining example in the newspaper world 'of that hereditary principle for which he did not conceal his admiration'.

Bill Berry was then forty-eight, at the height of his vigour, with his great natural ability strengthened by more than thirty years' experience of journalism. Although the problems facing him were immense, he quickly decided that the way to make a real advance lay in reducing the price of the paper to one penny – exactly as the Lawsons had done when *they* took over; yet he could not take this bold step before he had improved the content and re-equipped with new presses.

On the human front, his method was not to fire people, as other newspaper tycoons did, but to make the best of the team he had, and to strengthen it gradually by drafting in new recruits. His most surprising move, in many people's eyes, was to retain Lord Burnham's nephew, Lt. Col. Edward Lawson ('Fred'), not on the editorial side, but as General Manager. Lawson himself was amazed, and used to joke that his survival must have been due solely to the fact that he was the one man who could find his way about the labyrinth of the old building. In fact, Berry retained him not out of kindness or simply to maintain the family involvement, but because he was extremely competent and a skilful organiser. He also had an outstanding touch with people, and, even when he became Lord Burnham, was quite capable of returning to the office late in the evening, slipping off his dinner jacket and going down to the printworks still wearing his bow-tie to talk round the men causing a problem.

Another key survivor was the Editor, Arthur Watson, who was then forty-seven and had been in the chair since 1924. A tall man – taller even than Berry – he was well-built, vigorous and upright in every sense of the word, with a large, dark moustache which turned white as he grew older. In both appearance and conduct he was a nineteenth-century editor, punctilious in his dealings with the staff, and a good disciplinarian, but with few contacts outside the building. He was also extremely austere: a teetotaller, a nonsmoker, he had no indulgences except a passion for high-powered cars, which he drove at terrifying speed. He was strikingly different from his brother Alfred Watson, who at that time was Editor of the *Statesman* in Calcutta, and expressed such forthright political and social views as to provoke two attempts on his life (the second, in 1932, forced him to retire, with severe gunshot wounds).

It is hard to imagine Arthur Watson provoking any such attack, for he had practically no views about anything except gardening, and almost always spoke in a whisper. Yet behind his modest exterior lurked many admirable qualities: he was patient, shrewd and loyal, an excellent judge of character, and he never shirked unpleasant tasks. If he was rather limited, he was also perfectly fair and never made a mistake. It was said that whenever he had to tick someone off, he did it in the kindest possible manner, but at the same time left the person in default acutely conscious of his or her shortcomings, and that even when confronted by impossibly bad copy, would react no more violently than by murmuring, 'It won't do.'

A pleasing glimpse of Watson in action was left by Leonard Marsland Gander, a lively and adventurous fellow who had previously worked in India. Returning in 1926 to London from Bombay, where he had been chief reporter on the *Times of India*, and had covered for *The Daily Telegraph* the story of the attempted abduction of Mumtaz Begum, favourite dancing girl of the Maharajah of Indore, he went to 135 Fleet Street in search of a job.

> I inquired at a glass-fronted cubicle in the dark front hall for Mr Watson . . . There was the usual pause for internal telephoning, and then I was taken to a waiting room on the first floor. I sat there quaking. After a minute or two a large, bespectacled man, who towered above me, strode briskly in and began talking in a quiet and friendly voice. I explained myself, and answered a few questions about India, wondering all the time who he could be. I did not think it possible that a great editor, immersed in his important work, could find time to see a nonentity of twenty-four from Bombay. Unable to restrain my curiosity, I asked him outright. Yes, it was Mr Arthur Watson.

After two preliminary interviews, and summoned to a third, Gander was startled to find himself offered the job of 'Wireless Correspondent' at nine guineas a week. Accepting, he asked that the title should be changed to 'Radio Correspondent', and that he should be furnished with a portable typewriter. To his surprise, both requests were granted.

Low-keyed though he might be, Watson was a first-class technician, thoroughly familiar with every aspect of newspaper production, and never happier than when working against time on the stone (that is, in the composing-room). His expertise was the result of thorough training, for he had started work on the Newcastle *Daily Leader* (which was edited by his father Aaron) and had done most journalistic jobs by the age of twenty. When he joined *The Daily Telegraph* as a parliamentary reporter in 1902, at the age of twenty-two, he was the youngest member of the staff. In the First World War he became a major in the Royal Artillery; and when he returned, Lord Burnham, seeing how he had matured into a capable leader, first made him Night Editor, then Assistant Editor, before appointing him Editor on the sudden death of his predecessor, Fred Miller.

With engaging candour, Watson later described how nervous he had been about the arrival of Sir William Berry, and how his 'shell of defensive apprehension' had melted before the 'frank and trusting reception' which he got from his new proprietor. Whether he realised it or not, Watson was precisely the kind of Editor that Berry needed: able but not ambitious, efficient but not aggressive, and above all willing to work under a proprietor who took the closest interest in the day-to-day running of the paper.

The relationship established between the two men set a pattern which became the hallmark of the Berry family's reign at the *Telegraph*, adopted not only by William, but by his son Michael too. At the takeover in 1928 Watson was in effect demoted: with an Editor-in-Chief coming in above him, he was still known as the Editor, but in fact suffered some loss of authority and control. Other, more independent-minded men might not have been able to accept such a limitation; but Watson could, apparently without discomfort – and so, in due course, could all his successors, on both the daily and Sunday newspapers which this branch of the Berry family ran.

Keeping Watson in position, Berry began to draft in new men of his own. Among them was Cyril Lakin, a flashy and good-looking young Welshman who had been called to the Bar and had picked up some elements of journalism on the *Western Mail* in Cardiff. In the dim corridors of 135 Fleet Street, Lakin's flamboyance blazed out to great effect: according to Leonard Russell, he wore 'expensive, square-shouldered suits with enormously wide lapels and double-breasted waistcoats', and 'danced about on the balls of his feet like a middle-weight boxer', not least when playing golf near East Grinstead in orange plus-fours. In 1929, undeterred by Lakin's lack of experience, Berry made him Literary Editor and Assistant Editor, in charge of the leader-page and twice-weekly book-review pages, and word got about that he was the Crown Prince, who in due course would succeed Watson as Editor. Whether or not this was ever the intention, Lakin ended the rumours by moving to the *Sunday Times* – but not before he had recruited some admirable book-reviewers, among them Rebecca West, Cyril Connolly and Cecil Day Lewis.

Although many of the full-time editorial staff had grown old, a few young men were just setting out on lifetimes' service to the paper. Among them was Edward Harwood, who had been taken on as an office boy in February 1924 after coming thirteenth in a national essay competition. By the end of 1927, at the time of the takeover, he was a junior assistant in the library, and under the Berry regime he helped start the new cuttings library. From 1933 to 1940 he was Deputy Librarian, and then, after a spell of war service, Chief Librarian from 1945. On 26 February 1974 a lunch was given for him at Kettners Restaurant in Soho to celebrate his fifty years with the firm. A spare, studious-looking man, with appearance and manner as dry as parchment, he was also a formidable compiler of crossword puzzles, and had published over 6,000 in various newspapers.

Another recent recruit was H. J. C. Stevens, who had been appointed Chief Accountant in 1927, at the age of twenty-nine. Tall and erect, with a harsh, hectoring, sergeant-major's voice, and something of the vulture in his appearance, he took such a grip of the company's books that he remained in charge of them for fifty years, and became the terror of journalists and management alike, concealing his devotion to the firm behind raucous and derisive comments on the outrageous nature of expense claims.

By the time Berry took over, the *Telegraph* was in both appearance and content a poor relation of the *Times*. Its long columns, twenty-five inches deep, gave it a dowdy, old-fashioned look which was not redeemed by any flair in its presentation of the news. The issue of Monday, 2 January 1928 was typical: twenty pages, poorly illustrated, with the front page given over entirely to advertisements, which included announcements of concerts, shipping movements and so on (Cook's Winter Sunshine Cruises promised 'glorious sunshine'). The news, scattered about the paper, began on page four, and took the form of anonymous, very short reports, no more than three or four paragraphs long, under uniform headlines set in small roman capitals. Here and there a gleam shone out from the grey background – SLEEPWALKING MILLIONAIRE STEALS BEGGAR'S CLOTHES – FOUND SHOT IN BATHROOM – but most of it was as appetising as suet. The leading articles, of which there were four, were made to look insignificant by the fact that the first (and presumably most important) did not start until more than halfway down the third column of the leader-page. As in the *Times*, the fourth leader was a light, humorous piece unconnected with the news.

The Court page, as usual, carried a long list of the movements of society figures: 'The Earl of Dunmore, VC, and the Countess of Dunmore have returned to London from the country' . . . 'Lord and Lady Armstrong will remain at Bamburgh Castle, Northumberland, till the end of this month.' It is a safe bet that the news of greatest interest to most readers was that about the weather. For weeks past the paper's picture-page had been given over almost exclusively to snow-scenes: the whole country had been gripped by arctic temperatures, and now, in the first issue of 1929, the photographs were again of sledging and skating parties 'in snowbound Britain'. Yet the forecasters were at last speaking of a break: milder air was coming in from the north-west and bringing the first signs of a thaw. It is perhaps not too fanciful to see that overdue change in the weather as a symbol of the fresh air that was on its way into 135 Fleet Street, belatedly blown in by new owners to revive a venerable institution. By the middle of the week half the country, it seemed, had been flooded, and the news was a good deal more lively: INCH AN HOUR RISE: MENACE OF THE THAMES and SNAKE IN AN AEROPLANE: KILLED IN MID AIR.

Already one of the *Telegraph*'s main strengths was well developed: its classified advertising. Packed into the back of the paper were columns and columns of small notices offering and soliciting jobs. Sixty years on, they give a sharp insight into the stratification of society between the world wars, when the middle- and upper-classes could still afford to employ servants on a lavish scale. Drapery, Dressmaking, Hairdressing, Millinery and a dozen other professions offered vacancies; there were opportunities for Typists, Lady Clerks, Chauffeurs, Motor Mechanics, Hotel Assistants and Barmaids; and under the general heading 'The Household' came separate sections for Cooks, Cooks General, House Kitchenmaids, Housekeepers, Companions and Helps, Governesses, Nurses, Butlers, Valets, Manservants, General Servants, Parlourmaids, House Parlourmaids and Married Couples. This great army of retainers ministered to a much smaller number of employers, and often advertisements for new staff indicated the size and strength of the household: 'Cook wanted in Oxfordshire – family three, staff seven' was a typical ratio. Nor, in those halcyon days, was it illegal to specify the sex, type or even size of the person required: 'A GOOD PARLOURMAID (English) as soon as possible. About 30. Protestant. Fairly tall. One lady. Staff five. Kensington Gardens.' Such calls for help provided the life-blood of *The Daily Telegraph*, and so many people called in person at the office that the paper set up an interview bureau in which prospective employers could size up those who had answered their announcements.

Yet advertisements were only part of the story. The affliction of the paper, in recent years, had been lack of editorial space. With sales and revenue falling, the proprietors had tried the traditional remedy of keeping the number of pages down and cramming those that they did run full of advertisements, with the inevitable result that little room was left for editorial matter. As Watson himself recorded, the staff had been 'extremely conscious' of the paper's weaknesses, but had been unable to do anything about them, as 'control had been too parsimonious'. Berry had the vision to see that in the long term parsimony was no use: customers must be given more to read, and from the first day of his tenure he increased the number of pages, opening up the editorial space, even though at first it cost him dear.

A leader in the *Times* hailed the takeover as 'something more than an event in the world of journalism', and Berry's friend (and rival) Lord Beaverbrook wrote to him on 6 February 1928: 'I think it shows an immense improvement.' But he went on to suggest that Berry should demand of the Conservative Party that the letters of Cabinet Ministers be made available to the *Telegraph* as well as to the *Times*, which until then had been the only recipient. 'It is a most unfair arrangement,' wrote Beaverbrook; but as he hated the *Times*, and was usually trying to stir up trouble for it, Berry no doubt received this advice coolly.

What he urgently needed were new readers, for some of those inherited from the Burnham era were of tremendous antiquity. One can no longer be sure whether the extreme longevity of *Telegraph* readers was as much of a joke in the 1920s as it became half a century later; but it must have been clear that Mr J. M. Nisbet, who surfaced in Huyton, Liverpool, during October 1928, was in a class of his own. 'I claim a record which, if it can be equalled, cannot be beaten,' he wrote, 'as I have been a reader since the issue of the first number.' Since 1855? It seemed impossible – and yet it was true. Born in 1840 – and therefore eighty-eight when he wrote the letter – Nisbet had been articled to a firm of publishers at the age of fourteen, and recalled that, 'where the Law Courts now stand was a shop', occupied by a firm of toymakers. Across its front, one day, had appeared a 'broad band of sheeting' on which was written, in huge letters, THE DAILY TELEGRAPH. At first the boy Nisbet was puzzled as to what this slogan signified, but later he realised that the building had been the first office of the newspaper.

Such veterans might well have been put off by drastic changes; but at first the new management did nothing radical, and with minor improvements the paper gradually increased its sales. Before the takeover, working (as Watson put it) 'in a straitjacket', the staff had rarely been able to find room for more than two readers' letters in any one issue. Now two whole columns were reserved every day for Letters to the Editor. News stories and features were made fuller, photographs larger. Gradually the paper began to look better.

At the end of May 1928 the whole Berry clan was shaken by a disaster. At 8.15 am on the twenty-third, Seymour, Lord Buckland, went out for a ride, as was his custom, on his estate at Bwlch, before settling down to his day's work. An experienced horseman, he had for years ridden to hounds; that day he was mounted on a favourite bay mare, and set off at a canter, turning in the saddle now and then to pass a remark over his shoulder to his groom Henry Weaver, who followed on another horse some twenty yards behind. Perhaps the exhilaration of the fresh summer morning made Buckland careless: at any rate, Weaver suddenly noticed that he was riding dangerously close to a line of telegraph poles, and shouted a warning. Buckland's horse shied to the left, and the rider, leaning out of the saddle the other way, hit his head on one of the poles. The blow fractured his skull and brought him crashing to the ground, killing him instantaneously. Only five minutes after he had left the house, he was brought back dead.*

Tributes poured in from leading politicians, including the Prime Minister (Stanley Baldwin), Lloyd George, Ramsay MacDonald, and the Leader of the House of Commons, T. P. O'Connor, who remarked that Buckland 'loved a great joke as hugely as a great stroke of business', and that 'he never took himself with any pretentious seriousness'. But it was his grimly splendid funeral that gave local people a chance to show the esteem in which they held

---

* Bill Berry had also been a keen rider, but had given up in 1926 when he too had a bad fall, breaking his collarbone and two ribs.

him. On the morning of 26 May his coffin was borne two miles through the park at Bwlch on a farm wagon covered with laurel. His brothers William and Gomer led the chief mourners, who followed on foot. At Llansantffraed Lodge the coffin was transferred to a motor hearse, which carried it through Brecon and over the hills to Merthyr. In every house along the route the blinds were drawn; the streets were lined with people, and little groups with bared heads stood at every crossroads over the Brecon Beacons.

In Merthyr the streets were so choked with mourners that the cortege could scarcely force its way through to the English Congregational Church in Market Square. In the chapel, only three women of special distinction were allowed to join the congregation of six hundred men, and bells tolled for half an hour before the coffin was carried in by six police officers under the command of the chief constable. After the service, the body was cremated at Pontypridd, a few miles down the valley.*

Buckland's untimely end let loose some malicious rumours. It was said that a cheer went up on the Stock Exchange in Cardiff when news of his death arrived; that a proposal was mooted for a statue to be raised to the horse that had killed him; that, when his body was laid out for the funeral, the people filing past the coffin could be heard remarking: 'First time the old bugger's ever been straight in his life!' Yet if his sharpness in business had been too much for some of his rivals, the fact remains that to this day he is remembered in his home town with immense respect and gratitude, and a statue of him (by W. Goscombe John) stands outside the public library.

Nor did his benefactions to Merthyr – so generous in his lifetime – cease with his death. Shortly before he died, he had made over a large sum to a trust fund for his children and grandchildren; even so, in his will he left unsettled property with a gross value of £1,116,447 (worth perhaps £20 million at 1990 values). He also left shares in Guest, Keen & Nettlefold worth £50,000 for the relief of the poor in Merthyr, and further gifts of a thousand second preference shares for each of the town's five schools, as well as a thousand shares to the Market Square Chapel. Further, he asked that his widow should continue to support the charitable institutions which he had favoured, and in particular the Merthyr General Hospital. His brothers did what they could to take his place in Welsh affairs, Gomer succeeding him as President of the hospital and William as Governor of Christ's College, Brecon; and in November

---

* Even today, all-male funerals are still common in Wales.

1928 they themselves handed over £5,000 for poor relief, since income from Buckland's will fund did not become available for two years after his death.

Meanwhile William, though faced with the huge outlay needed to modernise the *Telegraph*, made a substantial benefaction of his own. On 31 May 1928, only a week after his brother had been killed, he formally handed over twenty-three acres of land on the summit of St Anne's Hill, Chertsey, to the town of Chertsey, as a park for public recreation. By buying the land the previous autumn, he had saved it from the builder, and since then he had opened up the woodland to form walks and viewing places. When Molly Berry unlocked the gate leading to the hill with a golden key, the family's gesture was seen as no mere local event, but a national gesture towards conservation far ahead of its time.

In London Berry continued to make improvements in his new paper. But he was also active on the fringes of politics and, perhaps with an eye to his own future, saw to it that the Prime Minister, Baldwin, was given a good press. On 6 March 1929, at lunch with J. C. C. Davidson (who had been Secretary to Baldwin and Bonar Law, and by then was Chairman of the Unionist Party), he 'waxed very anti-Lloyd George . . . pinning his faith on Neville [Chamberlain] as first lieutenant to the PM'. As the meal was ending, he sheepishly asked whether, now that his brother was dead, it would be possible for him to be considered for a peerage. Davidson assured him that it would be 'more than possible', but felt that it would be better if the award were made after the election (which was due in May). So, for the moment, he had to wait.

Official reward for Berry's enterprise and success in the newspaper world – and for the sound Conservative stance of his journals – came in June 1929, when, in the few days of power granted to him before his defeat by Ramsay MacDonald, Baldwin created him a baron. He took the title Baron Camrose of Long Cross – Camrose being the hamlet near Haverfordwest from which the Berry family had come, and Long Cross the village next to his home, Barrow Hills, in Surrey. In thanking Baldwin effusively for his letter of appreciation, Camrose described how the Prime Minister had 'inspired in my brother Buckland great affection', and how he himself and his younger brother had

> had the satisfaction of giving our assistance to somebody for whom we have the greatest respect and in whose honesty of purpose and single-minded devotion to the welfare of the community one could only have the most unbounded confidence.

55

At the *Telegraph* one major limitation on progress was the size of the building at No. 135, which had no space for the extra staff whom Camrose wanted to take on. The whole site was large, amounting to one-and-a-half acres; but the office accommodation, which fronted on to Fleet Street, was quite inadequate for the new regime.

The old building, completed in 1882, had once been the last word in style and efficiency: it was faced with Portland stone and Aberdeen granite, and in the words of Leonard Russell, 'had the air of having escaped from the terrace of great clubs in Pall Mall'. Externally, it was distinguished by its clock – 'the first public clock in Fleet Street lit by electricity', a well-known landmark. Inside, its most imposing feature was the grand hall, more than ninety feet long and forty wide, which occupied the whole of the ground floor. The high ceiling supported by two rows of marble pillars, the black-and-white marble slabs on the floor, the counters and fittings of polished oak – all its features conspired to impress the stream of visitors who called to place advertisements.

Half a century later, the splendour had faded, and decrepitude had overtaken the building. Leonard Russell left a snapshot of the upper regions:

> On the first floor, among busts of Gladstone and Disraeli, and paintings of ruined temples by Panini and Spy caricatures of George Augustus Sala and Sir Edwin Arnold, the traditions of the place were guarded by a number of tottering old gentlemen ... Above this powerhouse was the vast library, running the length of the building, and here at five every evening the five assistant night editors took their places, to read the proofs in a silence and an atmosphere appropriate to a club library ... Above this magnificent room ... was a mahogany gallery, with one end of it partitioned off into a long, narrow room. Here, in the late afternoon and early evening, special writers in frock coats turned out a column or two, pen travelling with fatal calmness over the paper – they all wrote shorthand, and practically no one in the whole office used a typewriter.

Such obsolescence held no attraction for Camrose and his partners, who swiftly commissioned a new building from the architects Elcock & Sutcliffe, at a cost of £250,000. Under the supervision of Fred Lawson, work began in June 1929 with the demolition of the old façade, half at a time; and safety regulations were so relaxed that young George Ailles, who joined the firm that year as a fourteen-year-old messenger boy, was able to sit on the parapet during his lunch hour and observe operations with his feet dangling over the abyss of Fleet Street.*

Once again the façade was of Portland stone but a distinguishing feature of the new building was the grey Creetown granite, with a single black band running across it, used for the base; and this time the core of the structure was of steel and reinforced concrete. Contemporary reports described it as 'neither efficient modern nor pseudo-classical', but 'a really modern building full of originality and excitement, on a classical basis'. To the *Financial Times* it was 'perfectly sincere, full of spirit, great originality and a strong sense of unity in the decorative features. One gets the impression that this is the work of one who has been brought up on classical architecture, studied the art of ancient Egypt and Assyria, and then given to them a modern expressionism, relating them to the needs and conditions of the present day.'

As a further embellishment, the young sculptor Samuel Rabino-vitch, who had worked with Jacob Epstein, was commissioned to carve two modernist heads directly into the stonework on the façade, ninety feet above street level. The western head – stern, glum and emaciated – represented the past; the eastern one, with its beaming, open countenance, the future.

In a pamphlet produced on its own new premises, the *Telegraph* boasted that the building was the tallest in Fleet Street, and 'the most modern, up-to-date newspaper office in the British Empire'. (It immediately became fashionable as a vantage point from which to photograph St Paul's Cathedral, on Ludgate Hill half a mile to the east.) A particular point of pride was that, with the exception of three American lifts and some decorative Italian marble, it was 'constructed of British and Empire materials from top to bottom'. All rooms were fitted with 'electric synchronised clocks, central floor plugs to take desk light, wall or ceiling light, internal tele-phone, radio and heat'. Much was made of the new, high-speed lifts, which could go from bottom to top of the six floors in eight seconds. Built by Waygood-Otis, they were of 'the latest gearless type, operated by a most modern form of automatic control':

This control is unique. Passengers operate the lifts themselves, those in the car pressing buttons for the destinations required, and those on landings buttons corresponding to the desired direction of travel. The lifts will answer all such calls in correct floor sequence in each direction.

* He retired as General Manager fifty-one years later.

By the standards of the day, the reborn 135 Fleet Street was a palace, the very model of a modern newspaper office. Yet in one respect the new building bore a curious resemblance to the old. Since the well-being of the paper still depended largely on its classified advertisements, and since many of these were still brought in by hand, it was once again deemed essential that the entrance hall should be of splendid proportions. So it was that the new proprietors demanded – or anyway were given – a grand room two storeys high, dignified by great bronze doors, huge hanging lamps of bronze and frosted crystal, white marble walls and elaborate oak counters at which the paper's lifeblood could be received with both despatch and dignity. The impression of efficient modernity was heightened by a special device, the particular pride of Fred Lawson: a vertically mounted, rotating belt which whisked advertisements and letters straight up from the porter's desk through the ceiling to the higher floors (and which, if the truth be told, was constantly breaking down).

The stairwell, too, was clad in white marble, and the Editor's office, at the eastern end of the first-floor corridor, was decked out with oak-panelling, antique bronze wall-lights and 'a Tudor style brick fireplace'. The room was of necessity large and comfortable – the pamphlet explained – 'for here the Editor interviews men of public affairs, as well as the leader-writers and heads of department'. On the sixth floor was a canteen, an editorial dining-room with cloths, napery and flowers on the tables, and a bar at which a pint of beer cost sixpence, rather than the sevenpence or eightpence charged by pubs outside. Anybody in the building could place orders with the canteen by telephone, and a pot of tea and toast – or whatever the request might be – would be brought down to the caller's office by a waitress smartly dressed in black, with white apron and hat.

All this was very go-ahead; but nothing could match the splendour of the suite furnished for the proprietors on the fifth floor (the two words soon came to stand for the human inhabitants of that storey, the supreme power in the building, as much as for the storey itself). There, besides three sumptuous offices for the proprietors, were a smoking-room and a dining-room, panelled in what looked like walnut, with carved mantelpieces and floodlit ceilings, again the epitome of modern design.* Altogether, the

* When the Fifth Floor was damaged by fire after the war, it became apparent that the panelling consisted of nothing but a veneer of Australian pine one-sixteenth of an inch thick.

proprietors' accommodation was reckoned among the finest in the world – and it had one extra feature, of which no casual passer-by in Fleet Street could be aware. Outside the windows of the offices, in the recessed central section of the main façade, lay a small rectangular garden – a strip of lawn, with flowers along the back, invisible from below, but adding immensely to the attraction of the working environment.

If the inadequacies of the old building had been a constraint on progress, a still greater handicap was the state of the printing presses, which, though only five years old, were already obsolete, and lacked the capacity to produce the larger papers which the new management wanted. Another £250,000 was therefore invested in new machinery, and the back of the building was remodelled, again under Lawson's supervision. In the composing-room fifty-two Linotype machines were installed, for setting the type in hot metal, and below them, in the machine-room, five Superspeed presses of the latest design gave the proprietors the capacity they needed for printing not only *The Daily Telegraph* but the *Sunday Times* as well. 'FIVE IMMENSE NEW PRESSES FOR PRINTING THE DAILY TELEGRAPH' cried the headline in a supplement published on 19 November 1929. 'This supplement is the first issue from one of the big battery of presses – mechanical marvels capable of producing a forty-page paper at the rate of 40,000 copies per machine per hour – which in the New Year will be printing *The Daily Telegraph*.'

Flushed with its new strength, and no doubt hoping to dazzle readers with technical wizardry, the paper burst into a high-flown account of the miracles that took place every night:

> The machine room is now the centre of activity, with the big presses waiting for the word 'Go!' From the autoplate machines come the crash and metallic echo as the plates leave the great shavers; gongs sound once more, arc-lights fizz and flutter; one after another the presses begin to revolve; the revolution counters show flickering needles, the machines rumble, break into a hum, and then, going full speed . . . open to a full-throated roar . . . The first edition is being run off!

The new presses ran all-out for the first time on the night of 14 February 1930, and the paper which appeared on the fifteenth was the first with smaller, modern pages. Freed at last from technical restraints, Camrose could now play his ace of trumps and reduce the price of the paper to one penny. News of this momentous change was leaked exclusively to the trade journal *World's Press News* on 27 November 1930, and it was put into practice on Monday 1 December.

A cynic might say that the move was old hat. The Levy-Lawsons had done the same thing in 1855, and the proprietors of other newspapers had emulated them. Yet, even if the idea was not new, it needed some nerve, for it carried a substantial risk: if the reduction in price had misfired, it would have incurred very large losses. Many people doubted whether it was possible for anyone, no matter how dedicated, to raise the circulation of the paper as high as Camrose hoped without sacrificing its essential seriousness – but in the event the move proved a masterstroke.

As Camrose himself later remarked, at the time of the price-cut no alteration of any kind was made in the content of the paper; and in an interview with *World's Press News* Fred Lawson emphasised that 'while selling at the popular price, we shall remain a "quality" paper'. The only apparent innovation was a bold strap-line at the top right of the front page proclaiming 'PRICE – ONE PENNY'. The effect, however, was sensational: sales – under 100,000 in November 1929 – leapt to 175,000 in December and 200,000 in January 1930, before settling into a steady climb of 50,000 a year. *The Daily Telegraph* was on its way to power.

From the start the cornerstone of the whole enterprise was news: news, news and more news was packed in with a minimum of display. Reports were still short, and the great majority were anonymous. The layout, although better than before, remained dreary, the typography amateurish; but, dull as it looked, the paper began to outreach all rivals in the breadth of its coverage. News was Camrose's passion, and he made it the paper's greatest strength. Years later, when people sought to analyse the secret of his success, many imagined that by some brilliant intuition he had divined the mental and spiritual needs of the newly educated middle-classes, and catered to them accordingly. The truth – less mysterious – was simply that he gave them unparalleled value for money: by keeping the price of the paper down, and packing it with information, he produced a daily bargain which more and more people were glad to snap up.

No doubt other factors also worked in his favour. As his Advertisement Manager, George Simon, put it, people in Britain were 'overcoming the instability of the earlier post-war years and going in for more solid fare'. There was, he said, 'an increasing demand for quality in life' – and it was on to this demand that the revitalised *Daily Telegraph* latched with such success. Another favourable factor – in the eyes of Arthur Watson – was the moderate political view expressed by the paper. Many people, he said, were 'tired of newspapers which are constantly propagating causes, one after another, and working them to death. They dislike finding their morning paper full, day after day, of propaganda for the cause which at the moment is uppermost in the proprietor's mind. They want a real newspaper based on sound, steady but progressive principles.'

Gradually Camrose began to leaven *The Daily Telegraph* with modest novelties, not least travel articles by his friend Winston Churchill who was then in the political wilderness and eager to earn money from his pen. One series, published in the autumn of 1929, described a journey to America and Canada, and offered a beguiling blend of travelogue and history. 'To feel a country,' the author remarked at one stage, 'you have to nibble its grass and handle its trees.'

Another innovation was the serialisation of books. Camrose's method was to run a large number of short extracts, rather than a few long ones, and to take maximum advantage of one project by spreading it out over several months. Thus on 2 September 1929 a front-page banner heralded publication of the memoirs of Prince Bülow, who had been Chancellor of the German Empire from 1900 to 1909. The opening extract amounted to no more than 1,200 words about the Kaiser's build-up to the First World War, but it clearly represented something of a scoop. The first series of twelve pieces ran for a fortnight; then came another two-week dose in November, and a third in January 1930.

Occasionally a moralistic note, perhaps echoing lessons learnt in the Welsh chapels, sounded in the news columns. On 5 January 1930, for instance, the headline BAN ON SORDID FILMS introduced an item about a curb threatened by the Chief Censor, Mr Edward Short. 'Scenes which were possible and permissible in silent pictures become repugnant when augmented by sound,' wrote the anonymous correspondent. 'It has to be recognised that the introduction of sound into films by heightening realism makes unpleasantly vivid things which the silent film left to the imagination.' Yet on the whole Camrose remained extraordinarily self-effacing. He used his powerful position neither to promote his own importance nor to force views down people's throats. In comparison with rival Fleet Street giants like Rothermere and Beaverbrook, he was modesty personified. News, not sensation, was what he sold.

He also stood by his staff unflinchingly – as when, in 1930, Arthur Watson was threatened with prosecution by Scotland Yard for refusing to reveal the source which had leaked him news of a Cabinet decision to arrest the Indian political agitator Mahatma Gandhi. With the backing of Camrose, Watson refused to divulge the name of his informer, even when interrogated by the Director of Public Prosecutions; and it was just as well for the Government that Watson remained silent, since his man had been J. R. Clynes, the former trades union leader who had become Home Secretary.

For all his high journalistic ideals, Camrose was not above indulging in mild sales-gimmicks. He never descended to the mass-bribery then practised by the popular journals, which gave away silver pencils and insurance policies by the thousand; but he lost no opportunity of promoting the paper and emphasising its virtues. Thus on 5 November 1930 he celebrated the *Telegraph*'s seventy-fifth birthday by publishing an issue of twenty-four full-sized pages and a supplement of thirty-two smaller ones. This, he claimed, set 'a new record in British journalism', for the main newspaper and supplement together formed the equivalent of forty full-sized pages, the largest edition ever printed in one operation in Great Britain. Messages of congratulation from the Prime Minister, Ramsay MacDonald, the Lord Mayor of London and lesser luminaries set a seal on the event.

Later in November 1930 the *Telegraph* claimed that it was opening 'a new era in household catering economics' with 'a remarkable innovation in advertising' which appeared on the women's page: the Harrods' Food News, giving details of prices and special offers. In February 1931 the paper announced another new feature: the Children's *Daily Telegraph*, 'an attractive illustrated section' for junior readers. 'The interests of the modern boy and girl are immensely varied,' ran the heavy-handed trailer. 'It will be the happy task of the editor of the children's section to give youthful readers informative articles, notes and news presented in a manner calculated to stimulate their interest in passing events and also the wonders of the world in general.' Behind this announcement one can detect the close interest of the Editor-in-Chief, whose own rather cursory schooling had left him with a strong didactic streak: a wish to educate as well as to inform, which he passed on to his sons and grandsons.

Camrose's energy and capacity for work were immense. In 1928, besides running the *Sunday Times* and putting *The Daily Telegraph* back on its feet, he had become involved in a tremendous circulation battle with Lord Rothermere, who, during a tour of the United States, received a message to the effect that the Berry brothers' newspaper empire had outgrown his own. This so incensed him that he sent orders for the launch of a vigorous counter-attack, which even Camrose, in his mild, measured prose, described as a 'very extraordinary and unprecedented campaign'. Rothermere's aim was to undermine the Berrys in the provinces by starting up new evening papers or buying titles already in existence. As Camrose later remarked, 'Nearly every newspaper of consequence received a tempting financial offer', but most of them 'stood firm and defied the threatened competition'. Rothermere's precipitate assault stirred up some frightful rows, notably in Bristol and Newcastle, and in private Camrose remarked to J. C. C. Davidson that in his view Rothermere was 'gradually going mad'; but after four years of dogged combat the Berry papers emerged unscathed, and Camrose himself was not deflected from his major task of reconstruction at 135 Fleet Street.

So, with Camrose at the editorial helm, and Gomer in charge of advertising and promotion, *The Daily Telegraph* began its long climb towards a target which most people considered unattainable by a serious newspaper: a circulation of a million copies a day.

4 TOWARDS THE MILLION, 1930–39

For most newspapers the 1930s were a kind of golden age. In the words of the historian Franklin Reid Gannon, 'the random harvest of the Elementary Education Act of 1870 was methodically gathered': more and more people acquired an appetite for news, and, with radio and television both in their infancy, the only medium which could satisfy their hunger was the Press. In the second half of the decade, as the threat of war increased, there was an ever-growing demand for accurate information. It turned out that Camrose had taken over *The Daily Telegraph* at a most auspicious moment; and with the expert hand of its new proprietor on the controls, the paper climbed like an aircraft from one circulation record to the next – from 100,000 in December 1930 to 300,000 by 1932, to 500,000 in 1935, to 750,000 in 1939 – confounding critics who had claimed that such a performance would be impossible for a serious journal, and leaving its old enemy the *Times* far behind, stuck at the 200,000 level.

The new owners of *The Daily Telegraph* made the offices on the fifth floor of 135 Fleet Street the headquarters of their entire operation. On thick writing-paper, embossed with a grandiose version of their address – 'Daily Telegraph Buildings, Fleet Street, E.C.4.' – they conducted the business not only of that newspaper but also of the *Sunday Times*, even though the head office of the group to which the Sunday paper belonged, Allied Newspapers, was at 200 Gray's Inn Road.

Like that other Fleet Street giant Lord Northcliffe, Camrose had a habit of tackling the morning paper in his earliest waking moments. A secretary came to his house first thing, and he would dictate criticisms and suggestions for onward transmission to the office. Often staff there had barely settled at their desks when a blast came through on the telephone. As Watson remarked, 'The terms, in the freshness of the morning, were apt to be a little rasping, but it usually happened, when I saw him an hour or two later, that while the criticisms remained, the testiness had gone.'

Though now a millionaire, Camrose enjoyed walking to work; but whether he arrived in Fleet Street on foot, or swept into the small yard of Peterborough Court by car, a commissionaire would leap forward at the sight of him to detain one of the lifts and usher him in. For most of the staff, this was their only glimpse of the proprietor – a tall, dark, distinguished-looking man, invariably dressed in a sombre suit, and often hatless, before that became fashionable, slipping into the building, to be carried straight up to his eyrie on the fifth floor, where another commissionaire or a butler sat at a desk on the landing, receiving written communications and guarding the sacred portals.

To this sanctuary Camrose would summon any member of the staff with whom he wanted to confer – principally the Editor, who would be called up to his first meeting at about midday. Writing of his chief later, Watson recorded that their relationship was 'always good, if not always completely smooth'. He described Camrose as 'straight in the back and in the eye, soft-spoken, and with a quiet geniality which quickly made him popular'. Yet there was evidently a touch of pepper about him, too: he always knew exactly what he wanted, and did not mind expressing himself bluntly. Some people were disconcerted by his habit of saying very little when things were going well, but a great deal when they were not. If not reclusive, he was at least reserved, and never sought contact with lesser members of the staff: indeed, to most of them he became an Olympian figure, cut off from ordinary mortals by his wealth and power, and also by the physical nature of the working environment which he had contrived. Such was the awe in which people held him that even if he merely came through on the internal telephone, the recipient of the call would sometimes spring to attention and remain rigidly upright while he spoke to the great man. The sycophantic tendencies inherited from the Burnham era were intensified, with the result that whenever a command or request came down from on high, no matter how trivial, there was a blind rush to carry out the order, and no consideration of whether or not the idea was a good one. Any project that emanated from Camrose was a 'must', and into the paper it would go.

The main difference between him and other newspaper tycoons lay in his lifelong fascination with the details of his profession. He ran *The Daily Telegraph* neither to promote himself nor to force political ideas on his readers: he ran it because he loved journalism, and was passionately concerned to create and maintain the best possible news service. As Watson remarked, no one ever had 'a more inquiring mind . . . A reporter would come back with what he believed to be a complete answer to some question raised by him, only to be met by a new set of penetrating queries which sent him out again with the feeling that he had hardly pierced the surface of his subject.' It was Camrose's insatiable appetite for facts, his curiosity for detail, that came through in *The Daily Telegraph* and made it uniquely successful.

Prominence was naturally given to any story which portrayed the paper as a pioneer of new developments. Thus on 1 February 1932, under the headline CAPE TOWN CALLING, a report described how the Prime Minister had inaugurated the first telephone service between London and South Africa:

> The message came from the *Daily Telegraph* Cape Town correspondent, Mr G. M. Green. Our correspondent's voice came clearly, without any disturbing influence, over the 5,000 miles of land and sea . . . The 'line' was so perfect that the horn of a passing motor car outside the office in which Mr Green was sitting could be heard when he spoke.

Again, on 10 September 1933, when the paper published the first pictures to reach England of King Feisal of Iraq, an accompanying report made their acquisition sound like some exploit of Biggles crossed with a journey by Richard Hannay:

> The pictures were flown from Baghdad to Britain, a distance of 3,000 miles, in eighty-four hours. The airmen met violent head-winds and terrific thunderstorms. So bad was the visibility over the Mediterranean that the airmen flew only ten feet above the waves.

Even in England, heroic tales could be told of the efforts made to keep readers abreast of current events. On 15 March 1934 the heading TAKING THE NEWS TO LAND'S END launched a breathless narrative by Our Special Representative in Penzance which featured Guard Loveday and the unprecedentedly skittish cross-head, WE TOPPED 90:

> There was a brief roar, and then Reading had swept past into the night. The vans of the world's fastest newspaper train lurched and thundered down the tracks, whirling the *Daily Telegraph* into the West Country in time for Cornish breakfast tables . . .

'Now for some speed,' shouts Loveday, above the thunder of the train.

Another essential feature of the paper – perhaps stemming from the proprietor's Nonconformist background in Wales – was that it did not peddle smut. Whenever Camrose ventured into print himself, he emphasised that *The Daily Telegraph* was in the business of 'clean' journalism, and he never relaxed his efforts to distance himself and his paper from the salacious posturings of the yellow or gutter press. It was as if the motto of the humble *Merthyr Times – Salus populi suprema lex –* had been elevated to a higher plane.

News was, and remained, the foundation of the enterprise. Yet Camrose also made much use of feature articles by outside authors, and of these none was more distinguished than Winston Churchill, still languishing in the political wilderness. He and Camrose became close friends; and although the newspaperman – with one short-lived exception – never showed any desire to enter politics himself, he was deeply interested in every turn of the game. In March 1930, for instance, he responded readily to Baldwin's request that he should start up an evening paper to counter the socialist line taken by the *Evening News* and *Evening Standard.* Since Camrose was short of ready cash at the time, J. C. C. Davidson went to Bristol to see if he could raise £400,000 from the tobacco empire of the Wills brothers, but the scheme fell through.

It is clear that Churchill much valued Camrose's advice, in both political and literary matters. Already, in 1933, Camrose began his letters 'My Dear Winston' and signed them 'Yours truly, Camrose', or 'Yours truly, Wm. Camrose'; but ten years later he was signing off 'Yours ever, Bill', and Churchill was addressing him as 'My Dear Bill' in return. After the Second World War a photograph of the two men playing gin rummy as they sat side by side in an aircraft became one of the most treasured exhibits on the fifth floor.

Churchill, who always went on revising articles and books until the last possible moment, was a demanding contributor. 'I am sorry to find that in the Tannenberg series of articles two extracts which I quoted from other works have been printed without the quotation marks,' he complained to Arthur Watson on 21 May 1930. 'I should be so much obliged if you would let me know of any deviation you propose to make in future from the text. I ought really to be consulted.' In a brief masterpiece of evasion, Watson replied that it was so long since the articles had been set by the printer that the original copies 'cannot now be found without a prolonged search', but that 'certainly no quotation marks have been taken out by anyone here'. Evidently some other disagreement broke out in January 1933, for Fred Lawson felt obliged to write Churchill a soothing note: 'I am sorry there was a muddle on Friday when your telephone message was received. Sir Gomer was in the office, and could have settled the whole question if it had been referred to him.'

Besides Churchill's special articles, Camrose published serial extracts from several of his books; and, running a daily and a Sunday paper in harness, he could deploy the material in one or the other as circumstances best suited him:

> My Dear Winston, [he wrote on 20 April 1933] We shall probably start Lloyd George in the *Telegraph* on 10 May and I do not anticipate that he will run much beyond the end of June. On this basis we should be able to commence Marlborough say the beginning of the second week of July. If Lloyd George takes a longer time, then I should revert to the idea mentioned to you of publishing Marlborough in the *Sunday Times* . . .

Serialisations, in those days, were heavyweight affairs. The extracts from *Marlborough*, for which the *Sunday Times* paid £2,500, ran to 40,000 words, appearing in June and July 1933. The paper's Editor was then W. W. Hadley, Camrose's one-time benefactor on the *Merthyr Times*, and Churchill worked closely with him on the text; before the series began he wrote enthusiastically to Fred Lawson: 'I was very pleased to see the fine advertisements in so many papers . . . I trust indeed that the public will be satisfied with the quality of the work.'

Another essential feature of the *Telegraph*, outside the main news, was the Peterborough column, published at the foot of the leader-page. An amalgam of gossip, news and comment, usually with the emphasis on politics and the arts, this assembly of short, independent stories was a revival of a feature which had been conceived in 1888, but had vanished during the First World War. In its reincarnation, it first came out under the headline 'London Day by Day' on 17 February 1929; and the signature 'Peter-borough' suddenly appeared, without explanation, on 2 November that year. The first editor was Victor Gordon-Lennox, who ran the column for three years before moving on to become Diplomatic

Correspondent, and under him it was nothing if not opinionated.

Gordon-Lennox specialised in scathing attacks on avant-garde writers and artists. Whether or not the puritanical attitude of the column derived in part from his proprietor, it is no longer possible to say; but, under his aegis, Peterborough had no time for anyone who broke the bounds of traditional morality.

In April 1929 the column carried a ringing denunciation of Radclyffe Hall's *The Well of Loneliness*, the lesbian novel whose publication in England had been banned by the Home Secretary. The main result of the suppression – the diarist noted sourly – had been to stir up interest in the book overseas: translations had already been commissioned in French, German, Dutch and Danish, and the author was considering offers from publishers in Czechoslovakia, Sweden and Spain. Besides, 60,000 copies had already been sold in English. 'All of which is very depressing,' the paragraph concluded, 'and shows how difficult it is to control public morals by regulation'.

Peterborough's dislike of Radclyffe Hall, however, was as nothing compared with his hatred of D. H. Lawrence. On 29 June 1929, under the heading A DISGRACEFUL EXHIBITION, he declared:

> Probably no greater insult has ever been offered to the London public than the exhibition at the Warren Galleries in Maddox Street of 25 paintings by Mr D. H. Lawrence . . . So long as the exhibition remains open, it must be a standing source of amazement that the authorities permit the public display of paintings of so gross and obscene a character . . . To pretend that such objects can be justified on any artistic grounds is sheer nonsense. Mr Lawrence's qualifications as a painter appear, to the normal mind at least, negligible, and his subjects, lacking all sort of restraint, are of a character such as has never been seen in London before.

When the police, alerted by this broadside, closed down 'the disgusting show', Peterborough crowed with self-righteous delight; and after Lawrence's death in May 1930 he wrote that the author's case called 'not so much for censure as for pity. The man was ill, the mind diseased, and the two maladies slowly gathered strength together . . . He had genius, which might have raised him to a high plane among lesser mortals, but alas, the kink in the brain developed early, and he came to write with one hand always in the slime.'

Simplistic moralising of this kind obviously fitted easily into the kind of 'clean' journalism that Camrose was eager to promote. Yet in the early columns of the reborn Peterborough, as in other parts of the paper, there sometimes appeared a curious streak of naïvety which reflected the proprietor's own lack of experience. Immensely successful though he was, he had worked on a relatively narrow front: he had never (for instance) been in the armed forces, or worked abroad. He seems to have found it acceptable that Peterborough should make cheap jokes about prominent foreign statesmen – as when, on 17 October 1930, the column reported that, 'like most of the prominent Bolsheviks, Stalin uses a false name. Since his real name is Joseph Sefdzhooghaashvilli, there is some excuse for it. He comes of good old Georgian brigand stock . . .' Later, Peterborough ridiculed Dr Engelbert Dollfuss, the Austrian Chancellor, by relaying the latest jokes from Vienna about his diminutive stature: that dachshunds were being groomed to provide him with a mount at military parades, and that he had sprained his ankle by falling off a ladder while picking strawberries.

Another weakness – in a journal out to capture middle-class readers – was that articles about and for women were devoted almost exclusively to the antics of the aristocracy. In June 1934, when Lady Camrose gave a dance for her daughters Sheila and Patricia, the *Telegraph* carried a news report which must, even then, have left many readers squirming:

> The terraced lawns twinkled with myriad fairy lights. Against the dark background tall rhododendrons glowed softly mauve . . . It was a wonderfully happy party. When the bacon-and-eggs stage was reached at three in the morning, the crowd of laughing boys and girls in the ballroom had not diminished perceptibly. Of them all, none seemed happier than the hostesses of the evening, the Hon. Sheila and Patricia Berry, who were dancing incessantly.

The *Telegraph* was on safer ground with its eulogies of the Royal Family – a subject which no amount of saccharine could make too sweet. When King George V gave his first Christmas broadcast at the end of 1932, Peterborough declared that it did not need very much imagination to 'picture the hush that fell on a large part of the civilised world when a BBC voice announced, "His Majesty the King"'. Everyone the columnist spoke to had, he said, been greatly impressed by the 'virile vigour' of the King's voice, which most of them heard for the first time; but what moved them most was the 'note of fatherly affection' which ran through the message:

It is indeed the simple truth that the end of the King's broadcast, the concluding words, 'God bless you', was one of the great emotional moments that come seldom in a lifetime. Each home was a microcosm of the listening world. How many family circles acted, I wonder, as the one did of which I heard yesterday? Without a word, and with eyes here and there filling with tears, they rose and joined in the National Anthem with the BBC Orchestra.

Gordon-Lennox's successor on Peterborough was E. D. (Toby) O'Brien, who ran the column for two years before launching off into public relations; and his departure made way for a man who became one of the pillars of 135 Fleet Street, Hugo Wortham. It was he who laid down that a classic Peterborough paragraph should contain one fact, one generalisation and, preferably, one very slight inaccuracy – and as he ran the column for a quarter of a century, from 1934 until 1959, his word must stand.

Wortham came to Peterborough already well established as critic and author, with experience in many fields. Having worked as a foreign correspondent in Egypt from 1909 to 1919, he knew the Middle East well. He had been a leader-writer on the *Morning Post*, and joined the *Telegraph* as a music critic. He was a determined traveller, a gourmet with exacting standards, an authority on wine (of which he drank a great deal), and addicted to trains, riding on the footplate of the engine whenever possible. To Bill Deedes, who later worked with Wortham, 'in demeanour, tastes and occasionally attire, he was an Edwardian. The grey Derby hat, the summer buttonhole, his manner on entering a club, made a convincing picture.'

He was also an excellent writer. If his essays on music lacked the lyricism and originality of those by Neville Cardus, they were strong enough to be reprinted in book form, and read well to this day. In 1931 he published *The Delightful Profession*, a study of Edward VII which, if it tended to be over-respectful, nevertheless broke new ground, being the first unofficial study of the King. Another favourite subject was his uncle, Oscar Browning, the schoolmaster forced to leave Eton after a quarrel with the Head Master over his relationship with young George Curzon, whose intellectual abilities (Browning thought) were suffering neglect. Wortham described him as 'a joyous, epicurean don ... who records dining with pleasure off snails, frogs, porcupine, hedgehog and wild boar, who took lessons in Polish when eighty-five, and preferred his sermons long'. *Oscar Browning* came out in 1927, and was later republished as *Edwardian Eton and Cambridge*.

Wortham armed Peterborough with an edge and distinction which many observers feel it never recaptured after his death. So sharp did the column become that few Members of Parliament cared to cross its editor. Nor was he an easy person to work for, since he gave recruits no instruction, but led by example, his choleric temper often exacerbated by *premier cru* claret; yet almost everyone who served under him greatly valued the experience of working for such a professional. Camrose and Watson thought him deeply eccentric, but realised that he was an original creation, and, as such, a definite asset.

With the advantage of hindsight, it is easy to discern Wortham's favourite subjects in the Peterborough column: music, cricket, Eton, Egypt, horse-racing and above all wine featured constantly, but always in paragraphs that were topical and deftly turned. In the world of music, especially, his connections were such that he would often come out with magisterial reminiscences, as of the composer Richard Strauss: 'When I last saw him, he rolled off with immense relish the latest good stories current in Berlin.'

One paragraph, which perhaps can be considered quintessential, concerned a proposal by the London County Council to put up a plaque on the front of 182 Ebury Street, where Mozart composed his first symphony in 1764. Combining historical and musical elements, it moved effortlessly on to contemporary social gossip, as it recorded how Mozart's father Leopold had fallen ill, and how during his convalescence the family had gone to live in the village of Chelsea, out in the country. The house which became No. 182 was then the home farm of the Manor, and Mozart, being unable to play an instrument for fear of delaying his father's recovery, wrote his first three symphonies at the age of eight. 'No. 182,' the paragraph concluded, 'is now the home of Lady Peek and her son Sir Francis Peek ... It is beautifully panelled, and has a long, narrow garden, once the site of the cow-houses.'

Bill Deedes recorded that Peterborough's longest-serving editor knew exactly what Camrose and the paper's readers required of him:

They wanted supreme snobbery and the impression of learning without its difficulties, which meant that the latter had to be shallow and that the former had to be constant. Intellectually, the whole thing had to be on the level one would expect from the wife of a British officer or the wife of a commercial traveller. There is really nothing to choose between them intellectually.

The new editorial expertise at 135 Fleet Street was backed up by greater professionalism in the business of selling the paper. Advertising and circulation were at first the province of Gomer Berry and Fred Lawson, but in 1931 these two were powerfully reinforced by the arrival of a new Advertisement Manager, George Simon, who became a mainstay of the firm and remained one for thirty years. In a clever publicity campaign, accurately tuned to the mood and aims of the new proprietor, he brought out a series of illustrated colour leaflets depicting the paper's upward progress. 'A record climb', said one, which showed people watching a glider soar. 'New heights quietly gained, steadily maintained, by sheer pilotage of an efficient machine . . . Like the efficient sailplane, *The Daily Telegraph* is independent of auxiliary motive power.' Other pamphlets developed the theme, speaking of the *Telegraph* as 'piloted by the best of Business and Journalistic talent', climbing steadily 'on the sheer service it gives as a newspaper'. Later advertisements placed the paper 'in a class apart', 'in a class of its own', 'in a class by itself'. In general, the campaign reflected the understated strength and confidence which Camrose inspired in his staff.

His Circulation Manager, William Hill, an immense man six feet seven inches tall, had been in the Buckinghamshire Hussars, which Fred Lawson had commanded. Under him, the paper began to canvass actively for new readers, sending out teams, often led by retired naval commanders, who would go from house to house, especially in rural areas, showing copies of the paper and offering it free for three days in the hope of luring people to buy it. Hoardings in and around London were plastered with enormous, forty-eight-sheet posters proclaiming: IT ONLY HAPPENED AT 4 A.M. BUT IT'S IN THE DAILY TELEGRAPH.

From his earliest days in journalism Camrose had shown an exceptional grasp of the potential of advertising; and now, as the dictators in Germany and Italy flexed their muscles, he became more and more fascinated by the power of publicity and propaganda. In April 1935 he suggested that the Government should set up a Ministry of Publicity, as the members of the Cabinet were 'finding out what advertising can do for them . . . If I were asked who was the most successful . . . advertiser today, I should say Mussolini. I regard him as a wonderful advertising agent gone the wrong way.' After the Duce, said Camrose, he would name Hitler, and perhaps in third place Lloyd George, 'who has a wonderful eye for publicity'.

Sensing the potential of radio and (later) television, Camrose encouraged the publication of stories about technical developments in the field. The *Telegraph*'s first Television Correspondent was Leonard Marsland Gander, who, after a spell as Radio Correspondent, had been drafted on to general duties, only to return to broadcasting. When, in February 1935, the *Telegraph* installed its first television set – a 'low-definition model of only thirty lines' – Gander was appointed to cover the new medium as well, urged on by Oscar Pulvermacher, the dynamic and enthusiastic Assistant Editor recruited from the *Daily Mail*. Gander promised readers that they would be kept abreast of events in the field, but later recorded what a struggle he had had, as the earliest pictures were 'mighty poor . . . a mere shadowgraph produced on a gadget known as a mirror drum'; and in the paper he reported:

> Last night I watched the BBC transmission from London National in the *Daily Telegraph* office. These images dancing and gesticulating on a frosted screen in a darkened room were only the shadows of what is to come . . . As the set was tuned, strips of light raced across the screen. Slowly a jumble of spots and bars resolved into the caption 'BBC'.

Things improved greatly in the summer of 1936 when the BBC began to transmit high-definition pictures on 405 lines from Alexandra Palace. One of the first people in the office to show interest was Camrose – and Gander's account of his efforts to produce a decent picture reveals precisely the kind of knee-jerk reaction which any request from the proprietor produced.

By the time Camrose let it be known that he would like to see the new phenomenon, the BBC had equipped 135 Fleet Street with one of their latest fifteen-inch screens; but when Gander tested it, a week ahead of the proposed inspection, all he could get on it was 'a hideous tweed pattern'. Interference, he knew, came from all the machinery in the building, but this seemed to be something altogether worse, and in the end he traced the trouble to the radiotherapy unit at St Bartholomew's Hospital, less than half a mile due east:

> Lord Camrose's visit was still a week off and there was time to do something. So I rang up the hospital and spoke to an extremely sceptical doctor, who declined to believe my improbable story. However, he did agree to a test, which proved beyond question that I was right . . . So, as a magnanimous gesture, he agreed to switch off the radio therapy at the time fixed for the demon-

stration. Lord Camrose entered the room and stayed for slightly less than two minutes. He asked three questions: How much does the set cost? How long are the programmes? Is that the biggest screen available? After that he said 'Thank you' and departed. Treatment of the patients at St Bartholomew's could be resumed, though I must add that Lord Camrose knew nothing about this.

A subject about which Camrose came to know all too much was Nazi Germany; and it is to his undying credit that *The Daily Telegraph*, under his direction, took a positive stand against the rise of Hitler and Fascism. In doing so, it stood out in sharp contrast with two of its competitors at either end of the social scale. At the bottom was the *Daily Mail*, whose proprietor, Lord Rothermere, was openly pro-Nazi, in frequent personal communication with the Führer, and whose man in Berlin, George Ward Price, often appeared to be acting as a public-relations assistant to Hitler and his cronies, so partisan were his despatches. At the upper end of the scale, the *Times* lost its head and its way in one of the most lamentable episodes in the paper's history. Having convinced himself that Hitler did not want war, the Editor, Geoffrey Dawson, went out of his way to pamper the Nazis. 'I do my utmost, night after night, to keep out of the paper anything that might hurt their susceptibilities,' he wrote to H. G. Daniels, his senior correspondent in Europe, on 23 May 1937. The paper's support for the policy of appeasement drove its correspondent in Berlin, Norman Ebbutt, to despair: time and again, the despatches on which he had laboured were spiked, and he was reduced to a policy of feeding information to diplomats or rival journalists, in the hope that it would somewhere see the light of day.

No such blindness inhibited the *Telegraph*. When the Nazis came to power in January 1933, its man in Berlin was Eustace B. Wareing, who soon began to report the excesses of the new regime with an accuracy that stung Hitler's colleagues, principally Dr Josef Goebbels. In February 1934 Wareing was joined by Hugh Carleton Greene, then twenty-four, chubby-faced and six feet six, younger brother of the novelist Graham Greene, and of the distinguished doctor Raymond. Having already worked for the *Times*, Hugh Greene could see better than anybody the difference between the two papers. As he later recorded, 'In the *Daily Telegraph* office . . . the News Editor, Robert Skelton, was completely at one with the views of his men in Berlin; the Editor, A. E. Watson, was massively imperturbable, and the leader-writers . . . understood Hitler's aims very well.'

This effective co-operation soon produced results. In Germany the issue of Monday, 7 July 1934, was confiscated by order of the Reich Minister of the Interior, Dr Frick, and the paper was banned in the country until 27 July. The incident drew a characteristically exaggerated outburst from Goebbels, who bitterly attacked all foreign correspondents, and those of the *Telegraph* in particular, for 'the worst form of revolver journalism', for 'establishing lie-factories which poison the world', and for 'emptying the slop-pails of cowardly falsehoods'. In London, a vigorous leader, headed BURKING THE TRUTH IN GERMANY, struck back with the observation that 'Dr Goebbels's real grievance against the foreign correspondents is that he has not been able to impose upon them the same close muzzling order which he imposes upon the German Press.' This was perfectly true. Goebbels's own lie-factory was under efficient control: censorship of German newspapers and radio was already strict, and the only way people could find out what was really happening in Germany was by reading foreign journals or listening to outside broadcasts.

That ban on the *Telegraph* was the first of many. Another was imposed in January 1935, and others in 1936 and 1937. Italy, too, declared the paper prohibited. Yet the Berlin correspondents continued to file, and by April 1935 the *New York Journal* was declaring that the *Telegraph* had superseded the *Times* as the mouthpiece of the British Government.

The paper's realistic attitude did not prevent Lord and Lady Camrose joining the English contingent which flocked to the Olympic Games in Berlin during the summer of 1936. Other guests invited from London by the Nazi hierarchy included his brother Gomer, by now Lord Kemsley (having been made a baron earlier that year), who sailed in his yacht to Kiel and went on to Berlin by train. There were also Sir Robert Vansittart, Permanent Head of the Foreign Office, and the American millionaire Henry Channon, always known as 'Chips', who by then was a Conservative Member of Parliament. With typically naïve optimism, the Nazi leaders imagined that a splendid festival and a few stylish receptions would convert recalcitrant Englishmen to their way of thinking, and persuade them that the new Germany was a perfectly civilised country. To this end, the leaders threw a series of immense parties, none more lavish than that given on 10 August by Joachim von Ribbentrop, whose appointment as Ambassador to London had been announced that morning. Six hundred people, including the Goerings, the Hesses and the Camroses, sat down to a champagne dinner at the Ribbentrops' villa in the fashionable suburb of

Dahlem, and afterwards people danced until dawn to the strains of a Hungarian gipsy band.

Camrose published nothing about his visit to Berlin – and it was not his habit to break into print except on occasions of special importance to the paper. Yet it is clear that he was not carried away by the grandeur with which the Olympics had been staged; unlike Channon, who thought the Nazis marvellous, Camrose did not lose his head, and his paper maintained its critical stance so staunchly that, when war at last broke out, he was among the 2,300 people listed by the Gestapo whose arrest was to be automatic after the Wehrmacht had invaded England.

As the stature of *The Daily Telegraph* grew, so, too, did that of its proprietor. He never became exactly a public figure, for his nature was too retiring, and he never sought the limelight; yet his position as owner of a leading daily paper, and his close association with Baldwin, Neville Chamberlain, Churchill and other leading politicians, ensured that foreign statesmen and diplomats kept a close eye on him. He was constantly in Whitehall, either going of his own accord to give advice, or summoned for policy discussions.

Another confidant was the author and politician Harold Nicolson, who in November 1935 was elected National Labour MP for West Leicester, and on 7 April 1936 wrote to his wife Vita [Sackville-West]:

> Lunch at the Soviet Embassy. Evidently Mr Maisky [the Russian Ambassador] thought the time had come to collar *The Daily Telegraph*, which consisted of Lord Camrose, the Editor of the DT, the Foreign Editor of the DT . . . What a foolish thing to have done, to have asked us in a bunch like that . . . Terrible lunch. Began with caviar, which was all to the good. We then had a little wet dead trout. We then had chicken in slabs surrounded by a lavish display of watercress. We then had what in nursing homes is known as 'fruit jelly'. There was vodka and red wine and white wine and Curaçao. Maisky filled his glass with each separate form of liquor but never drank anything but water.

On the whole, Camrose kept his private life so well separated from his professional existence that very little mention of it appeared in the Press, and even regular readers of the *Telegraph* could discern hardly anything about his background or family. One fact they did know was that he had become a keen sailor, and owned a 550-ton semi-diesel yacht, the *Sona*, in which he generally went cruising in the summer. Camrose's voyages were planned and executed on a lavish scale: often he would entertain on board during Cowes Week or at Deauville, and if he wanted to cruise in the Mediterranean, he would send the yacht ahead to avoid a tedious passage down the Bay of Biscay, and himself go on board at Cannes. (The *Sona* came to a violent end, when she was acting as a troopship during the Second World War and a lone German airman dropped a bomb straight down her funnel off the South Coast; and a faintly improbable story is told of how Camrose, walking along the cliffs near Swanage towards the end of the war, spotted the wreck of a ship lying in the water below and recognised it as his own. He is supposed to have been so astonished that he turned to a woman who happened to be passing and said, 'Madam – do you see that wreck? It was once my yacht.')

When the new liner *Queen Mary* sailed from Gourock in the Firth of Clyde for her preliminary trials in April 1936, it was natural that Camrose should be among the passengers invited to see how she performed. After forty-eight hours of speed trials and fuel-consumption tests – during which the Olympic gold-medallist Lord Burghley ran the 425 yards round the promenade deck in fifty-eight seconds, wearing ordinary leather shoes, trousers and a light singlet – Camrose proposed the health of the liner at a dinner party, saying that she was a wonderful ship, and that it had been a wonderful voyage.

Famous though he had become, he never turned his back on Wales, never lost his affection for the town from which he had come. In May 1935 Merthyr celebrated the Silver Jubilee of King George V and Queen Mary in great style, and among numerous other entertainments 250 members of the Ex-Servicemen's Club sat down to dinner as guests of Lord Camrose and Sir Gomer Berry, in premises which had been the gift of their brother, the late Lord Buckland. In proposing a toast to their benefactors, the Chairman referred to the great kindness shown to Merthyr by her 'brilliant sons', and the company sang 'For they are jolly good fellows'. Next day, in schools all over the borough, 14,000 children were presented with Jubilee mugs and laid into a splendid tea – after which (according to the *Merthyr Express*) they 'gave ringing cheers for the King and Queen, and followed with cheers for Lord Camrose and Sir Gomer Berry'. In terms of Merthyr's esteem, the brothers came close behind the Royal Family.

Occasional scraps of information about the Berrys crept into the national Press – most often the *Evening Standard*, whose anonymous gossip columnist, writing at the direction of his own proprietor, Lord Beaverbrook, trotted out tributes to Camrose every time his birthday came round on 23 June. 'He has many advantages,' said one paragraph, in characteristically clipped sentences:

> One is a good family devoted to their father. Another is wide personal popularity, such as few men in his position have known. For the power of the newspaper proprietor has usually proved an insuperable obstacle to personal popularity. Lord Camrose, has, too, the gift of zest and natural high spirits. Such advantages make the path of life easy for a man . . . Lord Camrose does not betray the volatility of his fellow countrymen from Wales. His bearing is calm and dignified, and he is the most handsome of the newspaper proprietors . . . But Lord Camrose's mind seizes on the concrete points of a situation with the speed and facility that distinguish Mr Lloyd George.

By this time the family was spreading out and increasing. Both the elder sons, Seymour and Michael, had grown up highly presentable copies of their father: tall, dark and handsome, though Seymour was the better looking of the two. He was also the more urbane and sociable, Michael being landed with an acutely shy nature which made him inclined to stammer, and to mutter rapidly with his mouth twisted slightly to the right. Both had gone to Christ Church, Oxford, and both began their careers on Allied Newspapers' provincial journals. Seymour worked in Newcastle, Manchester and Glasgow, before joining *The Daily Telegraph* in May 1933. In November that year Michael went to Aberdeen, and later to Glasgow, but he did not come to the *Telegraph* until after the Second World War. No doubt it was an excellent way to learn the trade – to start at the bottom and go through the various departments; yet there was also an element of escapism in the young men's eagerness to work outside London. As outsiders occasionally saw, Camrose had a tendency to be tyrannical with his sons, and he had the Victorian habit of regarding any male member of the family under the age of about fifty as still a boy. When Michael, half a century later, explained his readiness to work in Aberdeen by saying 'The great thing was to get away from Pop!', he made the remark as a joke; but it contained a kernel of truth, and hinted at the fact that Camrose, from the sheer power of his personality, drove his sons away and in on themselves.

At first, however, Seymour did very well. His father liked to maintain tight overall control of the *Telegraph*, but as he was often out of the office, calling on senior politicians, he was frequently obliged to delegate. Beneath him in the hierarchy, after Arthur Watson, came the Assistant Editor, Oscar Pulvermacher, a good, tough, lively organiser. Alongside him, Seymour worked as an ideas man, and first-class he was, frequently coming up with original projects for the paper's writers to tackle. Soon, when Camrose was away for any length of time, Seymour began to deputise for him.

For the family as a whole, the years 1934 and 1935 proved a period of rapid change. In September 1934 Camrose bought the Crown lease of 25 St James's Place – a substantial and stylish house with a garden overlooking Green Park – and later that autumn there were laid the foundations of a double alliance between two powerful clans. On 6 November the engagement was announced between Sheila Berry, Camrose's second daughter, and Freddy, the second Earl of Birkenhead, son of the redoubtable F. E. Smith.

The couple were married at St Margaret's, Westminster, on 1 May 1935, and the reception was held at 25 St James's Place, where extensive renovations had been completed just in time. In the autumn came news of another link between the same two families: the engagement, announced on 20 September, of Michael Berry to Lady Pamela Smith, Birkenhead's younger sister. Scarcely a week after that Camrose bought Hackwood Park, a splendid Georgian house standing at the centre of a 2,500-acre estate some two miles south of Basingstoke in Hampshire. A week later Patricia, his second daughter, announced *her* engagement to Roger, son of Field-Marshal Sir Philip Chetwode.

It is impossible not to be struck by the way in which the successive proprietors of *The Daily Telegraph* seemed to match each other in their rise up the social scale. Just as the first Lord Burnham, on the tide of success, moved from Bloomsbury to Mayfair, so Camrose graduated from the relative modesty of Seamore Place to the much more imposing St James's. In the country, just as Burnham had forsaken Newmarket for the splendour of Hall Barn, so Camrose abandoned the luxurious but essentially suburban Barrow Hills for the truly rural grandeur of Hackwood. (By a strange twist of fortune in 1934, the need to raise death duties forced the Burnhams to sell some 3,000 acres of the Hall Barn land to Lord Kemsley, who had recently bought the neighbouring estate, Dropmore.)

Hackwood was not, as *The Daily Telegraph* described it, 'a comfortable family house'. It was palatially large and grand. It had belonged to the Dukes of Bolton since the eighteenth century, but

The *Telegraph's* new building *above*, opened in 1882 at 135 Fleet Street, was the last word in newspaper offices, and the pillared entrance hall *below* one of its glories. *Top right*: Spy cartoon of Edward Lawson, first Baron Burnham.

Top right: Lord Burnham at Hall Barn with King Edward VII, on the King's last big shoot in January 1910. Top left: Camrose in his heyday and below his brother Gomer, the first Viscount Kemsley. Left: At the wedding of Michael Berry and Lady Pamela Smith, on 7 January 1936, the bridegroom's brother Seymour was best man.

Above: Lord Camrose playing gin rummy with Winston Churchill during a wartime flight. *Middle left*: Hackwood Park, near Basingstoke, bought by the first Lord Camrose in 1936, later became the home of his son Seymour *below*. Oving House *bottom left*, near Aylesbury, was bought by Michael Berry in 1955.

The *Telegraph* Berrys: Michael and Lady Pamela *above*, Michael after he had become Lord Hartwell *below left*, his favourite photo, and *below right* his son Adrian.

in 1907 it had been let to Lord Curzon, the former Viceroy, whose widow had continued to live there intermittently after his death, with many of the rooms closed. A handsome stone building, part seventeenth century, part Regency, with a grand, pillared portico in the centre of the north front, and linked to two wings by curved colonnades, it had a magnificently timbered deer-park extending to 800 acres, and, inside, was distinguished by its large and intricate Grinling Gibbons carvings, said to be the finest in any private house in England. Basingstoke was then a modest market town of some 12,000 people, not yet ringed by coils of bypass or invaded by the roar of traffic on any nearby motorway, and far enough off for Hackwood to seem in the depths of the country. The predominantly arable farming and the gentle hills both made for good shooting: like Lord Burnham, Camrose had become keen on field sports, and he now enhanced his estate by the plantation of new coverts specially laid out for shooting, to which, somewhat eccentrically, he gave no names, but assigned the numbers one to nine. Closer at hand, he embellished and enhanced Hackwood's immediate environs, the most striking feature of which was (and is) the Spring Wood, a lovely wild garden of trees intersected by grass paths and dotted with follies.

A new country estate was one thing, a new daughter-in-law something else. Lady Pamela Smith was no ordinary catch. Her friend Elizabeth Harman (later Lady Longford) remembered her at the age of sixteen as 'an enchanting wood nymph, with flashing black eyes, shining dark hair, an elfin face, pointed chin and a mischievous imagination . . . Life was never dull, always dramatic in Pam's company.' All who knew her were struck by her dark good looks, which she herself cheerfully attributed to gipsy ancestors, and everyone could see that she had inherited many traits of character from her father, to whom she had been very close.

As Lady Longford remarked, 'All the Birkenheads were life-enhancers', and none more so than Pamela. Although only twenty-one when she became engaged, she was already a veteran in terms of public performance and exposure in the Press. On the death of her father, in October 1930, the *Telegraph* had described the 'wonderful affection' which he had had for her, and the intimacy or mutual understanding that made them perfect companions. By the age of ten (the report went on) Pamela 'was already possessed of a mentality more than equal to that of most young women of twice her years', and she had inherited, among other gifts, her father's 'impish sense of humour, and not a little of his audacity'.

A tendency towards exhibitionism manifested itself in Pamela at an early age. One of her first appearances on the London scene was when she acted the part of the Peter Pan statue in Kensington Gardens in a 'Pageant of Hyde Park' arranged by her mother for the benefit of a London hospital. 'She was in her early teens,' the *Evening Standard* reported, 'but was the figure to the life . . . She has three great gifts: beauty, brains and wit.'

In 1931 she went to Paris to stay with a family and learn French, and by that winter she was being described as 'quite the most interesting girl who has been going about in London lately'. The following April, aged seventeen, she herself launched into print, with some characteristically pugnacious remarks in the *Queen*, given in the form of an interview headed, THIS DEBUTANTE BUSINESS AS I SEE IT. 'The modern man?' it began. 'What I have seen of him so far makes me think that he is conceited, bad-mannered and uninteresting, and it is a positive torture to have to sit next to him.'

In April 1932 the Peterborough column – with no inkling that she would one day marry the proprietor's younger son – reported that she had been chosen to take part in a 'matinée of French living pictures, in which she would represent Madame Récamier, whose salon attracted the intellectuals of France in the 18th century'. In May she appeared as a model in the salon of the couturier Chanel. Soon she was in the news merely for falling victim to chickenpox, and in December 1934 a rumour spread that she was engaged to Lord Glenconner, who was fifteen years her senior and had recently been divorced by his wife.

Her wedding to Michael Berry, in the chapel of Gray's Inn, on 7 January 1936, was hailed as the first important society wedding of the year. The day before, the *Telegraph* had devoted over a column of newsprint (and the *Times* half a column) to a list of the wedding presents. From Margaret, Countess of Birkenhead's 'long white ermine coat and household linen; six silver candlesticks and table silver to match, with two George III centrepieces and a George III tankard to Michael', through Lord and Lady Camrose's 'diamond and ruby bracelet, and to their son a fitted dressing case and other luggage', to Mr and Mrs A. E. Watson's 'a silver box', the list read like an irresistible challenge to burglars. The Winston Churchills gave glass, Lord Beaverbrook diamond earrings, Lord and Lady Desborough the works of Conrad, and the Marquess and Marchioness of Anglesey an early edition of Samuel Richardson's novel *Pamela*. The groom's present to the bride was a diamond tiara, hers to him a gold cigarette case.*

---

* This is now in the Cartier collection at the British Museum.

At the wedding service the bride was given away by her brother, the second Earl of Birkenhead, and Seymour Berry stood best man to his brother. The church held only 130 people, but there was room for many more at the reception in Gray's Inn Hall. After their honeymoon, the young couple went to live in Cadogan Place. Their first son, Adrian, was born in June, 1937, and some vivid glimpses of their happiness are preserved in the diaries of Chips Channon. 'We lunched with Eleanor Smith – unpunctual, untidy, vivacious,' he wrote on 19 May 1937; [with] 'her sister Pam, pregnant, luscious and original; and their mother Margaret Birkenhead. They all attacked the Archbishop of Canterbury [over the Abdication], deplored the present persecution of the Duke of Windsor, and were as gay and provocative and quick as ever.' In October the same year Channon saw Michael and Pamela arrive back from the South of France and thought the young couple 'gay, dark, vivacious and charming'.

Since the *Telegraph* did particularly well whenever the news became compelling, it fared better than ever during the Abdication crisis, towards the end of 1936. Now Camrose's friendship with Baldwin was handsomely rewarded by the fact that J. C. C. Davidson, who held full responsibility for all press arrangements, chose the *Telegraph* to be the recipient of special confidences. He made it his business to see that the paper was 'completely informed of all developments', and the result was (in the words of the author Frances Donaldson) 'that it was *The Daily Telegraph* and not the *Times* which emerged with most credit from the crisis'. To Chips Channon, 'the Astors and the Berrys vied with each other in traducing Edward VIII and intrigued against him for months out of a common puritanism'. Yet even if there was a grain of truth in this, Camrose found himself in the same dilemma as all patriotic Englishmen: it was impossible to support both the constitution and the renegade King. Camrose stuck with Baldwin, and afterwards Davidson wrote that prime ministerial confidence in him had not been misplaced: 'Nothing secret was disclosed, and of course I made no effort to influence the paper's attitude.'

In 1937 Camrose further strengthened his position at the *Telegraph* with two far-reaching changes. In the first, in January, he and Gomer dissolved their partnership and went separate ways; and in the second, in September, he took over the fading *Morning Post*, thereby assimilating one of the *Telegraph*'s rivals.

His thirty-six-year association with Gomer had been extraordinarily fruitful, and now they parted entirely without rancour.

In Camrose's own statement, published on 5 January 1937, he ascribed the change to the 'great expansion' of their newspaper and publishing interests. He himself had acquired his brother Lord Kemsley's interest in *The Daily Telegraph*. He had also bought 'the major portion' of Lord Iliffe's shareholding, although the latter remained a shareholder and a 'continuous director'. In exchange, Camrose had sold to Kemsley his own shares in Allied Newspapers (which included the *Sunday Times*); he had resigned from the Allied board, of which Kemsley had become Chairman in his place. Camrose retained control of Amalgamated Press (the magazine group) and the *Financial Times*, and Iliffe took over Kelly's Directories, which until then all three had shared. The only newspaper on whose board Camrose and Kemsley remained together was the Cardiff *Western Mail*, in which they both had a sentimental as well as a financial interest; but Camrose was at pains to emphasise that, far from having had any row, the three former partners remained on the closest of terms. The only reason for making the new arrangement, he told *World's Press News*, was 'to render their various interests independent of one another, so that the property of each may be clearly defined, their interests simplified'.

Many people were surprised by the deal, because it appeared to give Kemsley such a large share of the family cake. In all he acquired eighteen newspapers (five of them national, including the *Sunday Times* and the *Daily Sketch*), while Camrose ended up with only two, the *Telegraph* and the *Financial Times*. In fact he would very much have liked to retain the *Sunday Times* as well, and to have run it in harness with the *Telegraph*; but, to justify a purchase to the outside shareholders of Allied Newspapers, he would have had to give an enormous price for it, and could not make the necessary financial arrangements. Yet the deal left him with what he most wanted: more time to concentrate on the title closest to his heart. For him, the most important effect of the rearrangement was to give him sole command of the *Telegraph* (for Iliffe had never taken any part in its editorial direction). Another important change was that the *Sunday Times* and the *Telegraph* became separated, although the editorial staff of the Sunday paper still used the offices at 135 Fleet Street, and the paper was still printed there. As Camrose made clear in interviews given at the time, the *Telegraph* was still a private property, and no public shares would be issued.

In his book *British Newspapers and their Controllers*, published in 1947, Camrose himself set out the financial basis of the company after the rearrangement:

The Daily Telegraph Ltd. is a private company with a capital of £240,000. This sum, of course, comes nowhere near the actual amount of money employed, nor does it approach the sum paid for the paper when it changed hands [from the Burnhams] . . . The Preference capital formerly owned by my previous partners is now held by other interests controlled by me, but the whole of the Ordinary shares and the bulk of the Preference shares belong to me and my family . . . My two sons, Seymour Berry and Michael Berry are . . . the owners of all the Ordinary capital, but under the Articles of Association of the Company, I am Chairman and Editor-in-Chief for life or for as long as I choose to retain those positions.

By 1937, in other words, Camrose *was* the *Telegraph*. With a daily sale of over 500,000 copies (more than double that of the *Times*), and a reputation steadily growing, the paper had become an extremely valuable property – and within a few months of the reshuffle its success was further consolidated by the absorption of the ultra-Conservative *Morning Post*.

This was the oldest newspaper in London – founded in 1772 and more ancient, even, than the *Times* – and Camrose enjoyed pointing out that once, when it was a mere stripling in 1798, it had had the audacity to take over a paper called the *Telegraph*. By 1937, however, it was in terminal decline, with sales and advertising going slowly down in a vicious spiral.

News of the impending takeover broke on 28 July, when the directors of the *Morning Post* announced that they had accepted an offer for their holdings from Lord Camrose. They had been a curious crew, including Sir Edward Cunard and (until his death the year before) Rudyard Kipling, and the enterprise was sadly run-down, the editorial staff working on a single floor in Tudor Street, off Fleet Street, above the Argus Press, which printed the paper. Camrose let it be known, as usual, that he had not imposed himself, but had been invited to move in. The date for completion of the transaction was first set as 27 August, but in the event the amalgamation did not take place until 1 October, and in the interval rumours flew: that Camrose was planning to turn the *Post* into an evening paper, and that his son Michael (who by then was Managing Editor of the *Financial Times*) would run it.

As things turned out, none of these rumours had any foundation: what Camrose planned was a straight absorption. But to those working on the *Post* the news that it would cease to exist came as a savage blow, and its last night was vividly recalled by J. C. Trewin, until then the paper's chief reporter:

> It came as a desperate shock when, on the evening of 30 September, all going mildly according to plan, we were summoned to the sub-editors' room, the biggest in the office. The entire staff met, most people unaware. In retrospect the meeting was a highly theatrical event; in fiction it might have been, but it came through as a painful improvisation at which everyone tried, unsuccessfully, to cheer his neighbour (a few could afford it; the majority could not).
>
> H. A. Gwynne [Editor for the past twenty-six years] entered quietly. A minute later we knew from his few words, deeply felt and with no kind of histrionics – always against his temperament – that the next day's issue of the *Morning Post* would be its last as an independent journal, a history of 165 years. Within half an hour we knew further, from a distribution of letters in the Foreign Room – a queue outside it was as blithe as a meeting of the Suicide Club – which of us would be crossing to the *Telegraph* and which of us would leave Tudor Street that night, more or less compensated but unemployed.
>
> I was in the second group. Not many wished to go home. People loitered in the corridor, hung about the stairs. The evening's routine passed with the unreality of dream. Just before eleven the drama critic S. R. Littlewood (I had been his deputy for four years) brought a farewell theatre notice: the play was called, all too symbolically, *The Last Straw*.

Next morning a lugubrious valedictory leader by the Editor announced that the paper had come to the end of the road. For a long time, it said, the *Morning Post* had 'fought a losing battle'. In the past year alone it had lost £40,000. The takeover would assure 'the continuance of clean and responsible journalism, in an independent newspaper, unassociated with any combine'. Camrose had shown 'the utmost consideration' for members of the editorial staff, nearly half of whom would be retained. Gwynne was said to have received a pension of £5,000 a year – the same as his working salary, and a phenomenal sum for a pension at the time. Lesser mortals like J. C. Trewin felt as if they 'had been bludgeoned from behind while walking along quietly in the sunshine', and it was years before they could look on the *Telegraph* with anything but fear and mistrust.

The Daily Telegraph
and Morning Post

No. 25,691 Daily Telegraph
No. 31,582 Morning Post

TODAY'S WEATHER:
Thundery; rather warm

BROADCASTING:
Page Twelve

LONDON, FRIDAY, OCTOBER 1, 1937

LONDON LATE EDITION

ONE PENNY

PERSONAL

BIRTHS

MARRIAGES

GOLDEN WEDDING

DEATHS

IN MEMORIAM

1914–1918

PERSONAL

PERSONAL

CONCERTS, &c.

B.B.C.

PROMENADE CONCERTS
SIR HENRY J. WOOD
B.B.C. SYMPHONY ORCHESTRA

BEETHOVEN CONCERT

FRANK BISHOP

FRANCES ALLCOM
PHILIP WARDE
COLOGNE CHAMBER TRIO

DOROTHEA ASPINALL

WAIATA MAORIS

MUSIC, SINGING, ELOCUTION, &c.

MARIA LINKER

EDUCATIONAL

UNIVERSITY CORRESPONDENCE COLLEGE

LONDON MATRICULATION

PITMAN'S COLLEGE

METROPOLITAN COLLEGE

BUSINESS POSITIONS
THE CIVIL SERVICE
ALL EXAMINATIONS

CLARK'S COLLEGE Ltd.

UNIVERSITY TUTORIAL COLLEGE

LONDON MATRICULATION

SPECIAL CLASSES FOR SPECIAL UNIVERSITY ENTRANCE

ST. JAMES'S SECRETARIAL COLLEGE

LONDON COLLEGE OF SECRETARIES

HOW TO PASS MATRIC

STRAND TUTORIAL COLLEGE

THE FINEST START
KENSINGTON COLLEGE

MRS. HOSTER'S

AERONAUTICAL ENGINEERING

SCHOOL OF ECONOMICS, DUNDEE

JOURNALISM OR STORY-WRITING:
A HOBBY or a CAREER

WRITING FOR THE PRESS

EDUCATIONAL

EPSOM COLLEGE

PARIS ACADEMY
of DRESSMAKING and MILLINERY

24, OLD BOND STREET.

REVILLE

McCABE ACADEMY OF DRESSMAKING & MILLINERY
157-161, REGENT STREET, W.1

MANNEQUIN SCHOOL

TRUMAN & KNIGHTLEY LTD.

THE GABBITAS THRING
SCHOLASTIC AGENTS

SCHOOLS AND TUTORS

GABBITAS, THRING & CO. LTD.

PUBLIC & PREPARATORY
SCHOOLS YEAR BOOK

PATON'S LIST OF SCHOOLS

SCHOOLS AND TUTORS

PATON

COOK'S SCHOLASTIC SERVICE

SCHOLARSHIPS

PRIVATE SCHOOLS & COLLEGES

CLUB ANNOUNCEMENTS

RANELAGH CLUB
HIGHLAND GAMES

UNIVERSAL CLUB

KEMPTON PARK CLUB

RIDING, &c.

WINES

On 1 October 1937 the joint paper appeared under the title *The Daily Telegraph and Morning Post* – a double-decker, gothic masthead even more cumbersome than the one originally devised by Colonel Sleigh in 1855. The first leader, entitled A WELCOME TO OUR NEW READERS, was just that. They could rest assured, it said, that the paper sought 'to adhere to the highest journalistic standards':

Among those standards we include the strictest scrupulosity in the presentation only of real news, carefully collected by accredited and responsible correspondents. We include also the fair presentation of the case of both sides in matters of controversy ... *The Daily Telegraph and Morning Post* stands for clean journalism in every sense of that word and for journalism free from the slightest taint of corrupt influence.

The leader went on to call the *Telegraph* 'a fearless and independent Constitutional newspaper', and another article on the same page, signed by the veteran J. B. Firth, recalled for new readers the declaration printed in the first issue of all, on 29 June 1855, which announced that the purpose of the journal would be to act as 'a loyal champion of the Sovereign and the Constitution'. Here was the Camrose creed writ clear: clean, patriotic journalism, and real news only.

How seriously the readers took these high-flown claims, it is impossible to know; yet in a couple of weeks some of them at least were fortuitously vindicated, when Camrose sued the Fascist newspaper *Action* for libel. With a reckless disregard of reality, the rag had implied that he was a Jewish financier, with no sense of patriotism or loyalty to the Crown, and that in running *The Daily Telegraph* he had allowed his duty to the public to be subordinated to his own financial interests. The case was heard by Mr Justice Hilbery, and Mr Roland Oliver, when he opened for the plaintiffs, said, 'It is the custom to look upon the *Telegraph* as a pillar of tradition and respectability.' Camrose, giving evidence, was asked by Oliver: 'Are you in any sense a Jew?' – to which he answered: 'No, in no sense whatever.' The result – which must have seemed inevitable to most of the people involved – was that Camrose and the *Telegraph* won. They were awarded £20,000 damages: £12,500 to Camrose and £7,500 to the company.

Among the dozen or so staff who transferred from Tudor Street to 135 Fleet Street was J. C. Johnstone, a trenchant writer of leaders who settled well into his new slot. With him came Bill Deedes, who, although only twenty-four, had already served as

War Correspondent for the *Morning Post* in Abyssinia, and by 1937 had become the paper's Political Correspondent. Since the *Telegraph* already had a political specialist, Deedes at first found himself with little to do; but then Camrose sent for him and asked him to revive a scheme launched by the *Morning Post* the year before – the Christmas toy fund for children.

This had come into being as a result of the visit made by King Edward VIII to distressed areas of South Wales on 18 November 1936. The King had been received with wild enthusiasm, and after his tour, which included a visit to the derelict steelworks at Dowlais Top, above Merthyr, he had made his celebrated remark that 'something must be done'. (In fact, he said that something must be done *for these men*; but history truncated his words, and so made them more emotive.) The response of the *Morning Post* had been to send Christmas presents anonymously to children in the worst-hit areas – an idea which proved highly popular.

Camrose, much taken with it, put young Deedes in charge of the scheme for 1937 – and a formidable undertaking it proved. The aim was to provide a new toy – 'delivered as nearly as possible on Christmas morning' – to each of 150,000 children in the poorest districts of Durham, Tyneside, West Cumberland, South Wales and Monmouthshire. Although the front of anonymity was preserved – so that children would not, in theory, know where their presents had come from – in fact the paper solicited contributions from readers, and sent out to teachers for the nominal rolls of some 4,000 classes. Soon Deedes found himself travelling to distressed areas to collect material for background articles – and one of his first destinations, which he tackled with some trepidation, was Merthyr and Dowlais Top, where the unemployment rate was forty-three per cent. Before he went there, Arthur Watson warned him that the defunct steelworks had belonged to the Berrys, but he wrote a straightforward piece about the place, and heard no word from on high.

Once again, public response to the toy fund was enormous. King George VI and Queen Mary, the Queen Mother, sent in donations, and thousands of private letters poured into 135 Fleet Street. Big department stores contributed generously by handling the presents and giving well over nominal value. When the Queen Mother herself visited the office on 10 December 1937, she was received by Camrose and Fred Lawson and taken to the sixth floor, where she inspected nearly five hundred presents. Camrose told her that since the appeal had been launched at the beginning of the week, money had been coming in at the rate of £1,000 a day, and she was shown 2,300 letters which had arrived that morning. The first envelope she picked up contained an anonymous donation of 2s 6d, and the stirring lines

> A drop less beer,
>   A bit less baccy –
> Half-a-crown,
>   And a youngster's happy.

Altogether, the scheme succeeded wonderfully – not least in creating a wholesome, humanitarian image for the *Telegraph* and its proprietor. When teachers began sending in letters of thanks, these, at Deedes's suggestion, were taken down to Hackwood by despatch rider, and in due course Camrose responded with a grateful note. In 1938 the scheme was repeated, again with conspicuous success: readers sent in £23,000 – the equivalent of £500,000 today – and 227,000 children received presents. Once again Deedes was despatched to Merthyr, where he saw a grubby child of about seven crying as she peered into a toyshop window; and in the hope of enlisting public sympathy, he wrote a description of her. As he recalled fifty years later:

> I overdid it. Generous readers got in touch, wanting to adopt the child, to pay for her education, and sent cheques marked for her especial benefit. The Chief Accountant, H. J. C. Stevens, was enraged by this complication. 'You and your little Rosie!' he snarled, and held it against me for years afterwards.

Playing Father Christmas to the nation's children was an agreeable pastime; but weightier matters were pressing, and throughout 1938, as Europe slid towards war, the *Telegraph* continued to score with the catholic nature of its news and the excellence of its foreign reporting. As always in times of political uncertainty and international crisis, the public appetite for solid information was insatiable, and sales continued to climb.

In April 1938 the *Telegraph* again gave a platform to Winston Churchill, who had been contributing to the *Evening Standard* but had recently been given the sack 'because his views were not in accordance with the policy of the paper'. In a letter dated 4 April, Churchill suggested a fortnightly political article. Camrose's reply was cautious. 'It is a little difficult for us to enter into a definite agreement for any long period ... having regard to the fact that our policies might well be at serious variance,' he replied. He suggested a trial period of six months, at £70 an article, 'but reserving the right of non-publication in such cases as we decide'. Churchill agreed to these terms, and the arrangement worked so well that it was twice extended, first to a year and then to fifteen months. When the series ended, on 22 June 1939, the author wrote to Camrose hoping that he had been satisfied with the articles, and concluding: 'Alas, they have mostly only proved too true.'

As the menace of Hitler loomed larger, Camrose found his loyalties uncomfortably divided. Close as he was to Churchill, he was also a friend and fervent admirer of Neville Chamberlain, who had become Prime Minister in 1937; and when, after Munich, public confidence in Chamberlain sharply diminished, he was in a difficult position, for he felt certain that Churchill should be brought back into the Government. He also had the bad luck – at that critical moment – to fall seriously ill. He had suffered for some time from gout, and now found a refugee German doctor who claimed to have a patent cure. The remedy worked, in that it put paid to the gout, but it nearly put paid to the patient as well. The doctor, not realising that Camrose had already had jaundice, gave him an extra-strong dose, which put half his liver out of action, sent him into a coma, and left him permanently diabetic. Apart from this, he recovered and in 1938, to speed his convalescence, he sailed for a holiday in South Africa. Even there, his thoughts were continually of newspapers. Staying at the Mount Nelson Hotel in Cape Town, he summoned the *Telegraph*'s correspondent George Aschman, whose task it became to take him up the South African daily papers every morning, including the one on which he himself worked, the *Cape Times*. And what did Camrose do when he got them? He went through them column by column, story by story, criticising the layout, sub-editing and selection of news – even though he was 6,000 miles from home, and the papers were no concern of his.

At 135 Fleet Street the Munich conference produced a crisis. On 15 September, the day on which Chamberlain flew to meet Hitler for the first time, the *Telegraph* carried a forceful piece by Churchill saying that 'only the most blunt, plain, even brutal language will make its effect', and that 'whatever words are used must carry with them the conviction that they are spoken in deadly earnest. This is no time for bluff.'

For the next morning, J. C. Johnstone wrote a tough leader condemning the whole idea of Chamberlain's mission; but in the middle of the day Seymour Berry, who was in charge in his father's absence, found himself summoned to 25 Park Lane by Sir Samuel

Hoare, the Home Secretary. By the time he arrived, Hoare was at lunch, and kept him waiting two hours. When finally told that the Government would be angry if the *Telegraph* criticised its latest attempt at a settlement with Germany, Berry himself was so furious that he hurried back to the office bent on publishing Johnstone's leader as it was. There, however, others persuaded him that it should be toned down, and it appeared in a modified form, though still hostile to the Munich enterprise.

As if to soften the blow of the paper's defection, Peterborough carried a vivid description of Chamberlain arriving back at Heston aerodrome after the visit. The pictures on television were 'extraordinarily clear. The Prime Minister's machine and the escorting plane did a half-circuit of the aerodrome. [After a close-up shot of steps being placed to the cabin door] Mr Chamberlain emerged . . . a smiling – it would not be too much to say a buoyant – figure as he acknowledged the cheers, or rather the clapping, of the bystanders . . . a triumph for television.' When Chamberlain came back from his second visit to Hitler, on 30 September, to announce 'Peace in our time', Peterborough was again a close observer. As the Prime Minister brought out the 'No more war' declaration from its envelope, 'a gust blew out a foolscap sheet. For a moment it was the most striking object on the screen. A producer of genius could not have arranged it to greater dramatic effect.'

If coverage from Berlin was first-class, that from Vienna was even more vivid, for there the paper had an exceptional correspondent in the form of G. E. R. Gedye, who had fought in the First World War, been wounded, worked in Intelligence and served on the Rhineland Inter-Allied Commission in Cologne before becoming a journalist. Since 1922 he had reported from Central Europe and from 1929 had represented *The Daily Telegraph* in Austria. By nature radical, he took a sharp, sceptical view of Fascism, and was uniquely well informed on his subject, having first-hand knowledge of many people, events and places, not least the concentration camp at Dachau, which he had visited on Hitler's birthday in 1933.

Eventually, in March 1938, with the increasing Nazification of Austria, Gedye's vigorous, combative reports inevitably led to his expulsion. His despatches about the *Anschluss* – Germany's pact-cum-takeover of the country – early in the month were the final straw, and he was ordered to be out of the country by the twenty-eighth. A posse of Gestapo officials, sent to the station to make sure he boarded the train for Prague, spent half an hour searching his luggage and pushing wires down his hollow cane fishing-rods in a vain hunt for secret documents or foreign currency;

friends had brought a chocolate cake, a bunch of red roses and a bottle of 'Barack – the Duke of Windsor's own Apricot Brandy', made in Budapest, to send him off, and when the train pulled out, they saw his dachshund leaning from the window, one paw raised in a derisive Nazi salute.

For the next few months Gedye reported for the *Telegraph* from Prague; but then, in the summer of 1938, the imminent publication of his book *Fallen Bastions* proved too much for Camrose and his minions to stomach. When, in July, Gollancz advertised the book in their list for the spring of 1939 as telling 'the uncensored truth', they scarcely exaggerated, for the author had given rein to his deep loathing of Fascism, particularly in the chapters dealing with Hitler's rape of Austria, and included some scathing criticisms of Chamberlain; the publisher's notice so alarmed Arthur Watson that he wrote telling Gedye that the book (which he had not seen) seemed 'very undesirable'. Gedye refused to change his text, but offered to resign immediately – an overture which the paper rejected. When the book came out in February 1939, Watson ordered him to return to London immediately, even if it meant chartering his own aircraft. Gedye came, and was interviewed by Watson and Lawson. This time he did resign, and was given six months' severance pay – one of the very few journalists ever to be dismissed from the *Telegraph* under the Camrose regime.

The passionate, almost desperate, tone of the book was set by the last words of the author's Foreword: 'There is still time, but, I think, only just time. That is why, at whatever cost, I had to write this book – while there is time.' *Fallen Bastions* received immediate acclaim and went through several editions, the publishers rapidly reducing the price from 16s to 7s 6d as they scented the onset of publicity that would make it a bestseller. In April a note in the *New Statesman and Nation* diary said that Gedye had got the sack for including 'information and comments which *The Daily Telegraph* refused to print'. This Watson immediately refuted in a letter to the Editor, saying that Gedye had published a 'violently worded commentary on events in Central Europe', and that by taking such a partisan attitude had 'destroyed his value to us as a reporter. As a result Mr Gedye resigned by mutual arrangement.' This gave Gedye a good chance to hit back from America, where by then he had joined the *New York Times*:

Mr Watson writes that I 'resigned by mutual arrangement'. It is correct. It is equally correct that Herr Hitler invaded Czechoslovakia 'by mutual arrangement' with President Hacha . . . A man may not, it seems, write as he pleases about Mr Chamberlain and remain a foreign correspondent of *The Daily Telegraph*. Lord Camrose, the owner of the paper – who, I was told, had read my book and was 'extremely angry' – has acted, of course, entirely within his rights. I have no grievance. But is the newspaper-reading public satisfied? For me, the final rape of Czechoslovakia last March (which my book foretold), the humiliating picture of Britain's Premier running through Europe in search of allies to help him lock the Central European door now that the Czechoslovak horse has been stolen . . . and, above all, the rooted distrust of Mr Chamberlain which I find pervading all circles, official and private, in the United States, are for me full justification of my efforts to give in my book such warnings as I could.

It was a nice point. One of the *Telegraph*'s key principles was that, although opinion might legitimately be expressed in leaders and signed leader-page articles, the news must remain absolutely pure, uncontaminated by the reporter's own convictions. Although Gedye had sought to distance the remarks made in his book from his ordinary journalism, he had clearly broken one of the paper's fundamental rules. And yet, if he had not so savagely criticised a friend of the proprietor, would Camrose have reacted as he did? As it was, Camrose clearly found it intolerable that the Prime Minister should have been insulted by one of his own correspondents.

In fact, as Gedye's predictions proved ever more accurate, the paper moved further from the Government over Germany, and Camrose was forced by events to modify his support of Chamberlain. On 30 June 1939 a small posse of politicians, consisting of Harold Macmillan, Harold Nicolson and Anthony Eden, delivered to Peterborough Court a letter suggesting the formation of a War Cabinet. Obligingly enough, on 3 July 1939 the *Telegraph* devoted its first leader to a demand that Churchill be brought into the Cabinet, saying that his presence there was urgently needed. 'No step would more profoundly impress the Axis powers with the conviction that this country means business.' The article was 'quite threatening', thought Chips Channon, 'and the PM is taken aback by it'. Chamberlain sent for Camrose the moment he read the article, and explained – without convincing his visitor – exactly why he did not think Churchill's inclusion in the Government would make his task any easier. 'I am vexed that Camrose, who

The Daily Telegraph

and Morning Post

NO. 26,375   TUESDAY, APRIL 25, 1939   LONDON LATE EDITION   ONE PENNY

BIRTHS, MARRIAGES, DEATHS
& IN MEMORIAM NOTICES,
PERSONAL AND CONCERTS,
TOURS, CRUISES, &c.

ON BACK PAGE

BRITISH AMBASSADOR TO WARN HITLER

SIR N. HENDERSON'S MISSION IN BERLIN

CONSCRIPTION IN ENGLAND IF PEACE PLAN IS REJECTED

RUMANIA SEEKS CREDIT TO BUY ARMAMENTS

Sir Nevile Henderson has returned to his post as Ambassador in Berlin with instructions to make important representations to the German Government before Herr Hitler speaks on Friday.

(1)—Ambassador will urge the acceptance by Germany of President Roosevelt's peace plan and

Emphasise that were it to be rejected, the British Government, in carrying out its non-aggression policy, would be forced to introduce conscription.

In London yesterday the Rumanian Foreign Minister, M. Gafencu, saw Mr. Chamberlain and Viscount Halifax, the Foreign Secretary, and will continue his talks to-day. One of his objects is to obtain credits for the purchase of arms in England.

The Soviet Vice-Commissar for Foreign Affairs, M. Potemkin, has been appointed to undertake a special mission to Turkey, last night arrived in Rumania.

FUEHRER'S VIEW OF BRITISH STRENGTH

BY OUR DIPLOMATIC CORRESPONDENT

GERMAN CLAIMS

Partly Approach Desired

M. GAFENCU'S DAY

Talk With Premier

From to-day THE DAILY
TELEGRAPH AND MORNING
POST will print news on the front page.

The daily news—home and foreign is now so vital in the national life that it is obviously wrong that the most important page, the one which is seen first by the reader, should be occupied by advertisements.

Actually the custom of printing advertisements on the front page of daily newspapers has for many years been peculiar to this country. On the contrary, our country, the contrary, has become the invariable rule.

We believe that the new arrangement will be found both convenient and appropriate.

In every other respect THE DAILY TELEGRAPH and MORNING POST remains exactly the same paper as before.

Births, Marriages & Deaths and all other advertisements formerly on the front page will, as future, be found on the back page.

SOVIET ENVOY TO TURKEY

SENT ON SPECIAL MISSION

FROM OUR OWN CORRESPONDENT

MOSCOW, Monday.

JOURNEY BY WAY OF RUMANIA

A SIGNIFICANT ROUTE

From Our Own Correspondent

BUCHAREST, Monday.

ARMS ORDERS

British-Backed Credits

AXIS TACTICS

Sidelight on Albania

CABINET HEAR TO-DAY'S BUDGET PROPOSALS

Sir J. Simon to Speak For 90 Minutes

DEBATE MAY LAST TILL 11 P.M.

Socialist Questions On Mediterranean

By the POLITICAL CORRESPONDENT

The Cabinet met at the Prime Minister's room at the House of Commons last night to consider the Budget proposals.

Sir John Simon, the Chancellor of the Exchequer, will rise at approximately 3.45 p.m. to-day to present the Budget, which will be the second since his appointment as Chancellor.

MR. CHURCHILL MAY SPEAK

MR. BURGIN AT CABINET

CABINET AND COMPULSION

PRINCIPLE IS IN PRINCIPLE

U.S. AMBASSADOR NOT RETURNING

HITLER'S MOVE AWAITED

From Our Own Correspondent

WASHINGTON, Monday.

EGYPT'S FAITH IN BRITAIN

PROMISES GUARANTEED

From Our Own Correspondent

CAIRO, Monday.

ENVOY'S RETURN TO BERLIN

STATEMENT BY PREMIER

M. COULONDRE'S PLANS

From Our Own Correspondent

PARIS, Monday.

News Summary: Other Pages

HOME

EMPIRE

FOREIGN

FINANCE

SPORT

TO-DAY'S WEATHER: Bright intervals; showers—Page 14.

BROADCASTING: Page 8.

NEW AMBASSADOR TO U.S.

APPOINTMENT OF LORD LOTHIAN

The Marquess of Lothian has been appointed British Ambassador in Washington in succession to Sir Ronald Lindsay, it was announced last night. Sir Ronald, who is 61, is retiring this summer.

THE MARQUESS OF LOTHIAN

U.S. WELCOMES THE APPOINTMENT

OPINION IN CAPITAL

From Our Own Correspondent

WASHINGTON, Monday.

GERMAN WARSHIPS OFF SPAIN

SEEN FROM LINER

From Our Special Correspondent

ABOARD THE RAMPURA, Monday.

CRUISER AT BILBAO

BARCELONA, Monday.

---

20 WAR CANOES TO MEET KING'S SHIP

Red Indian 'Welcome At' Vancouver

PLANS FOR BRITISH COLUMBIA VISIT

FROM OUR OWN CORRESPONDENT

OTTAWA, Monday.

THE RETURN JOURNEY

NAVY'S SEND-OFF FOR THE KING

EARL OF PERTH LEAVES ROME

CIANO BIDS FAREWELL

From Our Own Correspondent

ROME, Monday.

DUKE OF ALBA'S RETURN

used to be such a firm supporter, should now have committed himself,' the Prime Minister wrote to his sister on 8 July, calling the drive to recruit Churchill 'a regular conspiracy'.

From Berlin, Hugh Greene, now joined by another young correspondent, Anthony Mann, had continued to file excellent, objective despatches, until the irritation which they caused the Nazi authorities flared up in April 1939. The immediate pretext for the outburst was a major innovation at the *Telegraph*: the switch of the front page from advertisements to news. On Tuesday 25 April, without warning, the paper appeared in its new form, with a panel on the front explaining that 'the daily news – home and foreign – is now so vital in the national life that it is obviously wrong that the most important page, the one which is seen first by the reader, should be occupied by advertisements'.

The change took all but one or two senior executives by surprise. Camrose had been planning it for months, but had decided to go ahead only a few days before, and did not announce his intention until Monday evening. That must have been a hectic night, for the new format sent shock waves through the rest of the thirty-page paper: the columns on the leader-page were made wider, and reduced from seven to six; the page opposite, on the right-hand side of the centre, which had previously carried the main news, now became the second news page; the personal announcements which had appeared on the front now went to the back, and so on. The response from readers was overwhelmingly in favour, and once again sales jumped ahead.

Only in Berlin was there a howl of protest. On the day of the change the Nazi news bulletin let fly a blast of outrage:

> The London *Daily Telegraph* has for weeks held the leading place in the Press campaign against Germany by printing scandalous anti-German reports. This paper, which used to be considered one of the serious papers of Great Britain, has now definitely broken with its tradition by devoting the whole of its front page to political agitation against the Axis powers.

This last sentence was demonstrably untrue: the front page carried several stories not about Germany at all. The main headline was BRITISH AMBASSADOR TO WARN HITLER – SIR NEVILE HENDERSON'S MISSION TO BERLIN, but there were also pieces about the Budget, to be presented in the House of Commons that day, and about the race to have the World's Fair in New York ready in time for the opening. Yet since very few citizens of the Reich would get a chance to read the *Telegraph*, the lie was immaterial. No doubt Goebbels was still more chagrined to see that on the following day, along with the news that conscription would be introduced for 450,000 men between the ages of eighteen and twenty, the paper printed a translation of the Nazi outburst, with the helpful explanation that the term for political agitation (*Hetze* – literally 'baiting' or 'rabble-rousing') was a favourite word in Nazi polemics at that moment.

It seemed hardly surprising that, ten days later, Greene was ordered to leave Germany, along with five other Britons, one of whom, Barbara Henman, had been working for the past fifteen months as secretary in the *Telegraph*'s office. The paper ran a leader which claimed that Greene's removal had nothing to do with his work but was purely a reprisal for the expulsion from London of Dr Roesel, leader of the Central London branch of the Nazi Party in Great Britain, and London correspondent of the *National Zeitung*, the paper closely connected with Goering. The Foreign Office also said that the matter was one of pure reprisal. Yet there can be little doubt that Goebbels had been needled beyond endurance by the persistent accuracy of Greene's reports.

Ordered to be outside the territory of the Reich by 24 May, Greene left Berlin by the Nord Express the previous day, seen off by a large contingent of British and American colleagues and friends, who threw a party on the platform of Friedrichstrasse station. A few minutes later, when the train stopped briefly at the Tiergarten (the Zoo), another party gave him a second send-off there. Back in England, he was able to contribute authoritative analyses of the situation in Germany, and for a while he took the sacked Eric Gedye's place in Prague, later writing of him that although he was 'a wonderful reporter, he sometimes allowed his crusading instincts to run away with him'.

Of course, not all the news in the *Telegraph* was about the imminence of war. 'Marianne Mayfair', the pseudonymous doyenne of the women's page, continued to twitter inimitably about social events – such as Lady Priscilla Willoughby's wedding to Sir John Aird in April 1939: 'Spring flowers from Cliveden, Lady Astor's Thames-side home, decorate No. 4 St James's Square, which she has lent for the reception following the marriage . . . Two charming family gifts have a personal flavour. One is a patchwork quilt embroidered by herself from Lady Cecilie Goff, Lady Priscilla's aunt . . .' There was also plenty of good, old-fashioned, real news. BURNED GIRL'S INFATUATION – NOTE TO CURATE – LOCKED

CHURCH ran the headlines on a page lead, about an eighteen-year-old domestic servant who died after being found with her clothes alight in the church of St Marius Chad, Longton, apparently driven to distraction by her love for the curate, the Reverend W. A. Goater.

Then, on 13 June 1939, came the proud announcement that the sales of *The Daily Telegraph* had passed three-quarters of a million – an increase of more than 100,000 copies a day during the past year. Over the previous months Camrose had become increasingly irritated by hints and innuendoes that the British Press was, as he himself put it, 'largely controlled by Jews, and that unknown international financiers were exercising a secret and sinister influence on our national affairs'. The aim of such rumours, needless to say, was to discredit any newspaper like the *Telegraph* which opposed the Jew-hating, Jew-baiting Nazis; and now, using the announcement of record circulation as a pretext, Camrose popped up from behind his parapet with an entire page on 'London Newspapers – their Owners and Controllers'. His article was so long that both Peterborough and the Letters column were displaced to other pages – an almost unparalleled departure. Besides several thousand words, he published photographs of nine leading newspaper proprietors, including one of Kemsley, but none of himself, and indulged in some mild self-congratulation in describing how the *Telegraph* had grown under his ownership. He even went so far as to predict that 'the round million a day is a figure to which we may hope steadily to climb'. His article can only be described as exhaustive, but it certainly made its point, and put paid to the idea of a Jewish conspiracy. Such was the interest it generated, in fact, that the author later expanded it into a booklet, which sold 40,000 copies, and after the war into his book *British Newspapers and their Controllers*.

More and more, however, the news reflected the approach of war. Air-raid sirens will be tried out in London tomorrow – 'the test will consist of the "Air Raid Warning" signal – a warbling or fluctuating note'; the demand for air-raid shelters is growing; the King and Queen will sail to Canada on a liner escorted by warships, rather than (as first planned) on the battlecruiser *Repulse*, which, it is thought, should not leave home waters. Conscription is announced, and greeted by a leader entitled ON A WAR FOOTING: 'If any doubt could remain of the extreme gravity of the times, it must be dispelled by the announcement which the Prime Minister was constrained to make to the House of Commons yesterday.'

When Hitler invaded Poland, and Chamberlain announced on

the morning of 3 September 1939 that the nation was at war with Germany, nobody could accuse the *Telegraph* of having failed to do its patriotic duty. Camrose was perfectly well aware that many people decried his newspaper for being dull and grey; but he had no hesitation in defending the position which he had achieved after ten years at the helm:

> I am not boasting when I say that *The Daily Telegraph* is in a field of its own. Such is the fact. It has not the many-million appeal that other penny London morning papers have. It is more staid, it is not so flippant, and some people may say it is not so bright. But it has achieved a public which is responsible, authoritative and influential – a public unique in the history of morning newspapers.

Did Camrose realise that he became known to some of his staff as Lord Copper, after the press baron in Evelyn Waugh's novel *Scoop*, published in 1938? It is true that the cognoscenti – among them Bill Deedes, who had worked with Waugh in Abyssinia – knew that the model for Copper was Beaverbrook, and that the *Daily Beast* sounded much more like the *Express* than the *Telegraph*; yet many features fitted *any* press magnate, and enough fitted Camrose precisely for the name to be transferred to the master of 135 Fleet Street. Camrose may not have spent his days trying to draw the head of a cow, stumped by the problem of whether the horns should go above or below the ears; but the proprietor of the *Telegraph* was a lord who lived in great style and lurked high up in his own sanctum; his name began with a C; the Waygood-Otis lifts at 135 did whiz up and down in exactly the manner of those in the Megalopolitan building; and the staff certainly said 'Up to a point, Lord Camrose', or words to that effect, when they wished to avoid telling him that he was wrong.

5 AT WAR, 1939–45

It was ideal for the daily papers that Chamberlain's fateful broad-cast should have fallen on a Sunday. On Monday 4 September 1939 they had a clear field, announcing the first offensives in Europe. The *Telegraph* had a strong front page, led by the three-column headline GREAT BRITAIN AT WAR – THE KING'S MESSAGE TO THE EMPIRE. The two right-hand columns carried news of fierce fighting in Poland, and in the centre of the page, at the top, was the text of King George's announcement: 'In this very grave hour, perhaps the most fateful in our history, I send to every household of my peoples, both at home and overseas, this message, spoken with the same depth of feeling for each one of you as if I were able to cross your threshold and speak to you myself.'

Already, on the previous Saturday, the paper had published a whole-page map of Europe, showing frontiers, lines of communi-cation and so on; and now it was ready with a main leader-page spread, headed HITLER'S GRIM SIX-YEAR RECORD IN TECHNIQUE OF PERFIDY. The first leader began: 'With conscience clear, with no purpose to serve but the saving of liberty itself, Great Britain and France are at war with Germany.' In the past few days the paper had rapidly redeployed its foreign correspondents as best it could. One of them was Clare Hollingworth, then in her late twenties, who went to Fleet Street to be given her first assign-ment, and was startled to hear Arthur Watson, in the silence of his dim, panelled room, say, 'Go tonight! You must go to Warsaw tonight.'

Back at her flat in Buckingham Palace Road, she set about packing, but decided that she needed a better suitcase; so at 2.00 am she telephoned Harrods, which then ran a twenty-four-hour service, and ordered a new one, which was delivered to her door an hour later. Thus equipped, she left at once to become number two to Hugh Greene in Warsaw, and reported the opening of the war from Katowice, where she saw Hitler's tanks roll into Poland.*

Had it been given a free run, the paper would now have established a prodigious sale, for the war produced what every circulation manager dreamt about — really strong news every day. Public hunger for information was higher than ever, and the *Telegraph* was organised to meet the demand: its war reporting was second to none, and the circulation soared briefly to 914,000 copies. Yet for Camrose — as for every other proprietor — the war proved a time of intense frustration, in which shortage of newsprint put an artificial limit both on the number of pages in each day's paper, and on the number of copies that could be printed. Within a few months the paper had shrunk from over twenty pages to eight: then it went down to six, and finally, on Saturdays, to four. The circulation was similarly forced down to a wartime low of 648,000.

The reduction was voluntary, rather than enforced by Government, and sprang at first from prudence, later from necessity. The first cut, made by mutual agreement between the newspaper proprietors, came in as soon as the war started. For a few months fresh supplies of newsprint continued to arrive from Canada, but it soon became clear that the proprietors must form a co-operative to ensure the fair distribution of whatever paper could be obtained, and in May 1940 they set up the Newsprint Supply Company, which worked for the industry as a whole and proved, in Camrose's own words, 'a brilliant success'. It was this body, he later wrote, which ensured that the British Press remained more or less intact — and he made a strong case for the national importance of newspapers in war, claiming that the failure of French papers 'to perform their national duty' in 1940 had been 'one of the decisive factors in the fall of France'.

Many members of the *Telegraph* staff, of course, were called up into the armed forces. Fred Lawson served in France and Belgium, and in 1941 commanded the Yorkshire Division before he became Director of Public Relations in the War Office a year later. (In 1943, on the death of his father, he succeeded to the family title as the fourth Lord Burnham.) Seymour and Michael Berry both went into the army and served with distinction. (They joined up

---

* Over the next fifty years Clare Hollingworth proved herself a reporter of exceptional courage and tenacity, covering wars in every corner of the world for the *Telegraph* and other papers. In the summer of 1989 she was in Peking as a freelance correspondent, and at the height of the riots was seen up a lamp-post in Tiananmen Square, still, aged seventy-nine, determined to secure the best possible vantage-point.

as volunteer 'Austrian recruits' when Hitler invaded Austria in March 1938. As Michael put it, 'We decided he had gone too far, and that we should bring our full might to bear against him as supernumeraries.') Later Seymour also became a Member of Parliament, representing Hitchin from 1941 to 1945. Their father was too old for active service – sixty in 1939 – and Arthur Watson was a year his senior: between them, the two veterans, with the able help of George Simon, held the fort at 135 Fleet Street for the duration of hostilities. Yet within three weeks of the outbreak of war Camrose took up his one and only political appointment, as Chief Assistant to Lord Macmillan, the Minister of Information and Controller of Press Relations.

With the war in its infancy, a feeling spread that the Government was starving the public of information to an unnecessary degree. As the *Daily Herald* put it, the Cabinet seemed to be 'treating this war as if it were no concern of the British people'; there was a general idea that some responsible person, who understood news thoroughly, should become involved, and other newspapers welcomed Camrose's appointment. 'It may be,' said the *Daily Mail*, 'that now the public will be trusted with the truth.'

In Whitehall Camrose seriously alarmed his subordinates by ordering the destruction of all unnecessary or obsolete paper – his habit was always to tear up everything possible – and, to general surprise, he left office after less than a month, announcing in the House of Lords on 25 October 1939 that he had arranged for himself no longer to occupy an official position, and that the reconstruction of the Ministry of Information had gone far enough for him to claim release from the public-spirited mission which he had accepted. Such was Camrose's one brief period in Government service. Yet there was no feeling that he had let the Government down, or defaulted by his swift withdrawal. Far from it. On 1 January 1941 his name appeared at the head of the New Year Honours List, in which he was made a viscount – Viscount Camrose of Hackwood Park, in the County of Southampton. Here was recognition that, even if he was not a member of the administration, his work and achievements were of national importance. One man who did not share this view was Frank Waters, General Manager of the *Scottish Daily Express*, who wrote in a sour note to his wife that Camrose had managed to 'scramble up another rung of the society ladder with a viscountcy . . . [He is] aiming at an earldom, which he'll get if the war goes on long enough, by kow-towing to the Conservative Party. As Editor-in-Chief of the *Daily Telegraph* he's carefully suppressed every twinge of conscience that the paper has had – and there have been many – over major issues of High Policy. The Conservatives now have him well and truly gagged.'

That was unfair. Camrose happened to be a good friend of Churchill, who had become Prime Minister in 1940, to admire what he was doing, and to be thoroughly patriotic. Churchill found strength in their friendship, and often rang the paper late in the evening to find out the news in the first edition. Once he came through to the Night Editor, Brian Roberts, and demanded that a story be killed, on the grounds that its publication would be damaging to public morale. Roberts refused, but then thought he had better cover himself by ringing Camrose – who, true to form, backed him up. 'Roberts,' he said, 'remember that *you* are the Night Editor, not Mr Churchill.' Years later Churchill himself recorded that in those dark days Camrose's 'unfaltering confidence helped to sustain all those who knew him . . . Nothing ever shook Lord Camrose, and "worry" was a word that found no place in his vocabulary.'

In November 1940, on the death of Neville Chamberlain, the Editor-in-Chief made one of his rare forays into print, with a eulogy of the Prime Minister whose career had come to such an ignominious end. 'One of the most honest, self-sacrificing statesmen who ever achieved the glory of being first minister of the Crown in this country,' he wrote.

October 1940 brought an innovation of lasting significance to the *Telegraph*: the start of a Manchester edition, printed in the north. For several years Camrose had been planning such a move, for demand had kept increasing, and papers produced in London inevitably reached northern readers late. Now two further considerations lent urgency to the idea. One was that train services had been reduced, so that the papers destined for the north had to leave London even earlier, and so missed much important news; the other, that if the *Telegraph* presses in London were damaged or destroyed by bombs, some alternative means of production, at least, would be available. Luckily Kemsley's company Allied Newspapers had, at Withy Grove in Manchester, the largest printing works in the country, and Camrose arranged with his brother that from 1 October 1940 the northern edition of the *Telegraph* should be printed there, its contents being transmitted by special telephone-line from Fleet Street. The paper opened an office in Manchester, and the Assistant Editor Oscar Pulvermacher – who, for all his dynamism, was none too keen on bombs – went up to run it.

Especially in wartime Manchester, Pulvermacher struck a stylish note. Always immaculately dressed, usually smoking an expensive cigarette, he was a close friend of Malcolm Sargent and other leading musicians. He lived at the Midland Hotel, only a ten-minute walk from Withy Grove, and yet, in spite of petrol-rationing, somehow always had an office car and driver to take him back and forth. In the evenings he would leave the office as soon as he had seen a proof of the leader-page, entrusting the front page to lesser mortals; and on one memorable occasion in 1942 he departed with instructions to the Chief Sub-Editor: 'I'm going now. I don't want to be disturbed for anything except the surrender of Hitler.' Flamboyant as he was, he could also be something of a mischief-maker – as when John Barbirolli came over from New York to take up his job as conductor of the Hallé Orchestra in 1943. Barbirolli went to the *Telegraph* office for the sole purpose of delivering a message for Pulvermacher from Alex Faulkner, the paper's correspondent in New York, but Pulvermacher refused to see him, and left him standing in the lodge, because he thought the job with the Hallé should have gone to his friend Malcolm Sargent.

Pulvermacher must have thought the timing of his move to the north fortunate, for only a couple of months later, on 29 December 1940, the building in Fleet Street became one of the first to suffer in a German air-raid. In spite of the vigilance of the aircraft-spotting team, set up on the roof by H. J. C. Stevens, a shower of incendiary bombs which fell on and around No. 135 started several fires, and the women's page editorial department on the third floor was burnt out. Other bombs penetrated the composing-room and the machine-room below, but were promptly doused. Gas and electricity failed. Neighbouring buildings caught fire and one next door, in Wine Office Court, was so gutted by flames that it collapsed, burying a fireman and a soldier beneath the rubble. Nevertheless production of the paper went on throughout the night, and next day the Duke of Kent came to inspect the damage, accompanied by Sir Walter Monckton, Director-General of the Ministry of Information.

A few days later Lord Haw-Haw – the traitor William Joyce – gave out on German radio that the building had been destroyed. Alas for him, this was fantasy – and in fact the greatest change which came over the office during the war was that the whole of the façade was painted a darker colour, to stop it showing up so clearly in moonlight. The building had another lucky escape in September 1944, when a parachute mine came down on the pavement just outside, between the *Telegraph* and the *Express*, but did not explode. The arrival of this contraption – which one man mistook for an overturned taxi – was not reported in the paper, in case information about where mines were landing might improve the despatchers' aim.

Camrose's own property did not escape so lightly. In the Blitz of May 1941 his London home, 25 St James's Place, was twice damaged by bombs: the first time, the windows were blown out, but on the second occasion the building was severely damaged, and he decamped to a suite in the Dorchester Hotel. This became the temporary home of many other rich people, its construction of steel and concrete giving it the reputation of being one of the safest buildings in London. In the country, he handed over Hackwood to the Canadian Army, who used the house and grounds as a military hospital and erected temporary wards, holding 750 beds, on the south lawn.

When a further reduction in the consumption of newsprint became essential in March 1941, Camrose himself explained the paper's policy. The choice was stark: either to go below six pages and come out with only four, or to reduce the number of copies printed – and it was the second alternative that he chose. As usual, he laid out the position with painstaking, almost pedantic, precision:

In contradistinction to other penny papers, *The Daily Telegraph* will, therefore, be maintained as a six-page paper. To do this means, unfortunately, a substantial reduction in the number of copies which can be printed, with the newsprint available. The war has led to a spirit of co-operation unknown in normal days, and we hope that in this spirit those readers who are fortunate enough to get their copies regularly will share them, wherever practicable, with less fortunate friends ... Far better that five people should read a *Daily Telegraph* true to its character and traditions than that six should read what could in four pages be, at the best, only an approximation to it.

Although based in London, Camrose did manage to slip abroad now and then. In May 1940 he was cryptically reported to have been 'somewhere in France', visiting the British Expeditionary Force as a guest of Lord Gort; and in October 1942 he travelled to America, where he had a brief audience with President Roosevelt, talked to Cordell Hull, the Secretary of State, and discussed wood-pulp supply problems with officials of the American Production Board.

Reduced in length though it was, the paper nevertheless managed to publish many graphic descriptions of the war – and few were more vivid than its reports of the mass air-raid on London carried out during the brilliantly moonlit night of 10 May 1941. On Monday 12 May, under the headline NAZI BOMBERS WRECK HOUSE OF COMMONS, the lead story described how many of London's most famous buildings, including the House of Lords, Westminster Abbey and the British Museum, had been damaged when German aircraft unloaded their bombs indiscriminately over the centre of the capital in what the Nazis described as a reprisal for the 'methodical bombing of the residential areas of German towns, including Berlin'. The *Telegraph*'s reports claimed that the enemy had lost at least thirty-three planes and 160 trained personnel, 'the highest penalty they have paid in night raids on this country'.

'Much damage was done, and many lives were lost,' said the first leader, 'but morning found those whose homes are in the bombed areas more than ever determined to carry on there . . . Frightfulness will not readily admit defeat, and will develop every form of horror it can invent. But the past assures us that it will always be baffled by the "grim and gay" British temper, and our national capacity for meeting the need of the hour.' The next day – 13 May – found the leader-writers in still more spirited form. 'Hitler has chosen to fight with the methods of the Vandal and the Hun,' they thundered. 'He makes his bid for immortality with Attila . . . Humanity has once again to defend itself against an invasion of barbarism, against hordes driven on by the passion of the tiger and the ape.'

It was on 13 May 1941 that there broke one of the most sensational stories of the war: Hitler's Deputy, Rudolf Hess, had parachuted into Scotland, apparently in an attempt to make peace. That day, and for the rest of the week, the *Telegraph* made the most of the story, reporting the extraordinary events near Glasgow and the panicky reaction of the German leaders to Hess's disappearance. NAZI PARTY SPLIT cried the front-page lead on the fourteenth: the article suggested that 'serious dissensions may have broken out in the Nazi hierarchy', and that 'an extreme state of tension seems to have been reached within the party'. The leader that day, entitled DEPUTY DESERTS, declared: 'In all the nightmare murk of treachery and bloodlust which is the history of Nazism, there has been no event so amazing as the flight of HESS from HITLER'; and the paper eagerly picked up a remark made in Cairo, about 'the first rat to leave the sinking ship'.

Yet within a few days the *Telegraph* became as baffled as everyone else by what had happened. The trouble was that no sense of any kind could be got from the prisoner: it soon became clear to his interrogators that he had no proper peace plan, and very little idea of Hitler's intentions; and even though these facts were concealed from the Press, the sheer absence of news about him was both frustrating and inexplicable. By Thursday 15 May, people were beginning to fall for the line put out by Hitler – that Hess had been ill for some time, and was suffering from delusions, so that he could not be taken seriously – and in its attempt to prevent the story degenerating into farce, the *Telegraph* was driven to the expedient of attacking him violently in a leader: 'Hess more than any other man but Hitler is responsible for the abominations of the concentration camps and the Gestapo. He lived and throve and made himself important by murder, torture and persecution.' Yet, after the drama of the man's sudden arrival, no fact of the slightest interest emerged, either from or about him: everyone presumed that he would make startling revelations, but none came. Many people found it incomprehensible that, no matter what he might have said, Churchill did not make tremendous propaganda capital out of him, if need be by inventing damaging admissions. But the Prime Minister refused even to make a statement to the House of Commons, and after a feeble joke by Peterborough – that Hess, who had helped Hitler compose *Mein Kampf*, was now writing a sequel of his own, *Mein Dekampf* – the story quickly faded from the news.*

Most war stories, of course, had their origins overseas, and correspondents such as Christopher Buckley (later killed in Korea) quartered the globe like the hounds of heaven. Often their where-abouts were not precisely identified – 'From Our Correspondent Somewhere in Iraq', 'From Our Special Correspondent at a Flying School' – but probably none covered more ground than Leonard Marsland Gander, who by the middle of 1943 had visited eighteen countries and travelled more than 50,000 miles during the previous two years. Hugh Greene, between other assignments, was able to turn his earlier experience in Berlin to good effect in a series of telling propaganda broadcasts. On 3 October 1941 he sent out a bitingly sarcastic message (in German) to Funk, the Nazi Minister of Economics, lamenting the fact that they could not join forces for a drink, as in the old days, and then suddenly rounding on 'my old friend':

* Nearly half a century later, the Welsh surgeon Hugh Thomas produced the extraordinary but plausible theory that the prisoner was not Hess, but a double, and that Churchill knew, or at least strongly suspected, that an attempt had been made to dupe him.

I will say this about you, Funk. You're a crook, but you have got a sense of humour, which is more than can be said about the rest of your gang. I remember how fascinated I was, the first time we met, to see you putting down alternate glasses of beer and brandy for several hours without stopping, until you fell asleep in the corner and snored . . . No, Funk. I ought to have known that you would never get into trouble for telling the truth.

In September 1942 Greene made Goering his target, having heard that the Reich Air Minister had bought a palatial house in Appelviken, the smart residential suburb in neutral Stockholm. A few days ago, said Greene, he had heard a well-known German industrialist inquiring about jobs in Sweden. When asked if anything was wrong, the man replied, 'Oh no, not at all – yet. But I'm afraid that all prominent Party members will be shot when the day of reckoning comes, after our defeat.'

Such outbursts sound crude now; but no doubt at the time they carried a punch, not least because they were so obviously well informed.

No newspaper could have been more patriotic than the wartime *Telegraph*; besides printing every scrap of news for which it could find room, or suppressing for the time being facts whose appearance might have damaged the Allied cause, it also published information, maps and plans disseminated by the War Office and Air Ministry – for instance, a series of silhouettes of German aeroplanes, beginning with four different views of the Ju52, 'the most important German troop carrier', put out as a guide to Local Defence Volunteers and others in the identification of enemy aircraft. 'It is suggested that the Local Defence Volunteers and other citizens should paste the series of pictures on cardboard and hang it in a prominent position for easy reference,' said the accompanying note.

In spite of Camrose's assurance that the paper would not go below six pages, in January 1943 it was forced down to four. There was room for only one leader now, instead of four, and everything had to be scaled right down. Yet still the Editor made it his policy to run serial extracts from forthcoming books – for instance, Charles Graves's *Seven Pilots*, from which three pieces appeared before publication in 1943.

One idea which eased production difficulties was the 'A' and 'B' advertisement system. Camrose was always keenly conscious of the value of small advertisements to the paper: he knew from his own experience how long it took to build them up, and to establish the confidence of readers. Now crisis threatened, for there was so little space that far fewer announcements than usual could be printed. The solution – for which the Company Secretary H. J. C. Stevens claimed credit – was to split advertisements into two streams – A and B – and to run each stream in half the copies printed every night, spreading them as evenly as possible through the editions. This meant that any one advertisement would be seen by only half the paper's readers – but at least it was a way of keeping the backlog within bounds (after the war the period of waiting increased at one point to eight weeks).

Another feature of the paper which survived the war in a truncated form was Peterborough. Like his proprietor, Hugo Wortham was well past the age to be called up, and so was able to carry on in control of his column. A great many of its paragraphs naturally referred to the war – as when he commended Churchill for pronouncing foreign words 'in the classical English way. For him Nazis are Nazis, not Natzis, just as Mozart used to be Mozart, and "Moat-sart" was looked on as an affectation.' Yet Wortham's preoccupations – Eton, cricket, racing – remained wonderfully consistent, and the entertainment value of his column was enormous, especially when so much of the news was grim.

When James Joyce died in January 1941, Peterborough let loose a predictable blast against modern writing – 'I always thought that Lewis Carroll, in "The Jabberwock", turned gibberish to better account than Joyce'. A proposal that Eton's traditional school dress of top hat and black tails should be abolished excited his special alarm, and in April 1942 he reported that an American passing through the school had been astonished by the boys' appearance, remarking, 'What's this – an OCTU for undertakers?' In April 1942 he revealed that the celebrated racehorse Nearco, unbeaten during its career, was living in a £500 air-conditioned dugout on a stud-farm near Newmarket. In September 1943 the death (from wounds) of Hedley Verity provoked an account – told to Wortham by the famous slow bowler himself – of Monday, 25 June 1934, when overnight rain, followed by sun, had made the Lord's wicket perfect for spin, and Verity had taken fourteen Australian wickets in a day, the greatest of his career. As always, Peterborough was on the lookout for members of royal families, and in February 1944, under the headline NAVY'S GREEK PRINCE, revealed that the 'tall, fair and good-looking' Prince Philip of Greece, then a lieutenant in the Royal Navy, had 'signalled his return to London' by visiting the Distinguished Strangers' Gallery in the House of Commons.

Other stalwarts who served out the war at 135 Fleet Street included Ralph Cooper, the Night News Editor (always known as Archie), and his assistant, Eric Stowell. Cooper was a mild-mannered and exceptionally kind man, who had two main claims to journalistic fame. First, in January 1911, as a junior reporter for the London News Agency, he had scooped all rivals with his report of the siege of Sidney Street, in the East End of London, in which two anarchists defied the combined might of the police and the Scots Guards for several hours before incinerating themselves. Arriving on the scene rather late, Cooper found all the other journalists trapped in a pub, from which the hail of gunfire prevented any escape; he, by good fortune, found himself lying on the floor with the Scots Guards in the upper storey of a bottling plant – from which he was able to telephone graphic, shot-by-shot reports an hour ahead of anyone else. His second celebrated exploit consisted in departing (at half-an-hour's notice) to cover a revolution in Madeira: having missed a plane at Croydon and a liner at Southampton, he pursued the ship down the Solent in a chartered speedboat and had himself hauled on board.

A firm believer in the value of shorthand, Cooper was said to think in it; and in the Newsroom he was courtesy personified. On one occasion a new reporter was sent to interview a crusty police commissioner late at night, and returned complaining that he had been insulted and thrown downstairs. 'Bit of a rebuff,' murmured Archie. 'Try someone else.' Having joined the *Telegraph* as a reporter in 1915, he served the paper for almost fifty years, the last twenty-nine of them (from 1935) as Night News Editor.

His assistant Eric Stowell was another likeable and conscientious man, but manifestly much more tense – perhaps as a result of his gruelling service in the Royal Artillery during the First World War. As a noncommissioned officer he was wounded and won the Distinguished Conduct Medal; then he was commissioned, and won the Military Cross. After the war he became Editor of the *Daily Dispatch*, and he joined the *Telegraph* in 1931; he was good and quick at his work but he never enjoyed strong health and often gave the impression of being under strain.

In 1943 the paper gained a particularly valuable recruit in the form of Colin Coote, a highly intelligent and experienced journalist, who had been working – with great reluctance – as a leader-writer on the *Times*. In his memoirs, published under the killer title *Editorial*, he gave a stark account of the miseries of life under the Editor Geoffrey Dawson during the late 1930s: the atmosphere in the office, he wrote, became 'quite horrible', and after numerous disagreements he reached a compromise, whereby he was obliged to write leaders only about disarmament, his views on Nazi Germany being impossibly at odds with those of his chief. When war broke out, Coote wanted to join the army, even though he was already forty-six, but could not, for his wife was dying of cancer: instead, he took a part-time job in the War Office, as assistant to the Director of Public Relations, and for a while he was able to combine this civilian role with continuing to work for the *Times*. As a means of raising extra money to pay for his wife's treatment, he also made some broadcasts. Soon, however, the management of the *Times* objected to these outside earnings, and proposed that his pay should be reduced to no more than a retainer. He refused 'with some indignation, and left with a handshake which was far from golden'. Then one night he met Camrose at a dinner of the Other Club and confided to him that he had lost his job – whereupon Camrose promptly said, 'Come to us'. Coote turned quite white, for although the possibility of his joining the *Telegraph* had been discussed at earlier dinners, he hardly expected such a quick reaction; but, once he had got over the shock, he agreed, and moved to 135 Fleet Street. Whether or not Camrose already saw him as a potential Editor, and a successor to Arthur Watson, is no longer clear; but for the moment Coote wrote leaders, immensely relieved to be working in a more realistic and congenial atmosphere.

By 1943 Camrose was bored with the war. The paper shortage made journalistic innovation impossible: with the news demanding every inch of space, it was a waste of time thinking up ideas for stories. He was therefore delighted when, in a governmental reorganisation, the Foreign Secretary, Anthony Eden, suggested to Churchill that he should become Minister of Information. Camrose longed for just this kind of responsible job, which he could have done admirably – and he was correspondingly disappointed when deprived of the chance by Beaverbrook, who, although ostensibly a friend, was bitterly jealous of his success, and now persuaded Churchill that, in spite of appearances, he had never properly recovered from his illness of 1938.

In the spring of 1944 he did make space in the paper for an excellent idea which combined education with fund-raising – the Daily Telegraph Prisoners of War exhibition, which was staged in the grounds of Clarence House, in the Mall. Put together with the help of the Red Cross and St John War Organisation (whose funds it was designed to boost) this was opened by the Duke of Gloucester on 2 May. 'Jackboots in the Mall, barbed wire and bayonets in St James's', began the paper's marathon report.

Under May skies, and surrounded by the throb of a free city, men and women met in the replica forecourt of a German prison camp to express their concrete sympathy with the men who suffer behind wire. A Nazi lookout post glowered down upon them. Nazi guards in steel-grey uniform paced every exit. Drab huts formed a rectangle of unrelieved monotony around them. But behind the barbed wire, behind the lookout post and behind the bayonets was evidence of how the British spirit has conquered the turgid Nazi regime.

After the formal opening by the Duke, Camrose himself held forth, drawing attention to the ingenuity with which servicemen had contrived to 'defeat the awful tedium and monotony of prison life'. His main theme, however, was the great effort they were making to prepare themselves 'for the happy day on which they return to this country'.

More than 34,000 have written home to say that they would like to educate themselves for their future after the war. In reply the Red Cross and St John service has sent to the camps over 220,000 educational books. Out of these 34,000 men, between 6,000 and 7,000 have already written and submitted their papers for professional and trade examinations. Of this number nearly 5,000 have passed outright, many with distinction.

When I tell you that these examinations include accountancy, law, agriculture, medicine and engineering, you will realise the serious nature of the work our men are doing in an environment so depressing and discouraging. Some idea of what all this work means may be gathered from the fact that over a hundred societies and institutions in this country hold examinations for prisoners of war, and many of them supply special study courses free of charge.

As one further illustration of this process of what has been happily described as 'qualifying for freedom', no less than twenty-two separate languages are being studied by our prisoners in Germany today. After that, who shall say that the British race is not interested in foreign languages?

To touch on the lighter side of this service to the camps. I read in one of the publications issued by the Red Cross that among the requests for educational supplies a group of medical students at one camp asked for some pickled dogfish. Another group asked for a skeleton. They did not ask in vain. To the everlasting credit of the Red Cross and St John it should be known that without any delay both the pickled dogfish and the skeleton were promptly supplied.

On he went, extolling the strenuous efforts made by the Red Cross to send out food parcels, and repeatedly praising the fortitude of the prisoners. In every way the speech was typical of Camrose: full of information, fired by enthusiasm for education, earnest, heartfelt, low-key, its sentences precise but pedestrian, leavened by one or two very mild jokes (but with each carefully signalled), it exactly expressed the personality of the man who ran *The Daily Telegraph*.

Another arena that lent itself to philanthropy was the Royal Albert Hall, in which the *Telegraph* sponsored a series of wartime concerts. One of the grandest occasions, attended by the Queen and her two daughters, the Princesses Elizabeth and Margaret, was staged on 25 March 1944 to celebrate the seventy-fifth birthday of the conductor and impresario Sir Henry Wood, and to raise funds for a national memorial to him in the form of a new concert hall in London. Wood himself conducted four of the items in the programme, and was presented to the Queen during the interval. Camrose gave an address, launching the appeal for funds, and the evening made a profit of £8,000.

An equally cheerful event, also sponsored by the *Telegraph*, was the concert to mark the seventieth birthday of Sir Thomas Beecham, on 2 May 1945. Again this was held at the Albert Hall, Beecham himself conducting the Royal Philharmonic Orchestra and the Luton Choral Society; and the proceeds of £2,400 went to the foundation fund of the Royal Philharmonic Society. In a birthday speech obligingly described by the paper as 'brilliant', Beecham hailed Camrose as one of his oldest friends and the *Telegraph* as 'for many years almost the mouthpiece of music in England'. At the start of his career, he said, when he first 'entered the musical arena in those rash, impulsive days', the paper's music critic had been among his most stalwart backers.

For another concert in 1945, given by the young violinist Yehudi Menuhin and the London Symphony Orchestra, Camrose and *The Daily Telegraph* defrayed all the expenses so that receipts could go to the St Mary's Hospital appeal for furthering research into the uses of the miracle-drug penicillin. (Later that year the paper gave both editorial and financial support to the Penicillin Train, a travelling exhibition designed to show what the drug could achieve: during a tour of the Midlands and South Wales, the train collected £2,000 for research, and in October 1945 Camrose, Iliffe and other notables inspected it at Paddington Station.)

In the course of the war Camrose's philanthropic thoughts seem to have turned often to Eton, and he made several bequests to show his appreciation of what the school had done for his sons. His aim was to provide bursaries for boys whose parents could not otherwise afford to send their sons to Eton, and, on a smaller scale, to enable boys to travel abroad during the holidays, so that their grasp of foreign languages would be improved. His first donation, of £1,000, was made in July 1939. Then, early in 1940, he proposed to give £5,000 over a number of years, and in February 1945 the Provost and Fellows gratefully accepted an offer of £15,000 – although it is no longer clear whether this amount included the sums paid already. In any event, his subventions were extremely generous: by 1988 his benefaction had grown to the sum of £1.6 million, and during that year twenty-eight boys received assistance worth £65,000.

With the advance of the Allied forces up through Italy in the spring of 1944, the news became ever more optimistic. Day after day the paper was able to lead with rousing headlines: EIGHTH ARMY ADVANCES FIVE MILES IN A DAY . . . MASSED TANKS DRIVE ALONG ROME ROAD . . . KESSELRING'S LOSSES EXCEED 50,000 MEN . . . ROME FALLS: MOPPING UP AT DUSK . . . GERMANS QUIT THEIR WHOLE TIBER BANK. In May 1944 the paper for once made a mistake, insouciantly printing the names Omaha and Utah as two of the answers in the crossword puzzle. Within hours men from MI5 were in the building, suspecting that an attempt had been made to leak information about the imminent invasion of France, which had been planned for months, in the deepest secrecy, using those very words as codenames for landing-beaches. Camrose certainly knew many wartime secrets: for instance, he had been aware of the fact that the Allies were deciphering the Germans' Enigma messages at least since 1941. But of course no breath of it had appeared in the paper, and now this mention of vital names was completely accidental.* On 6 June the war news was mostly

---

* The compiler of the crossword, a retired schoolmaster, had happened to hear the names used by American servicemen billeted near him, and thought they would fit in well.

of Italy, the main story from Northern Europe telling of bomb and rocket raids on German radio installations. Next morning, splashed right across the top of the front page, was the news that the invasion force had gone in at dawn the day before, and the liberation of Europe was under way. According to the paper's representative at Westminster, 'it was a House of Commons subdued in the presence of events that determine history' which heard from Churchill 'the momentous news that the great assault on Europe had begun'.

The war dragged on for almost another year. By the beginning of 1945 the staff of the *Telegraph*, like their readers, had developed such a hatred of Nazi Germany that events which gave rise to controversy later, such as the bombing of Dresden, excited only satisfaction and hope at the time. The sole desire of most people was that the enemy should be finished off, by any means. On 15 February 1945 the paper reported 'one of the most devastating twenty-four-hour periods of aerial warfare ever known', the chief events being the mass raids on Dresden by British and American aircraft. Dresden was represented as a vital rail centre, and no words were wasted on the civilians who might have died in the raids, or the lovely baroque buildings which might have perished beneath the hail of fire-bombs. The *Telegraph*'s Air Correspondent quoted an Air Staff officer as saying, 'Give us a month of reasonable weather, and we will paralyse the railroad system of the German armies in the East and in the West.'

In April, with headlines growing larger and larger, the news was almost too good to believe: RUSSIANS STRIKE FOR BERLIN: 28 MILES NOW . . . WORLD AWAITS FINAL NAZI SURRENDER . . . MUSSOLINI EXECUTED BY PATRIOTS . . . and then at last the nightmare drew to an end. GERMANY'S FINAL SURRENDER IS IMMINENT proclaimed a banner headline on 7 May 1945, followed, on 8 May, by an even bigger one, right across the top of the front page: GERMANY CAPITULATES! 'This is VE-Day,' began the lead story. 'The war in Europe is over. After five years and eight months, "complete and crushing victory" has, in the words of the King, crowned Britain's unrelenting struggle against Nazi Germany.' A feeling of scarcely imaginable relief flooded the paper. Besides news of the German surrender, the front page reported a frenzied outburst of rejoicing in New York, where a premature announcement of the capitulation had sent the city 'mad with joy'.

The first leader, set across two columns (an almost unprecedented device), paid a glowing tribute to Churchill:

SIFTA SALT

The Daily Telegraph

4 A.M.

This is the Gin
Gordon's

No. 28,048 LONDON, WEDNESDAY, MAY 9, 1945 *and Morning Post* Printed in LONDON and MANCHESTER PRICE 1½d.

NATION'S VE OUTBURST OF JOY: ALL-NIGHT CELEBRATIONS

ROYAL FAMILY 8 TIMES OUT ON PALACE BALCONY

Mr. CHURCHILL: 'NO GREATER DAY IN OUR HISTORY'

A GREAT NATIONAL OUTBURST OF RELIEF AND THANKSGIVING AT THE END OF NEARLY SIX YEARS OF WAR IN EUROPE WAS EPITOMISED YESTERDAY, VE-DAY, BY TREMENDOUS SCENES OF REJOICING IN LONDON, WHICH BEGAN IN THE AFTERNOON WITH THE PRIME MINISTER'S ANNOUNCEMENT OF THE END OF HOSTILITIES AND CONTINUED ALL NIGHT.

Eight times within 10 hours, in response to the enthusiasm of huge crowds, the King and Queen, Princess Elizabeth and Princess Margaret stepped out on to the balcony of Buckingham Palace. On one occasion they were accompanied by Mr. Churchill, who later, addressing a throng of 100,000 people in Whitehall, declared: "In all our long history we have never seen a greater day."

Of the vast numbers of people who set out from home in the morning, tens of thousands made their way towards Buckingham Palace.

They cheered at every opportunity—the changing of the Guard, arrivals for an 11 a.m. Investiture, Mr. Churchill's appearance on his way to lunch at the Palace.

"ADVANCE, BRITANNIA"

Outside the Palace at 3 p.m. a great silence fell on the multitude, and through amplifiers came the open-ing words of the Prime Minister's broadcast.

Announcing the signing of the act of surrender at Rheims at 2.41 a.m. on Monday, and that the signature in Berlin would take place during yesterday, he said that hostilities would officially end at one minute past mid-night—00.01 hours this morning.

Japan remained to be subdued, Mr. Churchill con-cluded. "Advance, Britannia! Long live the cause of freedom. God save the King."

"God bless him!" came the echo from the great throng; and then their pent-up feeling broke loose.

They paraded in rejoicing, vociferous columns along the Mall and in the parks; they waved flags, blew whistles, pelted one another with confetti, and they persistently roared their desire to see the King.

From the dim interior of the Palace the Queen, the King, Princess Elizabeth and Princess Margaret stepped into the sunlight on the balcony and stood hand-in-hand

PICCADILLY CIRCUS JAMMED

Crowds pouring towards Piccadilly Circus, time-honoured centre of public revelry, packed all the approaches. By five p.m. no traffic could get through.

Meanwhile, at Westminster, the Prime Minister had made in the House of Commons a statement in almost the same terms as his broadcast, and at Buckingham Palace, again answering the people's loyal call, the Royal family once more appeared on the balcony at 4.15.

Then, in the Row Room of the Palace, his Majesty exchanged congratulations with the Prime Minister and the War Cabinet. About 5.30 the Royal family, together with Mr. Churchill, again went out on the balcony.

After leaving the Palace, the Prime Minister, at 5.55, addressed a tremendous crowd at Whitehall—estimated to number 50,000—from the balcony of the Ministry of Health. It was then that he referred to "no greater day" in our history. He appeared a second time about 10 o'clock and addressed the throng.

Outside Buckingham Palace the crowd again saw the Royal family on the balcony at seven o'clock.

At 9.30. when the King and Queen and the Princesses appeared on the balcony for the fifth time, the police estimated that the crowd numbered 100,000.

After dark the Princesses, escorted by Guards officers, walked among the people. They again appeared on the Palace balcony with the King and Queen at 10.45 and shortly before midnight. Finally, just before the floodlights were switched off about 12.30 a.m., their Majesties went out on to the balcony for the eighth time.

Scenes in London—P5

BUCKINGHAM PALACE WAS FLOODLIT

PRINCESSES OUT IN NIGHT CROWD

The floodlighting of prominent London buildings and public places last night, including Buckingham Palace, St. Paul's, the Houses of Parliament, Trafalgar Square and Piccadilly Circus, aroused great enthusiasm among the crowds still cele-brating VE-Day.

British family members regained tens of thousands of men and women to go to the London hotels, all their King and Queen on the VE-Day, for which were the joy of peace in Europe.

A vast crowd was assembled outside Buckingham Palace throughout the day and until a late hour a joyous and colourful crowd whose enthusiasm rose to a crescendo of patriotic fervour at the occasional appearances on the balcony of the smiling King and Queen and the Princesses.

Whole Empire Hears King's Broadcast

Britain and the whole Empire heard the King's voice on the radio at nine o'clock last night.

His Majesty's broadcast, the full text of which appears on P4, while telling of the overthrow of Germany, con-tained a reminder that war has yet to deal with the Japanese. "Let us remember those who will not come back, their constancy and courage in battle, their sacrifice and endurance in the face of a merciless enemy."

PREMIER SANG WITH CROWD IN WHITEHALL

At 10.30 last night Mr. Churchill appeared for the second time that day on the bal-cony of the Ministry of Health building in Whitehall. When he appeared the crowd, which had his hand his band, broke into "For he's a jolly good fellow"

The Guards' band which had been playing in the crowd suddenly struck up "For he's a jolly good fellow" as the crowd. When the strains died away, Mr. Churchill began singing "Land of Hope and Glory," and the crowd joined in the singing. The Guards' band took up the strains.

"The word 'Victory,' is the signal. "We may allow ourselves a brief period of rejoicing." After a moment the Premier was singing "Run Rabbit Run" with the crowd—and in a moment more he was conducting the singing of "Roll out the Barrel."

GERMAN FLEET TO GO TO ALLIED PORTS

The Admiralty announces that German war-vessels of all kinds have been ordered by the surrender to the German Fleet:

All German and German-con-trolled warships, auxiliaries, merchantmen and other craft at sea are being ordered at Power their position in plain lan-guage, giving their position, and are being given orders to proceed to Allied ports as directed. They will remain in harbour or anchorage until instruc-tions are received.

All warships, auxiliaries, mer-chant ships and other craft in harbour are being ordered to remain in harbour.

ADMIRALTY ORDER

LEADERS MAY MEET SOON

URGENT PROBLEMS

By Our Diplomatic Correspondent
There is evidence that a meeting of Marshal Stalin and President Tru-man was foreseen in the letters of the Three Powers.

There is no official confirmation, but there is every likelihood that within the next few weeks there will take place a meeting of the three Allied leaders to discuss the outstanding problems of Europe.

2.40 a.m. SURRENDER SCENE AT ALLIED H.Q.

GERMANS SIGN CAPITULATION IN BERLIN

MOSCOW STATEMENT

The unconditional sur-render of Germany to Russia, and simultaneously to the Western Allies, was announced by Moscow radio shortly before 2 a.m. (BST) to-day. The capitulation was signed in Berlin.

The Moscow statement said: "The unconditional surrender of all German armed forces on land, sea and air has been signed."

The German High Command will immediately issue orders to all forces on land, sea and air under the German High Com-mand to cease military operations after 11.01 p.m. Middle European time.

The announcement added that the capitulation was signed in Berlin.

DRAMATIC 15 MINUTES THAT ENDED WAR

HUMBLED GERMANS

From DOUGLAS WILLIAMS,
Daily Telegraph Special Correspondent

RHEIMS, Tuesday.

This is how the war in Europe was ended. At 2.41 a.m. yesterday, in the war room of Gen. Eisenhower's battle headquarters in this ancient city, two German delegates, acting jointly on behalf of Doenitz as head of the Reich, unconditionally surrendered all German land, sea and air forces to the Allied armies in the West, and simultaneously to the Russian armies in the East.

The German delegates were Adml. Hans Georg von Friedeburg, C.-in-C. of the German Navy in succession to Doenitz, and Col.-Gen. Gustav Jodl, Chief of Staff of the Wehrmacht.

All forces, both Allied and German, cease operations on one minute after midnight on Wednesday morning.

The end of the war took place amid sombre simplicity and with the least possible ceremonial in a classroom 30ft square of the Ecole Professionelle, a French commercial school facing a busy shunting yard, from which Gen. Eisenhower for the past three months has directed the operations of his vast armies.

Against a background of brilliantly lit battle maps 15 men sat round an old oak table chequed and scarred by the knives of thousands of scholars. Dilapidated yellow pine chairs were ranged around, and each place was marked with a name card and furnished with a writing tablet and pencil and common china ashtray.

MAPS SHOW WAR'S LAST MOVES

The walls were covered with large-scale battle maps on which were still to be seen the front-line positions of the war's final hours marked in coloured chalk.

Searing Klieg lights, installed for the benefit of film and Press photographers, threw the faces of the partici-pants in the solemn ceremony into harsh relief. A calendar marked the date, May 7, 1945.

The Germans, three in number—Maj. Wilhelm Oxenius being also present as A.D.C. to Jodl—sat along one side of the table.

Facing them, reading from left to right, were Lt.-Gen. Sir Frederick Morgan, Maj.-Gen. Sevez, representing the French Army, Lt.-Gen. Bedell Smith, Gen. Eisenhower's Chief of Staff, Maj.-Gen. Ivan Susloparov, Russian repre-sentative, aided by a junior officer as interpreter, Gen. Carl Spaatz, of the American Air Force, Air-Marshal Sir J. M. Robb.

At the foot of the table sat another Russian dele-gate, Col. Ivan Zenkovitch, and Maj.-Gen. F. R. Bull, an American officer on Gen. Eisenhower's staff. On master of the British Army, circulated around the room as Master of Ceremonies, and also acted when required as German interpreter.

(Continued on P. 6, Col. 3)

SEYSS-INQUART ARRESTED

WAR CRIME CHARGES

Seyss-Inquart, German Gauleiter of Holland, has been arrested.

Himmler and Goering, reported to have been hiding, have turned up again, and it is believed they will be brought to trial.

Among those charged with responsibility as war criminals are...

KING LEOPOLD'S LIBERATION

SENATE'S MESSAGE

From Our Special Correspondent

In communication from the Belgian Government it is stated that King Leopold III, held in Germany, is now free.

LATE NEWS

QUISLING POLICE CHIEF FOUND

Oslo, Tuesday.—Jonas Lie, former Norwegian quisling Police Minister, has been found.

THE DAILY TELEGRAPH

This Morning's News

VE-Day
Nation's VE-outburst of joy; all-night celebrations. Royal family eight times out on Palace balcony.—P1.
Mr. Churchill: "No greater day in our history."—P1.

Europe
2.40 a.m. surrender scene at Allied H.Q.—P1.
Germans sign capitulation in Berlin.—P1.

3 Years Ago To-day

No words can express what this country owes to him. At every turn of the war he has been able to express the feelings in magnificent language and to direct the actions with unflinching resolution of a people whom he loves in a cause worthy of them and him.

Yet for once the leader-writer misjudged the mood of the people. 'After so long a period of struggle and suspense,' he wrote, 'the news may seem too big to evoke at once outward signs of exhilaration.' Not at all. That day, far from feeling numbed, the people of Britain went wild in what the paper of 9 May called the 'nation's outburst of joy'. The 'tremendous scenes of rejoicing' in London began in the afternoon, when the Prime Minister announced the official end of hostilities on the wireless, and they continued without a break throughout the night. For the first time since 1939 prominent buildings such as St Paul's Cathedral and the National Gallery were floodlit, thus bringing the era of darkness to a symbolic end. Crowds flooded Piccadilly Circus, blocking every approach so effectively that by 5.30 pm no traffic could get through; yet the densest throng was the one which seethed in the Mall outside Buckingham Palace, greeting the repeated appearances on the balcony of the Royal Family and Churchill with 'wild expressions of delight', and unshaken by the broadcast made at 9.00 pm by the King, who warned that although Germany was beaten, the Allies had yet to deal with the Japanese, 'a determined and cruel foe'. Rising to the occasion on 9 May, the *Telegraph* threw its normal restraint to the winds and revolutionised its front page by printing an immense photograph of the Royal Family and the Prime Minister on the palace balcony, across the top of all eight columns.

It was a measure of Camrose's closeness to Churchill that on VE night, 8 May, he dined with the Prime Minister at a small family party in the Annexe to No. 10 Downing Street. Only Churchill, his daughters Sarah and Diana, and Diana's husband, Duncan Sandys, were present. Next morning Camrose recorded the highlights of the evening in a vivid memorandum. Hearing that a huge crowd had assembled in Parliament Street, Churchill went out to address them at 10.30 pm, wearing his favourite boiler suit. Camrose went with him 'on the long walk from the Annexe through the various Government buildings, and the roar of enthusiasm which came up from the crowd at the sight of him and his grandson, Julian Sandys, was deafening.' The crowd responded to his speech by singing 'Land of Hope and Glory' and 'For He's a Jolly

Good Fellow', and afterwards Churchill returned with Camrose to the Annexe. Among the secrets which the Prime Minister confided to his friend was the fact that the Americans had advanced 120 miles farther than he had agreed with Stalin that they should, and that they would 'have to come back that distance'. Churchill also revealed that 'he had agreed the European line with Stalin', and that although 'it was not all that he could wish, it gave some guarantee for the future'. When Camrose left at 1.15 am, the Prime Minister still had a pile of files before him, 'all of which he said would be dealt with before he went to bed'.

Nowhere in Europe can hostilities have closed on a more satisfactory note than at the Hotel Metropole in Brussels. On 15 May 1940 Hugh Greene had fled the city in a great hurry, two days before the Germans arrived, leaving behind a scribbled note which acknowledged a debt of 2,213 francs and four centimes. This was placed in a file, and, as the years of the war rolled on, written off by the cashier as a dead loss. Then in July 1945, to the amazement and delight of the staff, Leonard Marsland Gander suddenly walked into the hotel, asked for the bill, and paid it.

6 NEW HEIGHTS, 1945–54

'Today I began on *The Daily Telegraph*,' wrote Malcolm Muggeridge in his diary on 1 June 1945. The author and journalist was forty-three, and after a varied career – which had included spells in Moscow and Calcutta, besides six years as an intelligence officer during the war – was none too sure that he had done the right thing in signing-on as a leader-writer:

It was somewhat drear – old Watson seated at his desk; Bailey, another old veteran, and I discussing the day's news, Watson then disappearing to see Lord Camrose, the proprietor, and returning to say he required one leader on Syria and one from me on Burma. On Burma I duly tapped, writing almost automatic, after so many years easily coming, complete rot.

Muggeridge found the 'whole effect' of 135 Fleet Street 'very twilit' – and it is hardly surprising. Not only was much of London in ruins: rationing was still in force (of newsprint as well as of food), and austerity very much the order of the day. Besides, the hierarchy at the *Telegraph* were growing old. Camrose was sixty-six, Watson sixty-five, Fred Burnham fifty-five, and even George Simon fifty-two. Yet Muggeridge settled in well. Sharing an office with J. C. Johnstone, whom he came to like very much, he put a much-needed spark to some of the ancient tinder lying about the place, his mischievous, imaginative intelligence crackling among the dusty, dry brushwood of fixed ideas and attitudes.

With the war in Europe over, one of Camrose's main concerns was to ensure that the Conservatives were returned to power in the General Election of 5 July, so that Churchill would continue as Prime Minister. The *Telegraph* certainly did its best for the cause, with supporting leaders and reports on the progress of the campaign; it claimed that 'apart from the Socialist and Liberal party fanatics who provoked it, nobody wanted an election at all', warning electors to remember 'the responsibility falling upon those parties who did choose to imperil national unity and strength before the job of winning the world war was done'. The *Telegraph* also sounded a note of caution, pointing out that the result of the poll was unpredictable, as constituencies had changed so much since before the war, and 'a great part of the electorate is quite unfamiliar with elections, and another substantial part is serving overseas'.

Camrose himself was far from sanguine, and had begun discreet negotiations for disposing of the *Financial Times*, afraid that a Labour win would put an end to financial journalism, and perhaps to the whole capitalist system. In July he duly sold his controlling interest in the paper to its smaller stable companion, the *Financial News*, for £743,000; and in October that year, in a curious double transaction, the *Financial News* as a company took over the *Financial Times*, but as a newspaper was taken over by it and ceased separate publication. Camrose later confided to one of the FT's managers that this was the greatest mistake he ever made.

In spite of its proprietor's political worries, the *Telegraph* did not seem galvanised by any sense of urgency. On the eve of polling day a leader-page article demanded SHALL WE SELL THE NATIONAL INTEREST FOR A PINT OF SOCIALIST DOGMA? But when the editorial itself remarked that 'No leader has ever deserved better of his country' than Churchill, it reflected the widespread feeling that the idea of the people rejecting him seemed inconceivable.

When they did just that, giving Labour a landslide victory, and an overall majority of 153 seats in the Commons, an air of stupefaction invaded the paper's columns. Reporting that Allied and foreign countries were 'showing some natural bewilderment at the dismissal of Mr Churchill by the electors', they went on to say that the decision seemed 'at strange variance with the warm gratitude which every man and woman in the country felt towards him'. Muggeridge recorded that there was 'great consternation' in the office. 'Even Watson seemed troubled; not in himself – I don't think he cared much either way – but at the thought of having to venture up to a stricken fifth floor.'

Churchill's defeat was a great blow to Camrose. But only ten days later, on 7 August 1945, momentous news took his mind off home troubles. ALLIES INVENT ATOMIC BOMB, cried an enormous headline. FIRST DROPPED ON JAPAN. Faced with a story of immense impact, the paper was at its best. The news was that 'the first atomic bomb, a single one', had been dropped on Hiroshima, 'a town of twelve square miles on the Japanese mainland', and that it had had over 2,000 times the blast-power of the largest weapon ever used until then; but the *Telegraph* consolidated the story by assembling an absorbing display of background information. This explained how the first test of the new device had taken place only three weeks earlier, at 5.38 am on 16 July in the New Mexico desert; how an agreement between Churchill and President Roosevelt had enabled research to be carried out in the United States and Canada, safe from German air attacks; how different pieces of immensely complex knowledge had been brought together from different fields of science into a single, workable plan. The paper reported Churchill's arresting phrase, that this revelation of the secrets of nature had been 'long mercifully withheld from mankind', and the ferocious warning of Roosevelt's successor, President Truman, that if the Japanese did not accept the Allies' surrender terms forthwith, they might expect 'a rain of ruin from the air, the like of which has never been seen on this earth'. Besides its admirable coverage of the main news, the paper had space to report, on that same day, that in the fourth Test Match at Lord's, stopped by bad light, the young Australian all-rounder Keith Miller had defied England's bowlers, helping his side to a score of 273 for five wickets.

On that same day, 7 August, Churchill paid Camrose a visit at 135 Fleet Street and they had a wide-ranging talk. The atomic bombs were naturally high on their agenda, and the fallen Prime Minister confided that he had tried to persuade the American President Truman not to disclose details of design or manufacture to Stalin. Churchill thought that, with the secret in their hands, the Americans could dominate world politics for the next five years; and he said that, if he himself had stayed in office, he would have urged Truman to use this power to make Stalin behave 'reasonably and decently' in Europe.

Camrose saw that his old friend's disappointment at losing the chance to shape the future of Europe was 'very deep indeed', and now and then Churchill 'found it difficult to conceal his bitterness at the way the people of England had treated him'. The conversation touched on the possibility that Churchill might write an account of the war, but he expressed doubts about publishing such a work in his own lifetime.

A week later, on 15 August 1945, the front page splashed the news of Japan's unconditional surrender. A panel beneath the main headline pointed out that the war had lasted 'three weeks short of six years'. Alongside, an anonymous despatch from New York reported that outside the Imperial Palace in Tokyo wailing crowds were beseeching the Japanese Emperor to forgive them for their failure; and another story recorded that in London 'continuous blasts from the sirens of ships in the river and railway engines roused people who had been unaware that peace had returned'. The State Opening of Parliament, already planned for that day, fortuitously provided the occasion for uninhibited rejoicing.

Camrose, by now, dominated his paper completely. On 23 June, his sixty-sixth birthday, the anonymous sycophant at the *Evening Standard* had loosed off his usual gushing broadside: 'He will be regarded as one of the greatest newspaper proprietors . . . The force of his personality is felt throughout the organisation. And he is also a very popular figure, with innumerable friends . . .' All this was true. Yet Camrose puzzled Muggeridge, who saw him as a rather sad man, and thought that he seemed little interested in anything but money – not in a selfish way, but in general terms. One day in December 1945 Muggeridge recorded how Camrose appeared unexpectedly at the editorial conference:

> He had been walking about the City – strange, on a Sunday afternoon, this millionaire newspaper proprietor wandering about the ruined City. He was really a touching figure, asking about the American Loan, and whether the terms might have been easier, and then going off again.

Later, discussing with Camrose the life of Kipling which Freddie Birkenhead had written, but which had been suppressed by Kipling's daughter, Elsie Bambridge, Muggeridge said he thought that the author should redraft the book, or threaten to; whereupon Camrose asked, 'very characteristically, "Was it worth it?" because the book would not make much money'.* Again, at lunch on the fifth floor one day the talk turned to Calouste Gulbenkian, the Armenian oil magnate who lived in a Lisbon hotel. Camrose (Muggeridge noted) seemed slightly annoyed when Ulrich, the Portuguese Ambassador, said that Gulbenkian had between £200 and £300 million.

> 'Is he happy?' Camrose asked eagerly. And Ulrich (to my delight) replied, 'Yes, I think so.' I weighed in to say that I never could understand this business of the burden of wealth, being always

---

* Through Mrs Bambridge's agent, Camrose demanded compensation for the author, which he eventually secured. But, in the opinion of Michael Berry, suppression of the book shortened Birkenhead's life. The biography was eventually published – and serialised by *The Sunday Telegraph* – in 1984, after the deaths of the author and of Mrs Bambridge.

myself in the position of wanting to shoulder some. This also didn't please Camrose, but did his son Michael, sitting beside me, immensely.

In due course Muggeridge came to like Camrose. Compared with the other newspaper magnates for whom he had worked – Beaverbrook and Rothermere – the laird of 135 Fleet Street seemed a relatively simple person, straightforward and honest:

His aspirations had been well satisfied by becoming rich and a lord, whereas the other two continued, till the days of their deaths, to be tormented by unrealised hopes and unaccountable fears. Camrose, it is true, might have liked to go a notch or two up in the peerage, or accumulate another million or two, but as long as his brother and former associate didn't, it bothered him little. The contentment with his achievement and status made him seem more like a lord than most lords.

He told me once how, travelling in an American plane, a fellow-passenger, hearing he was a lord, asked him where his castle was. I could see the questioner's point; Camrose looked like a man who lived in a castle . . . In my experience, aspirants quite often make more convincing versions of what they aspire to be than the originals they copy – for instance, Isaiah Berlin as a don, Evelyn Waugh as a country gentleman, Orwell as a proletarian and Camrose as a lord. For one thing, they take more trouble over their costumes and getting word perfect.

One facet of Camrose which his staff rarely saw was his generosity. Towards the end of 1945 he heard, to his consternation, that Churchill considered himself hard-up and thought that he might have to sell Chartwell, his home in Kent. At once Camrose proposed an ingenious plan to solve the problem: he and a group of friends would buy the house and arrange matters so that Churchill could live in it until his death, whereupon it would pass to the National Trust, who would maintain it as a memorial. The speed with which this 'noble and princely plan' (as Churchill himself called it) went through bore witness to Camrose's stature and powers of persuasion. To raise £50,000 for the purchase price, and the further £35,000 needed by the National Trust as an endowment, he himself put up £15,000 and cajoled sixteen others into contributing £5,000 each. All but two paid up within three minutes of hearing his idea, and the two laggards with minimal further delay.

At 135 Fleet Street no one was better placed than Muggeridge

– a newcomer with a fresh eye – to observe the peculiar structure which Camrose had devised for the running of his newspaper. Watson's editorial authority, he saw, was 'strictly limited', because effective control was in the hands of the Berry family:

> This meant, in those days, Lord Camrose with, for supernumer-aries, his two sons, always referred to in the office, in true Victorian-patrician style, as Mr Seymour and Mr Michael. Some time after our editorial conference, Watson would be summoned to the fifth floor to give an account of his editorial intentions and to receive his instructions. Later, the news editor would be similarly briefed. In this way, the two satrapies were kept separate and independent of one another.

This odd system – which survived unchanged for the next forty years – had many anomalies, not least the fact that, when there was a strong News Editor, the Editor had no jurisdiction over large areas of the paper, including one of vital importance, the front page. Some people thought that Camrose had deliberately imported an American idea and set up the system on the principle of divide-and-rule – and certainly, in later days, it did encourage inter-departmental skirmishing. Yet, as his own personal authority was unchallenged, and needed no artificial support, it seems more likely that the division sprang from a straightforward desire to keep news and opinion separate, rather than from any need to water down the authority of his executives.

Although Muggeridge saw Camrose as the dominant personality at 135 Fleet Street, the old man had already begun to hand over the day-to-day running of the paper to his son Michael, who worked in an adjoining room. Camrose himself spent much time on his other businesses – the Newsprint Supply Company, Amalga-mated Press, Kelly-Iliffe's and the Imperial Paper Mills. He began to travel a good deal, spoke often in the House of Lords, and set out to write a book. He also liked to recruit new members of the staff, or to appoint existing ones to new jobs. At the end of 1947 the foreign correspondent John Wallis returned to London after a year reporting the troubles in Palestine. Soon he found himself called to the fifth floor, where he was thanked for his good work and keenly questioned about the situation in the country he had just left. Then came the real business of the day. 'Now, Wallis,' said his proprietor expansively. 'What would you say if I offered you Paris?' To which Wallis replied, 'Honoured and delighted,

Sir!' – and to Paris he went, as chief of the bureau there.

One man who got in on the old-boy network was Gordon Shepherd, who, after finishing the war as a lieutenant-colonel in Intelligence, married a Viennese girl, added her name to his (becoming Brook-Shepherd), and stayed on in the Austrian capital directing Intelligence in Central Europe. Demobilised in the spring of 1948, he came to London in search of a job, and through a friend, Alan Pryce-Jones, who had just become Editor of the *Times Literary Supplement*, arranged an appointment at 135 Fleet Street. His first contact there was Eric Stowell, by then the Chief Assistant Editor in charge of news, who struck the newcomer as 'the worst example of a Camrose slave, practically crossing himself every time he mentioned the great man's name'. Mastering his revulsion at the 'awful, servile approach' which seemed to pervade the building, Brook-Shepherd persevered. Luckily for him, the Russians at that moment moved into Czechoslovakia, and Camrose, with some prescience, foresaw that the Soviet occupation might well bring down an Iron Curtain across Eastern Europe, so that the paper would need strong representation in that area.

Summoned to the fifth floor, Brook-Shepherd met Camrose, whom he found rather remote and grand, and his son Michael. When they asked if he would join the paper, and he protested that he had never done any reporting, they brushed aside his doubts, saying that he had good contacts, could draft telegrams, and so on. They then sent him to see the Foreign Editor, S. R. Pawley (known as 'Pop', from his avuncular appearance). He, none too pleased to have an amateur thrust on him from above, handed Brook-Shepherd a despatch just in from Madrid, about the collapse of some stands in a bullring, and asked what treatment he thought it needed. After a few moments' perusal Brook-Shepherd said he thought the piece was all right as it stood – a verdict which seemed to throw Pawley, but which nevertheless got him a job, with no training, previous experience or journalistic qualification of any kind. A few weeks later, in April, came the Soviet blockade of West Berlin, and Brook-Shepherd, hastily despatched to reinforce the office there, found that he did indeed know all the right people. Foreign reporting came naturally to him, and in June he was appointed *The Daily Telegraph*'s correspondent in Vienna. Camrose's method of staff selection, though old-fashioned, paid off handsomely, for during the next two years, before the Iron Curtain closed down, Brook-Shepherd was able to travel extensively in Eastern Europe, sending back reports of a high calibre, and laying the foundations of a lifelong career with the *Telegraph*.*

Much of the greyness which pervaded the *Telegraph* sprang from the rigid operation of the Newsroom – the hub of the building. This was the domain of the News Editor, Alex Maclaren, a martinet who ran the place to an absolutely fixed set of rules. Reporters were expected to come in at 10.00 am and leave at 6.00 pm. Their copy had to be written in short paragraphs and in conformity with the precepts of the Style Book. Once a piece was finished, the author took it up to the main newsdesk, where Maclaren or one of his senior assistants went through it as though conducting a tutorial. The article would then be sub-edited to the same inflexible formula. Jokes were not allowed. Any attempt at originality or stylistic felicity was ruthlessly suppressed – and if anyone was rash enough to complain, he or she could be referred to the inexorable demands of the Style Book.

In this slim volume, with its small, looseleaf pages clipped into a green cardboard cover, the dour collective mentality of *The Daily Telegraph* was graphically displayed. First came a list of words barred in headings – 'us/our' for 'Britain', 'comma, as substitute for and' – then a list of words 'overdone in headings' (new, plan, pleas, talks, move), then a whole range of barred expressions, many with a preferred alternative, or with a reason for exclusion, in brackets: Aeroplane (plane, aircraft) . . . Blast (explosion) . . . Blaze (fire) . . . Boom (opposite of slump) . . . Bulgar (Bulgarian) . . . Dash (for hurried journey) . . . Girl (for woman) . . . Landslide (in elections) . . . Luxury as adjective (in luxury flats, liners) . . . Overall (except as garment) . . . Overwhelming (not to be used to describe majorities) . . . scholar (for schoolboy) . . . Student (for Oxford or Cambridge undergraduates) . . . Tragedy (for sudden death) and so on. After a list of permissible and forbidden abbreviations ('Never U.K.'), there followed a section on general pitfalls: '*Bonham Carter*, Lady Violet; all others Bonham-Carter (hyphen) . . . *Burglary* applies only to dwelling-houses at night . . . *Commando* is a unit, not a man . . . *Cran*: always explain (750 herring)'.

---

* In later years – to the incredulity of colleagues, he seemed to wield an influence out of proportion to his status in the hierarchy, and this gave rise to stories that he had somehow saved Michael's life, either literally or financially, or by taking the blame at a court martial for some family misdemeanour. All these rumours he dismissed as absolute fiction: one reason he remained on easy terms with Michael (he himself said) was that he never had any ambition to become Editor, of either the daily or the Sunday paper; and once, when Michael said to him, 'I don't suppose your hat's in the ring, is it?' he merely answered, 'No.'

Extensive though these prohibitions were, they sometimes had to be reinforced by special notices posted in the Newsroom – one, for instance, laying down that only Malays ran amok.

Instructions for sub-editors were no less precise: paragraphs should average six lines, with a maximum of ten. Sentences were to be kept short, and number about three to the paragraph. An informative cross-heading must be written-in every four or five paragraphs, immediately above the passage to which it referred.

The intention of all this was admirable: to make everything as precise as possible, and to eliminate mistakes. Yet it was in the inflexible application of its own rules that the paper rendered itself ridiculous. Thus, nobody was allowed to use the expression 'he told me'. The only formula permitted was 'he said to me'. Never mind that the word 'said' had occurred five times already in the paragraph: in it must go again.

When the Style Book came nearer home, the less-than-generous nature of the organisation became evident. Under the heading *Daily Telegraph, The*, were the following instructions: 'Name, including THE, in caps and small caps at every mention: THE DAILY TELEGRAPH. No other paper is given definite article with cap T as part of title.' Under 'Newspapers' came another dose of the same medicine: 'No British newspaper and no newspaper proprietor anywhere are mentioned without special instruction. Similarly when family of newspaper proprietors figures in news'.

Here was the least attractive feature of the Camrose regime: its curmudgeonly attitude to rivals. The ban on mentioning other newspapers often led to absurdity – as when, unable to name the *Times*, even in the midst of controversies with which readers were already familiar, *Telegraph* reporters were forced to use evasive expressions such as 'another newspaper'.* No one, from Camrose downwards, seems to have been aware that the practice earned the paper nothing but ridicule and contempt – and if any member of staff had realised it, he would certainly not have made a fuss, for, as always, the proprietor's every wish was law.

Foreign correspondents were naturally expected to observe the niceties of the Style Book, but they were furnished also with a separate set of instructions. 'We have room only for the best news,' began the section on 'News Coverage'. 'No story should exceed *300 words* unless it is of paramount importance . . . The limit for average-value stories is *150 words*. Many excellent front-page

---

* Later the practice was sent up by Bernard Levin, writing in the *Times*, when he referred to 'A Daily Another Newspaper'.

stories are no longer than *50 words*.'* A simple code, based on trees for outward messages, flowers for inward ones, was designed to preserve some measure of privacy and conceal intentions from rivals. Thus a cable from the office prefaced 'Cedar' meant 'We are very interested in . . . send all you can get', whereas 'Eucalyptus' meant 'Paper extremely tight. Please keep to essentials.' For the correspondent, use of the word 'aconite' warned that a first-class story had broken, and 'heliotrope' that messages were being censored.

Whenever Camrose went out to a formal dinner in London, the Newsroom would stand by to report the event, especially if some leading politician was scheduled to make a speech. It was a rigid, if unwritten, rule that the reporter would make himself known to Camrose and ask how much he thought the occasion was worth. If he said, 'Half a column', or 'A third of a column', the reporter would immediately write a piece, telephone it through, and dash back to the office to make sure that all was well. One thing of which he could be certain was that his contribution would not end up on the spike, for the sub-editors would mark any contribution connected with Lord Camrose with the legend MUST – DO NOT CUT OR ALTER, and it would go through the mill bearing a charmed life.

One night a young reporter called George Evans carried out just such an assignment. Returning to 135 Fleet Street, he found his story already in type and on the desk of Archie Cooper, the Night News Editor. Glaring at Evans over his half-moon spectacles, Cooper told him the piece was too long. Evans demurred. 'Well,' said Cooper, 'what did Lord Camrose say?' 'A short half-column,' Evans answered, 'and that's what I did.' 'Good Lord!' cried Cooper in alarm. 'Why didn't you *say* "a short half-column"?' – and into the paper it went, his lordship's instructions interpreted to the letter, regardless of what the Night News Editor himself might think.

It was maddening to everyone concerned, but to Camrose most of all, that the progress of the *Telegraph* was artificially held back after the end of the war. Even though hostilities had ceased, paper-shortages had not, and it was not until the autumn of 1946 that print-runs were once again unrestricted. On 23 September,

---

* Defending this parsimony, Michael Berry pointed out that, with paper rationing still in force, space was at a premium, and it was an occasion for celebration when the paper was again able to advertise, 'Ten Pages a Day'.

the first 'free' day, the circulation rose to 999,751 copies; this, however, was a fluke, and it was not for another eight months that the magic target of one million was reached.

On 16 October 1946 Camrose left London on a secret mission. Ostensibly he and Lady Camrose sailed from Southampton for a holiday in America on the maiden passenger voyage of the *Queen Elizabeth*, which until then had been used only for troop-carrying. Since he had witnessed the trials of her sister ship the *Queen Mary* before the war, it seemed natural that he should be on board. Other passengers were the Birkenheads, the Rothermeres and the Shipping Correspondent of *The Daily Telegraph*, who sent back breathless reports ('The liner is doing a steady 29½ knots . . .') and was given much more space in the paper than he would have got if his proprietor had not been present.

Even Camrose's staff in Fleet Street thought he was making a recreational visit to America. What he was doing, in fact, was acting as the personal agent of Winston Churchill, with power to negotiate the sale of his epic account of the Second World War – a plot which he and the author had been hatching for more than a year.

Camrose's message to prospective bidders in the United States was that, after a period of uncertainty when Churchill had thought that he might never write the book, the author had changed his mind and decided to go ahead. Having set things up with Churchill's American literary agent, Emery Reves, and floated the bait on the waters, Camrose sat back and waited, staying in the Plaza Hotel on 59th Street, overlooking Central Park, and parrying inadequate offers. At last, on 27 November, he cabled Churchill to say that Henry Luce, proprietor of *Time*, *Life* and *Fortune* magazines, had, together with the *New York Times*, offered $1,150,000 for serialisation in the United States, and that the publishers Houghton Mifflin were offering $250,000 for the book rights. The serial deal was the largest ever made between an editor and an author, and, when the news came out, it caused a sensation, with chagrined correspondents pointing out that Churchill's fee would amount to *five shillings per word*. The arrangement was that, after serial extracts had appeared in *Life* and the *New York Times*, Houghton Mifflin would publish the successive volumes in book form in the United States. In England, publication rights would be controlled by *The Daily Telegraph*, the money, in due course, being paid into the literary trust which Churchill had established for the benefit of his children and grandchildren.

Given that Camrose was so close to Churchill, he was obviously the man to do this huge deal on his friend's behalf. When he returned to London at the end of November with a preliminary two-page letter of agreement, he was so delighted by his coup that (according to *Time*) everyone on the staff of the *Telegraph* 'got a jubilant mimeographed note from the boss and an extra week's pay'.* In April 1947 representatives of the American journals concerned travelled to London to complete their arrangements, and the final American contract was so complicated that it ran to eleven pages.

Soon afterwards, on 8 May 1947, Camrose was at last able to publish the news which he had so eagerly anticipated: that the *Telegraph* had broken the one-million barrier, with a net daily sale for the month of April of 1,001,047. 'This is the first time in the newspaper history of the world that any quality newspaper has achieved a million sale,' crowed a front-page announcement; and, as always at moments of peak achievement, the proprietor wheeled himself out from behind the parapet of 135 Fleet Street like a piece of heavy ordnance to put down a barrage of statistics on his long-suffering readers.

The nearest comparable quality newspaper circulations, he wrote, were to be found in the United States, where the *New York Times* and the *New York Herald Tribune* had a weekday average of 540,306 and 352,154 respectively ... In July 1939, 'before the war tension had become severe', the *Telegraph* had reached 768,000, a gain of 100,000 over the previous July ... The highest point in other years was 913,997 in June 1940 ... Now, in 1947, the effect of paper-rationing was still so severe that the *Daily Mail* could print only 24.64 per cent, and the *Daily Express* 24.71 per cent, of the pages they had enjoyed before the war, while the *Telegraph* fared worst of all, with only 22.6 per cent.

The long leader-page article gave full rein to Camrose's passion for statistics; but it also enabled him to restate the main points of his philosophy:

By the side of the 'big battalion' sales of the popular dailies, *The Daily Telegraph* figure of a million seems a comparatively small total. But surely it is a healthy sign of the times that a paper of its character should make solid progress against the more sensational note of some of its contemporaries. Obviously the

* Michael Berry later dismissed this report as highly improbable. Yet he himself did give every member of the staff an extra week's pay when the circulation of the *Telegraph* passed one million copies a day, and another to mark the paper's centenary in 1955.

contents of the paper do not make such a wide appeal as those of the newspapers which seek to entertain more than to inform. They never can do so. Neither is the manner in which the news is presented calculated to attract sensation-loving minds.

On the other hand, *The Daily Telegraph* has proved that there is a consistently growing section of the public which appreciates a paper aiming to be of steady, balanced character and which, while vigilant in enterprise, does not try to distort news or views to sensational ends. That is the standard of journalism which we have set out to achieve, and it is always for our readers to decide how far we have attained it.

Towards the end of the article, Camrose allowed himself a little speculation about whether the sale of his paper might ever grow to 3,500,000, 'and the *Daily Mirror* come back to 1,000,000'. But he hastened to assure everyone that 'never under my control will the paper change its character in an attempt to force a rapid increase in the number of its readers'.

His passion for facts manifested itself still more strikingly in his brief (and only) book, *British Newspapers and their Controllers*, which came out in July 1947, dedicated to 'M.A.C.' – his wife. The book was an extension of the author's article of 1939 (see page 98), and he brought it out, as he himself explained, to pre-empt the Royal Commission on the Press, which, after many delays, had been set up to examine the industry. Having 'investigated exhaustively', he wrote, he had found 'none of the mystery or indirect ownership so widely alleged by those who agitated for a Commission'; and in a series of vigorous sideswipes he pointed out various errors made, and misconceptions held, by other people involved. The book was very uneven, a curious mixture of history and autobiography, with a tremendous weight of detail about circulations and shareholdings, not only of the national newspapers but of the main provincial organs as well, the whole laced with solemn, full-page photographs of the principal proprietors. In essence it was a corrective outburst, by a professional deeply involved in journalism, against interference by ill-informed and woolly-minded amateurs.

By the spring of 1948 Churchill had completed his first volume, *The Gathering Storm*, and the sub-editor landed with the unenviable task of carving it up for serialisation was H. D. Ziman, known to all as 'Z' – a man with a powerful intellect, and one of the greatest bores ever to send people fleeing down the corridors of

No. 135 (according to the novelist Anthony Powell, 'an Homeric bore, perhaps captaining the British team'). Born of émigré Polish parents, and taken to New Zealand as a baby, Ziman won scholarships to Rugby and Oxford, where he read Greats. He joined the *Telegraph* in 1934 after experience on the *Liverpool Post* and the *Times*, and worked industriously as leader-writer, foreign correspondent and features sub-editor before being commissioned into the Middlesex Regiment in 1939. Later in the war he transferred to Intelligence, and later still became a war correspondent for the *Telegraph*, reporting with the Canadian forces after D-Day.

Although in fact a kind man, Ziman was implacable towards those whom he conceived to be his enemies, and there were always plenty of these in the office. But it was his normal manner, rather than his animosity, that made people run. In the words of another colleague, David Holloway, 'he was cursed with a wide knowledge and a good brain, and a compulsive need to share his wisdom, or rather to ensure that everyone else should be corrected so that they might be in a similar state of enlightenment'. In his high, penetrating voice, and looming ever closer to a victim pinned in a corner, Z would hold forth interminably, telling immensely long anecdotes, usually with a snuffling sort of chuckle to show how clever they and he were.

In the late 1940s he had no greater enemy than Hugo Wortham, still editor of Peterborough, and on 9 February 1948 Malcolm Muggeridge recorded in his diary: 'Curious episode in the office: H. D. Ziman, a Jew, hit Hugo Wortham, secret anti-Semite. Both greatly agitated afterwards. Whole incident sinister, I thought.' Evidently the dust-up sent shock waves through the building: a week later Z told Muggeridge that ever since the incident the Editor, Watson, had been treating him 'very cautiously, as though he was expecting that Ziman might slosh him one too'.

Whether or not Z ever had a chance to bore Churchill over the extracts from his book, history does not relate. What is known is that Churchill much annoyed Z by forcing him to change some of the work he had done – and it is a fair bet that the sub-editor's colleagues had their ears mercilessly bent as the saga was related. They would have been amused if they had known how different a tone their tormentor adopted when he sought a favour from his partner in literary endeavour. Thanking Churchill on 29 November 1948 for signing his copy of *The Gathering Storm*, Ziman wrote: 'This volume and its successors – if I may hope for further favours to come – will occupy a particularly proud position among books inscribed for me by the writers.' (In 1956, unable to stand Z's contributions to leader-writers' conferences any longer, Watson's successor Colin Coote solved the immediate problem by creating him Literary Editor.)

In London, Camrose took to throwing an immense party at the Savoy Hotel to celebrate each general election. The first, on 23 February 1950, was certainly the biggest party in town, as well as the largest in the sixty-year history of the hotel. Camrose took over all the public rooms on the Embankment side and invited 2,000 guests, whom he and Lady Camrose received in the Ballroom. They were a motley crew, including stars of stage and screen – Leslie Henson, Hermione Gingold, Alexander Korda, John Mills, Hermione Baddeley, Valerie Hobson and Noël Coward – but also Lord Wavell, the Duke of Marlborough, A. P. Herbert, the miners' leader Will Lawther and the boxer Freddie Mills; and their political affinities were well enough mixed for each new result to be greeted by a cacophony of different responses. According to the next day's *Telegraph* (which carried a picture and report of the party on its front page), when the first result was displayed – Salford West, traditionally the earliest to complete its count – the Labour success 'aroused excited comment'. It was left to the Communist *Daily Worker* to record that the Socialist win was greeted with 'boos and anguished groans'. The *Telegraph* kept its end up by reporting that the 'greatest spontaneous cheer' of the night burst out at 3.00 am, when it was announced that the only Communist candidate for London, Mr P. Piratin, had been decisively defeated in Stepney.

On the whole, though, it was a grim night, which gave the Berry camp little cause for rejoicing. 'To the Savoy at 10.30 pm, to a vast Camrose election night party,' wrote Malcolm Muggeridge in his diary. 'Practically everyone I've ever heard of there, champagne flowing, ran into numbers of people, whole thing slightly macabre, an eve of the battle of Waterloo flavour about it – the bourgeoisie shivering before the deluge to come.' Hopes that Churchill might be returned to office faded early in the night, and the only consolation was that the slender Labour majority left Attlee's position precarious, making it clear that another election would not be long delayed.

The Socialist victory must have seemed a poor reward for Arthur Watson, whose marathon stint as Editor came to an end, after twenty-six years, on 1 April 1950. With his shining pink face and quiet voice, his imperturbable good manners, he reminded Muggeridge of a family solicitor:

He was not a dazzling person, intellectually or in any other way, but a very good one, who occupied an important, and often difficult post with credit and much more shrewdness and independence of judgement than people gave him credit for.

His successor, Colin Coote, was very different – a clever, complicated man, already fifty-six when he took over, who provoked widely varying reactions among his subordinates. In appearance he was immensely distinguished, with a long, noble face; and many admired him for his quick, incisive mind and his ability to turn out precisely-phrased leaders with minimum delay; but others saw him as an attractive lightweight, a charlatan, even – a man who felt that he should have edited the *Times*, and who never had the slightest interest in *The Daily Telegraph*, which he saw as socially and intellectually inferior, a poor second-best. Muggeridge could not stand him, and, when he himself was in the editorial chair on a Sunday would groan, 'Oh, if only I shared the Editor's *utter* indifference about what appears in this newspaper!'

Coote had the good fortune to be brought up bilingual in English and French: family connections in France and a French-Swiss nanny saw to that. At Rugby (where his housemaster was the father of the poet Rupert Brooke) and Balliol he was an outstanding footballer. No sooner had he taken his Oxford degree, in 1914, than he was commissioned into the Gloucestershire Regiment and sent to the Italian front, where he added another language to his repertoire and won the DSO, only just missing a VC. On almost the last day of the Great War he was gassed – an experience which left him with such an implacable hatred of the Germans that more than forty years later he wrote to Sir Alan Lascelles, former Private Secretary to King George VI and Queen Elizabeth II: 'I can't say my dislike of the Boche has faded. I can hardly bear to be in the same room as them . . . I had quite an interesting Armistice Day [1918]: lungs liquefied by phosgene and given a fortnight to live. But here I still am.'

After a spell as a Coalition Liberal Member of Parliament, Coote joined the *Times* as the paper's correspondent in Rome; but his bent was not so much for reporting as for commentating, and he was soon brought back to London, where he wrote sketches of proceedings at Westminster and became the chief political writer. His own experience of Italy under Mussolini had given him an intense dislike of Fascism; and when the *Times*, under Geoffrey Dawson, began to champion the policy of appeasement, his discomfort became acute – as has already been mentioned. A colleague who worked with him in Printing House Square described him as 'a rather irritable, handsome man, with a disdainful and sometime querulous voice', known in the building as 'Captain Coote'.

In purely political terms, the *Telegraph* gave Coote a comfortable base. By the time he became Editor, his own views were solidly Conservative, and he found no difficulty in criticising the opposition at home, the Communist regimes abroad. Pointing out that both Mussolini and Hitler had begun their political careers as socialists, and that 'Stalin still professes to be one', he wrote:

I am not one of your bitter politicians. I believe that most men and women, to whatever party they belong, are fundamentally decent and mean well for their country. But where the Socialist party have gone wrong is in tying themselves to a theory which in our country will not work. I have seen governments trying to work the theory in many lands. Inevitably it works out as dictation.

Ideologically, Coote was right for the *Telegraph*. Besides, he shared Camrose's immense regard for Churchill, whose sayings he selected and published in a fulsome tome.* Why then did he feel that the *Telegraph* was beneath him – or at least give that impression?

He was by no means alone in doing so. At that time – 1950 – and for at least the next twenty-five years, the idea survived that in social and political terms the *Times* was the only newspaper which mattered. Such was the power of tradition, such the reputation of the Thunderer. No matter that it had made itself abjectly ridiculous in the years before the war – and again after it, by its sychophantic attitude to Russia. No matter that its circulation was less than a quarter of that of *The Daily Telegraph*. There yet persisted the notion that the *Times* was the organ which represented the views of the Government and the ruling class, and that the rest of the Press counted for little beside it.

Camrose never saw things in this light: his aim was to forge ahead and push his own journal as far past the magic million as it would go. In his view (and in any logical view), the *Times* had already been left far behind. Coote, however, could not accept that numerical superiority was enough: once rebuffed in Printing House Square, he found the *Telegraph* for ever *faute de mieux* – and a good many of his staff went about with similar chips on their

* *Maxims and Reflections of Winston Churchill*, 1947.

shoulders. (Peregrine Worsthorne, who moved over from the *Times* as a leader-writer in 1953, also felt that he had 'come down in the world', and regarded his transfer as 'a disappointment, like leaving the Brigade of Guards and joining the Royal Warwickshire Regiment'.

In Coote this feeling produced an Olympian detachment, a lack of commitment, which riled many junior colleagues, and which came through – inadvertently – in his autobiography, *Editorial*. The early parts of the book, about his childhood, school, university, war service, and work in Italy, were admirable: lively, amusing and sometimes waspish. Yet when he came to his time at the *Telegraph*, his writing went dead as mutton.

Oddly enough, Coote was far more forthcoming in an essay called 'The Editor's Job' which he contributed to a symposium about newspapers* published only a year after his book appeared. In this he wrote that the essential duties of an editor were to keep his paper independent of all outside influences, and to maintain the purity of the English language; but he added an engagingly modest autobiographical note, which suggested – as *Editorial* had not come within a mile of doing – that he recognised the relatively small nature of his own contribution to the *Telegraph*:

> The greatest quality which an Editor can possess is luck. I speak feelingly, because I have had more than my fair share of that. A tremendous increase in the means of the average British citizen involved a tremendous tendency towards a paper of the kind with which I was associated. A famous doctor of my acquaintance, when asked the reason for his success, replied, 'I try to avoid doing my patients any harm.' It was very easy to avoid doing my paper any harm. My job was that of stroking a confident and well-trained crew with an intelligent and sympathetic cox on a fast and favourably flowing tide. In such a case, the main task of an Editor is not to catch any crabs, such as pomposity, impatience, prejudice, unfairness or conceit.

The main crabs which colleagues felt that Coote caught were idleness and aloofness. Instead of going round the building, encouraging by his presence, he would sit in his room reading thrillers, which he would hastily shove into a drawer of his desk whenever anyone came in, or tucking into the exceptionally luscious sandwiches with which his second wife furnished him. His aloofness

---

* *Fleet Street: the Inside Story of Journalism*, 1966.

was manifest in one small detail: he took pride in the fact that he never used a typewriter. It is true that his handwriting, though minute, was neat and legible, and could always be deciphered by a secretary. Yet his refusal to use a machine meant that every article he wrote had to be typed by someone else, often against the clock, before it went to the printer – a state of affairs which most other journalists found grossly unprofessional. He was also thoroughly vague about details of how the newspaper was produced, never venturing into the composing-room; and his ignorance of typography was total. Once, when a young features sub-editor, Nicholas Bagnall, came to his office full of enthusiasm for some article on which he had been working, Coote said, 'All right – let's put the headline in something good and big. Put it in Baldini!' After thirty years in journalism, he had failed to grasp either that there was no such typeface as Baldini, or that of every type which did exist (and Bodoni was one commonly used at the *Telegraph*), many sizes were available, each precisely measured and designated by a system of points.

Yet Coote suffered from a fault more dangerous to an editor than mechanical ignorance. This was a habit of pretending to know everything, of refusing to be surprised. Whatever anyone told him, he had already heard – a foible that led directly to the loss of many good stories. Thus in January 1957, when Anthony Eden resigned as Prime Minister because of ill-health and anti-Suez feeling, everyone expected that his successor would be Rab Butler. It so happened, however, that Kenneth Rose, who was working on Peterborough, went one evening to a concert where he met Sir Robert Boothby, already a senior figure in the Conservative Party. 'Take it from me,' said Boothby, 'it's going to be Harold Macmillan.' Yet next day, when Rose told Coote that he had heard from an extremely good source who the next Prime Minister was going to be, the Editor merely replied, 'Yes, yes: it's going to be Butler.' Rose persisted, 'That isn't what *I* heard,' but Coote told him he was wrong, and Peterborough missed a scoop.

Not all Coote's foibles were obvious when he took the editor's chair in 1950, but his appointment was by no means popular. 'Heard that Watson had retired . . . and would be replaced by Coote,' noted Muggeridge in his journal on 3 April 1950. 'Everyone very sorry about this.' In the days that followed, much manoeuvring took place, for Camrose asked J. C. Johnstone to become Coote's deputy, and, when he declined, offered the post to Muggeridge, who accepted it 'with mixed feelings'. Muggeridge felt that his own dislike of Coote was reciprocated, and on 6 May, after a grand farewell dinner had been thrown for Watson at Claridge's, he reported: 'Huge gathering of *Telegraph* staff. I was at Camrose's table, the usual speeches, Camrose's better than I expected ... Coote went in for some rather far-fetched undergraduate humour.' In spite of his misgivings, Muggeridge settled down as Deputy Editor, and soon established himself as a favourite with the rest of the staff, who found him a delightful companion, as stimulating as he was amusing, and as highly-coloured in his ideas and opinions as the rest of the paper was grey. (Unfortunately he stayed for only two years before leaving to edit *Punch*, and his successor, Ivor Bulmer-Thomas – Coote's choice – lasted an even shorter time. Although liked by colleagues, he was one of the few men who fell out with the Berrys, and was sacked.)

Anyone who wanted to disparage Coote could point out that his power and importance were severely limited by the peculiar structure which Camrose had devised. Not only was the Editor working under an Editor-in-Chief: he also had no control over the part of the paper which contributed most to its success – the news. In comparison with the editors of other newspapers, his position was very weak – and many people were surprised that anybody would take on a job so circumscribed. Equally, it is clear that Camrose had deliberately chosen, in Coote, a man who would work within the framework which he himself found comfortable.

Even at seventy, Camrose himself was highly active: besides running the *Telegraph*, he was still Chairman of the magazine group Amalgamated Press, which in the year ending 28 February 1951 made a record profit, before tax, of £4,367,000. In his statement at the annual general meeting he lamented the fact that the 'colossal sum' of over £2,250,000 would go to the Government in tax, but he consoled shareholders by telling them: 'We have our eggs in many baskets ... We are not entirely dependent on the periodical publishing business for our earnings.' In retrospect, he seems to have been curiously uninventive about saving money: every year he complained about the huge amounts of tax levied, and indoctrinated his son Michael with the idea that there was no point in the *Telegraph* earning vast sums, as they would all be taken away in tax. Thus, in the year ending 31 March 1951, the *Telegraph* made a profit of £464,000, and in the next year only £386,000. As things stood, under the company's articles of association, Camrose could hold the office of Chairman and Editor-in-Chief for life, if he wanted, and he also had the right to appoint one of his lineal descendants, or the wife of one, to succeed him in any of his offices. The ordinary shares were all held by his sons;

and, as the diarist in the *Evening Standard* remarked, the paper was 'certainly secure against any takeover bidder buying up the shares on the Stock Exchange . . . If any outside bidder came along offering to buy up the family's holding, I believe he would be quickly shown the door.' For the moment, everything seemed impregnably secure; yet if Camrose had transferred the ownership of the paper to some form of charitable trust, its long-term future might have been very different.

So great was his own confidence, however, both in himself and in his family, that he specifically rejected this option. As he himself wrote in 1947:

> Some newspapers today have created trusts intended to ensure that the future ownership and control shall not pass into the hands of undesirable proprietors who might change the character of the papers. I do not feel that such legal instruments are necessary or that they will achieve their object. I have already taken what I consider effective measures to perpetuate the paper in its present form, so far as that can ever be achieved, by handing over the voting control to my two elder sons . . . who, except for the years of the war, have been in journalism all their adult lives. I have retained the chairmanship for my lifetime, or for so long as I choose to occupy that position, and I feel that mine is a more realistic policy than that of leaving the last word in the hands of inexperienced people, however distinguished they may be.

In the autumn of 1951, as the Labour Government stumbled to defeat and another General Election loomed, the *Telegraph* once more threw its weight behind the Conservative campaign; but it also treated the whole business for what it was: a splendid news opportunity. On polling day – Thursday, 25 October – the front page announced that the paper had planned a 'most comprehensive scheme' to give the latest election results: special trains, and trains rescheduled to leave later than usual, would 'ensure the inclusion of the most up-to-date news'. Late editions would also be flown to many parts of the country, and large screens had been erected in Manchester and London for the immediate display of results. The paper's information bureau maintained a twenty-four-hour service.

The leader-page sought, not unskilfully, to raise apprehension among the electorate. Under the heading A DAY OF VITAL DECISION, the first leader claimed: 'What has emerged unmistakably in the course of the election campaign is that our country has reached one of those decisive turning-points in history on which the whole shape of the future depends.' Alongside was a sterling blast of good sense from J. C. Johnstone, who pointed out that 'in an attempt to confuse the electorate, the official Socialist organ* has recently formulated "Twenty Questions for the People". All the questions contain a catch, and all depend on ignorance, prejudice or unwariness to attain the desired effect. They epitomise the methods of Socialist propaganda.'

Possibly these articles and their predecessors had some influence. Election analysts were predicting a swing of three per cent to the Conservatives. In any event, the election gave Camrose the pretext for another colossal party at the Savoy, again for 2,000 people.† In sheer size this celebration was the equal of its predecessor, but it excelled the earlier party in grandeur and high spirits, for as the night wore on, it became increasingly clear that this time Labour was on the way out. Again, it was the biggest party in London, and again Lord and Lady Camrose received their guests in the Ballroom, helped by Seymour and Michael. This time, however, Camrose had arranged a private parlour, an inner sanctum for special friends, and observers were thrilled that among such relatively common species as Harold Nicolson, Lord David Cecil, Lord Beaverbrook, Donald Wolfit, Joyce Grenfell and Robert Morley, they spotted that exquisitely rare bird of passage, Greta Garbo. She, the *Telegraph* reported, was seen wearing a black swagger coat and sitting alongside Cecil Beaton, with whom she had been having 'a country idyll' at Broadchalke, his house near Salisbury. Her neckline 'plunged and plunged right down to her waist', and she, who was supposed never even to smile, astonished everybody by throwing back her head and letting out a loud laugh.

There was a good deal of laughing all round. In those days, before electronics had superseded mechanical display systems, thirty specially trained operators were needed to keep the enormous main information board and several subsidiary ones posted with the latest results, each of which had to be written up on cardboard. Every Tory win was greeted with howls of delight, and also with blasts on a hunting horn, sounded by a reveller in the restaurant. Evelyn Waugh spoke of the sound of the English county families baying for broken glass; here the upper- and middle-classes were

---

* Which the *Telegraph*, of course, could not bring itself to name.
† The planning of these occasions was most elaborate. For that of 1959 there were forty-one different guest-lists. Of the 3,984 people invited, 1,953 accepted, 1,194 refused, and 837 did not bother to reply.

baying for Labour blood, but, as in *Decline and Fall*, they were well fuelled with champagne, and it is safe to assume that the racket was much the same.

By 5.00 am on Friday, when a special late edition was printed, the Conservatives had gained eleven seats, and the Socialists' lead in the House of Commons had been wiped out. A narrow Conservative win seemed likely; and it was not until the following day that the paper could proclaim, 'Victory but no triumph for the Conservatives. Defeat but no rout for the Socialists'. Yet Churchill was Prime Minister once more, and to Camrose personally that meant a great deal.

The year 1952 thus opened on a cheerful note; and when, at the beginning of February, a major news story presented itself, the paper rose to the challenge as only the *Telegraph* could, with excellent reporting and first-class background information. The event was the royal tour of the Commonwealth, to be made by Princess Elizabeth (then twenty-three) and her husband the Duke of Edinburgh, who left London on the first leg of their journey on 1 February.

To send them off (the *Telegraph* reported), the largest gathering of the Royal Family ever seen at London airport came together at Heathrow on a freezing winter's day. The Chairman of British Overseas Airways Corporation, Sir Miles Thomas, met the royal party in the newly-decorated VIP lounge, and 'there was a tremendous cheer from the crowd as the King, in a thick overcoat over his grey suit, carrying his bowler hat', led them all out towards the plane. This was an Argonaut airliner, specially converted into a 'flying flat', its beds fitted with foam-rubber mattresses, its semicircular lounge with chairs and tables. Another cheer went up as Churchill, in a stovepipe hat set at a jaunty angle and a thick scarf, was summoned to inspect the special aircraft; and when it took off, the King (bare-headed in the biting wind), the Queen and other members of the Royal Family watched from the roof of the airport building until it was out of sight.

The romance and uncertainty of early intercontinental flying come through strongly in the reports of the Argonaut's progress. At 1.15 pm it passed over Paris, flying at 289 mph and 19,000 feet. Lunch (of turtle soup, hors d'oeuvre, grilled steak and strawberry melba) was served still over France. Its first stop was at El Adem, the desert airfield in Libya. News of its safe arrival was immediately telephoned from London airport to the King and Queen at Buckingham Palace. After an hour for refuelling and a change of

THE DAILY TELEGRAPH AND MORNING POST, FEBRUARY 7, 1952

8-PAGE MEMORIAL SUPPLEMENT

The Daily Telegraph

4 A.M.

Imperial
FOR BETTER LETTERS

No. 30,139 LONDON, THURSDAY, FEBRUARY 7, 1952   and Morning Post   Printed in LONDON and MANCHESTER   Price 2d.

DEATH OF KING GEORGE VI

PEACEFULLY IN SLEEP AT SANDRINGHAM

LAST WALK IN GROUNDS ON PREVIOUS EVENING

NEW QUEEN FLYING HOME: IN LONDON TO-DAY

PROCLAMATION TO-MORROW: PRIME MINISTER ON RADIO TO-NIGHT

HIS MAJESTY KING GEORGE VI DIED IN HIS SLEEP AT SANDRINGHAM HOUSE IN THE EARLY HOURS OF YESTERDAY MORNING. A SERVANT FOUND HIM DEAD IN BED AT 7.30 A.M. AN ANNOUNCEMENT FROM SANDRINGHAM, REPEATED IN A SPECIAL ISSUE OF THE LONDON GAZETTE LAST NIGHT, SAID:

The King, who retired last night in his usual health, passed peacefully away in his sleep early this morning.

Princess Elizabeth, who immediately became Queen, was informed of her father's death while she was at the Royal hunting lodge near Nyeri in Kenya. A thunderstorm delayed for two hours the departure of the plane which is to bring her to London, where she is expected at 4.30 p.m. to-day.

The Accession Council, which consists of members of the Privy Council summoned with others, "notables of the Realm" such as the Lord Mayor of London, to act on the demise of the Crown, met at 5 p.m. yesterday to decide on the accession proclamation. This will be read at 11 to-morrow at St. James's Palace, at Temple Bar and on the steps of the Royal Exchange in the City.

The Queen, who is 25, is expected to take the Royal oath before a second meeting of the Council to-day. She was proclaimed Queen Elizabeth II of Canada in Ottawa yesterday. Prince Charles automatically becomes Duke of Cornwall.

Mr. Churchill will broadcast on all B.B.C. wavelengths at 9 o'clock to-night for 15 minutes.

OUT SHOOTING ON PREVIOUS DAY

The King, who was 56 and in the 16th year of his reign, was born at Sandringham. During what proved to be his last stay there he was out shooting on Tuesday morning and afternoon, and appeared to be in good health. In the evening he walked in the grounds.

The Queen-Mother and Princess Margaret accompanied him when he went to Sandringham last Friday. On the previous day he had gone to London Airport to see his elder daughter and the Duke of Edinburgh leave for Nairobi.

Queen Mary was informed at Marlborough House of her son's death. The Duke of Gloucester, who was at his home at Barnwell Manor, Northants, went to Sandringham on hearing the news. The Princess Royal was told at St. James's Palace. The Duchess of Kent returned from Germany last night and the Duke of Windsor leaves New York in the Queen Mary to-day.

The Prime Minister and Sir David Maxwell Fyfe, Home Secretary, were given the news by telephone. A Cabinet meeting was held. The House of Commons and the House of Lords met formally for two minutes and adjourned until after the Accession Council, when M.P.s and Peers began to take the Oath of Allegiance to their new monarch. The two Chambers are expected to meet on Monday for addresses of condolence and then adjourn until Feb. 19.

Subject to the wishes of the new Queen the body of King George will lie in state in Westminster Hall from Monday until the funeral, the date for which has not yet been fixed. Carpenters at Sandringham finished making the coffin of oak from the estate last night.

CINEMAS AND THEATRES CLOSED

The effect of the news from Sandringham was felt immediately throughout the nation. All cinemas were closed and the Lord Chamberlain directed that theatres should be shut for the day and also on the day of the funeral of the King. B.B.C. programmes were cancelled except for news bulletins. There will be a restricted programme from to-day until after the funeral. The Stock Exchange and Lloyd's closed, courts adjourned and a number of public dinners and other functions were postponed. Flags in every town were at half-mast.

All sport stopped except for the four Football Association Cup-ties. Saturday's Rugby Union International between England and Ireland at Twickenham has been postponed. Football League and Rugby League fixtures will be played or arranged. National Hunt racing was suspended.

As soon as the news became known a crowd began to gather outside Buckingham Palace, and was there until late at night. Ambassadors were calling throughout the day to sign the visitors' book as an official expression of their sorrow, and messages of sympathy flowed in from every quarter.

Mr. Churchill issued a statement from 10, Downing Street last night asking that there should be no public gathering at London Airport when the Queen arrives from Kenya.

A recent portrait of his Majesty King George VI.

LYING-IN-STATE ON MONDAY

PARLIAMENT TO SEND CONDOLENCES

By our POLITICAL CORRESPONDENT

Parliament is expected to send condolences to Queen Elizabeth and the Royal Family on the death of King George VI to be moved in both Houses. Lords and Commons on Monday next, Feb. 18.

The body of the King will lie-in-state in Westminster Hall from Monday until the day fixed for the funeral. These arrangements are provisional until Queen's definite regarding her wishes and those of the Sovereign are known on her return.

7.30 a.m. DISCOVERY BY SANDRINGHAM SERVANT

FROM OUR SPECIAL CORRESPONDENT

SANDRINGHAM, Wednesday.

The King was found dead in his bed at Sandringham House at 7.30 this morning. He had died as he slept peacefully during the night.

A short while before he retired after a family dinner party last night the King took a last walk in the grounds. He admired the calm and quiet of the evening and was looking forward to a day's shooting to-day.

MEDICAL VIEWS ON CAUSE OF DEATH

Hot BOVRIL beats the weather

The common cold menace is at its worst this time of year. Take soothing action —double up your resistance with Hot Bovril.

The Beef in BOVRIL keeps you glowing

As SAFE as ...

MICHELIN TYRES

ROYAL PLANE OVER SAHARA AT 3 a.m.

UGANDA DEPARTURE HELD UP BY STORM

The Argonaut airliner Atalanta, in which the Queen and the Duke of Edinburgh are flying home from East Africa, was early to-day heading across the Sudan for Libya. It was due at El Adem, Libyan desert airfield, at about 6 a.m.

After an hour's stay for refuelling, the airliner was taking off again for the 1,550-mile stage of the journey, and was expected to arrive at London Airport about 4.30 p.m. to-day.

PROCLAMATION AS QUEEN ELIZABETH II

NEWS BROKEN BY DUKE

QUEEN'S FORTITUDE

FUNERAL ESCORT & BEARER PARTY

RETURN OF QUEEN PREMIER'S PLEA

ROYAL FAMILY CANCEL PLANS

DUCHESS FLIES HOME

BISHOP OF NORWICH

LATE NEWS

INVITATION FROM DR. MOSSADEQ

Today's Weather

crew, it took off again for Nairobi. 'Early this morning,' the
Telegraph's report went on, 'the plane was flying over the eastern
Sahara, and at 2.30 was 1,197 miles from Nairobi. It was flying
at 17,000 feet in a clear sky. Winds encountered earlier had been
left behind. At 12.15 am Captain Ballantine radioed: "Calm air.
Steady flight. Their Royal Highnesses have retired and are reported
sleeping soundly."'

At Eastleigh, the RAF airport outside Nairobi, Frank Harvey
was in position to report on 2 February: 'From the bitter cold of
the London winter Princess Elizabeth and the Duke of Edinburgh
emerged into the brilliant warmth of what might have been a
perfect English summer's day'; and a photograph sent by wire
showed the Princess reaching over to take a bouquet from a
three-year-old African boy who, overcome by the occasion, had
forgotten to hand the flowers to her.

Had it proceeded as planned, the royal tour alone would have
provided good copy for weeks; but fate decreed otherwise, and
suddenly, only five days later, there burst the stunning news that
the King had died in his sleep at Sandringham in the early hours
of 6 February. DEATH OF KING GEORGE VI cried the biggest
headline the *Telegraph* had ever run, across all eight columns on
7 February. No News Editor, no proprietor, could have hoped for
a more dramatic conjunction of events: the Monarch's life snuffed
out; the fact that he had been out shooting, apparently in good
health, the day before; the discovery of his body by a servant at
7.30 am; his elder daughter, suddenly Queen, hearing the news at
a hunting lodge in the wilds of Africa, 5,000 miles from home;
the curtailment of her tour; her dash for England; the funeral
arrangements at Sandringham, in London and Windsor . . .

The *Telegraph* chose to run thick, black, mourning rules down
between its columns – the normal rules turned upside down, so
that their bases printed heavy lines. The effect was hideous, and
made the choked type hard to read. But, as always, the content
was highly professional. Not only was much of the body of the
paper (including the entire Peterborough column) given over to
royal news: there also appeared, as if by magic, an eight-page
memorial supplement – the result of clear-sighted planning.

To the end of his life Camrose remained a dedicated professional.
The very least that can be said of him is that he never succumbed
to delusions of grandeur, and never made a fool of himself. In
this he differed sharply from his brother Lord Kemsley, whose
square-clipped moustache increased his resemblance to one of the

Marx brothers, and who became ever more foolishly plutocratic as his power and wealth increased. (It was said that Kemsley's second wife, whom he married in 1931, was the mainspring of his social posturing.) Unlike his brother, Camrose did not flaunt silk ties and pearl tiepins, or travel in a high-bodied Rolls-Royce, or keep one lift at the office reserved for his use only, with its doors standing open five minutes before he arrived. Nor did he style the *Telegraph* 'A Camrose paper' (all Kemsley's publications bore his name on the front). He remained dignified, unostentatious and hard-working. Nevertheless, by the beginning of the 1950s he too had become very grand.

He never returned to the house in St James's Place, which had been totally destroyed by bombs.* Instead he bought a short lease of 24 Carlton House Terrace, one of the enormous, white-stuccoed houses between Pall Mall and the Mall. Number 24 had three main floors, two attic storeys, double front doors flanked by pairs of Ionic columns, and a large garden. 'Like all Camrose residences, much more like a club than a private dwelling,' noted Muggeridge after a huge party there.

Nowhere was Camrose more of a swell than in the world of sailing. From 1947 he was Vice-Commodore of the Royal Yacht Squadron, and so in charge of the Squadron's accounts, which he would present with a lucid and witty speech at the annual general meeting. In place of the sunken *Sona* he had acquired an immense successor, the *Virginia*, a twin-screw vessel of 712 tons, 180 feet long, with a crew of thirty (including a chef), a teleprinter and a ship-to-shore telephone. Though twenty years old when he bought her, she was luxuriously comfortable and fully equipped for long-distance expeditions, having already crossed the Atlantic and cruised in the Baltic. Among the world's largest yachts listed in Lloyd's Register, she ranked twenty-third, and in the United Kingdom was second only to the *Shemara*, owned by Sir Bernard Docker – a rating which occasioned keen rivalry between the two families. On one voyage, from Cannes to Corsica and Sardinia, members of the Berry family were delighted when, with the *Shemara* moored alongside them, the appalling Lady Docker fell overboard into the harbour.

When the *Virginia* made her formal arrival at Cowes week, in August, she was greeted with a nine-gun salute, marking her owner's status as Vice-Commodore. Camrose gave cocktail parties

---

* Seeking compensation from the Government, he was offered £12,000; but after his death his son Michael secured £70,000.

on board; and at the one held on 3 August 1952 the guests included the Duke of Edinburgh, who had been racing his own Dragon-class yacht *Bluebottle*. In the winter Camrose sometimes cruised in the Mediterranean, but in the summer and autumn he tended to stay closer to home, visiting Cowes, Deauville or Le Touquet, and some outsiders found it faintly absurd that a yacht as big as a Channel steamer should spend so much time in cold, unglamorous, northern waters.

Whenever she did anchor off the French coast, the staff of the Paris office were put on their toes, for, come hell or high water, the daily papers from London had to be on his lordship's breakfast-table every morning. By special arrangement they were flown to Le Bourget in the early hours; Eric Johnstone, the European Sales Manager, would then drive out to pick them up, motor on to Le Touquet, and take them to the foot of the gangplank (without, however, ever being asked to cross it). By the time they reached the *Virginia*, they must have been the most expensive papers in the world. Other members of the staff were more fortunate and found themselves invited aboard; Adrian Secker, number three in the Paris office, once acted as a postal courier and finished up staying the night. His chief memories were that Lady Camrose was a most cosy and motherly hostess, and that a prodigious amount of port was drunk after dinner.

At the age of seventy-four Camrose was still an enthusiastic journalist. By now he had handed over much of the *Telegraph*'s routine to his sons Seymour and Michael, but he came to 135 Fleet Street most days, and took a close interest in every issue of the paper. The routine he had devised remained the same as ever. Just before 1.00 pm Eric Stowell, the Assistant Editor in charge of news, would ascend to the fifth floor; with Seymour, Michael or Camrose himself, he would minutely dissect last night's paper, and discuss stories to be covered that day. Then, going down again, he would dictate a memorandum for the Newsroom noticeboard, allotting praise or blame for past performance. Praise was rare, and whenever any did appear, it was in the passive tense: 'The piece about x *was liked*'. Everybody knew what that meant. Once, after young George Evans had been despatched to interview a seventeen-year-old who had been taken on as a valet and trainee chef by the Queen, he was criticised for having used the boy's Christian name: 'Evans's story on the Buckingham Palace trainee was liked, but we should in future avoid using the diminutive or familiar.'

At 6.00 every evening the Editor would go up to discuss the

leaders for that night, and at other times Camrose saw the senior managers who ran the business side of the paper – principally Fred Burnham, who had become Managing Director at the end of the war. A few senior members of the editorial staff were invited to lunches on the fifth floor, but most of the rank-and-file had no contact with their boss. If he did run into a junior employee, he was unfailingly civil.

There seemed no reason why his comfortable routine should not continue indefinitely: but in fact the old order came to a sudden end. At Hackwood on 9 June 1954 Camrose fell ill with a gastric attack, and was taken to the Royal South Hants Hospital at Southampton. At first there seemed to be little cause for alarm. A telegram from Churchill – SO SORRY TO HEAR YOU ARE IN HOSPITAL. HOW ARE YOU GETTING ON? – evoked a cheerful answer: MANY THANKS PROGRESS GOOD HOPE RETURN HACKWOOD TUESDAY – BILL.; and on 14 June he dictated a characteristic suggestion for a Peterborough paragraph:

> We printed the short obit on Saturday of C. F. Adams of Boston, aged 85 I think. I believe his grandfather and great-grandfather were both Presidents of the United States. He was one of the veterans of the yachting world, and very well liked. Had a yacht called *Resolution*. Among other things was Chairman or President of the Employers' Liability Company (of London) in America. Daughter was married to Pierpont Morgan Junior's son, Harry Morgan. Had been over here many times. Lord Knollys knows him well.
>
> Could be a paragraph for Day by Day.

It was. Peterborough printed the memorandum verbatim – but posthumously, for in the early hours of 15 June Camrose died suddenly of a heart attack. The news commanded the top centre of the *Telegraph*'s front page, where normally a photograph was published. In Fleet Street the flags flew at half-mast, and Harold Nicolson wrote in his diary: 'He was a staunch friend and a wise counsellor. He showed that one could be a Press Lord and a Gentleman. He was an example to the newspaper world.'

Such sentiments were echoed on an immense scale in the obituaries. *The Daily Telegraph* devoted most of its leader-page to tributes, and other papers were generous alike with their space and their praise. Uniquely among press barons, Camrose attracted no criticism or enmity at his passing: every appraisal was favourable, and almost all were enthusiastic. *Truth* called him 'one of the most urbane and courteous self-made men who ever lived'; the *Times* said that he had had the gift of green fingers, 'for making journals grow healthily'; the *Daily Mail* hailed his 'outstanding achievement' in leaving so great a newspaper as his monument; the *Daily Express* spoke of his 'honest and purposeful character'; the *Western Mail* hoped that his story would 'evoke the pride of the Welsh people and inspire the young men of the Valleys to bring equal honour to their country'; and the *Financial Times* remembered him as a stickler for accuracy, who 'would have put to shame the most exacting of Eton headmasters'.

The *Telegraph* itself published a tribute from Winston Churchill, who wrote:

> This is a great grief to me. Lord Camrose was one of the best friends I have known during my long walk through life. For thirty years, in peace and war, we have been intimate companions. Patriotism and an earnest desire for a stable yet progressive society were his unswerving guides.

Yet even this public salute paled beside the note which the elder statesman wrote – most unusually – in his own hand on 16 June:

My dear Lady Camrose,
I know how you and Bill were devoted to one another, and depended upon each other in all the joys and griefs of human existence. His life and career do him honour achieved by few. His work remains as a living monument which will long endure for the good of our hard-pressed country . . . Please accept my most fervent sympathy. I know your courage.

Yours affectionately,
Winston S. Churchill.

In her reply, Lady Camrose neatly returned the Prime Minister's compliments by writing: 'You could have had no more devoted admirer than Bill. He would, I know, have laid down his life gladly for you.'

Camrose's funeral took place at the Wokingham Crematorium on 18 June, and at his memorial service, held in St Paul's Cathedral on 23 June – his birthday – the Prime Minister and Lady Churchill were among the distinguished congregation, 2,000 strong. Almost the last to arrive was Lord Beaverbrook, and it fell to Kenneth Rose, one of the forty ushers, to escort him the full length of the aisle to a pew at the front. Rose's journeys up and down the aisle gave him a unique chance of observing the family *en masse*. 'The Berrys look an awfully rough crew when seen together,' he noted in his diary. (Two years later, on 3 May 1956, Churchill returned to St Paul's to unveil a green-marble plaque, placed in the crypt as a memorial to Camrose. Once again he was stylishly dressed, in a new-looking, braided frock coat and wing collar, but by then, at the age of eighty-five, he had grown very old and shaky. After praising his former comrade's 'steadfast loyalty', his foresight and pertinacity, and borrowing Bunyan's phrase to describe him as 'valiant for truth', he betrayed his own frailty by concluding, 'It gives me very great pleasure to unveil this plaque to my old friend, Lord Curzon.')

A more homely service took place at the Market Square Congregational Church in Merthyr, where members of the family took their places in Pew No. 47, which traditionally had been the preserve of the Berrys since Bill's childhood. Several of the local mourners remembered him from those far-off days, and many more came to pay their respects to one of the town's most famous sons. The lesson was taken from Ecclesiasticus, Chapter 44 – 'Let us now praise famous men' – with its wonderfully appropriate phrases – 'Rich men furnished with ability, living peaceably in their habitations' – and the minister, the Reverend R. M. Ellis Gruffydd, declared that every memory of the deceased would be 'a monument to things of integrity, nobility and worthiness'.*

On 25 June 1954 the *Telegraph* printed a whole page of eulogies culled from other papers. None was more realistic than that from the *Times*, which said that Camrose's achievement had been founded on qualities that all could emulate:

> The hardest of hard work, complete business integrity, a courage and confidence which neither obstacles nor reverses could confound, and a determination to apply in his chosen world of journalism the highest standards of cleanness, reliability and truth. He never stooped to do a shady thing, nor shirked to do a hard one.

Yet it was the Danish *Berlingske Tidende* which created the most memorable phrase, when it wrote: 'It is one of the big trees in the forest of the world Press that has fallen.' The *Telegraph* itself declared that by the death of Lord Camrose it had lost the man

---

* Had Camrose lived another year, he would have been made a Freeman of Merthyr – an honour accorded to his brother Lord Kemsley on 28 April 1955.

who 'gave it new life and over a quarter of a century of inspiration', and the main leader concluded: 'Despite the sorrow of his passing, his work must go on. The standards which he set must endure. Endure, under providence, they shall.'

7 SECOND GENERATION, 1954–60

The King is dead – long live the King! But the new monarch of 135 Fleet Street was not the man whom most people had expected to succeed. After a promising start, and having often deputised for his father, the elder son, Seymour, had fallen victim to hepatitis during the Italian Campaign, and this led to complications which made it impossible for him to work regularly. Friends were extremely sad that this should have happened to a man so engaging and attractive: those who had worked with him thought him a still better natural journalist than Michael, with greater talent and imagination. For a while the pretence was maintained that all was well. But once the old man had gone, the truth quickly came out: on 15 June 1954 – the day of Camrose's death – the *Evening News* reported that Seymour had not enjoyed good health for some time, and that his younger brother Michael would probably become Editor-in-Chief – as indeed he did. Formally, Seymour, the new Lord Camrose, became Chairman of *The Daily Telegraph*, but it was his brother who took up the reins.

Michael was then forty-two: tall, dark, and even in middle age painfully shy, with a habit of muttering very fast out of the right-hand corner of his mouth. Less sociable and outgoing than Seymour, less easy and forthcoming in conversation, he nevertheless had a lively sense of humour, which for most of the time remained hidden behind a solid and gloomy façade – and when he did laugh, he had a curious way of tucking the laugh back over his shoulder. He was essentially serious and hard-working, and endowed with a formidable sense of duty.

Training for this, his life's work, had begun at an early age, when his father had made him copy out the leading articles in the *Sunday Times*, and count up the advertisements in that paper and its rival the *Observer*. At Eton he acquitted himself most creditably. A science- and then a history-specialist, he worked his way up into Sixth Form, ending as Captain of the Oppidans – the senior boy in the school, apart from the Collegers, or scholars. Thus it fell to him, in 1930, to organise the celebrations for the Fourth of June.

For two halves (or terms) at the end of 1929 and the beginning of 1930 he was Oppidan Editor of the *Eton College Chronicle*, the school magazine, and for his last year he was a member of Pop, the self-electing oligarchy of boys with specialist powers and privileges.

Having left Eton in the summer of 1930, he went to Christ Church, Oxford, where he read PPE, yet where, by his own account, he learnt very little. His tutor was the outstanding economist Roy Harrod, and Berry was said to have been one of his most able pupils; but, partly because Harrod spoke in the ultra-academic manner then fashionable, and partly because Berry himself was so idle, he 'only understood what Harrod was talking about in the last fortnight before Schools'. All the same, in the summer of 1933 he got a second-class degree, and that autumn began work on one of his father's provincial papers, the Aberdeen *Evening Express*. On his first day he was set to work checking the cricket scores – and since, in his own words, 'nobody plays cricket in Aberdeenshire, that showed what they thought of me'. On his second day, however, things went better: he was transferred to general sub-editing, and in the evening the Chief Sub-Editor said to him angrily, 'Why didn't you tell me you'd done this before?' – one of the nicest compliments anyone had ever paid him.

Next he worked as a reporter on the Aberdeen *Press and Journal*, then moved to Glasgow, where he put in a year on the *Daily Record* as a sub-editor, followed by a spell as picture editor. When the Editor of the *Record*'s sister paper, the *Sunday Mail*, fell ill, David Anderson, Editor-in-Chief of the group, who much admired Michael, suggested that he should take over. Camrose felt that his son was not yet experienced enough to be an editor, but with Anderson's backing Michael got the job, and so began what he later jokingly called his 'finest hour'. The *Sunday Mail*, he admits, was 'a pretty low-class paper', and the staff consisted of himself, the man who produced the serials, occasionally one reporter, and a secretary – reinforced by an army of sub-editors who came in on Saturdays. Being his own master, Michael could write what he wanted – and he did turn out a great deal. In the copies of the paper which went to his father, he was supposed to mark everything that he had written; but he had the sense to leave pieces of dubious taste anonymous or pseudonymous: as he remarked, 'Father was not a great one for making comments, unless you'd done something perfectly frightful. But he seemed pleasantly surprised by the way things went.'

With this formative experience behind him, Michael moved to

Manchester, as a sub-editor on the *Daily Despatch*, and then to London, where he worked as a gossip writer on the *Daily Sketch*. As the Abdication approached, the whole staff knew more or less what was going on, but were forbidden to reveal the true facts; then, when the news broke, Michael was given two whole pages in which to describe the background. He found the exercise great fun; but already he had decided that he was by nature not so much a writer as a sub-editor, 'and a rather good one at that!' His last big job before the war was as Managing Editor of the *Financial Times*, which he thoroughly enjoyed. In general, his strategy at the start of his career was to learn the newspaper business as thoroughly as possible, but at the same time to keep out of his father's way – partly because he liked being on his own, and partly because he felt that his father did not want him at the *Telegraph* before he was some use. As he said later, he would not have liked to work as a junior under his father as Chairman and Editor-in-Chief.

At the outbreak of war he was called up into the 11th (City of London) Light AA Brigade, a territorial unit of the Royal Artillery, and rose to become a lieutenant-colonel. At first, during the Phoney War, he commanded a detachment guarding radar installations at Canewdon, in Essex. Later he became an anti-aircraft gunnery instructor, and then, after a staff course at Biggin Hill in May 1940, a G3 on AA Command, before being appointed Brigade Major of the AA brigade at Exeter. After eighteen months there, he did the full staff course and was posted to COSSAC, the organisation formed to plan the invasion of Europe, in which he spent the rest of the war – first at Norfolk House in London, then as an observer during the Sicily landings, and finally in France, Brussels and Germany. Although claiming that 'nobody could imagine a duller war than that', he was nevertheless twice mentioned in despatches and won the MBE for meritorious service in planning. When hostilities ceased, he became G1, Coal – but there was no coal. Then he was made Assistant Economic Adviser to Fifth Corps – but his advice was never asked. So his war service came to a close, and at the end of 1945 he returned to Oxford for a couple of months, hoping to 're-educate' himself (at the age of thirty-two). He made arrangements to lodge in his old college, but at the last moment heard that if he occupied the room, he might deprive some younger person of a place, so in the end he took digs in Merton Street, together with his brother-in-law, Freddie Birkenhead, who was writing his life of Kipling. Reading a lot, and going to see his old tutor Roy Harrod once a week, Michael found that he too wanted to write a book – and in due course he produced

Party Choice, subtitled 'The Real Issue between the Parties', which was published in 1948.

This modest work, of only 120 pages, gives some fascinating (if involuntary) insights into the character of its author. The introduction disarmingly begins, 'The motive for this book was my own ignorance', and all through *Party Choice* a reader has the feeling that the writer is writing not merely to instruct others, but also to work out his own ideas about economics and politics. The book has the air of a lecture, fluent enough, as if being made up as it goes along, with some cosy philosophical reflections thrown in along the way.

The author's purpose (he wrote) was to examine Socialism and Conservatism. He had left out Communism 'because it is frankly a gospel of tyranny, hate and atheism'. He had also omitted Liberalism, 'because though I understand what Liberalism was, I cannot understand what Liberalism is'.

The first aim of any political party, Berry maintained, should be 'to achieve a high material standard for the maximum number of people'. The 'decisive freedoms' are those of an individual to choose 'his work, his home, his leisure, and how he shall spend his money . . . Happiness may be encouraged by comfort, but does not flow from it. Happiness is rather the elation of good work well and loyally done and the sense of personal fulfilment in sustaining many different interests in life.'

Quoting from J. M. Keynes's seminal work *The General Theory of Employment, Interest and Money*, Berry referred to the book's 'masterly analysis' and the fact that 'its basic theory is now accepted by the majority of economists round the world'. At that point, with typical self-deprecation, he added a note in italics:

The rest of this chapter, though I hope simply expressed, is a trifle technical. The argument, finishing on page 26, is that, for the most part, unemployment can be cured single-handed by the Chancellor of the Exchequer in his monetary and budgetary policy.

Berry went on to demonstrate the inefficiency of nationalisation and to defend the idea of profit: 'Profit-seeking is a perfectly normal habit which everybody in the land pursues.' Wealth, he thought, must be allowed to pass on from one generation to the next, but not without some surrender. 'New generations must, for the most part, depend on their own efforts', but the incentive to work must be encouraged, not stifled. For these and other economic reasons, he concluded that

> Socialism is inferior to Capitalism. Socialism was in origin a doctrine of statics – an idea merely to share out differently a cake of given size, without any clear ideas on cake-making ... It presumes that wealth exists without being continuously created.

A critic might have said that this was all conventional stuff, even if expressed with commendable clarity. But when he came to the difficult question of Britain's colonies, Michael took an enlightened view. He had been horrified by the way in which the Labour Government's precipitate withdrawal from India had plunged the sub-continent into civil strife, and now remarked:

> The job of Britain ... is not to make haste in converting all Colonials into dark-skinned Englishmen governing themselves under English constitutions. The evolution of the Colonial peoples must be in accordance with their, not our, traditions.

Towards the end of the book he observed that 'it is better to be an empiricist than a doctrinaire', and went on to conclude that, once the immensity of the task of governing Britain had been recognised, 'there is some excuse for hesitancy and good ground for humility'.

Here, then, was the new Editor-in-Chief of the *Daily Telegraph*, clearly portrayed: a Conservative, but not a blinkered one; a capitalist with a healthy contempt for Socialism; and what one colleague called 'an unreconstructed Keynesian' – which, no matter how fashions in economics might change, he remained for the whole of his career. This was one of the most striking facts about Michael Berry: from the moment he took over in 1954, to the moment he lost control of the family business in 1985, his outlook scarcely changed at all.

Certainly his assumption of power changed nothing in the building. He had been working there for some time, in any case, and members of the staff were used to seeing him shuffle into the lift on his way to the fifth floor. Now he might come and go with still greater regularity, but the chances of him speaking to any member of the staff were minimal – unless he found himself accidentally trapped in the lift with one, in which case he might force out some

154

question of numbing banality (perhaps about the food in the canteen) before fleeing for the sanctuary of his private suite. His shyness was so acute that it immediately communicated itself to casual acquaintances and made normal conversation almost impossible.

Just as he kept his own offices unchanged, with their 1930s panelling and their ancient *Telegraph* contents bills for decoration, so he maintained his father's routines to the letter. A butler dressed in black still guarded the entrance to the fifth floor. The Assistant Editor in charge of news, now known as the Managing Editor, still came up to see him soon after his arrival around midday, and descended bearing his complaints or commendations, as well as suggestions for the day. A memorandum still went up on the Newsroom board every day saying that such-and-such a story was, or was not, liked. The Editor still came up at 6.00 pm to discuss staff, features and the night's leaders. Some members of the staff still involuntarily stood to attention when they spoke to the new proprietor on the telephone.

Others felt that Michael would have preferred to run – had it been given to him – a rather different paper. He did not demand, and was sometimes disconcerted by, the subservience with which he was treated. He did not realise that his slightest remark was liable to be followed with absolute slavishness. One day, for instance, he mentioned that at Eton he had been taught never to begin a sentence with the word 'but'. Everyone agreed that it was not a bad rule – but he had never dreamt that it would go into the Style Book and receive the status of holy writ. The trouble was that his shyness prevented him from communicating with any except a few senior members of staff, and made it impossible for him to take the temperature of the building. Still less could he face the embarrassment of ordering his employees to be less sycophantic. The result was that things carried on much as before.

As under his father, staff described his method as one of 'divide and rule'. Again, this was not quite accurate. Michael had plenty of personal authority, and did not seek to weaken his subordinates' positions by playing one off against another. But he did form the habit of seeing each man separately, of hearing what he had to say, of keeping the information to himself, and of taking important decisions on his own. This in turn reduced the power of his managers, and limited their scope for innovation.

The staff, all too well aware of his isolation, sought to crack it by giving him a lunch soon after he had taken over. The event, organised by the Night Editor, Brian Roberts, took place at a hotel near Piccadilly Circus on a very hot summer day, but its chances of success – slim anyway – were undermined by the fact that the guest of honour passed out as he was introduced to his hosts. Feeling dizzy, he asked to sit down, but even then fainted away, and came round to find himself lying half-in, half-out of a window, with his tie undone, gazing into the solicitous eyes of a senior sub-editor, who, he remembered, had just been given his notice. After a couple of stiff brandies he felt better, and managed to make his speech; but the staff, not knowing that he was prone to faints of that kind, were disconcerted by the whole episode.

Even though things might seem the same, Berry had begun making careful innovations. 'I don't want a new broom,' his father had told him when he came to 135 Fleet Street in 1946, and from the start he moved cautiously, conscious that senior members of the staff were much older and more experienced than he was. (This did not prevent him being nettled when he asked to see the Saleroom Correspondent, the immensely erudite A. C. R. Carter, who inquired, charmingly, 'And how do you like journalism?') He found the *Telegraph* weighed down by taboos: all headlines had to be in capital letters, the Labour Party had to be called the Socialist Party (on the grounds that it was just that), any cartoon making fun of the Establishment had to be cleared with the proprietor, and he himself was not allowed to run a parliamentary sketch, depicting exchanges in the House of Commons, because it would take up too much space. But he soon began, as he put it, to test the length of his rein, and this was readily extended. When, for instance, he told his father that he had established a 'Nuts' Fund', to take on idiosyncratic writers who did not fit easily into the paper's structure, Camrose was delighted.

Berry's first task, as he saw it, was to remove political bias from the news, and it took longer than he expected to train reporters to write objectively, especially when they contributed constituency reports during General Elections. Often sub-editing such reports himself, he sent several back to be re-written. Eventually he was rewarded when the *Telegraph* became the first paper to emphasise the impartiality of its news stories by printing below them the catchline, 'Editorial Comment – Page X'. After his father's death, Berry took care to observe the Camrose dictum that re-launches were anathema for any paper: readers (he believed) should never be confronted with some drastic change of policy in a single issue, but it was quite legitimate that if they looked back over a period of a month or two, they might be surprised. Liberalisation therefore proceeded gradually.

From his sanctuary on the fifth floor Berry could gain little idea of relationships down in the engine-room; but at that time they were not easy. Early in 1954 he had recruited as Deputy Editor Donald McLachlan, a lively professional journalist (and former schoolmaster) whose background is more fully described in the next chapter.* McLachlan had been working as Foreign Editor of *The Economist*, and welcomed the chance to join a larger paper, but soon found that he had mixed feelings about the Editor, Colin Coote, who for some reason always referred to him as 'McLufflin'. In a fragment of autobiography – alas incomplete – McLachlan left a vivid glimpse of his early impressions of No. 135:

There was a mysterious process round about 6.00 called 'Going Upstairs'. The Editor disappeared for half an hour or more to 'Mr Michael' – 'the young man', Coote used to call him. It was many weeks before I discovered what went on at these *tête-à-têtes* on the fifth floor, because Coote and Michael Berry both preferred to have their day off on Sunday [so that there was no chance for McLachlan, when deputising, to go aloft]. The thought did cross my mind that Coote – who never seemed quite sure of himself – was a bit jealous of his relationship with the proprietor, and did not want me to realise within what limits the Editor of *The Daily Telegraph* exercised his power.

Later McLachlan came to the conclusion that his suspicion was unworthy, but he recorded it because it gave 'some idea of the sense of authority up aloft which prevailed in that office'. Another curious feature, he found, was the nightly news conference, which took place in the office of the Assistant Editor (News), 'a nervous, white-haired, slightly pompous but very likeable little man called Stowell'.

I was early informed that he had shown great gallantry in the war, so that I should not think of him as a timid stooge – which was certainly my first impression . . . Opposite him sat Brian Roberts, the Night Editor, a dark, fierce little Welshman, as different from Stowell as a terrier from a rabbit. Intense, impatient, irritable (or he put it on), he was a product of the *Mail* newsroom at one of its toughest periods.

---

* McLachlan had been recommended by Brendan Bracken, Chairman of *The Economist*. At first Michael Berry suspected that Bracken had been trying to get rid of him, but later he changed his mind.

McLachlan had little time for Coote: he thought him idle, and could not bear his habit of saying 'I know, I know', when confronted with new information. Yet the great machine which the first Camrose had created ran on so smoothly that for the time being little alteration in the paper was perceptible to readers.

The younger generation of the family soon found that they did not want to live on quite the same scale as their father. The Michael Berrys were already established in some style, with an eighteenth-century house in Cowley Street, almost within shouting distance of the House of Commons. Since 1945 they had also owned a country house at Kidmore End, near Reading, where one of Michael's hobbies had been the cultivation of a grass tennis court which he himself maintained in immaculate condition, not allowing play to take place unless the surface was in perfect order. Then, in March 1955, they moved to Oving, in Buckinghamshire, described by Richard Crossman as 'a most wonderful house with a view over the whole plain of Aylesbury'. Molly Camrose still owned half of Hackwood, the other half having been given, in shares of one eighth, to her children, and Seymour lived there at weekends. In 1955, when the family disposed of 24 Carlton House Terrace, he took a suite at the Dorchester as a London *pied-à-terre*; and in 1958 his mother, who had severe arthritis in both knees, sold the yacht *Virginia* to President Tubman of Liberia. (Like her predecessor the *Sona*, the *Virginia* came to an inglorious end. Refitted at a cost of £70,000, renamed *The Liberian*, and equipped with a 12-inch gun, she became the personal warship of the President, who took pleasure in sailing along his shores and intimidating the commanders of his coastal provinces. In 1967, however, with Tubman on board, and under a Dutch captain, she hit the rocks three times in succession in Las Palmas harbour. That skipper was dismissed; but the new one, a Liberian, fared no better. Again the yacht struck some rocks, and this time, after ten days, she sank.)

In the background, however, one feature of the new generation was profoundly different. Old Camrose had received an incalculable amount of help from his wife Molly, but her assistance had been almost entirely private. In contrast, the back-up which Michael got from Lady Pamela was, if not exactly public, at least conducted so as to attract attention from leading public figures. Entertaining was Pamela's passion. Into her stylish parties she poured an immense amount of thought and energy. Her food and wine were the best that money could buy, and at her lunch- or dinner-table the conversation was as stimulating as any in London.

By the end of the 1940s, she had established herself as one of the two most celebrated hostesses in the capital, locked in none-too-good-natured rivalry with the other, Ann Fleming, wife of the writer Ian; and friends who were lucky enough to receive invitations from both made invidious comparisons between the two. Richard Crossman contrasted 'Pam's hard-boiled, political, journalistic atmosphere' with that of Ann Fleming's parties, which he found 'full of a kind of smartness and journalistic elegance'. Evelyn Waugh, on the other hand, told Nancy Mitford: 'Mrs Fleming is aristocratic and corrupt, Lady Pamela is neither.'

Waugh, at first, was a great admirer. 'I have just come back from a weekend at Pamela Berry's,' he told Nancy after a visit to Kidmore End in August 1946. '[John] Betjeman came over and read poetry. Most enjoyable.' A year later he again reported: 'I spent the weekend at Pam Berry's and was never so sumptuously fed or delicately flattered.' Gradually, however, his attitude became mocking and derisive. In April 1949 he wrote to Nancy: 'Are you having a good influence on young Pam Berry? I suspect not. I have my eye on her for the church. Lay off.' In April 1951 he described her as 'a sort of booster for paganism', and in 1955 confessed to Sir Maurice Bowra, 'Lady Pamela has faded from my life like a little pat of melted butter.'

Lady Pamela's appearance was striking. Most men found her handsome rather than beautiful, and she herself cheerfully attributed her dark good looks to the gipsy Smiths in her ancestry. (Once on holiday in the Mediterranean, when the bureaucratic port authority at Maritima, in Sardinia, required her and her friends to fill up forms with the names of father, grandfather and great-grandfather, Elizabeth Cavendish impressed the locals by entering 'Tenth Duke of Devonshire, Ninth Duke of Devonshire, Eighth Duke of Devonshire'; but Pamela simply wrote 'Tenth Gipsy Smith, Ninth Gipsy Smith, Eighth Gipsy Smith'.) 'Pamela in excellent form,' noted Muggeridge, after he and his wife Kitty had entertained the Berrys to dinner in January 1954. 'As Kitty and I agreed afterwards, she is not witty, but immensely droll; not clever, but shrewd and tough. Dresses always exactly like a gipsy, with heavy, glittering metal on her dress.' Other people thought that she *was* clever. Certainly she was immensely spirited and energetic, with much of the dominating personality that had made her father so formidable; and the urge to stir people up was clearly one of her motives in entertaining on such a scale.

Her salon consisted mainly of politicians, writers and journalists; but people noticed that although she courted politicians of all parties, she also despised them as a breed, preferring writers, and journalists especially, whom she regarded as more glamorous creatures. Hating the idle rich (among whom she included her brother-in-law Seymour), she liked creative, hard-working, self-made people best. Once in a newspaper interview she remarked that she herself 'would loathe to be in Parliament', because 'it has such a turgid effect on women'. She also said that she would not like to be a journalist, but this was because she was 'completely untrained. Look at all the silly women who say, "I think I'll go into journalism" – and know nothing about it.' She became annoyed if anyone described her as a political hostess, and once burst out: 'I don't know why I'm tagged with the label of political hostess – or indeed as a hostess in any accepted sense. The only entertaining I do is of so vague a character that it hardly merits such a portentous description.'

Defending her own extravagance, she would point out that in her parents' day 'the dinner table played a great part in politics', and that 'many political decisions must have been reached over the dinner table'. But, she feared, with the decline and contraction of the dinner party, 'conversation and wit are becoming lost arts'. Among contemporaries, she named only Richard Crossman, Michael Foot and Sir Isaiah Berlin as having 'true elegance of style and wit'. All three, needless to say, were her frequent guests.

Gossip was her delight. As Peregrine Worsthorne (who had joined the *Telegraph* as a leader-writer in 1953) recorded,

> She never made any effort to go through the motions of what less naturally intelligent women strongly imagine to be serious political conversation. She loved to hear (and to tell) all the gossip, public and private, and felt no need to disguise her pleasure in such matters behind a mask of intellectual solemnity.

Soon she became renowned for her mischievous – some would say malicious – wit. Frank Giles, Editor of the *Sunday Times*, recalled how, when he had set up house in Little Venice – the fashionable area between Paddington and Maida Vale – she asked him where he was living. When he told her, 'she looked complacently round her pretty, panelled drawing-room in Cowley Street, close to the Houses of Parliament and Westminster Abbey, and said, "It sounds very nice, but you'll have to find a flat in London, won't you?"'

People described her soirées as 'coruscating'. Brilliant they were; but the coruscation was often as hard as the glitter of diamonds,

The front of the new building under construction, 1929.

Right: The front of the new building, finished in 1930, and *below* the new front hall.

Top left: One of the directors' offices in the new building, with a portrait of the first Lord Camrose on the wall. *Below left*: the garden on the fifth floor balcony, and *below* Arthur Watson, editor of the *Daily Telegraph* from 1924 to 1950, who bridged the Burnham and Berry eras.

Editors of the *Daily Telegraph*, clockwise from top left: Colin Coote, Maurice Green, Max Hastings and Bill Deedes.

Editors of the *Sunday Telegraph*, clockwise from top left: Donald McLachlan, Brian Roberts, Peregrine Worsthorne and John Thompson.

Leading editorial
lights on the *Daily
Telegraph*, clockwise
from top left:
Peter Eastwood,
Colin Welch,
Michael Wharton,
Peter Utley,
H. D. Ziman,
Hugo Wortham and
Malcolm Muggeridge.

Senior managers: H. M. Stephen *top left*, H. J. C. Stevens *top right*, Alan Rawcliffe *bottom right* and Hugh Lawson.

Goodbye to No. 135: *Sunday Telegraph* staff line up on the balcony with the Editor, Peregrine Worsthorne, in the centre, before their move to the Isle of Dogs in 1987.

and she herself would drive the conversation on relentlessly, wrenching it away from idle chatter and forcing it back to matters of political contention. Peregrine Worsthorne gave a vivid idea of the high voltage that fizzed round her table:

My first luncheon party under her roof . . . was in honour of Walter Lippmann, the veteran American pundit, at the height of the Suez crisis. Pamela started the general post-prandial conversation by shouting down the table: 'Oh, Perry, do tell Walter why you think his attack on Anthony [Eden, the Prime Minister] was so fatuous.' And such was Pamela's personality that Mr Lippman had no choice but to pay attention to someone else's views on a basis of equality . . . When under Pamela's wing, one was carried effortlessly and instantly into the stratosphere of high society and high politics: into altitudes which are usually reached only after years of toadying and social-climbing.

No one disputed the glamour and excitement of Lady Pamela's parties, but people could see that Michael Berry himself found the whirl of social activity at Cowley Street a strain: often he would miss parties altogether, or arrive late and slip out early, with the excuse – frequently valid – that he had to put the paper to bed. Having no small talk, he found himself uncomfortable at drinks parties. As he put it, 'I don't like standing about in clumps. I'd much rather get my knees under a table'. The fact that he was partially deaf in one ear made large gatherings still more of an ordeal.

On the face of things, the Berrys were a strange couple: she going out of her way to attract attention, he doing everything he could to avoid it; and many people wondered why Pamela entertained so feverishly. One reason, undoubtedly, was that she wanted to help her husband. She felt that he *needed* to meet politicians, even if he did not much enjoy it; and certainly, without her efforts, he would have been even more cut off than he was. Yet the political commentator Paul Johnson, whom Pamela befriended even in his days as a socialist, saw her party-giving (and her work in the world of fashion) as a *pis aller*, an outlet for energy that could have been better spent. Her trouble – she herself confided to him – was that she had a good brain but had never been trained to use it. Her father had fired her with a thirst for knowledge; but ideas imparted while he was shaving before his full-length mirror were no substitute for higher education, and she resented her lack of knowledge bitterly. In Johnson's view, what spurred her on to such efforts as a hostess, at least in part, was intellectual insecurity.

Another matter of keen debate was the role – if any – which Pamela played in the conduct of *The Daily Telegraph*. The ambiguity of her position was well conveyed by Alan Brien, who became Theatre Critic of *The Sunday Telegraph* on its inception in 1961. When he first met Lady Pamela, he wrote,

> It was widely believed in Fleet Street that Lady Pam actually ran *The Daily Telegraph*, and that Mr Michael . . . was a kind of monosyllabic, dummy front-man, and I think it is true that she often acts as a kind of exotic pilot fish, swimming ahead, fending off bores, steering in talent, exploring new territory, testing the water. She is his radar. But just because she does not make the final decisions, she is free to be indiscreet, provocative and apparently irresponsible – or, rather, responsible only to herself.

This was an acute observation. It was not true (as some people believed) that Michael would refuse on principle to take telephone calls from his wife while he was in the office; but it was true that she very seldom came to Fleet Street and had little direct influence on the content of the paper – for if ever she did suggest something to him, it was most likely that, out of sheer obstinacy, he would do the opposite. Nevertheless, the mere fact that she associated with leading politicians, and was constantly stirring up gossip, inevitably created ripples from time to time; and of course, if she wanted some favour, like getting Peterborough to mention a protégé, she might lean on a particular journalist – just as any other proprietor's wife would. She also expressed vehement views on articles in the paper: once at a party, when Colin Welch had written a leader sympathetic to Richard Neville and the hippy magazine *Oz*, she cried out: 'A DREADFUL leader – quite dreadful!' and gave him a dressing-down in front of the assembled company.

Politicians who did try to exercise direct influence on the Press usually found they could make little headway, no matter what their allegiance might be. In January 1967 Richard Crossman discovered, to his rage, that a 'brash young man' from *The Sunday Telegraph* was preparing a hostile profile of him. Crossman wrote to Berry asking 'if it was his normal practice to do a hatchet job on a leading politician'; the answer was that no such directive had been given, and that the profile would portray Crossman as a rough diamond, '"with emphasis on both rough and diamond"', whatever that may mean'. On another celebrated occasion

R. A. Butler and Lord Salisbury called at Cowley Street in the hope of pulling the daily paper into line behind them: attempts at serious conversation were ruined by Lady Pamela's border terrier, which, even though she had left the room, kept coming up to Butler and begging him to throw a ball.

It was in the field of fashion that Lady Pamela cut ice in her own right. In March 1954 she became President of the Incorporated Society of London Fashion Designers, and threw herself with gusto into the task of promoting British fashion houses and fabrics. In July of that year she twisted the arm of R. A. Butler, then Chancellor of the Exchequer, so effectively that he lent her his official residence, No. 11 Downing Street, in which to throw a party for overseas fashion buyers, with the Duchess of Kent as the guest of honour. Along with the Butlers, Lady Pamela herself received the guests, and the whole affair was so stylish that the *Guardian* declared, 'Paris couldn't have done it better.'

The observation touched a nerve. Pamela was maddened by the fact that people saw Paris as the capital of fashion. 'Everyone goes wild about the Paris collections,' she complained to the journalist Quentin Crewe, 'but London fashion shows pass almost unnoticed.' The main trouble, she thought, was 'the idiotic reaction of the English to the word Paris. It means brothels and excitement . . . anything Parisian must be better than anything British.'

It was to shatter this illusion that she launched herself into action on behalf of the London fashion houses. After No. 11 Downing Street, her second *mise-en-scène* was still more ambitious: the Mansion House, traditional headquarters of the Lord Mayor of London, where no fashion show had ever been held before, and where the City of London gold plate went on show for the evening. In January 1955 – clearly at her instigation – *The Daily Telegraph* announced that it had set out to discover the country's best-dressed women. The judges would be the Duchess of Marlborough, Lady Pamela Berry, Mrs Thorneycroft (wife of the President of the Board of Trade), Cecil Beaton, Simon Elwes and Winefride Jackson, the paper's Fashion Editor. Readers were invited to send in nominations, and in due course the panel selected ten women, without placing them in any order, but including Beatrice Lillie, the Countess of Westmorland, Margot Fonteyn, Mrs Cavendish-Bentinck and the Countess of Dalkeith. The whole proceeding drew a waspish letter from Pamela's friend Nancy Mitford, who wrote to the Editor of the *Telegraph* from Paris:

Sir – I attribute the choice of the ten elegant Britons to Mr Simon Elwes's love of a pretty face, Lady Pamela Berry's love of English clothes, the Duke of Marlborough's love of horses, and Mr Cecil Beaton's love of a joke. Have I solved the puzzle?

Yours faithfully,
Nancy Mitford

Unabashed, Pamela secured as her next venue Lancaster House, in St James's, whose palatial State rooms had not been used for a private party since 1913. To them she lured an astonishing collection of important people, including the Lord Mayor of London, half the Cabinet and four ambassadors. Among the throng, unfortunately for her, was Randolph Churchill, who, notwithstanding the fact that he was godfather to her son Adrian, gave her a spiteful blast in the next issue of *Truth*. Calling the show 'an entertainment of inconceivable silliness', he implied that she had been hard put to it to dredge up a quorum, and claimed that 'those who did attend looked frumpy and dowdy ... The whole performance made a mockery of the British fashion industry.'

Nothing could have been more wounding than that last sentence, and she struck back in a vigorously rude letter at his 'malice unredeemed by wit', his 'pyramid of abuse', and his 'impertinent taunt that the French, Austrian, Italian and United States Ambassadors had been "gathered together from the dreg-ends of the London season"'. Fashion, she declared, 'like art, is a matter of taste, and that is evidently not a quality with which Mr Churchill is conversant'.

This exchange led Churchill to deny a report, made by the *Daily Express*, to the effect that he had been reinstated at the tables of London's two most stimulating hostesses, Lady Pamela Berry and Mrs Ian Fleming. 'Lady Pamela Berry is still, of her own volition' – he wrote in a letter to the Editor – 'not on speaking terms with me.'

Anything but downhearted, Pamela forged ahead with further fashion shows, in the Fishmongers' Hall – where she used the drawing-room in which hung the celebrated portrait of the Queen by Pietro Annigoni – and in Hamilton House, Piccadilly. Here the guests of honour were the Queen Mother and Princess Margaret, and it seemed thoroughly appropriate, in various ways, that it was Lady Pamela, in a dress of crimson wool with black braiding, and seated beneath an eighteenth-century yellow canopy, who deputised for the Queen Mother at the rehearsal.

Fashion apart, Pamela found another outlet for her energy in recruiting distinguished overseas lecturers for the English-Speaking Union, and as a member of the Advisory Council at the Victoria and Albert Museum. Most of her activities had no connection with the *Telegraph*, but sometimes she helped Michael to entertain on behalf of the paper. One notable occasion was the election-night party of May 1955 – again held at the Savoy – when the Conservatives returned to power with an increased majority, and with their new Prime Minister, Sir Anthony Eden, confirmed in office (Churchill having at last resigned, aged eighty, on 5 April). Another big night was the eastern-hemisphere premiere of Michael Todd's film *Around the World in Eighty Days*, which took place in London on 12 June 1957, in aid of the Newspaper Press Fund Festival Appeal of which Michael Berry was Chairman.

The paper had a tenuous but legitimate connection with this project. In the first edition of the novel the author, Jules Verne, included a note disclosing that the inspiration for his story had come from a report in *The Daily Telegraph* of 11 May 1872 to the effect that the completion of a railway in India had made it theoretically possible to travel round the globe in eighty days. Perusal of that issue of the paper does not in fact reveal any such report; nevertheless (the story went on) Verne later heard that he had committed a solecism. The Reform Club, in which his hero Phileas Fogg was supposed to have made his wager, did not then take *The Daily Telegraph*, disliking its politics; and so, in later editions of the book, it was the *Morning Chronicle* which gave Fogg his idea.

The film set out to restore the *Telegraph* to its rightful place in the saga. The opening sequence showed four men reading the paper in the Reform Club, and in later scenes newsboys held up copies as they shouted out news of Fogg's progress. A mock-up issue was made, dated 11 May 1872, with news (erroneously) displayed on the front page, and the banner headline FOGG ARRIVES IN SAN FRANCISCO; and this page, when blown up on the sixty-by-fifty-two-foot screen, was, as the producer claimed, 'the biggest *Daily Telegraph* you'll ever see'.

In June, when Todd flew to London to arrange details of the premiere, Lady Pamela gave a lunch party for him – an event bitchily described by her rival Ann Fleming in a letter to Evelyn Waugh:

> It was a disappointment you did not lunch with Lady Pamela Berry the day you were expected, it's always a treat to see you and I anticipated a clash with the guest of honour, Mr Mike

Todd; at one moment he turned to his hostess and said, 'I'd like to bite your tongue out.' I encouraged him and said we should all be grateful but alas, he lost his nerve.

Since Waugh's correspondents often became infected with his own habit of farcical exaggeration, in their efforts to amuse him, it is hard to know how much truth this letter contained; yet Lady Pamela remained on good terms with Todd, and the premiere proved a huge financial success. Every seat was sold, the most expensive costing a hundred guineas apiece (and the first two had been bought by Mr Todd and his wife of the day, Elizabeth Taylor). Michael and Lady Pamela Berry received their guests in the foyer of the Astoria Cinema in Charing Cross Road: the Duke of Kent and Princess Alexandra, ambassadors, Cabinet Ministers, film stars and others.

The film, however, was only the start of the evening. After it, buses took the guests to Charing Cross pier, where a small fleet of boats was waiting to ferry them to the Festival Gardens fun-fair in Battersea Park. Alas, the weather was foul – provoking Ann Fleming to send another caustic description to Evelyn Waugh:

> Those of us who wished the maximum pleasure embarked at midnight from Charing X pier in a flotilla of river steamers, rain was falling, and the cabins and bars were filled with Jewish film producers, publishers and interior decorators. On each deck was a brass band playing 'Rule Britannia'.

Pelted by rain, and by deluges of publicity pamphlets dropped on them from the bridges, the revellers were sodden by the time they reached Battersea, and the downpour half-ruined what would otherwise have been a memorable evening, but did not prevent the exercise making a profit for the Benevolent Fund of £14,000.

At 135 Fleet Street Michael Berry had continued to make innovations, of which the most significant was the introduction of a humorous column called 'Way of the World'. On the whole he was strongly opposed to any kind of frivolity in the main body of the paper, and he had no time for elaborate, flowery writing, least of all in the news. The *Telegraph*, in his view, contained a great deal of reading-matter, but most people did not have much time to read it. This meant that everything must be succinct. As he himself said, 'You don't want a lot of high-falutin waffle before you get to the point. If you read the whole of the first paragraph of a story – eight or nine lines – and still don't know what it's about, that's no good.' He seemed to suspect that anyone who wrote in a long-winded fashion might actually be mendacious, and he certainly did not see style as an asset or a help to understanding. His appetite for facts was insatiable, and some of his writers, realising this, managed to work quite tendentious ideas into the paper by dishing them up disguised as hard-fact stories.

One of the problems which Michael inherited from his father's time was a brilliant young man called Colin Welch, who, after winning scholarships at both Stowe and Peterhouse, Cambridge, had joined the paper as a leader-writer in 1950 at the age of twenty-six, Arthur Watson's last appointment. It was Michael who had told Watson to take Welch on; but the trouble with him was that he was far too funny. Instead of soberly dealing in facts, as a good *Telegraph* journalist should, his mind piled castles of fantasy high into the air. Like another Muggeridge, he was a fount of merriment. He was also a wonderful mimic, and his face accurately reflected what was going on behind it: sardonic and faintly mocking beneath a stack of tousled hair, it looked as though its owner was perplexed only by the problem of which joke to tell next.

With his apparently incurable tendency to be flippant, Welch had his Editor-in-Chief worried. Berry saw that he had wonderful talent, but could not bear to have writers performing antics in leading articles. As he himself said later, 'When he was writing descriptively, he was marvellous; but I did find his style quite unsuitable for serious leaders.' His solution was ingenious, and a lasting success. Since Welch was always wanting to be satirical, Berry said to him one day, 'Go away and write a satirical column.' The result was Way of the World, which first appeared on the page opposite the leader on 18 October 1955, with the name 'Yorick' at the foot; but after an impassioned complaint from a provincial paper which already had a column with that signature, the name was changed to 'Peter Simple', from a feature once carried by the *Morning Post*.

So was born a new world, often filled with savagely ironic comment on the lunacies of modern life, but peopled also by Councillor Dunt (Soc.) of the Stretchford (Staffs) Borough Council, Colonel Marsh-Staggage, late of the Independent Minority, General Nidgett, Daphne Dutt-Pauker, the Hampstead Thinker, and a cast of others who sprang fully-fledged from the imagination of Colin Welch, and, later, from that of his collaborator and successor, Michael Wharton.

Wharton joined the *Telegraph* in 1957, and recorded his own recruitment in characteristically whimsical fashion. He was staying with Constantine and Theodora Fitzgibbon when Colin Welch arrived on a visit:

> He mentioned that he was thinking of getting a full-time collaborator for the Peter Simple column. I made no particular response to this. It was good old Theodora, of course, who suddenly shouted, 'Can't you see, you fathead? He's offering you a job.'

The difference which these two made to the *Telegraph* was incalculable. How, before the advent of Peter Simple, could it have published a paragraph like this?

> My own memories [of the NAAFI] are distinctly nostalgic. I think of those stolen moments spent listening, when nominally barrack-room orderly, to Debussy's String Quartet, until brought to my senses by an angry shout from the RSM, who was creeping about on all fours, looking for mouseholes.

How, without Peter Simple, could the paper have published a take-off of Jennifer's Social Journal, the pride of the *Tatler*?

> I long one day to see Jennifer in hell – not from the slightest ill-will, of course, but just to see her 'do' it. The Devil, a striking figure in black ... very witty and amusing ... Dr 'Chips' Faustus, who is a great personality and said to be very clever ... Left early after enjoying a cocktail with Miss Lucy Borgia, one of 1498's youngest debutantes, very soignée in black velvet.

Only the existence of Peter Simple made it possible for the paper to give such a blistering verdict on the Russian leaders Bulganin and Khrushchev, who came to England in April 1957. The column described the visit (which was still in progress) as a 'mounting fiasco', recalled how the British, 'weak in discrimination', had fallen in large numbers for Ribbentrop before the war, and concluded hopefully that 'Khrushchev, it seems, is too gross fare even for us'.

> Bulganin [a politician had reported] is a charmer: genial, homely, provincial ... just the sort of man you might see at any West Country pig-show, straw in mouth, hat tilted back, knobbly stick in hand, hanging over a rail and absent-mindedly scratching the back of – well – Khrushchev.

Introducing a selection of pieces from Way of the World some thirty years later, Wharton modestly explained that 'this little book ... is in chronological order, and pomposities and facetiae follow each other with bewildering inconsequence, just as in the daily column, and, indeed, in life'. In fact the creation of Peter Simple made it possible for one writer, at least, to say what he wanted, and moreover to say it with humour and polish, free from the suffocating restrictions of the Style Book and the sub-editors. The column quickly established a following, and Michael Berry considered it an extremely useful addition to the paper. Until then, he felt, the staff of the *Telegraph* 'had always been known as dyed-in-the-wool, top-hatted Tories, and this at last attracted the attention of people in the middle, politically, and even of left-wingers like Tom Driberg'.

Once Way of the World had made its mark, Berry took up another project still dearer to his heart: the Parliamentary Sketch. For years he had nursed the idea of a daily report on Parliament done in a humorous fashion, yet giving readers an accurate idea of the nature of important debates, the arguments used on either side, and the outcome. His aim was not that the piece should lampoon one or two speakers – as later authors seemed to think – or that it should score easy points by referring to the different subjects arising at Question Time; rather, he meant it to give a balanced report on major issues.

His first choice, as a potential author, was Alistair Forbes, who was then contributing a political column to the *Sunday Dispatch*. Berry asked him to do a couple of trial pieces, and invited him to come and discuss them at 7.00 one evening. At 7.15, as he waited, a message arrived from a secretary to say that Forbes could not keep the appointment – and that was the last he heard of him in the context. Forbes's lack of manners, however, soon became Berry's gain, for his next choice proved ideal: in Colin Welch he found a perfect author for the new feature. Welch grasped the idea at once, and deployed his brilliantly amusing descriptive powers so effectively that the sketch went a long way towards relieving the heaviness of the news pages. (From the start Berry's intention was that if the House of Commons produced nothing sketch-worthy during the day, the writer should ring the office to ask the Night Editor whether he really wanted a piece that night; but later authors sometimes failed to observe this protocol, wrote anyway, and were chagrined when their articles were spiked.)

*   *   *

It was a departure from the paper's usual pro-Government stance that provoked one of the most acrimonious political rows of the 1950s – the affair of the Smack of Firm Government. For this attack on Sir Anthony Eden – which in retrospect many people saw as the beginning of his downfall – Lady Pamela Berry took a lot of blame. It was widely said that she had been disparaging Eden at her parties, that her remarks had come to the ears of Eden's wife Clarissa, that in consequence the Edens had cut the Berrys, and that Pamela had therefore put the *Telegraph* up to writing the article. It is true that she was hostile to Eden; but it was certainly not true that she ordered or even suggested the piece, whose genesis was more complicated.

The leader-page article, published on 3 January 1956 and entitled WAITING FOR THE SMACK OF FIRM GOVERNMENT, was an unusually tough one. 'Why are the men who triumphed at the polls last May now under a cloud of disfavour with their own supporters?' it began, and it went on to express the dissatisfaction that people of all ranks were feeling with the performance of the Government, but more especially with Eden. The passage that became famous read:

> There is a favourite gesture of the Prime Minister's which is sometimes recalled to illustrate this sense of disappointment. To emphasise a point he will clench one fist to smack the open palm of the other – but this smack is seldom heard. Most Conservatives . . . are waiting to feel the smack of firm Government.

Its author was Donald McLachlan, the Deputy Editor who had joined the paper less than eighteen months before. In that period, he later wrote, he had 'never come across a single instance of Lady Pamela's influencing the policy of the paper', and he himself had met her only twice. It was on the second occasion, at a lunch party in Cowley Street during November 1955, that the talk had turned to Eden. Lady Pamela complained that a *Telegraph* sketch about the Commons debate on the defectors Burgess and Maclean had presented Eden's speech as a parliamentary triumph; and when McLachlan defended the author on the grounds that it *had*, in its own terms, been a triumph, she, according to McLachlan, 'seemed piqued and dropped the subject'.

Yet it was from Michael, not from Pamela, that the initiative for the article came. Some time in December it occurred to him that it would be a good idea to run a piece assessing Eden's performance as Prime Minister during his initial six months of office, out of the shadow of Churchill for the first time. He talked to Coote about it, suggested that McLachlan would be the best man to write it, and that they should run it on the first day of the new year. McLachlan, however, found the piece hard to write, and on 28 December asked Kenneth Rose (who was then on Peterborough) to lunch at Brooks's, where he confided that he had been disturbed by the Berrys' petty malice towards Eden, manifest at their own lunch party, and showed him a draft. Rose made several 'cosmetic suggestions', all of which strengthened the case against Eden, and which were, he believed, accepted. Even so, McLachlan was unable to complete the piece in time for New Year's Day, and it came out two days later, on 3 January. The idea for the celebrated catch-phrase had come to him at lunch with Ann Fleming, when Eden had kept emphasising points with his characteristic gesture of punching one fist towards the other palm, without actually making contact.

The leader caused an immediate stir. Dining out on the night of its publication, Rose found himself next to Sir Linton Andrews, Chairman of the Press Council and, as Editor of the *Yorkshire Post*, a dedicated supporter of successive Conservative administrations. 'I was distressed to read today's attack on the Government,' said Andrews – and then, after a long pause: 'Because I cannot think of any answer to it.' Two days later, again at dinner, an old friend of Rose's, who was then one of the Prime Minister's private secretaries, dismissed the article as 'a typical piece of Lady Pamela's spite', and could not be convinced that she had not ordered it. That was the general view taken, and on 8 January the *Sunday Express* carried a leader attacking Lady Pamela's attempt at petticoat government.

Such was the price she paid – however undeservedly in this instance – for constantly promoting gossip and intrigue. In fact, all the article had done was to crystallise the feelings of unease which had been troubling many people, and McLachlan afterwards told H. B. Boyne, the distinguished Political Correspondent of the *Telegraph*, that in writing it he had had no intention of starting an 'Eden must go' movement; yet this was precisely what he set in train, and the long-term effects of his leader were profound. Boyne believed that it began Eden's 'overt downfall in the Conservative Party's esteem, and the country's'.

The author was embarrassed by the strength of the reaction which he had provoked. He later wrote a letter of apology to Eden, who graciously accepted it, and asked the McLachlans to lunch in the country. Later still, in Barbados, the Edens invited them for drinks, and all seemed forgiven.

* * *

During the 1950s the foreign news coverage of the paper was much strengthened. Donald McLachlan had not had a very high regard for the *Telegraph* when he was at the *Economist*, preferring the *Times* and the American press as sources of information; but from the mid-1950s there was rapid improvement. The paper did not as yet have a correspondent in Moscow, but elsewhere it was strongly represented, employing about thirty of its own people abroad and many more 'stringers' – journalists working primarily for foreign papers, who wrote for the *Telegraph* as a sideline. In London a reserve of 'firemen' was always available – experienced reporters who could be whipped out to any trouble-spot at zero notice (hence the expression 'to fire-brigade' an event – to cover it by sending a man from London).

In the United States the paper maintained offices in Washington and New York, where the Chief American Correspondent was Alex Faulkner, who had joined the paper in 1929 and worked for it in Paris before crossing the Atlantic (in all, Faulkner represented the *Telegraph* for forty-five years). On the Continent, the Chief Correspondent for Southern Europe, based in Rome, was Anthony Mann, another veteran (in terms of experience at least), who had reported from Vienna and Berlin before the war, from Copenhagen during it, until he was interned, and afterwards from Germany and Paris, his assignments including the trial of the Nazi war criminals at Nuremberg. A true European, he had married a German girl, was fluent in five languages, could get by in four more, and was in every respect a typically professional *Telegraph* foreign correspondent.

Another of that ilk was John Wallis, chief of the *Telegraph* bureau in Paris. His exceptional contacts ensured that he was always astonishingly well informed, and usually at least one jump ahead of the competition – as he showed on the night of 12 May 1958, when he rang Ricky Marsh, then Night Foreign Editor, and said he thought he ought to be in Algiers first thing next day. Asked if he was sure, he said he was as sure as he could be, and Marsh immediately gave him authority to go. He flew down overnight, and the coup which ended in the fall of France's Fourth Republic began as he arrived in the morning, the only British newspaper staff correspondent on the scene.

The Paris office, at 20 Place Vendôme, was one of the *Telegraph*'s post-war glories. During the war the building had been some minor Luftwaffe headquarters, and one day, just after hostilities had ended, the War Correspondent Douglas Reid was drinking in the Ritz Hotel, across the square, when he saw that an angry crowd had gathered round No. 20, where some last-minute resistance appeared to have been encountered. With great presence of mind he went over and said that the owner of the building, who was being beaten in a corner, was a close personal friend of his, and that moreover these offices had been requisitioned for *The Daily Telegraph*, which would occupy them forthwith. Thus the paper took a lease on the building, at a very favourable rent – and with it came several Mercedes typewriters abandoned by the German airmen. The *Telegraph*'s three correspondents occupied one of the large rooms at the front, with a magnificent chandelier, and surrounded by slightly curved eighteenth-century mirrors which threw back hundreds of reflections.

Here, one day, old Lord Camrose played a joke on John Wallis and his assistant Ronnie Payne, who were taking the air on the balcony. When he came through on the telephone, and asked if they were busy, Wallis of course replied, 'Frightfully.' But Camrose – who was in his favourite haunt, the Ritz Hotel, right opposite, immediately countered, 'Oh no you're not! I can see you on the balcony. Come over and have a drink.' So over they went, for champagne cocktails.

Now, with the second generation in charge, Lady Pamela made heavy use of the Paris office. Her fashion work often brought her to the French capital, and in those days of currency restrictions, when travellers were allowed to take practically no money abroad, she relied on the office to settle any bills she might incur (though of course she would pay the firm back in England). She also made a habit of dragooning members of the staff to smuggle packages back to London on her behalf: usually expensive underwear, but once at least a whole ham.

Staff members in Paris frequently found themselves called upon to run errands. When the Berry family went on holiday to their villa in the South of France, they themselves would fly down to Nice, but someone would bring their car – loaded with food and baggage – over on the ferry, and Jacques Taffoureaud, the office manager, would drive it down to the south. In Paris itself, Ronnie Payne frequently came under pressure to do the family's bidding.

One night Pamela, staying with Sir Gladwyn and Lady Jebb at the British Embassy, proposed to walk down the Faubourg St Honoré with the Ambassador and his wife to open the British Fashion Week. 'I *do* hope you'll be there,' she cooed at Payne over the telephone. 'It's going to be *such* fun, and you can write one of your very amusing articles about it.'

She had picked a bad evening. The Algerian crisis was at its height, and the French Prime Minister, Michel Debré, had just been on the radio saying that rebel paratroops might drop on the city that night. Tanks were moving into Paris, airport runways had been blocked. Payne, alone in the office, clearly could not leave his desk; but when he apologetically said as much, she replied, 'Oh well – if you're going to take *that* attitude . . .' and rang off.

In the event he was at his desk until 4.00 am – and by then a complaint had evidently reached London. That day the front page of the *Telegraph* was covered with French news, and Michael Berry rang Payne at his flat on the Left Bank to congratulate him. 'I wanted to say that your coverage was far superior to that of any other paper,' he muttered. 'I'm arranging for you to be paid a bonus.' He left Payne with the clear impression that he, and not his wife, was Editor-in-Chief of the newspaper.

On another occasion Lady Pamela summoned Payne to the bar of the Hotel Crillon to witness the great reconciliation which she was about to effect between her friend Nancy Mitford and the veteran journalist Sam White. The two had been at loggerheads ever since the appearance of the novel *Don't Tell Alfred*, in which Nancy had created a character, Amyas Mockbar, who was clearly based on White. 'The Fiend in human form,' she called him, 'a brigand if ever there was one, whom I can't help rather loving.' Upset by this, and by nasty remarks about Mockbar's Jewishness, White had written some spiteful retaliatory pieces about the author.

'Be sure you're there,' Pamela told Payne, 'because I'm going to make them kiss,' and when he arrived at the hotel at midday, she asked him to order champagne. 'I want you to bring Sam over the moment he comes in,' she said. Presently White appeared, giving characteristic upward twitches of his right elbow – not, as strangers thought, a sign of intoxication, but the legacy of a motorcycle crash when a despatch-rider during the war. 'I certainly won't kiss that bloody Mitford woman,' he growled as he came in – but kiss her he did, such was the strength of Pamela's personality.

By the second half of the 1950s, the staff at 135 Fleet Street had been to some extent rejuvenated by the introduction of new blood – Welch, Worsthorne, their colleague John Applebey, and, on the Peterborough column (a traditional starting-ground), Kenneth Rose, Philip Goodhart, Alistair Horne, and Fred Burnham's second son Hugh Lawson (who soon transferred from editorial into advertising and management).* Yet many of the old-timers were still

* The sudden death of John Applebey, from leukaemia, was a severe loss to the paper.

soldiering on, not least Peterborough himself, Hugo Wortham, who by now had become a cantankerous old man, past his best, but still the inspiration of the column. His habits, by then, were absolutely fixed: he would arrive late in the morning, a dapper little fellow, vermilion in the face, wearing a bowler hat (usually a grey one) at a rakish angle. His assistants were also expected to wear bowlers: young Rivers Scott, who joined in 1955, was soon taken aside and reprimanded for wearing a trilby. 'On Peterborough,' his mentor told him, 'we wear bowlers.'

At his desk, particularly in the afternoons, Wortham would emit a continuous rumble, talking perhaps to himself, perhaps to his subordinates (who could say?); and when he left in the evening, he usually did so abruptly, without telling anybody that he was going. The only way to determine whether one of his exits was the last of the day was to look at the hat-stand. If the grey bowler had gone, Wortham had too.

Scott found him 'a fantastic man, the last of the Edwardian rakes', who could work in a completely professional fashion even when three-parts pickled, as he usually was. He was a man of fastidious habits, and once was appalled when, at a party, the Minister of Transport, Ernest Marples, thrust him a glass of champagne out of which he had already drunk. To some of his juniors he seemed exceptionally selfish and vindictive – and certainly he resented it when a subordinate happened to know the important people from whom the column's news derived. Once when the Aga Khan had invited Kenneth Rose to tea at the Ritz a telephone message came through asking him to arrive at four-fifteen rather than four-thirty. Wortham was incensed. 'You've no right to have tea with the Aga Khan without telling me!' he said. 'I'm going in your place.' 'Well,' answered Rose coolly, 'the Aga Khan will be very surprised to see you, as this is a purely private invitation.' Another tremendous row broke out when Rose announced that he was going to Wagner's *Ring* at Bayreuth with the Duke of Kent, a close friend. At the last moment Wortham told him that, since the office was so short of staff, he could not go. 'In that case,' said Rose, 'you'll have to sack me.' In the end he went, and kept his job.

Life on Peterborough was not always easy. Wortham's work-methods were chaotic, and sometimes great drifts of paper would lift off from his desk and blow across the room. Randolph Churchill would ring up to dictate incoherent paragraphs late at night, roaring with irritation at the obtuseness of the person taking down his words. Michael Berry (who took a close interest in the column) would send down cryptic notes of criticism or suggestion, usually scrawled in his spiky handwriting, barely decipherable. 'What's this Armenian fellow doing talking to the Archbishop?' he once demanded. The 'Armenian fellow' was the leader of the Armenian Christians, on a visit to his flock in England.

Wortham's most famous moment came at one of the Christmas lunches given on the fifth floor by old Camrose, who always asked twelve guests (under the new regime, numbers swelled to fifty or sixty). Camrose himself did not drink claret, but ordered some specially for Wortham, who claimed that the wine was not at room temperature. Next year Camrose instructed the butler – an old commissionaire who had been with him for twenty-five years – to 'warm it'. Wortham took one sip and said in a loud stage whisper to his neighbour, 'You know what they do with the claret here? They boil it'.

The family never forgot that. But they did not have to put up with Wortham for much longer. He retired early in 1959, already ill with cancer, and died that summer at the age of seventy-five, intestate, leaving £24,256. He had run Peterborough for twenty-five years, and gave the column a distinction which, many people feel, it has never achieved again. The sole recreation which he listed in *Who's Who* – 'anything highbrow' – had shone out agreeably in his work.

Another old-timer was Eric Stowell, the Assistant Editor in charge of news. By now his grip on reality was faltering, and this, combined with his staring blue eyes, caused him to be nicknamed Mad Stowell. A conversation recalled by Ronnie Payne illustrates the difficulty which young reporters found in communicating with him.

Stowell: 'Now, Payne: very good to see you. You've been doing a splendid job in Berlin.'

Payne: 'Actually, I've just come back from Suez.'

Stowell: 'Ah, yes. You did a splendid job in Suez. But you were in Berlin?'

Payne: 'That was for a week or two in the summer.'

Stowell: 'Ah, yes. And where are you living now?'

Payne: 'In Paris.'

Stowell: 'Oh, Paris! *I* know Paris. The river Wallis meanders through the middle of the city . . .'

He too stayed on past normal retiring age, but resigned through ill health in 1958, and died two years later at sixty-nine.

Coote, the Editor, who had either withheld his age from *Who's Who* or caused it to be withdrawn, was already well into his sixties, but showed no sign of retiring; he was still maddening his staff by his omniscience, and by his craven refusal to stand up for them when they got into trouble. It is impossible to say how many stories were lost through his claim to have heard them already, but the result of his infuriating habit was that many of his young Turks stopped telling him things. It also led to the celebrated incident of the Fall of the French Government.

One night when the French Government seemed likely to be defeated, Peregrine Worsthorne was required to write a leader on the political situation in Paris. Since no definite news of a vote had arrived by the time his article went to press for the first edition, he was forced to leave his conclusions open; but once the edition had gone, he set off for home and went to bed.

Some while later, his telephone rang. 'Small here,' said a voice. 'Night Editor of *The Daily Telegraph*. I thought you'd want to know the French Government's fallen.'

It was the last news Worsthorne wished to hear. But something had to be done. He rang Coote – also by then at home – and said, 'I hear the French Government's fallen.' Instantly Coote replied, 'I know. I'm dealing with it. You'd better rewrite your leader.'

Worsthorne began composing new phrases. Coote, meanwhile, rang the office and said, 'I hear the French Government's fallen.' The Night Editor, taken off-guard, reacted exactly as his boss had done, and said, 'That's right. We're just getting confirmation.' The moment he could, he rang John Wallis, the paper's chief correspondent in Paris. 'I hear the Government's gone, after all,' he said. Wallis, unable to admit that he, the man on the spot, had not heard so vital a piece of news, immediately agreed, and said that he was about to send details of the vote. In Fleet Street the front page was taken apart to make way for the new lead story and the leader-page was also brought back to take in the revised editorial.

But then, as Worsthorne struggled to complete a new draft, his telephone rang again; the caller once more announced himself as the Night Editor – but this time, in the background, Worsthorne heard drunken laughter, and suddenly he smelt a hoax. The voice was that of his friend Henry Fairlie, who, after dining well in Soho with John Raymond and Paul Johnson, had repaired to the latter's flat and decided to have some fun. Because, like all the best practical jokes, their ruse was psychologically acute, it very nearly came off. In the light of day, the concatenation of telephone calls and reactions seems absurd, but just before midnight, it caused chaos.

Coote was enraged, and saw to it that the paper severed relations with Fairlie, who at the time had been negotiating a contract to join it. But Coote was still more incensed when, years after his retirement, the story found its way into Atticus, the gossip column in the *Sunday Times*. He wrote the paper's Editor a huffy letter saying 'I did not, and could not have, told anybody to remake the front page', and claiming to remember no call from Worsthorne on the evening in question. But his denials rang hollow, and behind the scenes he leant heavily on Worsthorne to get some disclaimer printed. Worsthorne then rang Frank Giles, Editor of the *Sunday Times*, beseeching him to print a correction – which in due course he did.

The young men on the paper saw its curious structure in various ways. Ronnie Payne always liked to think of the *Telegraph* as 'a regiment with a rather sloppy colonel, who was absolutely fine on mess nights, and could talk to the officers, but never had anything to do with the troops'. To Colin Welch, it was 'like Wilhelmine Germany, with the supreme war lord doing one thing, and the Foreign Office signing a peace pact with whatever country the War Office was planning to invade the next day. And like the Kaiser, the supreme war lord of the *Telegraph* had far too much on his plate.'

Yet even Coote's most disgruntled critics had to admit that under his guidance – or at least under the guidance of Michael Berry – the circulation of the paper kept rising. Editorially, the 1950s were a decade of no mean success, and the year ending 31 March 1961 also proved exceptionally lucrative, with a profit after tax of £610,000.

At that stage the paper was in a very strong position, for its circulation was so much higher than that of its two main rivals, the *Times* and the *Guardian*, that it could afford to charge an extremely competitive rate for its advertising. Customers who placed advertisements in its columns reached far more high-class readers, at a far lower cost per reader, than in any other journal, and the advertisement department had not so much to solicit business as to turn it away. Yet in March 1955 there took place an event of evil omen – a strike by the electricians and maintenance men, in support of a demand for more pay – which brought all national newspapers to a standstill and kept them off the streets for almost a month. The shut-down exposed the risky position of the *Telegraph*, which, unlike many rivals, was not part of any group, and had no allied sources of income to sustain it through periods in which its own life-support of revenue from sales and advertising was cut off. The first Lord Camrose had felt so secure as not to need any back-up; but now, with the Fleet Street unions starting to flex themselves, his isolationist policy began to look dangerous.

There was not much that the management of the day could do to combat the strike. Nor did they ever make much headway with the area of land known as 'the Hole', at the back of 135 Fleet Street. The Hole was a bomb-site of half an acre, derelict since the war, directly north of (that is, behind) the *Telegraph*'s printing works. The paper had bought it in three different stages from the Goldsmiths' Company for a total of £35,000, with the idea of building a new printworks there; but the site was scarcely large enough, and difficult to develop, for the River Fleet ran right under it, and much work had to be done simply to keep the sides of the cavity shored up. Over the years several schemes were mooted, and at one stage piling for a new building began; but always difficulties or doubts supervened, and no new plant ever took shape. Eventually the firm sold the Hole for £1 million, and although they had nominally covered their outlay, they lost an asset of very high potential value.

In 1959 the Berrys sold off the magazine group Amalgamated Press, for which they received some £3 million, the proceeds being divided among thirteen members of the family. According to executives of the *Mirror* group, which bought it, the enterprise had been under-managed and allowed to run down. Cecil King, Chairman of the group, described old Camrose as 'greedy', and thought that he had taken too much out of the business; others felt that he had merely given it too little attention. Fortunately for the Berrys, King did not understand the business, and had had little experience of magazines. He asked for no accounts or forecasts, and so got none; but Michael could have told him that Amalgamated's leading titles were going to lose £1 million in the next year. In any event, it was a good moment for the Berrys to sell – even if it left Michael's branch of the family with only one newspaper asset. In 1947 his father had boasted that their eggs were in many baskets: now they were all in one.

The Sunday Telegraph

No. 1

STRIKE THREAT BY BEA PILOTS

Protest at Dismissal of Munich Crash Man

BALLOT FORMS GO OUT : REINSTATEMENT CALL

SUNDAY TELEGRAPH REPORTER

ON the eve of the third anniversary of the Munich air disaster British European Airways faces a threat of strike action by 750 pilots in protest against the treatment of Captain James Thain. He was commander of the Elizabethan airliner which crashed with the loss of 23 lives.

Ballot forms have gone out to B.E.A. pilots this week-end asking them if they are willing to stage a 24-hour strike. The result of the ballot will not be known for at least three weeks.

The action has been taken by the B.E.A. council of the British Airline Pilots Association. The Association is demanding that Captain Thain should either be reinstated in the Corporation or compensated, and that a new inquiry should be held into the accident.

If the pilots agree to come out in Captain Thain's support, it would be the first pilots' strike in the history of British civil aviation. It would cost B.E.A. at a conservative estimate, about a quarter-of-a-million pounds and cause the cancellation of about 400 flights.

The Elizabethan, carrying members of the Manchester United football team home from Belgrade, crashed on take-off at Munich on Feb. 6, 1958.

Capt. Thain was subsequently dismissed from BEA and his appeal was rejected in the end of last year. His airline pilot's licence is no longer valid.

Slush Warning

Matters have been brought to a head by a Ministry of Aviation circular after the danger of aircraft taking-off in slush. Capt. Thain blamed slush for the accident, but a German inquiry held that ice on the wings was to blame.

Capt. James O'Sullivan, chairman of the association, said: "We have tried negotiation but in vain. Our determination to see justice done is unshaken.

"So far in this association is concerned the accident inquiry is not complete, and while it is incomplete the association will never agree to Capt. Thain having to bear not only the wife blame and responsibility, but that he should be condemned is perpetuity.

"It is simply not good enough to say that steps have now been taken to warn pilots and operators of the dangers involved in take-offs and condemned runways.

British European Airways have for some time imposed slush take-off restrictions, although they have had their slight that the Ministry of Aviation recommendations on take-off action take-off distances restricted in slush can be disregarded at bonus ultra-conservative, in view of the corporation's operating experience.

Some pilots question this in view of their firm's ultra-conservative views in North America. In view of the corporation's restrictive interpretation of slush command and and Freeware airports. It was recently from Canada.

The Ministry's circular is based on calculations made by the American National Aeronautics and Space Administration. Practical research is about to be carried out in this country.

German Findings

The German commission of inquiry into the disaster reported that the twin-engined Elizabethan failed to get airborne because of ice on the wings. Capt. Thain maintained that slush on the runway prevented it from ever reaching unstick take-off speed.

A Ministry of Aviation inquiry found it could not rule out either slush or ice, or both, as the cause. British European Airways dismissed Capt. Thain for failing to ensure that the wings were free of ice and snow before a Wheeskfall.

The point about which he feels most bitter is that his airline pilot's licence has been allowed to lapse, through the BEA's refusal to give him any flying practice after the accident.

The man of practice is an individual is in general, profession and with the terrible onus of the accident, he has lost his means of livelihood.

Balance Tipped

The cause of the accident can never be proved conclusively. But the 1961, in the light of the technical data then available, the German inquiry tipped the balance against Capt. Thain.

Today it may be that it has tipped in his favour.

The recently-published Ministry circular does say of slush take-off: "It can be said that the deceleration

Continued on Back Page—Col. 3

Mr. Powell Heartens Back-Bench

HEALTH CHARGES SUPPORTED

BY OUR POLITICAL CORRESPONDENT

THE Government is assured of massive support from Conservative back - benchers when the Opposition launches its first major—and united—attack of this Parliament. The attack will be on the decision to increase health charges.

It will be fought on two days, Wednesday and Thursday. First it will be fought on the Opposition's censure motion, and then on the second reading of the Bill authorising the increases.

Mr. Enoch Powell, Minister of Health, will be in charge for the Government on both days. His handling of this, his first debate as a senior Minister, will be watched with interest.

Judging by his performance when he announced the increases last week, he will prove a formidable foe.

But his speech will not be wasted only for the quality of his handling of the controversy. It will be watched for signs he may give of his thinking on the future shape of the social services and role of the State in a prosperous society.

ADDING ANGER

The increased health charges, which Labour intends to fight bitterly on every stage, will add anger to the two-day debate on the economic situation coming tomorrow. But they are seen by Conservative back-benchers as the only way to hold taxation.

Mr. Selwyn Lloyd, the Chancellor of the Exchequer, will open the economic debate for the Government. His handling of the next few critical months could have a far-reaching effect on his standing in the Conservative party.

In some ways cross-currents of economic thinking are proving closer. Few Socialists now imagine the economy can be regulated in detail from Whitehall.

Among Conservatives there is a trend in favouring broad objectives, though much uncertainty about how it can be done in a democratic society.

A four-man deputation saw the Minister of Health at Westminster yesterday to protest against increased Health Service charges. The deputation consisted of Labour and trade union leaders, and included a local Communist party organiser.

THE SUNDAY TELEGRAPH AND ITS AIMS

TODAY appears the first new national Sunday paper for 40 years.

It is not its aim to improve upon some other paper. Instead it is being started in the belief that for educated people there is a sizeable gap in Sunday reading.

THE SUNDAY TELEGRAPH hopes to fill that gap.

On one side are two serious and voluminous newspapers whose emphasis is on magazine features; on the other are a larger number which in varying degree tend towards triviality and sensationalism.

THE SUNDAY TELEGRAPH will not neglect the wider range of reading for which the public has time at the week-end. While deliberately restricting its paging to a manageable size, it will also give a larger proportion of its space than other Sundays to succinct reporting and explanation of news, home and foreign.

To readers from one side of the gap THE SUNDAY TELEGRAPH will represent "the paper you can finish," and, to those from the other side, it will strive to be "the paper that will satisfy."

READERS of THE DAILY TELEGRAPH will find the format of the Sunday not unfamiliar. To provide a wide variety on Page One, news is carried over where necessary to the back. The rest of the news is larger in the centre spread and is continued in consecutive pages. All the main articles are brought together in the front of the paper while sport and classified advertising are moved to the end.

THE SUNDAY TELEGRAPH, however, is not merely the seventh day edition of THE DAILY TELEGRAPH. In a newspaper designed for Sunday a different emphasis is appropriate. A more detailed image of the new paper is contained in a "Letter from the Editor," on Page 8.

Rhodesian 'Show-Down' Warning at Chequers

By WALTER FARR
Sunday Telegraph Commonwealth Correspondent

SPECIAL ENVOYS went to London by Sir Roy Welensky are to issue a warning in talks yesterday that the situation in the Rhodesian Federation is nearing a "show-down point." A head-on clash between the Federal and State Governments can, they insist, be avoided only by drastic reductions of the concessions Britain proposes for Northern Rhodesian Africans.

It now appears to be touch-and-go whether the Federation can be saved in its present form. In addition to talks at Chequers there were discussions by Mr. Sandys, Commonwealth Relations Secretary, now in Salisbury, and Mr. Alport, Commonwealth Relations Minister.

Mr. Sandys, who was to remain in Salisbury for 10 days negotiating a new Southern Rhodesia constitution a firing squad, came to London early this week. He is presumably changing his plans because of the deadlock.

Sir Roy's envoys are Mr. Julian Greenfield, the Federal Minister of Law and one of the most powerful figures in the United Federal Party, who arrived in London last week, and Mr. "Taffy" Evans, one of Sir Roy's ablest negotiators.

Mr. Evans arrived in London yesterday. He was travelling incognito. He refused to answer any reporters' questions on arriving his visit.

Sir Roy's decision to send him is authoritatively stated to be a clear indication that Sir Roy feels

Continued on Back Page, Col. 4

LAST-MATCH DEFEAT FOR SPRINGBOKS

FROM OUR OWN SPORTS REPORTER

THE mighty Rugby Union men of South Africa will not return home unbeaten. For yesterday they met their final defeat at the very end of the 34-match tour of Britain.

Their conquerors were the Barbarians, a team of first-party selected players who each year thank the South Africans' ideal opponents. They won by 6 points to nil.

Thus yesterday the Springboks came from Doctor Maranga and Ngubo Mtanga, and lost at Twickenham to Cardiff. At the finish, Keith Oxlee, the South African fly half, dropped a goal.

But who can deny the South Africans' first-class record? They won 28 of the 34 matches, scoring a total of 476 points against a team 110.

Michael Melford—P.16

HANGING INQUIRY NOT LIKELY

By OUR POLITICAL CORRESPONDENT

A call for an inquiry on the Homicide Act, 1957, and the death penalty's value in protecting points is unlikely to be favoured by the Government, in motion tabled by Mr. E. Gardner, Q.C. (Billericay) and supported by 16 other Conservative M.P.s, makes the call.

No decision has yet been made. But the initial reaction is that the Act has not yet had time to be fully tested. Mr. Butler, Home Secretary, originally sustained a five-year trial period.

Editorial Comment—P.14

LATE NEWS

WEST INDIES BASES PACT EXPECTED

PORT OF SPAIN, TRINIDAD, Saturday.—An agreement whereby West Indies bases, leased to America in 1940, would be integrated into the United States defence plan is expected to be signed here Monday, was a qualified driver. They need an agreement service to lease.

LONDON PLAN OPPOSED

A special conference of London Labour Party decided yesterday to oppose the creation of a Council for Greater London, recommended by the Royal Commission. The area and functions of population and valuable value were held to be too large and unwieldy for the administration of local self-government.

GIRL'S CLOTHES ABLAZE

5-year-old Frances H. L. sq. toss from her clothing after Wolverhampton. Yesterday. She was playing with another child when her clothing afflame on a room heater. She was taken to hospital, where her condition is critical.

Phone Plan for Football Results

SAME PRINCIPLE AS TEST SCORES

Sunday Telegraph Reporter

Mr. Bevins, the Postmaster-General, is considering a telephone service for giving Saturday football results. He told me that this was one of a range of information services he was studying with the aim of getting private subscribers to use their telephones more.

At present they make no average one call a day. The Post Office is spending an investigation made in Europe and the United States to find out what can be done to increase this average.

Mr. Bevins believes also that informative services can be sold in businessmen. Stock Exchange and wool prices could be given.

TIME SHARE

The months-old current work on the same principle as dialling UMP for Test Match scores or WEA for weather. One snag yet to be overcome is that computer results could vary several minutes, the duration of the new local fixed-time deals.

A whirring might be found in the suggested introduction of 12-minute local fixtures could be cut into 6 a.m. on Mondays. This 12-minute call suggestion was met with protest that the Post Office has meant that local operators were overloaded.

CAPITAL NEED

There is definite hope that the Post Office will get more money to expand services. Current investment is above £96m, and next year it will be about £96m. Mr. Bevins said that a subsidy would mean an extra £16m, spared a year over the next year in an effort to catch up his expansion programme.

The Post Office, he said, was financing 73 per cent. of its capital out of its own resources. This was a better record than any nationalised industry.

No Revolution

OUR SCIENCE CORRESPONDENT writes: The weight of the latest satellite, 6½ tons or more than 15,000lb., does not imply any revolutionary advance in Russian rocketry. During the last three years the payloads of both American and Russian rockets have been increasing at a steady rate.

The Americans appear to be far-sweep one and two years behind the Russians. Their Saturn rocket, due for testing in 1961, will lift 1½ tons. The "Nova," for lunar voyages, aimed at 1964, will lift 200,000lb.

RUSSIA PUTS 6½-TON SPUTNIK IN ORBIT

Heaviest Space Vehicle Yet Launched

By DEREK WOOD
Sunday Telegraph Defence Correspondent

A 6¼-ton earth satellite was successfully put into orbit by Russia yesterday. This is the largest vehicle so far launched into space, and represent considerable technical achievement.

The previous largest satellite weighed nearly five tons, and was also launched by Russia. This is the ninth successful Russian space shot.

The new satellite is stated to have a rate of revolution round the earth of 89 min. 48 sec. Its top point of orbit is 203½ miles and its lowest point of orbit 118.8 miles. An "improved multi-stage rocket" is stated to have been used.

Prolonged Trials

It is probable that this latest satellite has been the subject of prolonged trials. At the time of President Kennedy's inauguration it was reported that a special launching would be made in Russia.

This earlier satellite means that a series of tests are now sufficiently advanced to enable the forseeable future of maintaining weapon-equipped satellites in space.

TAKEN TO CELLS

Attackers were taken to pavilion-neon cells to be dealt with by the Governor today. Thus the lights struck down and the film unbroken.

One of the warders, Edward Dunford, 32, of Tower Street, Edmonton, was treated in the Royal Northern Hospital for injuries to his jaw and right thumb, and three other officers were given first aid.

---

4 WARDERS HURT IN GAOL SCUFFLE

SUNDAY TELEGRAPH REPORTER

A PRISONER was attacked twice and four warders were injured as they went to his rescue in the chapel of Pentonville prison, last night. About 500 prisoners were watching a religious film, "The Tin Star."

Pairs and feet started flying. Lights were up and the alarm bell sounded. Four warders from other parts of the prison.

After someone had attacked the prisoner in the dock was pulled away, and from among 500 inmates in close the same prisoner. Other prisoners stood and watched.

Mr. Zarb Likely to be Freed this Week

FROM OUR OWN CORRESPONDENT
CAIRO, Saturday.

MR. JAMES ZARB is likely to be released within a few days. He is expected to be out on prison before next weekend.

The official reason given by the Cairo journal paper of Ahram is obviously localised story is the United Arab Republic's view appreciation for the part played by Professor Arnold Toynbee, the British historian, in a public debate in Montreal this week between Mr. Yusnee Herbez Israeli Ambassador to Canada.

Al Ahram says that one British news had found the courage to speak righteous words about Israel. Mr. Zarb, 42, a Maltese-born businessman was sentenced to 1956 on spy charges. Mr. James Swinburn, another Briton imprisoned at the same time, was released on 1959 after serving half his five-year term.

---

14 KILLED AS AFRICAN MOB FIGHT POLICE

FROM A SPECIAL CORRESPONDENT
LUANDA, Saturday

AT least 14 people, including 7 seven Portuguese policemen, were killed when 300 Africans armed with knives attacked a police station on the outskirts of Luanda, Angola, early today. Numbers of wounded have been taken to hospital, where armed patrol are on guard.

Other armed groups attacked civil and military prisons in the town. Dozens of arrests have been made.

In Lisbon, a Government communiqué said the Government of Angola had received reports from abroad that a was planned to upset public order in Angola," coinciding with an assault on the later Santa Maria. Photographers and correspondents who wanted the scene this morning were held for 45 hours.

In particular, the key to and safe deal would, it is believed, have to be the concession for the News of the World of Odhams' new shop.

OFFER EXPECTED SOON

The next development in the struggle is likely to be the dispatch to the Odhams board—and almost simultaneously to shareholders—of the Daily Mirror's formal offer. This is expected within the next few days.

It will obviously depend whether or not the Prime Minister this week decides to grant the Odhams request for an inquiry into newspaper and magazine ownership. Indeed, it is believed to have been held up till now only because the Prime Minister is considering whether to institute a full list of Odhams' shareholders.

Details—P.2

TRAIN KILLS TWO ON CROSSING

A woman hay-cart driver and a coal of 14 were killed when their van was ripped in two by a 60 mph express train on a level crossing at Moorends, near Doncaster, yesterday. Points were trying to find a driver of three of High Hazel Road, Moorends, was an car-maker.

Her companion, Terry Lewis, of Grange Road, Moorends, was a qualified driver. They need deliveries service to farms.

Daily Herald May go to News of the World

By Our City Editor

THE News of the World group is most now be considered a possible eventual owner of the Labour-controlled Daily Herald and the People. So far no counter bidder to the Daily Mirror in the battle for Odhams Press has yet emerged, nor seems likely to do so.

However, intimate to Sir Jeremy WY William Carr, chairman of the News of the World, and Mr. Cecil King of the Daily Mirror suggested a deal between their two shareholdings may now be possible. This could involve the purchase from the Daily Mirror of the Odhams empire once the Daily Mirror bid is successful.

Bus Ambush: Police See Three Men

FROM OUR OWN CORRESPONDENT

Three men were at Wimbledon police station yesterday helping police with their inquiries into the murder of a London bus conductor, Mr. George Beckett, who was found battered to death in a gully on Thursday.

Two of the three were in a van which was stopped by Fitting Squad cars in Camberwell Green and Camberwell. One of these men later was a detained for further inquiries, was taken from the Peckham area.

The body of the bus conductor was taken from a 93-bus near fares box which was almost certainly empty. All the coins were in the coach itself when the body was found.

Eichmann is Charged

From Our Own Correspondent
HAIFA, Saturday

ADOLF EICHMANN, who ordered by Hitler to find a final solution to the Jewish question, has just seen for the first time the charges accusing him of taking part in the extermination of millions of Jews.

This marks the beginning of what will be one of the legal battles of the century.

Eichmann faces the death penalty, which applies in Israel for crimes under the law for the mass murder of Nazis and for collaborators.

See Back Page—P.4

1,400 Deaths in Flu Epidemic

Sunday Telegraph Reporter

Influenza deaths in Britain in January totalled 1,453, and it is feared the total will grow for another week or so. In the last bad epidemic in February, 1959, deaths in four weeks were 1,292.

A Ministry of Health official yesterday thought that the differences between the January death rate and the epidemic's were "encouraging, but, he added cautiously "it is too early to make predictions."

BRITONS ESCAPE AVALANCHE TRAP

From Our Own Correspondent
VIENNA, Saturday

After being cut off for more than 24 hours British tourists today made their way to the canyon of Zuers and Lech on the Arlberg. An avalanche had blocked the only road through the resorts with the main railway lines.

About 3,000 British, French and German visitors were stranded there. Both Zuers and the town of Lech said that each had been cleared through the main railway village to open during the day. At Zuers, some avalanche danger had, at the night, the road was still closed owing to avalanche danger.

SIR PHILIP GAME

The death of Sir Philip Game, former Commissioner of Metropolitan Police and an Air Vice-Marshal at his home in Sevenoaks, Kent, was announced last night. He was 84.

Earl of Longford

The sixth Earl of Longford died in Dublin yesterday, aged 78. He is succeeded by his brother, Lord Pakenham.

Anna May Wong

Anna May Wong, the Chinese film star, has died of a heart attack at her home in Santa Monica, California. She was 54.

Obituaries—P.14

RUSSIA AGREES TO DELAY TEST TALKS

WASHINGTON, Saturday

The State Department announced that Russia has agreed to resume the Geneva conference on the banning of nuclear tests on March 21. This will give the new American Administration time to review its policy.

Cold Comfort

"Such action is cold comfort indeed to a man who has suffered and is suffering the loss of his inquiry, where the knowledge gene which the findings were based was inconclusive."

Capt. Thain fought to clear his name, and his wife, a trained chemist and physicist, carried out a series of experiments to help prove that ice could not have caused the crash. Her evidence was given to the Ministry inquiry which followed the German investigation. But a last-minute snag prevented the installed special equipment for clearing slush at both London and Preswick airports. It was south from Canada.

Labour Official expelled

Sunday Telegraph Reporter

Because he persistently criticised Capt. I. R. Maxwell, prospective Labour candidate for Buckingham, Mr. Ray Ballchambers, of Old Bradwell, has been excelled from the general management committee of Buckingham Labour Party.

He has been fall-time agent and president of the Party, and was on the executive of the branch at the last election, when Capt. Maxwell was chosen. "I am appealing to the National Executive of the Labour Party," he said yesterday.

Capt. Maxwell's utterance as candidate at the last general election has been criticised by a section of the National Executive of the Labour Party and the local party, as he had been a party member for less than a year.

It was also complained locally that he and his close supporters concealed that he was Czech-born.

OTHER PAGES

---

8 THE SUNDAY TELEGRAPH, 1961–70

At about 7.00 pm on the evening of 10 May 1959 Michael Berry got a severe shock. One of his cousins rang to tell him that his uncle, Lord Kemsley, had sold his newspaper empire to the Canadian magnate Roy Thomson, who had made a fortune from Scottish Television. Michael immediately asked if he could buy the *Sunday Times*, but the answer was, no, it had gone with the package. Neither he, the cousin, nor any of his brothers (Kemsley's sons) had known anything about the deal until it had gone through.* Michael was both astonished and hurt. The *Sunday Times* was still being printed on the *Telegraph* presses, and ever since 1937, when Camrose and Kemsley split their businesses, it had been clearly understood that neither would sell any paper without first offering it to the other. The obverse of this unwritten agreement had been that, so long as Kemsley owned the *Sunday Times*, Michael Berry would not start up a paper to compete with it.

Unwelcome though the news was, it at least cleared the way for a project which Michael had long cherished: to start a Sunday paper of his own. At once he began to think in more detail about a Sunday edition of the *Telegraph*. For a while he made no contact with Thomson, whom he did not know: but Fred Burnham, who was still Managing Director of the *Telegraph*, kept seeing the Canadian at dinners in the City, and Thomson kept saying how much he would like to meet Michael Berry. When this happened for the third time, Michael thought he had better take the initiative, so he rang Thomson and said: 'As the younger man, I'll come and see you.'

Both expected the call to be a purely social one; but the meeting

---

* Camrose had always said, only half in jest, that his brother never could resist a deal; but Kemsley seems to have been disconcerted by the after-effects of this one. 'It's the most extraordinary thing,' he said ingenuously, 'but since I sold the *Sunday Times*, nobody asks me out to dinner any more!'

– between a shy, abrupt Englishman and a Canadian with no small talk – was not at all relaxed, and soon developed into a ponderous game of one-upmanship. Thomson had failed to realise that Berry was not pleased with the way his uncle had sold out, and after a few stilted pleasantries crashed in with: 'I want to do a forty-eight-page *Sunday Times*, but I understand you can't print more than forty pages for us. Is that right?' Michael agreed, but said that it might be possible to install new machinery, even if it took some time. He added that he knew nothing about machinery – to which Thomson replied, 'Neither do I'. Thomson suggested that, rather than suffer a long delay, Berry might like to move the whole of the *Telegraph*, editorial as well as mechanical, up to the *Sunday Times* building in Gray's Inn Road, which Kemsley had begun but left incomplete. Berry would make a lot of money, Thomson said, by selling or leasing 135 Fleet Street. Michael said he would consult his brother about this, though he did not favour the idea of moving.

Thomson then asked if he could buy *The Daily Telegraph*. Michael said, 'No.'

'I'd give you a very good price for it,' said the Canadian. Again Michael refused.

'I'd give you a very good price *indeed*,' Thomson insisted – whereupon Michael hit back with, 'Would *you* sell the *Sunday Times*?'

'No,' said Thomson. 'It's a matter of prestige.'

As the meeting ended, Thomson left Berry with his theory of newspapers: 'There's no future in Fleet Street for a house without a daily, an evening and a Sunday.'

Afterwards Thomson was afraid he had offended Berry by his direct approach. (As he said, he always asked people if they would sell him their businesses, as a matter of course.) He thought that his visitor 'appeared to flush and cut short the interview' when asked if the *Telegraph* was for sale. Michael, in fact, was not at all put out; but the effect of the meeting was to steel his resolve to go ahead with a Sunday paper of his own. Since he had gained the impression that Thomson meant to withdraw the *Sunday Times* from the printing contract anyway, he decided to take the initiative himself. He therefore asked H. J. C. Stevens, the Company Secretary, to look out the contract and see what notice the *Telegraph* was obliged to give. Stevens's answer was 'Six months'; so, in the middle of December, he wrote to the *Sunday Times* terminating the contract immediately, and asking them to be out by the following June.

He was surprised to receive no reply. After a few days he got someone to telephone and make sure that the letter had arrived. It had. But for once Stevens had made a mistake: he had not realised that to the original printing agreement, made in 1931, there had been added in 1937 a supplementary one, extending the period of notice from six months to a year. The *Sunday Times had* realised this, and were playing for time in which to organise new printing arrangements. Thomson, by then in Canada, told his executives merely to acknowledge the *Telegraph*'s letters, saying that he would deal with them on his return. When he did answer, in January, Michael Berry, in turn, had begun to use delaying tactics, for although he wanted his new Sunday paper to roll as soon as the presses were free, he did not want to start it in January, the worst time of the winter for sales. With a launch date of 5 February 1961 in mind, he finally gave Thomson twelve months' notice on 25 January 1960, which meant that the last edition of the *Sunday Times* which could be printed at 135 Fleet Street would be that of 22 January 1961, and that there would be one spare Saturday – 28 January – for a trial run of the new paper.

Berry's motive in launching a Sunday paper was mainly commercial; even though the termination of the printing contract would cost him some £3,000 a week, he reckoned he could break even if he established *The Sunday Telegraph* with a circulation of 500,000. His initiative was by any standards a bold one, for in the second half of 1960 the *Sunday Times* had achieved a sale of just over 1,000,000 copies, the *Observer* was selling 738,000 copies a week, and the *Sunday Graphic* had been closed down with a circulation of 1,089,000. Yet financial considerations were not Berry's only ones: there was also the fact that a log-jam of able staff had built up on *The Daily Telegraph*, and it would be good for everyone's morale to have a fresh field in which to exercise their talents. Thus many of the senior staff on the new paper were *Daily Telegraph* men. With the birth of an infant imminent, each journal became known within the building by the short version of its full name – 'the Daily' and 'the Sunday'; and for the Sunday, Michael Berry created a structure that mirrored that of *The Daily Telegraph*. The Editor was in charge of the opinion pages, the arts and so on, and the Managing Editor had control of the all-important news. Each would report to him separately, just as their counterparts did on the Daily.

The Sunday's first Editor was Donald McLachlan, then fifty-one, who for the past five years had been deputy to Coote. A slim, angular man, with large spectacles, a pointed chin and a high forehead, and something bird-like about the forward crane of his head, he looked the don he was. His career had encompassed an unusual combination of journalism and teaching (he once remarked to his secretary Mary Cobban that in academia he was thought of as a journalist, whereas in Fleet Street he was regarded as an academic).

McLachlan's origins were modest. His parents, both from the East End of London, met in the course of their work at the Charing Cross Hotel, where his father was assistant manager, his mother assistant cashier. He was born with a squint, and after an operation at the age of fifteen, although his eyes appeared to be straight, he still saw double through one of them. From the City of London School he won a demy-scholarship to Magdalen College, Oxford, and there got a First in PPE. With that under his belt, he went as a temporary master to Winchester, where he was confirmed as a permanent teacher after only one half (or term). He then won a Laming fellowship, which enabled him to travel and work in Europe. After visits to Paris, Strasbourg and Geneva, he arrived in Berlin early in 1933, just as Hitler came to power, and worked with the *Times* correspondent, Norman Ebbutt, who was often ill. His experience there left him with excellent command of German, and a vivid idea of the menace of Fascism.

Back in England, he went to the *Times* to write leaders, but, finding that dull, in 1935 he returned to Winchester where he made an impact which many boys never forgot. The historian M. R. D. Foot, for instance, was taught by him in 1935 and 1936, during Mussolini's conquest of Ethiopia and the start of the Spanish Civil War. Nearly fifty years later he recalled how McLachlan had 'burst in on our settled English ideas with accounts of Poland and Germany under dictatorship and made us start wondering for the first time what systems of Government were . . . It was he who gave me an intellectual stimulus, a curiosity to know, that has enlivened and informed my life ever since.'

Foot recalled how, in a school with strong religious traditions, McLachlan stood out as 'a devout agnostic', and how, although divinity was a compulsory subject, he taught moral theory instead of theology. In all subjects 'his inquiring spirit seemed to place him well to the left of centre'.

For the two years 1938–40 he combined both his skills in one job by editing the *Times Educational Supplement*. Then for the war years he went into Naval Intelligence, emerging to become Foreign Editor of the *Economist* – from which, as already related, Coote recruited him in 1954.

As an editor, McLachlan's greatest asset was his ability to throw out ideas. He was always bursting with ideas, constantly scribbling them on tiny scraps of paper; and although many were crazy, most people agreed that the brilliant ones made the irritation caused by pursuing the duds worthwhile. (One of his maddest and most typical ideas – though nothing to do with journalism – occurred to him in 1940, when the country was threatened with invasion, and he was worried about how he and his wife Kitty would feed their three young children. If they were going to be hungry, he said, would it not be a good thing to get them in training, by going without a meal now and then? To which Kitty replied sharply that it would be time enough when food actually ran short.)

Another admirable trait was his eagerness to help young people, and his evident pleasure when they succeeded. He also defended colleagues strongly when they were threatened by libel actions or other pressures – in marked contrast with Coote. He was lively, energetic, a great encourager – and often splendidly naïve. 'Don't worry about the facts!' he cried when he found a young man struggling to collect information for a leader-page article about morale in the Brigade of Guards. 'Think of a headline, and write to that' – and he once boasted to a colleague that he himself had just written an 850-word article without a single fact in it. Once, however, his habit of writing to a headline landed him in trouble. At the last moment it was found that the chosen line would not fit into the space available. Because of the nature of the whole operation, the wording could not be changed. To reduce the type by one whole size was not acceptable, since it would have left the line looking weak. The only solution was to set the headline as originally planned, and reduce it photographically just enough for it to be squeezed in: a laborious and time-consuming process. When the feat was eventually accomplished, McLachlan was thrilled.

Another time he rang Ion Trewin, a young feature-reporter, at six o'clock in the morning and told him to proceed at once to Oxford, where he was to interview Norman Chester, a don at Nuffield College. Trewin, though startled, did as instructed, only to find that Chester was ill. Eventually, to the mutual embarrassment of journalist and subject, Trewin interviewed Chester in bed – but when he returned to London, he found that McLachlan had forgotten why he had sent him, and the piece was spiked. Wary of this kind of nonsense, staff-men on *The Sunday Telegraph* learnt to ignore requests from the Editor unless they were repeated: 'Only act if he asks twice' became the motto of the wise.

On yet another occasion, when the paper was young, he went ranging along the corridors, as usual, and burst into the office of the Literary Editor, Anthony Curtis, to find him and his two colleagues drinking champagne. 'Good heavens!' McLachlan exclaimed. 'Champagne at eleven in the morning?' 'Of course,' they said. 'Always! Do have a glass.' He looked astonished, but had one, and went on his way faintly scandalised by such apparent extravagance – nobody having let on that the bottle was merely a sample, and that the wine was being tested for possible use at a party.

No administrator, McLachlan would thoughtlessly keep a Cabinet Minister waiting in the anteroom while, as one colleague put it, 'he had a long, ruminative talk with the paper's cycling correspondent, or even with the man who went round the building delivering the evening papers'. One Tuesday morning, annoyed to find nobody in Peregrine Worsthorne's office, he left a note saying 'Why this desk unmanned, 11.15? DHMcL'. Returning half an hour later, he testily crossed out the '11.15' and added '11.45'. Returning yet again, in still greater irritation, he crossed out '11.45' and substituted '12.15'. What he forgot was that, the Friday before, he himself had despatched Worsthorne on a fortnight's tour of South Africa.

Also from the Daily, as Managing Editor, came Brian Roberts, described by McLachlan as 'a dark, fierce little Welshman', but known to all, on account of his decrepitude, as 'Scruffy'. The most striking thing about Roberts was his temper. Michael Berry thought him 'peppery'; others reckoned him downright rude. (The first time Berry saw Roberts, he mistook him for an office boy, so insignificant was his appearance; but, as the proprietor wryly remarked, he very soon discovered his mistake.) For thirteen years Roberts had been an irascible and domineering (but highly effective) Night Editor of the Daily, always liable to throw tantrums, scream abuse, snap pencils, stamp about and even burst into tears of vexation, but able at the same time to take difficult decisions instantaneously and drive production of the paper forward through the night. Sympathetic colleagues saw his outbursts as a form of release, an expression of his own perfectionism; more critical observers, while respecting his professionalism, thought him a menace, in that, although at moments of crisis he kept his own head, his antics made other people lose theirs. This had happened one night in November 1956, when three major news stories – the invasion of Suez, the Hungarian uprising and the US Presidential election – were all running simultaneously. Roberts's judgement and decisions had been first-class, but his extravagant behaviour drove half the sub-editors to distraction.

Now his experience and efficiency were harnessed to the task of creating a news team for the Sunday. With him, as News Editor, and in effect his deputy, came George Evans, who in the past ten years had covered many thousands of miles as roving reporter and diplomatic correspondent for the Daily. Another Daily man was Ralph Thackeray, known to all as 'Thack', a dour and laconic Lancastrian, who became Features Editor.

McLachlan was most annoyed to hear that Coote had offered the Deputy Editorship of the Sunday to Peregrine Worsthorne, one of the Daily leader-writers. Coote had no right to do this, as McLachlan soon made clear: instead, hearing that what Worsthorne wanted was to establish himself as a pundit, he appointed him to the nominal position of Assistant Editor, on the understanding that his real job would be to write a signed political column, which would appear on the leader-page.

As the team assembled and began to shake down, towards the end of 1960, arguments raged in all directions about what the contents of the new paper should be. Michael Berry himself had a very clear idea, which he outlined in a memorandum to McLachlan. The emphasis of the other serious Sundays, he wrote, was on well-written magazine features. A paper which concentrated on news should make an immediate impact, and the *Telegraph*, with its large news-gathering organisation at home and abroad, was particularly well placed to do this. Much, he thought, would depend on the degree of success achieved during the first three months.

McLachlan embraced his ideas enthusiastically, but he and Roberts fought like tigers over how precious space was to be divided between features and news. One item of which both McLachlan and Berry had high hopes was 'To the Point' – an assembly of very short leaders, each not much more than a hundred words long, which would head the opinion page, and (they hoped) attract more attention than the long-winded tracts run by the *Sunday Times* and *Observer*. The idea was to sum up matters of the day in a few, memorable, epigrammatic sentences. McLachlan canvassed almost every member of the editorial staff with his concept: 'Imagine, at dinner, you are sitting next to Lady Bloggs, and she turns to you and says, "Oh, Mr Hart-Davis – *do* tell me what you think of the Budget" (or Rhodesia, or the moonshot, or whatever was in the news). You turn to her, and in a few brilliantly-polished phrases encapsulate all that needs to be said on the subject.' Like many of McLachlan's ideas, this one sounded good at first – and everybody was exhorted to submit Points for publication; but since the extra payment offered was derisory, and most of the paragraphs offered were never used anyway, enthusiasm soon waned. Besides, the fallacy underlying the whole operation quickly became apparent – that leaders as short as those tended to be not so much memorable as jejune. Irreverent calls were soon heard for the column to be re-named 'Beside the Point'.

Another feature in which McLachlan took a close interest was the new gossip column, to be called 'Week by Week' and written by Kenneth Rose, who had moved across from Peterborough. Everyone agreed that a column was wanted, but the dispute about the pseudonym with which it should be signed was protracted, and not settled until a few days before publication. In a confidential memorandum to Michael Berry, Rose wrote:

> I have given much thought to a pen-name for the new feature . . . Here are some possibilities which I have rejected:
>
> Ajax; Apollo; Ariel (a rebel angel); Cerberus (all the secrets of the Underworld, but a dog); Clio (Addison used it in the original *Spectator*); Coningsby; Creevey; Ivanhoe . . . Crispin, with its flavour of Henry V, is a possibility, though there seems no apparent connection between the new paper and the Patron Saint of shoemaking . . .
>
> ALBANY is my best suggestion. It has the following points in its favour: 1. It is euphonious and easy to pronounce. 2. It has associations with London – and that part of London which is reputed to house the civilised and well-informed. If necessary, I am prepared to go and live in Albany.

McLachlan was not impressed, and in a note of 20 December 1960, wrote, 'If Albany falls by the way, there is a remarkable character in Boswell, Monboddo. He has views on everything, as you will have.' McLachlan and Roberts joined forces to hold out for Peter Pindar, the pen name of an obscure eighteenth-century writer. Not until 3 January 1961 was agreement reached. Then, in a note which would have seemed deliberately insulting from someone less casual in his dealings with staff, McLachlan told Rose that 'Albany' had been approved '*faute de mieux*'. Yet still not everyone was satisfied. On 26 January McLachlan sent for Rose, who to his surprise found that the latest objector was Lord Burnham. What about the present Duke of Albany? Burnham asked. Would he not be annoyed if his title was used? Rose pointed out that the man in question was German, and that the peerage had been suspended since the end of the First World War. Would not the signature

'Albany' be taken for that of the Duke? No, said Rose: he signed himself by his Christian name. What had Albany to do with Fleet Street? asked Burnham. It was a hive of informed gossip. What about the brand of cigarettes called Albany? What, countered Rose, about John Lawrence, the racing correspondent, being known as Marlborough? At last the Managing Director seemed satisfied, and Albany won the day.

As these preliminary editorial skirmishes continued, the circulation department mounted an extensive publicity campaign based on the slogan 'Filling the Gap'. *The Sunday Telegraph* fills the gap' shouted the posters – the gap being that perceived to exist between the two heavies, the *Sunday Times* and *Observer*, at the top of the market, and lightweights such as the *Sunday Express* lower down. On the daily front, the *Telegraph* had brilliantly exploited the gap between the *Times* (then selling 280,000 copies a day) and the *Guardian* (212,000) at the top, and mass-market rabble at the bottom: why should the same trick not be pulled on Sundays? McLachlan himself, writing of the concept, said that he 'hoped to win hundreds of thousands of readers straight away from popular rivals by offering a serious newspaper in attractive, readable, lively form'. Further, it was 'the calculation at 135 Fleet Street that the economic and social revolution in Britain has gone much further and deeper than most people realise. *The Sunday Telegraph* hopes to reveal the existence of a broad, serious readership in the new middle class that has not yet been tapped.'

Hopes were one thing, performance another. The planning of the new paper was grossly amateurish. Only one dummy issue was prepared, and the production of that devolved into chaos, with Roberts yelling abuse in the composing-room until ten at night, and then throwing in his hand – the only time colleagues had ever known him to do so. Had it been a real paper, very few copies of it could have been printed, for the first-edition time was hopelessly overrun. Almost worse was the new baby's appearance. So steeped were its staff in the traditions (and limitations) of the Daily that all they were able to create was a rather poor copy of the original, with cramped typography and tiny illustrations – anything but the attractive production which the Editor had been touting.

For the moment, however, its deficiencies were concealed from the public. Both inside and outside Fleet Street, excitement mounted over the launch of the first new Sunday newspaper for forty years. (Simultaneously, in a less-publicised but no-less-frantic scramble, the *Sunday Times* had whisked its staff and equipment out of 135

Fleet Street and was struggling to set up presses of its own in Gray's Inn Road – a feat which it managed with only hours to spare.)

With two days to go, Coote wrote McLachlan a generous note:

I send you and your team the most heartfelt good wishes on the eve of *Der Tag*, or, as it is sure to be, *le jour de gloire*. So far as I know, the Daily has grudged nothing to the new baby either materially or morally; and if, after the birth, you feel there is anything more we can do, please say so at once. Again, warmest and most confident salutations.

Yours ever, CRC

On the night of 4 February 1961 both the main television channels – BBC and ITV – included sequences showing production of the first number in their news bulletins. Mercifully, the chaos was less severe than that of the previous week, and 1,400,000 copies were printed. On 5 February 1961 *The Sunday Telegraph* was born.

Its appearance was disastrous. There was no picture at the top of the front page, and readers were dismayed by the dense thickets of type. Even with such mean space given to headlines or illustrations, there seemed very little to read, for the twenty-eight-page paper was packed with advertisements. The whole publicity campaign, on which thousands of pounds had been expended, was shot to pieces by one brilliant observation in next morning's *Guardian*. The only gap which *The Sunday Telegraph* appeared to fill, wrote the author of its London Letter, 'was that between Saturday's *Daily Telegraph* and Monday's'.

This was all too true, even down to the fact that the page order of the Daily had been replicated exactly, so that everyone should feel at home. Readers soon began to demonstrate that six consecutive days of the Daily were all that the human frame could stand. After a couple of months, as the curiosity value of the Sunday wore off, its sale fell away to 650,000 – scarcely more than half that of its parent. Michael Berry himself later admitted that he found this disappointing. Perhaps he had set his sights too high in the early days: after the first month, even with all returns deducted, the net sale had averaged a million, and there seemed a good chance that it would settle at 850,000 or (at worst) 800,000, certainly above that of the *Observer* at 715,000. This was the main ambition – to beat the *Observer*. So when sales dropped below that crucial point, the feeling of let-down was severe.

By no means everyone found the first issues disappointing. 'I thought you might like to hear the Prime Minister's views on the ST,' wrote Harry Boyne, Political Correspondent of the Daily, to Brian Roberts on 1 March. 'He likes it very much and particularly because it keeps pretty well to the DT format ... Although he didn't actually say so, I got the impression that it has already become his favourite Sunday.' Another old professional – Lord Beaverbrook – thought equally well of the newcomer. 'I send you a letter of warm congratulations on your success with *The Sunday Telegraph*,' he wrote to Berry on 13 March. 'Yesterday's issue was a first-rate production. And I particularly admire the vigour and strength of the leader column. Altogether you are well on the way to establishing another Sunday newspaper.'

Later Berry felt that many mistakes had been made – not least (*pace* Macmillan) in giving the new paper an appearance so like that of the old. 'Where we went wrong was in thinking that people would like an American idea – the seventh-day *Daily Telegraph*. We started off believing that news was paramount, but of course there often isn't any news at the weekend. If you look at a tape from one of the news agencies on a Saturday morning, you see there's nothing at all. That's why you're always praying for an earthquake!'

Writing about the event twenty years later, Berry recalled that he had been 'brash enough to ask the Prime Minister, Mr Macmillan, to give us a "leak" for our first issue', and thought that he had looked a little surprised. The botched launch, he wrote, 'proved very costly'. (Figures published later showed that the company spent £405,000 on launching the paper in 1960, and that in its first full year it lost £453,000.)

Gradually, however, the paper began to improve and to hit the longer stride that Sunday readers wanted. Its executives realised that, whereas all the Daily had to do was to report news really well, *their* job was to manufacture news as creatively as possible, and also to think up background features of genuine interest, rather than taking the easy way out by ordering turgid analyses of local politics from foreign correspondents in far corners of the earth.

One of its most successful features was Peregrine Worsthorne's column, on the leader-page. Until then, most of Worsthorne's writing on the Daily had been anonymous; now the column gave him a much better chance to deploy his originality. A most attractive person, both physically and mentally, he wrote as he dressed, with style and flamboyance; if it is hard, at this distance, to single out literary equivalents of spongebag trousers and Leander socks, they were nonetheless clearly apparent to contemporaries. Often, in the middle of dazzling intellectual argument, Worsthorne would reveal the most endearing naïvety. In particular, he had a talent for blithe but lacerating self-exposure – as when he described, in an autobiographical article, how, as a snobbish and 'rather pretty' boy at Stowe, he had been bullied by his loutish, common contemporaries and seduced on a sofa by George Melly.

In *The Sunday Telegraph*, as McLachlan later wrote, Worsthorne 'made a name for himself with his brand of stylish paradox, and, by keeping going week after week, he became a habit'. 'Paradox' was the word: often Worsthorne put the sub-editors in a spin by falling behind schedule (so that a headline had to be set before his article was finished), and then finding that, in the course of writing, he had argued himself round to face a direction opposite the one predicted. Once he was so late that, by the time he had finished, the rest of the leader-page was sitting on the stone in the composing-room fully made up, with a finite hole left in the middle. This meant that there could be no argument about the length of the piece, and Thackeray, the Features Editor, told Worsthorne he would have to cut thirty lines. 'But that's impossible!' cried the agonised author. 'It'll reduce the article to a foetus!' Thackeray, who was stubborn as a mule, besides being highly professional, moved off murmuring, 'Oh, come, come!', and in less than a minute had tailored the piece invisibly to fit the space; but for months after that he was known as the Foetus Editor.

McLachlan was always a supporter and encourager of Worsthorne. With Albany, on the other hand, he never came to terms. Considering the column snobbish, he would address Kenneth Rose as 'Viscount Albany' – and he was beside himself with indignation when, just as the new paper was launched, Lord Longford died, with the result that Rose's first assistant, Thomas Pakenham, became entitled to call himself Lord Silchester. 'The first day of Albany,' exclaimed McLachlan, 'and your assistant becomes a peer!' In the early days the column was ground between the conflicting orders of McLachlan and Michael Berry: the Editor told Rose that it should not contain any jokes, and that it should include more stories about the provinces; but when Rose went to Birmingham and wrote a paragraph about the French Consul-General there, the Editor-in-Chief struck it out, on the grounds that it was insufficiently metropolitan. Later Albany made some rude remarks about rich socialists who, in anticipation of a Labour government, had acquired bolt holes in the West Indies – and suddenly the paper found itself facing three legal actions. Lord

Bernstein sued for libel and received damages. Lord Rothschild, threatening an action for libel, received an apology. Lord Walston wrote to McLachlan expressing surprise that his paper had behaved more like the *Sunday Express* than a reputable journal – whereupon McLachlan suggested that they should dine at Brooks's to discuss the matter. This they did; but at the end of the meal McLachlan put his guest in a state of total confusion by abruptly saying that he had to go and leaving him to pay the bill. To the end of his time in Fleet Street McLachlan remained uneasy about the nature of the animal he had helped create; in a handing-over note left for his successor, he ungraciously remarked that he thought the Albany column 'wrongly conceived', but that this was 'one of the things of which I have failed to convince M[ichael] B[erry]'.*

From his own experience on the Daily, and from what the *Sunday Times* was doing, Berry knew that one of the best ways to build up the Sunday paper was to serialise important books: what one needed was a gripping and readable series of at least three extracts, for which one would not only pay a high price but also spend a lot more on promotion. By means of such an operation the paper might pull in 30,000 new readers, and, if it was lucky, keep a third of them when the serial was over.

One conspicuously successful serialisation was that of 'Chips' Channon's diaries, in 1963. Normally Thackeray did the cutting and preparation of serial extracts, but this book Michael Berry took on himself – and a hard time he had of it. As he went through the typescript, he found that a great deal of the original had been scored out. Seeing that these parts contained some of the best material, he persuaded Peter Coats, Channon's literary executor, to let him restore many passages. Still not satisfied, he met Channon's son Paul at White's Club and again asked for more material, this time with better results. To Berry's surprise, he got permission to print almost everything he wanted; but when, just before publication, Channon said, 'You do think I'm doing the right thing, don't you?' Michael, who considered the revelations 'perfectly appalling', hardly knew how to reply. Hugh Massingham, the paper's Political Correspondent, then wrote a 'marvellous introduction to the series, saying what a shit and bounder Chips had been'; but Michael became worried that Paul Channon, seeing it with the first instalment, would veto all further

* The column and its author both proved exceedingly durable. When this book went to press in the autumn of 1989, both were still in full flight, Rose having declined an earlier offer from Charles Douglas-Home to become a Associate Editor of the *Times*.

publication, and toned it down. Even so, the series caused a gratifying stir.

A still more satisfactory operation was the publication in full of the Denning Report on the Profumo affair, which shook Macmillan's Government in the summer of 1963. For weeks the nation had been agreeably scandalised by revelations of how John Profumo, Secretary of State for War, had lied to the Commons about his relationship with the call-girl Christine Keeler. In newspaper terms, the affair had everything: the downfall of a senior politician; the involvement (and later suicide) of the osteopath Stephen Ward, who held sex-parties at his cottage on Lord Astor's estate at Cliveden; the link between Christine Keeler and Eugene Ivanov, naval attaché at the Soviet Embassy in London; the man (alleged to be a Cabinet Minister) who had served at dinner parties naked except for a mask. Sex, spies, high society, low society, suicide, politics: what more could any editor ask for? *The Daily Telegraph*, needless to say, made full capital out of the affair, which provided a legitimate excuse to run seamy reports at length, day after day, while maintaining a pretence of outrage.

It was Michael Berry's suggestion that the Sunday should print the whole of the official report on the affair commissioned by the Government from Lord Denning, Master of the Rolls. The idea that a newspaper should publish a complete Government White Paper was entirely new, and nobody on the staff knew how the law stood on such a project; but once the plan had been conceived, its execution had to be pushed through as fast and as secretly as possible, in the hope that official permission would be forthcoming, or at any rate not specifically withheld.

The paper's solicitor, Peter Richardson, was set to making inquiries. Luckily, when he rang the Treasury Solicitor's office, he spoke to someone quite junior, who referred him to a Treasury circular which said that permission for publication of White Papers 'would not normally be refused'. McLachlan felt that to press for more information at that stage might be to alert other newspapers about *The Sunday Telegraph*'s intentions; so he quietly went ahead with printing posters and drafting in extra labour to prepare the supplement. Very soon, however, the Controller of the Stationery Office was on the telephone, saying that publication could not be allowed, because full copyright on the report was reserved. McLachlan quoted the Treasury circular mentioned above, and some inconclusive exchanges followed.

His next conversation was with the deputy Treasury Solicitor, Sir Harvey Druitt, who said that the position in law was perfectly clear: the copyright in such documents was reserved. Referring him to the circular, McLachlan said he had understood that permission to publish in full would be given unless the circumstances were exceptional. Druitt replied that he considered that the present circumstances *were* exceptional, and made it clear that he would not allow publication.

In further telephone conversations the argument shifted on to more practical ground. The *Telegraph* made capital out of the fact that a friend of the Managing Director had heard the Home Secretary say, the night before, that 'everyone in the country' should read the report. *The Sunday Telegraph*, McLachlan argued, would perform a useful public service by supplying the whole report, free, to perhaps 2,500,000 readers. The Controller of the Stationery Office seized on this number, and said it might be very useful to him in computing any claim which might arise for infringement of copyright. McLachlan himself wrote a brief record of the exchanges:

The Controller of the Stationery Office took the line that he had arranged an exceptional distribution of this paper through his branches, and that our supplement would involve him in loss. We replied that our publication would take the report into homes which never dreamt normally of reading, let alone buying, White Papers . . . The man from the Treasury Solicitors hinted that we might be subject on Saturday to an injunction, which would cost us a lot of money and ruin a good publicity stunt and a piece of journalistic enterprise. When I asked if he was threatening us, he hedged; but I made it clear that we must decide to print on Friday evening . . .

Michael Berry then suggested that if they were worried about loss of money to the Stationery Office, we might pay something to make it up. [Within an hour] the Deputy Treasury Solicitor rang back to say that it would cost £4,000, which represented an attempt to work out what the Stationery Office would lose in sales. So, on that basis, we were allowed to go ahead.

I was told later that the problem was put direct to Macmillan, who himself worked out on his blotting-paper what the sum should be. I also learned that we were very lucky to be dealing with the deputy Treasury Solicitor, as the Treasury Solicitor [Sir Harold Kent] was away owing to the death of his daughter. He was very tough, I was told, and would have had an injunction against us in no time.

So the supplement went through in September 1963 – twenty-four pages, plainly laid out, illustrated with black-and-white photographs, and bearing on the front the key quotation from the Home Secretary: 'This report should be read by everyone in the country . . . the most readable and absorbing Blue Book ever written.' Not everybody did read it; but the exercise was a spectacular journalistic success, a tribute to steady nerves and clever manoeuvring, and boosted the sale of the paper by fifty per cent, almost to a million copies. McLachlan later heard that the *Observer* had also thought of running the report in full, but that, when they formally asked permission, they had been refused. 'So this was a case of how the brutal, ungentlemanly approach succeeds, where the polite, constitutional approach fails,' he wrote. 'The *Observer* were livid about it.' In retrospect, he was surprised that a loophole in the law about government publications should have existed for so long without anyone else discovering it. Later, the relevant Treasury minute was amended to prevent any repetition of the exploit.

'Were our arguments about the public interest humbug?' he asked himself. 'From time to time I have an uneasy feeling they were. Certainly our motive was to promote the sales of *The Sunday Telegraph*, and promoting the public interest was hardly at the top of our minds. But certainly a lot of people got the whole of the Denning argument without sensational headlines or black type, and could sort out truth from rumour.'

The paper again launched into stormy seas when it bought world rights in the marathon official life of Winston Churchill, which was begun by his son Randolph in 1964. Since Camrose had been such a friend of Winston, and since the Daily had serialised his account of the Second World War, it was natural that the Sunday should be offered first refusal; little did anyone realise what nervous energy the project would consume, or what rows it would engender.

By the initial agreement, Winston was paid £50,000, and Randolph and the Churchill trustees were to receive £200,000, in five instalments; but work was not far advanced when the old man died, in January 1965; as Michael Berry put it, 'Old Churchill went down with his money. He liked tips in five figures.'

Supported by the efforts of various research assistants, among them the brilliant young historian Martin Gilbert, Randolph forged ahead with his huge task, working at Stour, his home near East Bergholt; but he was easily disheartened, and soon sent a petulant message to McLachlan complaining that nobody at *The Sunday Telegraph* seemed interested in what he was doing. The Editor responded by arranging to call on the author in his lair; on this first visit, he took his wife with him, and Kitty McLachlan later described how, after a meal, the company repaired to Randolph's study, where Gilbert was installed at what their host described as Disraeli's reading-desk and instructed to read aloud the jewelled passages about Winston's youth which had already been completed. Whenever he stumbled or mispronounced a name like Cholmondeley, Randolph corrected him sharply, in a way the McLachlans found cruel and humiliating: 'In *this* house, dear boy, we say *Chumley*'. At every interruption the pug dogs burst into a chorus of barking. Each time peace had been restored, Randolph would say, 'Box on, dear boy – box on.' It was not an easy evening; but some of Winston's letters from school were so poignant that Randolph was much moved, and tears coursed down his cheeks.

On a second visit, in very cold weather, Randolph took the McLachlans to his local pub, where he ordered buttered rum all round. But on his third visit Donald McLachlan went alone – and it was on this occasion, incensed by something he had said, that Randolph threatened him with a knife. As Martin Gilbert wrote:

> With a shaking and trembling of his whole body, Randolph rose from the table, turned away from the guests, strode over to the sideboard, picked up a carving knife, and turning back to the table, his face contorted with anger, shook the knife at the editor and bellowed more savagely than any of us had heard before: 'People like you should have been shot by my father in 1940.' Then, turning from the table, the knife still held high, he strode out of the room.

According to Gilbert, who wrote this account in 1982, the outburst was caused by McLachlan's remarks about the *Times*'s support for the policy of appeasement during the 1930s. In particular, McLachlan is alleged to have said that he not only approved of the way in which the Editor Geoffrey Dawson had censored Norman Ebbutt's despatches from Berlin, but had actively advised him to blue-pencil 'superfluous details' about the Nazi regime. As Kitty McLachlan quickly pointed out, there were several errors in this account. For one thing, Gilbert set the episode in 1968, by which time McLachlan had left *The Sunday Telegraph*. For another, the 'editor and his wife' did not turn white, or breakfast alone next morning and then leave: the wife was not there. For a third, McLachlan was not at the *Times* during the years of appeasement (1936–38), and in any case was a friend and former accomplice of Ebbutt. Yet, whatever the real cause of Randolph's fury, it boded ill for the success of his project with the *Telegraph*.

In the event, serialisation of the life of Churchill fell flat. As Michael Berry recalled, the paper did its best, giving the series from the first volume maximum publicity; he himself cut the extracts, and found the young Winston's letters to his mother fascinating. Yet, in purely journalistic terms, the enterprise came too long after the event. By 1966, when the first volume appeared, popular interest in Churchill was fading, and could not be revived on the scale for which the paper had hoped.

Then, in 1968, with only two volumes published, Randolph's health rapidly declined, and in June he died of a heart attack brought on by kidney failure. The question of who should succeed him gave rise to long discussions, mainly between Sir John Colville, Chairman of the Churchill trustees, Michael Berry, and representatives of the two book publishers involved, Heinemann in London and Houghton Mifflin in New York. Berry, having bought world rights, held the whip hand.

Freddie Birkenhead — Winston's godson and Berry's brother-in-law — immediately put in for the job on the grounds that he was a professional historian and already familiar with the family background. The others, however, managed to talk him out of it by emphasising the size of the task that lay ahead: at least three more volumes would have to be written, and each would have to be accompanied by two volumes of documents — nine tomes in all. For a man approaching sixty, and not in good health, the proposition (they said) was too daunting. Instead, they suggested that Birkenhead should write a one-volume appreciation of Churchill, using all the papers, but that it should not come out until all the volumes of the official life had been published. Birkenhead agreed, and began work.*

Both the book publishers were keen that Randolph's successor should be his son, young Winston: when pressed, they admitted that their main reason was that 'Winston Churchill by Winston Churchill' would look so striking on the dust-jacket. But Randolph had not wanted his son to take over; when he knew he was dying, he had told Berry as much over lunch at the Ritz. Nor did old

---

* In the event, Birkenhead never completed his book, which he left unfinished at his death in 1975. His son Robin, the third earl, took it over, but he too died (in 1985) before he could complete it. In 1988 the book claimed a third author — Sir John Colville — who began to prepare it for publication but also died in the attempt. The first part of it, covering the years 1874–1922, eventually came out in 1989, and the section written by Robin, spanning Churchill's career from 1924 to 1940, was privately printed the same year.

Winston's widow, Clementine, wish their son to inherit the biography. Someone else was needed. Michael Wolff, head of the research team, fully expected the mantle to fall on him, but in the end the monumental task was awarded to his assistant, Martin Gilbert.

Gilbert was then still only thirty-one, but already the author of ten books, of which the best known was *The Roots of Appeasement*. For the main biography, Randolph had proposed three further volumes. Gilbert now persuaded the *Telegraph* that there should be four, and a fresh agreement was made out on this basis. In the event, the new author found that he needed still more space to do justice to the immense archive of material at his disposal, and his relations with the paper became strained as he extended the number of extra volumes first to five and then to six. By the terms of his contract, he was not supposed to write anything about Churchill for other publishers, or any other book of a substantial nature, while the project was running; but in Michael Berry's view he kept infringing the agreement: 'The gaps between volumes grew greater and greater, deadlines were ignored, other books appeared, and in the biography he never made any attempt to stand back from the daily catalogue of events. Meanwhile memories of Sir Winston grew dimmer.'

It is characteristic of relationships between the two parties that Gilbert categorically rejects Berry's account. He points out that, at the outset, it was Seymour Camrose who encouraged him not to skip anything, but to write 'the true story of Churchill' in full; and that he devoted over twenty years of his own life to carrying out this mighty task, producing, in that time, six volumes of text and twelve of supporting documents, every one a book of immense length. As for the fact that the newspaper serials did not have greater success – this, he says, was due to the lack of skill with which they were prepared, especially the later ones. When he saw these, he was 'staggered' by what dull reading they made. 'The *Telegraph* people could have had marvellous extracts,' he said later. 'As it was, they never even read the books properly. There were wonderful pictures in the photographic archive, and they never used them either.'

Relations between the *Telegraph* and the Thomson group remained edgy. With the Sunday paper faltering, Thomson launched a *Sunday Times* colour supplement – the first such magazine in the United Kingdom, which came out in February 1962, edited by Mark Boxer, and immediately added 150,000 copies to the sale, even though the opening issues lost money heavily. Michael Berry had no doubt that the creation of the supplement was a deliberate attempt to finish off the new rival.

A year later – on 12 January 1963 – he hit back with his own first attempt at a colour supplement, a twenty-page, full-colour issue devoted to the visit of Pope Paul to the Holy Land. The experiment was highly fraught, for no firm in England could print the number of copies required, and the magazine was produced by Axel Springer in Hamburg. The paper despatched two photographers to Palestine, but their films were delayed, and twenty-four hours before press-time no photographs had reached the printers. Yet somehow the issue was scrambled together by a team consisting of John Anstey (brought in as Editor), Michael Berry, Ralph Thackeray and one of the Assistant Editors, Douglas Brown, an excellent writer who specialised in articles on foreign affairs and church matters. The result proved an immense success, lifting the sale of the paper through the million mark for the first time. The brief text began, 'It is scarcely too much to say that last weekend the whole of Christendom journeyed with Pope Paul to the Holy Land'; and once again Michael Berry's news sense had hit the bull's-eye.*

Pleased that the gamble had come off, even though it had cost £30,000, he put a brief note into the next issue of the Sunday paper saying that he intended to repeat the experiment from time to time – and by doing so accidentally set off a colour-magazine race. David Astor, proprietor of the *Observer*, took this announcement to mean that *The Sunday Telegraph* was going to bring out a regular colour supplement – perhaps not every week, but certainly often. The threat spurred him to start a magazine of his own, which, by strenuous efforts, he managed at the beginning of September 1964. Hearing of his plans in June, Berry decided to launch a spoiling operation. Calculations of possible circulation-increase and of the amount of colour advertising available suggested that it would be unwise to bring out a direct rival magazine, on Sunday: the *Observer*'s circulation, at 715,000, was still about 50,000 ahead of *The Sunday Telegraph*'s, and even if magazines boosted both papers, the *Telegraph* would still be number three among the heavy Sundays, and thus unlikely to win a profitable share of colour advertising. Berry therefore decided to bring his magazine out on a Friday – a move which added some

---

* This was the first colour record of the Pope's visit to appear in Europe. Even *Paris Match*, which chartered an aircraft as a flying process-room, could only manage black-and-white pictures on the following Monday.

85,000 to the sale of the Daily, and usefully removed some advertising from the competition. The magazine first appeared at the end of September 1964, produced in Bavaria, because printers could still not be found in England, and edited by John Anstey, who, with astonishing tenacity, ran it for the next twenty years. In 1976 it was moved to Sunday, to intensify the campaign against the *Observer*.

Colour magazines apart, Thomson himself did what he could to undermine the young *Sunday Telegraph* by spreading rumours among advertisers that it was not going to last long. Genial as he might seem in public, his animosity suddenly revealed itself when the McLachlans met him, by chance, at the inauguration of the London Hilton in April 1963. After the official ceremony, guests were free to roam all over the new hotel, and the lifts were jammed with people wanting to reach the penthouse on the top floor. Caught up in the rush, Donald and Kitty McLachlan suddenly found themselves face to face with Thomson, who glared at them through his pebble lenses; and Kitty, in an attempt to be friendly, said, 'When we get to the top, I suppose one of you two'll have to push the other off.' Thomson replied flatly, 'That won't be necessary. He's going down anyway.' 'On the contrary,' said Kitty, 'he's only just started going up.' On that barbed note the lift disgorged them, and they parted company.

It was partly in an attempt to stem Thomson's rumours that in January 1964 the Sunday announced its support for the first World Theatre Season, in which the impresario Peter Daubeny brought seven distinguished foreign companies to act in London as part of the celebrations for the 400th anniversary of the birth of Shakespeare. This ambitious event, presented in conjunction with the Royal Shakespeare Company, took place at the Aldwych Theatre between March and June. Possibly it did something to enhance the image of *The Sunday Telegraph* as a serious journal; certainly it led to fearful arguments between the paper and Peter Daubeny, a charismatic but highly-charged man who was insatiable in his demands for publicity.

On their way to one of the World Theatre Season productions, the McLachlans suffered a serious accident. Kitty was driving along the Embankment, and pulled up when signalled to do so by a policeman, on duty at an intersection where the traffic-lights were out of order. Hardly had they stopped when a car smashed into them from behind. Both suffered whiplash injuries in the neck. Donald, who had undone his seat belt to lean forward and pick up a pencil off the floor, was in a less vulnerable position, but even so had to wear a surgical collar for some weeks. Kitty's neck never fully recovered, even after several operations. The driver of the car that hit them escaped prosecution and never so much as wrote a line of apology.*

As the Sunday paper struggled to find its feet, a curious episode, most uncharacteristic of *The Daily Telegraph*, was being played out in Moscow. The paper's first correspondent there was Jeremy Wolfenden, a classical scholar and Fellow of All Souls, who was twenty-eight when posted to Russia in 1962. Unknown to his employers, he was a homosexual, and he had not long arrived in Moscow when a KGB agent compromised him by leaping out of a cupboard in a room at the Ukraine Hotel and taking photographs as he was going to bed with the barber from the Ministry of Foreign Trade. Wolfenden did what he could to resist the KGB's demands that he should pass them information about the Western community in Moscow; he warned colleagues not to discuss sensitive matters, and confessed to the British Embassy what had happened. They, evidently, passed on his information to London, for when he returned on leave, an officer of the Special Intelligence Service asked him to co-operate with the KGB, but also to report to the SIS whenever he was in England.

The *Telegraph* did not realise it at the time, but the term 'Our Man in Moscow' had taken on a new meaning. The strain of trying to keep both sides in play drove Wolfenden to drink: already a serious imbiber, he descended into bouts of alcoholism and deteriorated physically. In 1965, seeking escape from Moscow, he arranged a transfer to Washington, but he continued to drink heavily, and on 28 December he died, aged thirty-one, having apparently passed out in the bathroom and cracked his head on the basin as he fell. For years friends believed that the KGB had murdered him, but later research suggested that his death had been an accident, even if it had been precipitated by his involuntary venture into espionage.

By the early 1960s Colin Coote had become a senior statesman, in journalism and politics alike, who could fairly say that he had been friends of ten Prime Ministers, and that the two politicians

---

* In 1971 McLachlan drove a hired car into a tree and was killed near Gordon-stoun, in Morayshire. He had gone to Scotland to finish research for his biography of Kurt Hahn, founder of the school, and if Kitty had not still been suffering pains in her neck, which were exacerbated by long-distance travel, she would have been with him, acting as driver.

he had liked best were Churchill and Hugh Gaitskell. In 1962 he disgusted McLachlan by accepting a knighthood from Harold Macmillan. 'I've spent seven years trying to get our independence recognised,' McLachlan complained to Kenneth Rose, 'and now we're seen to be tied to the Tories!'* Coote himself claimed to have had some misgivings, but said that he accepted the honour because it acknowledged the paper's achievement, rather than his own. Even so, he did not mention the matter to his proprietor before news of it appeared in the paper. Coote's French connections made him a fervent European and a keen advocate of Britain's entry into the Common Market, so that under him the *Telegraph* strongly championed the move towards Europe. On the other hand, he had absolutely no feeling for, or understanding of, America. On the day after the Cuban missile crisis of October 1962, assuming that the Americans had lied as usual, he wrote a leader saying that President Kennedy was an excitable young man who had gone off his head. It took a good deal of argument, by Colin Welch and others, to turn him round.

Oddly enough – for he was more of an analyst and commentator than a gatherer or maker of news – it was Coote who introduced Stephen Ward to the Soviet attaché Eugene Ivanov and so (inadvertently) forged one of the links in the chain of events that set off the Profumo affair. In his memoirs, *Editorial*, he described how, when plagued by lumbago, he was recommended to an osteopath called Ward in Devonshire Street, and how his pain was miraculously 'tamed and then expelled'. Ward, he found, was a terrible chatterer and name-dropper; but among the stream of 'political imbecilities' which poured from him as he kneaded, there emerged also some sensible observations about black-and-white drawing and bridge. As a result, Coote first invited Ward to a bridge party at his house, and then sent him to do sketches of the leading personalities in the trial of Adolf Eichmann (for war crimes) in Israel. The drawings turned out well, and attracted favourable comment when used in *The Daily Telegraph*.

When Coote went for further treatment, Ward complained that he was unable to get a visa to visit Russia. It so happened that, a few days earlier, Coote had entertained a party of diplomats who had come for a tour of the *Telegraph* building. The Soviet representative had been Ivanov, who had struck Coote as 'an agreeable personality', with excellent English. What better solution

---

* A decade later the paper's Political Correspondent, H. B. Boyne, also accepted a knighthood.

of his obliging osteopath's problem, then, than to bring Ivanov and Ward together? The two met at a lunch which Coote organised: they got on well, and agreed that, when a visa came through, they would together plan the details of Ward's trip to Moscow. Before they could do that, however, Ward introduced Ivanov to his friend Christine Keeler . . . and events ran away with them. Later, Coote loudly protested his innocence in the matter – and there is no doubt that he acted in good faith. All the same, it seems ironic that so loyal a supporter of Macmillan should, by his meddling, have brought the Prime Minister to the verge of ruin.

When Coote at last retired, aged seventy, in the spring of 1964, the paper gave him a huge farewell lunch at the Savoy. Correspondents flew in from all over the world, and the menu reproduced in miniature the front pages of the first and last issues that he had edited. In a speech which gave much pleasure to all, Michael Berry sang his praises. Like Rolls-Royces, he remarked, Editors of *The Daily Telegraph* were built to last. In the past forty years there had been only two, and during fourteen years under Coote the circulation of the paper had climbed from 971,000 to its present level of 1,319,000 – a record of which anyone could have been proud.

Coote's successor was Maurice Green, whom Michael Berry had brought on to the staff three years earlier. Green, until his move an Assistant Editor on the *Times*, was the first man whom Michael had recruited as a potential Editor – and a hard time he had to bring him in. At Berry's first approach, after a long talk, Green declined his overtures, fearing (rightly) that even if he were called the Deputy Editor, he would in fact be number three in the organisation, with Berry and Coote both above him. But two years later, when Berry tried him again, he agreed to come.

Like Coote, Green was a Rugbeian, and a distinguished one. A classical scholar at both Rugby and Oxford, he was described by the *Financial Times* as one of the outstanding members of the Gaitskell generation at the university. Soon after going down he joined the *Financial News*, of which he became Editor at the age of twenty-eight. (The novelist Hammond Innes, who worked under him there, dedicated his book *Atlantic Fury* to Green and his wife Janet.) Five years later, in 1938, he moved to the *Times*, where at first he was in charge of the City and industrial pages. After war service in the Royal Artillery as an instructor at the School of Anti-Aircraft Defence, at Swindon and Rhyl, he returned to Printing House Square and became an Assistant Editor of the *Times*.

Green's appearance was deceptive: behind his pale face and rather meek façade, a keen intelligence was at work. His manner – studious, courteous, almost diffident – increased this misleading impression of vagueness. He was about as unlike the traditional image of a newspaper editor as anyone could be. When speaking, he would leave such long gaps between sentences ('Green pauses', they were called), as if searching for words, that people would say it was a pleasure to watch him think. He also had a disconcerting habit of staring into space over the shoulder of the person to whom he was talking. Michael Berry, maddened by this habit, once thought he would try an experiment to see if he could break the spell by doing the same thing. The result was agonising: both men gazed past the other for about two minutes, rigid with embarrassment – and in the end Green won, forcing his tormentor to break the silence. But then, as Green suddenly found his voice, he became (in Michael's words), 'quite gabby. It was like taking a cork out of an awkward bottle. There was plenty of fizz in the bottle once you'd opened it.'

Berry was drawn to Green partly by the fact that he was at heart an economist – unlike Coote, who had been more interested in the broad sweep of political philosophy. But *everybody* liked Maurice Green. He was easier to get on with than Coote, more obviously committed to the paper, and tougher at standing up to unwelcome pressures, whether from outside the organisation or from ambitious climbers within. Although he too, like Coote, had been passed over for higher promotion at the *Times*, he never gave the slightest sign of feeling that he had come down in the world. On the contrary, he set a demanding standard with his own writing, as a colleague recalled:

There never was a more ruthless eliminator of redundant words from sentences. He is most unsparing with his own. Some journalists start writing, and what they mean to say comes to them as they go along. Before Green puts pen to paper, he first removes from his mind what he does not want to say.

His interests were wide: the arts, books (he wrote enthusiastic reviews of each new volume of Lawrence Durrell's *Alexandria Quartet*), bicycling through Europe with his wife, fishing, shooting: so keen was he on shooting, in fact, that when *The Sunday Telegraph* was in the offing, he specially asked not to be considered for the post of Editor, because, if he got it, it would deprive him of his shooting on Saturdays.

Coote had not departed, however, without leaving his mark on the succession. Just as he had, *ultra vires*, told Ivor Bulmer-Thomas that he would become Deputy Editor of the Daily paper, and then promised Peregrine Worsthorne the same post on the Sunday, so now, without consulting anyone else, he had appointed Colin Welch Deputy on the Daily. Michael Berry was much put out, but did not feel he could countermand the appointment. Though still suspicious of Welch – the original Peter Simple, and now writer of the parliamentary sketch – as someone too clever and too imaginative by half, Berry did not know him very well; but, as the years went on, his reservations increased. Welch, he thought, was a brilliant man, who wrote wonderful Commons sketches, but was incurably frivolous, incapable of keeping jokes and fantastical notions out of serious articles. Worse, he had a habit of changing his stance on important political matters, so that a leader written one month would be contradicted, or at any rate weakened, by another published a few weeks later. 'You must look up what we said before,' Michael would tell him. 'If you want to change, you can, but not in one night. If you must box the compass, do it in four leaders, gradually moving round. Even if *you* don't remember what you wrote earlier, your readers will.' Michael could not help noticing that, when Green was in the chair, their evening editorial conference about the leaders took place promptly at 6.00 pm. When Welch stood in, he did not go up to the fifth floor until nearly seven, by which time the leaders had been passed, usually unamended, and it was too late to make changes.

Now, thanks to Coote's machinations, Michael was landed with Welch, who promptly gave up the parliamentary sketch, saying that it was incompatible with his new job. Many members of the staff thanked God for his presence – just as they thanked God for Peter Simple, which had now taken flight in the hands of Michael Wharton, and in 1962 had won the ITV 'What the Papers Say' award for the best column of the year, being hailed as 'consistently amusing and provoking'. Wharton was then in his late forties – a soft-spoken Yorkshireman, charmingly diffident in manner, who described himself (if he had to) as a Tory radical with Luddite implications. On good days he would write most of his column round the margins of that morning's *Telegraph* as he approached Fleet Street on a bus; but the headquarters of his imaginary cast – among them Jack Moron, Sir Rufus Grunt (C. Natterhurst) and Dr Spacely-Trellis, the go-ahead Bishop of Bevindon, all card-indexed – was a tiny office at the back of the building, in which there was just room for himself and his secretary, Claudie Worsthorne

(Perry's wife), who patiently answered all but obscene letters from his readers. People could not always tell whether or not Wharton was joking – a good sign – and once, when he wrote about gramophone records for learning Etruscan, as preparation for holidays in Ancient Etruria, he received a request for further details.

Often his main enemy seemed to be the intellectual idiocy of the Left; but one left-wing fan, Tom Driberg, pointed accurately to a wider horizon when he described him as 'a pre-1914 innocent consumed with despairing nostalgia for a legendary golden past'. Wharton's hankering for an older and better world was perfectly expressed in the piece he contributed to an otherwise serious feature called 'The Car I Like':

> Vast in proportion, noble and august in design . . . panelled in solid, well-polished mahogany, furnished with folding writing-table, compartments for brandy-flasks and other necessities of travel, it enfolds its passengers (six in complete comfort) in a dim, almost cloistral atmosphere . . . Wrapped in fleecy rugs against the cold, I issue orders through the braided speaking-tube with its silver mouthpiece, and the car makes its stately way through landscapes as nostalgic as itself.

In 1964 the Daily gained an especially valuable recruit in the form of T. E. Utley (always known as Peter). If his mind was one of the sharpest ever to distinguish the paper, his appearance was one of the least mistakable, for he had been blind since the age of nine: his right eye was obviously sightless, his left covered by a black patch which gave him a piratical look, and whenever he arrived, left or moved about the building, he was invariably on the arm of a lovely girl, usually a stunning blonde. Such was the power of his intellect that inability to read (except in Braille) seemed not to hamper him at all: at Cambridge he had won a starred First in history, and after that he wrote incisive leaders for the *Times*, the *Sunday Times* and the *Observer*. Yet it was on the *Telegraph* that he made his real mark as a Conservative philosopher and prophet. Together with Colin Welch, he sharpened the paper's traditional stance, and – often to the considerable disquiet of the proprietor – set about redefining Tory ideas.

At home in the mornings his wife would read him the papers, and in the office the process was continued by a succession of devoted and (it always seemed) outstandingly attractive secretaries, whom he chose, at least partly, by getting them to read test-pieces aloud. His powers of absorption were altogether exceptional, and his articles, which he dictated, were as clear and incisive as the voice in which he spoke them. Over the years he made a special study of Northern Ireland, and became so deeply involved in the tortured affairs of the province that he once fought an election campaign, with predictable lack of success, against the Reverend Ian Paisley.*

Invisible to readers, but with a presence very much felt within the building, another man had established himself in a powerful position. This was Peter Eastwood, who had risen through the ranks of the news organisation to be Night Editor, and over the next twenty years became the most hated man ever to work at 135 Fleet Street. That sounds an unkind verdict, but it is true: in an organisation which, on the whole, conducted its affairs in a gentlemanly fashion, Eastwood made himself uniquely unpopular.

In stature he was short and stocky, with large spectacles and thick fair hair, which he wore *en brosse*, cut short and brushed up and back, in a fashion that made people call him 'Bottlebrush'; at first sight he seemed inoffensive, for his manner was quiet and (at times) ingratiating. Unlike Brian Roberts (who had brought him on to the paper) he never shouted or abused people; but as those who fell foul of him soon found to their cost, the less he said, the more of a menace he could be.

His origins were utterly different from those of Coote or Green. No public-schoolboy, he was brought up at Batley, in Yorkshire, and after grammar school went straight on to the *Batley News* as reporter and sub-editor. After three years there, and a spell on the *Yorkshire Evening News*, he joined the *Daily Express* as a sub-editor under the legendary editor Arthur Christiansen, then at the top of his form, fizzing with drive and energy. 'In those days,' Eastwood recalled nearly fifty years later, 'you could walk in on a Monday, have a job by Wednesday and be out by Friday.' His next move, in 1938, was to the *Daily Mail*, where, through an administrative mix-up, he managed to stay until 1941, becoming Acting Chief Sub-Editor. Called up belatedly into the Gunners, he went out to India and Burma, and became a subaltern in the Indian Army, before moving back into journalism on the South-East Asia Command newspaper produced in Calcutta. After the atom bombs had been dropped on Hiroshima and Nagasaki, he went down to Rangoon to report the Japanese surrender, landing in Singapore in September 1945. There he helped to relaunch the *Straits Times*,

---

* Sad to relate, Utley fell out with the *Telegraph* towards the end of his life, and moved to the *Times* before his death in 1988.

and later started the *Sunday Times*, the first Sunday paper in the colony. His Far Eastern wanderings ended in 1948, when he returned to Britain, and after a few weeks with Reuters, joined the newsroom of *The Daily Telegraph*.

A man of wide experience, then – but also one of ruthless ambition, determined to work his way to the top. In purely technical terms, he was masterly: a superlative sub-editor, and by common consent the best Night Editor the paper had ever had. 'It was a joy to watch him handle copy,' one man (who much disliked him) recalled. 'He worked so fast that the effect was almost poetic. With a few strokes of his pen he could turn a loose, turgid piece into excellent, concise English. As Night Editor, he had a phenomenal ability to carry the entire paper – all thirty-two pages – in his head, and could organise it wonderfully.'

Never was this ability better demonstrated than on 22 November 1963 – the traumatic day, which no journalist will ever forget, when President Kennedy was assassinated in Dallas. It was a Friday, and Eastwood had had the day off; but at about 6.00 pm, as he was watching television at home in Hampstead Garden Suburb, an announcer broke into the programme to say that there had been a shooting incident in Dallas, and that it was thought the President had been wounded. At once Eastwood snatched up his telephone and rang Frank Walker, who was in charge of the news during his absence. 'It looks as though Kennedy's been shot,' said Eastwood. 'You'll want to increase the size of the paper. I'm coming in.'

Wearing a sweater and old trousers, he drove straight to Fleet Street, arriving about twenty minutes later. People were amazed at his appearance, having never before seen him in anything but a suit. But he reached the office before the news came via Reuters and this gave the paper a head-start. Other people on duty that night agree that he was magnificent; before he arrived, there was, if not panic, at least confusion, so vast did the story and its consequences seem. With a few quick decisions he redesigned the paper, threw out advertising, put on more pages, gave everybody definite instructions. With Stephen Barber filing from Dallas, and the other American correspondents from New York and Washington, with an entirely new Peterborough column, a new obituary and a new leader-page article by Richard Ryder on the Kennedy years, an immense number of words were set in type that evening. The Head Printer, Frank Baker, was a good friend and pulled out every stop. For once the compositors and Linotype operators forgot petty grievances and worked all-out, fired by the terrible immensity

The Daily Telegraph

4 a.m.

No 33776. LONDON, SATURDAY, NOVEMBER 23, 1963. *and* Morning Post Printed in LONDON *and* MANCHESTER. Price 3d.

PRESIDENT KENNEDY IS ASSASSINATED

Shot in the head in open car on Texas festival drive

FORMER DEFECTOR TO RUSSIA ARRESTED

LYNDON JOHNSON SWORN IN AS NEW PRESIDENT

From STEPHEN BARBER
Daily Telegraph Special Correspondent

DALLAS, Texas, Friday

JOHN FITZGERALD KENNEDY, 46, the 34th President of the United States, died this afternoon within half-an-hour of being shot in the head as he drove through Dallas in an open car. He was on his way to make a speech at a political festival.

The shooting happened as the President's car drove through cheering crowds. Shots rang out and he slumped down in his seat.

Mrs. Jacqueline Kennedy, who was also in the car, jumped up and cried: "Oh, no!" She cradled her husband in her arms as the car sped to nearby Parkland Hospital. Police motor-cyclists with sirens blaring cleared a path through the crowds, and the traffic.

At the hospital President Kennedy was given an immediate blood transfusion and a Roman Catholic priest was called to his bedside to administer the last rites. The President died 25 minutes after being shot.

VICE-PRESIDENT ESCAPES INJURY

Vice-President Lyndon Johnson, 55, who was sworn in later as the new President, was travelling in the car behind President Kennedy's but was unhurt. The Governor of Texas, Mr. John Connally, 46, who was in the President's car, was shot in the chest and head. To-night his condition was described as " serious."

Crowds waiting outside the hospital groaned as priests announced the President's death. Many people collapsed in tears.

Police to-night seized Lee H. Oswald, 24, chairman of a pro-Castro "Fair Play for Cuba" committee. Oswald, wearing a brown t-shirt, was taken screaming from a cinema. A shot was fired during the arrest. A Dallas policeman had earlier been shot and killed near the cinema.

Oswald, of Fort Worth, Texas, a former Marine, defected to the Soviet Union in 1959, and said he had applied for Soviet citizenship. He returned to the United States last year with his Russian wife. Police said he was the prime suspect in the assassination, but had known all knowledge of the crime. He was later charged with the murder of a policeman.

RIFLE 'SEEN AT WINDOW'

Eye-witnesses reported seeing a rifle being withdrawn from a window in a building overlooking the President's route. A TV reporter said: " A policeman fell to the ground, pulled his pistol and yelled: ' Get down." It is not known whether Secret Servicemen in President's bodyguard returned the assassin's fire.

Police found an Italian-made rifle with telescopic sights in a building nearby. Three spent cartridges were found beside the rifle.

President Kennedy, who was received by opposition in the Southern States to his Civil Rights Bill, had arrived in Dallas by air during a political tour of Texas. Thousands lined the streets as he drove to the town's Trade Market to speak at a lunch, and the President had the bullet-proof glass top of his car lowered so that he could wave to the crowds.

A woman witness, Mrs. Jean Hill, said in a radio interview that the President and Mrs. Kennedy were looking at a dog in the middle of the road, near an underpass, when the shots rang out. She said: " There were three shots. He grabbed his chest and fell over his wife. Jackie fell over him."

EMERGENCY OPERATION

The President was unconscious when he arrived at the hospital. Doctors found that the bullet had struck the President's neck, just below the Adam's Apple. There was also a gaping wound in the back of his head. An emergency operation was performed on his throat, to enable him to breathe.

About an hour after his death, President Kennedy's body, clothing stained with her husband's blood, sobbed quietly as doctors fought to save her husband's life. Before it was announced that he was dead, Mrs. Kennedy was led into a private room. She was later stated to be suffering from shock.

About an hour after his death, President Kennedy's body was placed in a bronze coffin to be flown to Washington. His body will lie in state and he will be given a state funeral.

CARS HURTLED PAST

The first that we of the Press knew that anything so terrible had occurred was when we saw the cars hurtle past the Trade Mart auditorium where we had been waiting to hear the President's speech. Sirens shrieking, the cars raced straight by to the Parkland Hospital, three miles away.

When the President's car reached the hospital his limp body, his wrist still clutching his arm, was gently lifted on to a trolley. On the floor of the car, spattered with blood, lay a bunch of flowers presented to Mrs. Kennedy earlier.

The horror of it all was accentuated by the golden sunshine. As if in Kennedy's honour, a grey drizzle had cleared away upon his arrival at Dallas Airport.

(Continued on Back Page, Col. 4)

Mrs. Kennedy bending over her husband in the back of an open car after he had been shot while they were driving through Dallas, Texas. (Other pictures: Pp 11, 13, 15, 19 & back page: the President's life in pictures—P14)

NEW YORKERS WEEP IN THE STREETS

FROM OUR OWN CORRESPONDENT

NEW YORK, Friday.

NEW YORKERS heard the news in shocked silence. Thousands were returning to their offices from lunch while more poured from skyscraper buildings to drift aimlessly in the streets.

It was as though they emerged from a devastating air raid.

The New President, U.S. Embassy Scenes and Foreign Tributes—P15

Obituary, Protests to BBC and Home's Tribute—P15

Pictures—Pp 11, 13, 14, 15 and 19

Security Blog Penetrated—Back Page

Special Article, London Day by Day and Editorial Comment—P16

'MONSTROUS,' SAYS SIR WINSTON

Sir Winston Churchill issued the following statement: "This monstrous act has taken from us a great statesman and a wise and valiant man. The loss to the United States and to the world is incalculable.

" Those who come after Mr. Kennedy must strive the more to achieve the ideals of world peace and human happiness and dignity to which his presidency was dedicated."

WALL STREET FALL

From Our Own Correspondent

NEW YORK, Friday. The New York Stock Exchange was closed by the Board of Governors to-and-afternoon to-day. At the close of trading the Dow Jones industrial index had fallen 21.16 to 711.49.

London Fall Expected—P15

Whenever there was a radio or television set a silent crowd gathered.

Many wept unashamedly, trying to comfort sobbing women. The tolls of St. Patrick's tolled

LATE NEWS

KENNEDY SHOOTING
(see this page)
Washington, Thursday.—
Shot which killed Mr Kennedy fired from the fifth or sixth floor front windows of a building. Oswald was employed in stock clerk, from distance of about 100 yards.

In Dallas, Texas, doctors said the condition of Mr. Connally, the wounded Governor, was "good" after an operation lasting four hours. He had not been told that Mr. Kennedy was dead.—R.P.

Mr. Kennedy's body and the casket in which it was carried. He was taken into the White House from the plane and later to his father's grave.—Reuter.

To-day's Weather
(Midnight Forecast)

GENERAL SITUATION: A small depression moving E. across N. England.

LONDON, S.E. ENGLAND, E. ANGLIA, E. MIDLANDS: Rain or drizzle, perhaps heavy at times. Wind light, becoming moderate or fresh. Max. 55F (13C).

CEN. S. and S.W. ENGLAND, CHANNEL ISLANDS, WALES: Rain or drizzle, patches of hill fog. Wind S.W., fresh. 58F (14C).

E. ENGLAND, BORDERS, EDINBURGH, CENTRAL HIGHLANDS: Rain at times. Wind S. or S.W. Outlook: Further rain or moderate, becoming milder. 46F (8C).

SEA PASSAGES: Irish Sea: Moderate.

ENGLISH Channel: rather rough.

JOHNSON TAKES OATH IN AIRCRAFT

FROM OUR OWN CORRESPONDENT

WASHINGTON, Friday.

MR. LYNDON B. JOHNSON, 55, was sworn-in as the 35th President of the United States at 3.39 p.m. (8.39 p.m. GMT) to-day within hours of President Kennedy's assassination. The new President will serve the remainder of Mr. Kennedy's term, until January, 1965.

The next Presidential election will be in November, 1964. Mr. Johnson took the oath aboard the Presidential plane at Dallas's Love Airfield when he was preparing to fly to Washington to take over the American Government.

He was sworn in by District Judge Sarah Hughes, the first woman judge in the Dallas Federal District. She was crying during the ceremony.

President Johnson arrived at a military airport in Washington to-night.

(Continued on Back Page, Col. 6)

QUEEN'S MESSAGE TO WIDOW

The Queen, who is spending the week-end with Sir Harold and Lady Werther at Luton Hoo, was informed by telephone of President Kennedy's assassination. The next morning she wired the following message to Mrs. Kennedy:

"I am deeply distressed to hear of the tragic death of President Kennedy. My husband joins me in sending our heartfelt and sympathy to you and your family."

COFFIN IS FLOWN TO WASHINGTON

From VINCENT RYDER and DAVID SHEARS
Daily Telegraph Special Correspondents

WASHINGTON, Friday.

PRESIDENT KENNEDY'S body came home to Washington to-night in a short, sad ceremony. [Picture—P19.] The Air Force Plane No. 1, which carried him to so many places around the world, brought the coffin from Dallas. President Lyndon Johnson travelled with it.

Mrs. Kennedy watched as the coffin was lowered with some difficulty into a Navy ambulance. Mr. Robert Kennedy, Attorney-General and the dead President's brother, jumped from the platform.

(Continued on Back Page, Col. 5)

of the news. As Eastwood remarked, 'If a story as big as that catches people's imagination, there is nothing they can't do.' Yet it was he who master-minded the night's operation, and produced an outstanding paper.

The trouble with Eastwood was that he had a fearfully abrasive effect on other people. On paper he was magic, with humans a disaster. One sub-editor of the day described his arrival at the *Telegraph* as 'like putting a tiger into a children's play-pen', and said that his whole history on the paper was 'littered with corpses'. Always, it seemed, he was starting wars with other people who were, or might become, rivals in his advance to power. First he fought Brian Harvey, the Features Editor; then his main enemy became Michael Kennedy, the Northern Editor (in Manchester); then his arch-opponent was Kenneth Fleet, the City Editor. None of these men picked rows with Eastwood. It was he who instigated the warfare – and the worst feature of it was that so many other people got caught up in the hostilities involuntarily. 'These dreadful conflicts, involving people against their will, went on all the time,' remembered one man, 'and the effect in the Newsroom was such that nobody could remain neutral. You were either an Eastwood man or an enemy.' The result was the futile expenditure of a great deal of nervous energy, which was very disruptive to the editorial production of the paper.

Rivalry between the two papers was always a source of friction. The staff of the Daily tended to regard their colleagues on the Sunday as amateur upstarts, who simply squandered the hard-won profits that their own efforts had gained. The Sunday, in turn, regarded the Daily as dismally hidebound and unadventurous. McLachlan got on well with Michael Berry – though finding him painfully shy – and during his whole time at the *Telegraph* had only one serious argument with him. This occurred when, in an uncharacteristic aberration, he had written a leader-page article which referred repeatedly to the English line of kings as the Stewarts. Edition-time was approaching when Berry called him in and pointed out the mistake on a proof. 'You're quite wrong,' McLachlan told him blithely. 'It's "ew", not "u".' For once Berry blew up. 'I'm NOT wrong!' he said sharply. 'And you can go away and change it.' McLachlan in turn flared up. 'Who IS Editor round here?' he snapped – and out he went, slamming the door, leaving Berry sitting at his desk, a little ruffled.

But if McLachlan liked Michael, he did *not* like Lady Pamela, who, he thought, resented the fact that he would not automatically accept ideas which she put up. Hardly ever in his twelve years on the two papers did she ask him to Cowley Street – he went once to a large cocktail party, and a couple of times to dinner – and he was riled by the fact that Peregrine Worsthorne and Hugh Massingham received far more frequent invitations. (Lady Pamela, for her part, did not dislike McLachlan, but she did find him a bit of a schoolmaster and thought him the wrong sort of person for her lunch parties, which, unlike her dinner-parties, she held purely for her own amusement and for lighthearted anecdotal badinage.)

The McLachlans lived at Bentley, in Hampshire, where Donald sought to foster team spirit by getting up a *Sunday Telegraph* cricket eleven against the village; but they also had a flat in London – first in Robert Adam Street, off the Strand, and then in Roebuck House, a new block near Victoria Station – and there they held small breakfast, lunch and dinner-parties, principally for the critics on the paper, whom they would introduce to distinguished out-siders – Rebecca West, Angus Wilson, the Harold Wilsons, Graham Greene, Cyril Connolly, Sidney Bernstein, John Betjeman, Clement Freud, Michael Adeane, Claus Moser and many others. At one stage Ted Heath, who lived close by, became a regular breakfast guest. These gatherings were by no means mere social occasions: just as Lady Pamela manipulated the conversation in Cowley Street, so McLachlan steered the talk in his Victoria flat. One morning soon after Labour had been returned to power in October 1964, Brigadier Godfrey Hobbs, Director of Public Relations for the army, was invited to breakfast, and there found Patrick Gordon Walker, the recently appointed Foreign Secretary. Since the two men had not seen each other since their schooldays, forty years before, they fell eagerly into gossip about old times, only to be pulled up by McLachlan, who said briskly, 'I didn't ask you here to talk about Wellington!'

Many people were startled when, in 1966, it became known that McLachlan was retiring, at the age of only fifty-six – by *Telegraph* standards, scarcely adult. Many people assumed that he had got the sack; in fact he left of his own volition, having always wanted to write. On 1 November 1965, in a characteristically modest and direct letter, he suggested to Michael Berry that he should step down next spring, even though the paper was still not doing very well:

I find myself in the difficulty that I do not really know whether I have failed or not. Clearly a paper that does not pay is not a success. On the other hand so many people say it is a good paper, and it is so obviously part of the Sunday institution now, that I feel something good has been achieved. But one thing I am certain of: if it is necessary to produce a popular paper, then I am not the man to do it – nor I fear are my principal assistants. The DT influence and its high standards are too strong.

Although Berry urged him to stay, he remained adamant that he wanted to be his own master, and in particular to write an account of Naval Intelligence during the Second World War. This was duly published in 1968, with excellent reviews, as *Room 39*, and McLachlan contributed articles to many newspapers and magazines on his favourite subjects – defence, the BBC, Intelligence work, spies and Soviet defectors – before his untimely death at only sixty-one. In 135 Fleet Street his lively mind, his energy, his enthusiasm were much missed. As he wrote in the *Evening Standard* in 1968, he had 'enjoyed editing enormously, and nothing in it more than getting other people to write, finding ideas, helping to work them out, and then enjoying the resulting satisfaction'.

In the middle and lower echelons of *The Sunday Telegraph* there were faint hopes that, as his successor, Berry might draft in a young, tough, professional outsider – somebody with fresh ideas, who would breathe new life into the paper and break out of the straitjacket it had inherited from the Daily. This was not to be: the new Editor was Brian Roberts, already sixty, and a veteran who had already done twenty-seven years' service with the firm.

Roberts did not endear himself to his staff, who found it hard to forgive his gratuitously offensive manner. His aggression seemed to spring, at least in part, from his own physical inadequacy. He was small and dishevelled, and, until he celebrated his elevation by getting a set of false teeth, had few of his own remaining – a defect which made him shush or bubble his 's's, so that he would refer (for instance) to his News Editor, Derek Sumpter, as 'Shumpter'. He also had other singularities of speech which, though he appeared not to notice them himself, were a gift to the mimics in the building: he habitually spoke of 'jimmicks' and 'shit-zophrenia', and referred to Close-Up, the paper's news-background team, as if the word were spelt with a z, a verb rather than an adjective. One of the legends about him was that, as Night Editor of the Daily on 6 August 1945, he had dismissed reports of the Hiroshima atom bomb as 'a typical American jimmick', and had proposed, until overruled, to suppress the story.

His rudeness appeared to stem also from his lack of judgement on matters outside the immediate news. As a news editor, he was first-class, with a real nose for a story; he was also an absolute stickler for accuracy, and had an admirable loathing of mistakes. Yet when it came to feature articles, he was out of his depth: he simply did not know whether a piece was any good or not, and, rather than risk a judgement, would hand articles to other people for a view. Whenever someone did press him for his own opinion, he barked out that he would be obliged if they stopped wasting his time.

What distressed the people who tried to deal with Roberts was the fact that he had an extremely good brain, if only he cared to exercise it: he had read Greats at Oxford, and treasured his Latin and Greek. The trouble, some thought, was that for much of the time his mind was elsewhere, and that at heart he was more of a farmer than a journalist. Certainly he used to head for his farm in Sussex at every opportunity, and cultivated no political or literary contacts of the kind that McLachlan (and most other editors) sought out in London. And yet, in spite of the irritation he caused, he made a perfectly effective editor, fitting easily into the traditional Berry structure. Even if, under him, the Sunday paper did not break new ground, it did not lose any either.

All through the 1960s Lady Pamela continued to entertain, to intrigue, to charm, to baffle and to infuriate. As a friend, she was absolutely loyal and tenacious, but her likes and dislikes were very swift, and if anyone put a foot wrong, she could be extremely sharp. In other people's houses she was a model guest, enthusiastic, friendly and modest; but in her own home she was dreadfully mischievous, and conducted the conversation like a maestro. Once, after Kenneth Rose had written something rude about John Sparrow, the Warden of All Souls, but the two men had made up their quarrel, Pamela saw them together at one of her parties. 'What!' she cried as she came up. 'You two talking to each other?' – and immediately the shadow fell again. Colin Welch, arriving to find the drawing-room packed, was seized by the arm and propelled through the throng. 'So glad you've come,' said his hostess. 'You must help me out. I've got the *most* frightful bore over here....' Such manipulation was all very well: the trouble, as Welch remarked, was that he could not help wondering whether, a few minutes later, Lady Pamela might not say exactly the same thing again, about him.

Only once, in her husband's experience, did Pamela lose her social nerve. One evening, in the middle of a cocktail party, she rang Michael in the office and said, 'Come at once! Cecil King's standing in the middle of the room, and I can't get anyone to talk to him.' Characteristically, Michael replied that it would be pointless for him to leave Fleet Street, as it would take him at least fifteen minutes to reach home, and by then the problem would have resolved itself. (Later the Berrys became friends of the Kings, and often dined with them.)

In the heady atmosphere of Cowley Street it was easy to gain the impression that Pamela was forming the papers' policy; and many ambitious young members of the staff imagined that their progress up the ladder in Fleet Street could be accelerated by cultivating her. Every one of them was wrong – for while Pamela went for clever, lively people with a flash of steel about them, Michael's preference – in his newspapers, at any rate – struck his employees as always for the solid, the reliable, the grey.* In spite of this fundamental difference, members of the staff derived great benefit from her entertaining, for she had an extraordinary knack of making senior political figures, from the Prime Minister downwards, feel privileged to meet even junior executives from the two papers. It was, the politicians somehow felt, their good fortune to talk to these bright young journalists, rather than vice-versa.

Even so, staunch Conservatives were dismayed by the way Pamela shifted her attention to Labour figures as soon as Harold Wilson's Government scraped into power in October 1964. 'She took up with terrible people like Balogh and Kaldor, simply because they were in office,' said one friend. 'You should have seen her kissing Marcia Williams [Wilson's secretary]!' Some people felt that she did it simply because it gave her the gratification of being near the centre of power – but in her defence, it could fairly be said that she was only doing what the *Telegraph* did anyway: that is, although the paper maintained its Tory stance in leaders, it turned the full power of its news-gathering machine on to Labour when Labour was making the news, and, as always, its strength lay in objective reporting. Others though felt that she gave quarter to Socialists because she preferred them anyway. Just as her father, F. E. Smith, had sided with Churchill and Beaverbrook against the grandees of the Tory Party, so Pamela was always a bit of a rebel, on the side of the fast set against the respectable set – a curious fact, considering that it was dull,

---

* Thirty-five years later he vigorously disputed the fact that the papers had been 'grey'. The term (he contended) referred only to their appearance, which derived from poor printing and the attempt to pack in as much information as possible. Most of the staff, however, felt that the adjective described the contents as well, all too accurately.

respectable people at whom the *Telegraph* was deliberately aimed. She also had a strong anti-royalist streak, and a complex about Buckingham Palace, to which she was not invited as often as she would have liked. 'You ought to *attack* the Royal Family!' she cried at Peregrine Worsthorne after he had written a sycophantic article about them. 'They hold the country back.'

One man with deep suspicions about Lady Pamela's motives was Harold Wilson. At a cocktail party given during the Labour Party conference in Brighton in the autumn of 1966, he was, according to Barbara Castle (then the Secretary for Employment), obsessed with 'plots' against him. He 'dilated to me about Ministers who went a-whoring with society hostesses, and was livid with Tommy Balogh for coming down specially to attend Pamela Berry's dinner . . . and even pursued Pam Berry out of the room to attack her for the biased reporting of the conference in *The Daily Telegraph* . . . "Mrs Ian Fleming is another one," he said darkly.'

Wilson's secretary Marcia Williams told a rather different story. In her memoir *Inside No. 10*, she described Lady Pamela as 'the centre of a perpetually mesmerised male audience', and said that Wilson enjoyed her company enormously, inviting her and Michael to dine at Chequers, and seeking her out at other people's parties; but even though, when he became Labour's leader, Pamela took on a wager that she would one day lure him to a party in Cowley Street, he never went there, except one evening when Michael invited him back to the house after a dinner of the Other Club at the Savoy. 'His most unusual Press relationship was perhaps with the *Telegraph* owners,' wrote Marcia Williams:

> Rigorously Tory, harshly anti-Labour, they managed neverthe-less to carry out their role with more dignity than most of those they support, and to carry on, too, some of the best old-style traditions in British journalism.

It was because of Wilson's 'respect for their independent contri-butions, however hostile politically, to the journalistic world' that in 1968 the Prime Minister created Michael Berry a peer. When Pamela learnt of the impending honour, she was delighted, and urged her husband to accept it. So, in the New Year Honours, he became Baron Hartwell of Peterborough Court in the City of London, and, as Marcia put it, 'a real Press Baron in his own right'.

On 1 January 1968 Richard Crossman recorded that his first duty was 'to ring up Pamela Berry and congratulate her on her husband, Michael's, becoming a newspaper peer'. Yet in general

Crossman found her hard to understand. A few weeks earlier he had written:

> I tried to talk to Pamela about Balmoral and the problems of the monarchy but what interested her was Harold and Marcia. She has an obsession about that . . . How is one to explain the Harold–Mary–Marcia triangle to a person like Pam?

By the end of the 1960s, the *Telegraph* seemed to occupy a position of formidable strength. The circulation of the Daily stood at 1,350,000, an all-time record, enabling its advertising rates to be kept down to a highly competitive level. The Sunday, though still struggling, had established itself as a paper of quality. One small reflection of this prosperity was the Information Bureau: an admirable institution, run by a team of eight or nine women, who answered inquiries free of charge from anyone who cared to ring. For the price of a telephone call any member of the public could track down elusive facts, names, dates or figures – and even without the benefit of computers or mechanical information systems, the staff were extremely efficient. The Bureau was expensive to run, but it created widespread good will, and it was much mourned when a later management closed it down on grounds of extravagance.

Yet behind the impressive façade of the 1960s, ominous signs of weakness were developing. In Fleet Street as a whole the *Telegraph* had a reputation for poor management – or rather, for having scarcely any management at all. In the opinion of David Cole, a Kemsley man who at the time was Managing Director of the *Western Mail*, 'the strength of the *Telegraph* was purely editorial, and the firm lacked any real commercial focus, any real comprehension of what needed to be done in the way of development for the future'. The flaw, Cole thought, had been apparent even in the days of the first Lord Camrose: 'That was why Amalgamated Press started to disintegrate. Camrose was a journalist and editor, rather than a businessman. Kemsley was the real businessman of that generation.'

In 1961 Lord Burnham had stepped down from the post of Managing Director, giving place to George Simon, the former General Manager; but he died only two years later, and an outsider, H. M. Stephen, was appointed to succeed him. Stephen – generally known as 'Steve' or 'HM', rather than by his awkward Christian name Harbourne – had been an exceptionally able RAF fighter pilot, winner of the DSO, the DFC and bar, and famous for having shot down five enemy aircraft in a single day, 11 August 1940. Since the war he had gained wide experience in newspaper management in the Beaverbrook and Thomson organisations – and oddly enough it had been he who had masterminded the rapid transfer of the *Sunday Times* printing in early 1961. Now, at 135 Fleet Street, he found himself in a very different environment.

For one thing, his starting salary of £6,000 a year, as deputy to Simon, was about half what any other national newspaper would have dared offer. For another, the managers had no budget, and practically no financial information on which to base their plans. The fact was that, like a Victorian factory-owner, Michael Hartwell took most major decisions himself, and his managers merely put them into effect. The result was that they too, like the editorial staff, were infected with the prevailing sycophancy, and sometimes shirked giving him unwelcome news, preferring to reveal only what they thought he would wish to hear. As one manager admitted later, 'Quite often, if we saw a minus sign on a set of figures, we'd put a little stroke down through it to make things look better.'

While things were going well, such peccadilloes could be lost in the current without causing serious problems. Yet a clear insight into the company's weakness was given in a report published in January 1967 by the Economist Intelligence Unit. The Unit surveyed the operations of several newspapers, but visited the *Telegraph* first, and came up with some startling observations; behind the restrained phrases, one senses shock, not to say incredulity.

The report emphasised that personal relations on the paper seemed to be exceptionally good, but was clearly puzzled by the lack of any formal structure. The Board, it said, consisted of the two proprietors, Seymour Camrose and Michael Berry, and the Managing Director, H. M. Stephen, but formal Board meetings were held 'very infrequently, and mainly for statutory purposes'.

All major policy decisions appear to be formulated during informal policy discussions between the proprietors and the Managing Director . . . The Unit found it impossible to prepare a chart of the management structure because in practice lines of communication and authority are not clearly defined . . . The enviable success of *The Daily Telegraph* is based on a brilliant formula, and there is no reason to think that the proprietors will change the formula while it is so successful . . . It was difficult to discover any clear-cut commercial policy. Naturally there is a desire to increase the circulation . . . but in our opinion the organisation is not planned or directed as a normal commercial business . . . There appears to be no formal basis for the selection of future management . . . There appears to be comparatively little interest in training within the organisation, and virtually no training of existing or future management is undertaken . . . There are no formal channels of communication between the top and middle management . . . Managers are not always consulted before important policy decisions are taken . . . Below director and general manager level there is an almost complete lack of costing information, and profitability considerations appear to be largely ignored. This is particularly noticeable in the editorial functions, where no reference appears to be made to costs at any time . . . Department heads who are responsible for spending very large sums have not always a clear knowledge of how much they have spent.

All this sounded like a recipe for disaster – as indeed, in the end, it proved to be; and at the time the report presciently remarked that although the paper's formula was brilliant, 'heavy reliance' was being placed upon it, and that 'there must be some doubt as to whether the organisation is equipped to handle a major change in the advertisement pattern, or more robust competition'.

Most proprietors would have been direly worried by such a diagnosis. Those of the *Telegraph* merely brushed the report aside as an irrelevance, and a bit of an impertinence, too. For once the Daily was less than honest in its presentation of the news: although much of the report's criticism was published in the paper, it appeared under the misleading headline GREAT DIVERSITY IN ORGANISATION OF THE PRESS, and a smaller headline saying '*The Daily Telegraph* – Personal Relations Good'. Elsewhere, the Editor-in-Chief poured scorn on the report, describing it in an article on 18 January 1967 as 'in many ways a depressingly superficial document'. He went on: 'Investigators would have avoided mis-statements if they had interviewed any member of the Board. The Managing Director twice asked to be seen, but his request was not acceded to.'

Berry's general line was that, in a relatively small business, there was no need for elaborate management structures, and that newspapers were in any case an unusual form of business:

A newspaper dies every morning and is recreated entirely new every night. It cannot be so closely fettered by the slide rule and the accountant.

This was Berry's view, and even the experience of losing his own business twenty years later did not change it. Then, as in 1967, he ridiculed complex responsibility-charts, 'in which X reports to Y who reports to Z, with the qualification that for specific factors he has to report to someone else', as 'a parody of the first chapter of St Matthew'.* Anyone coming into a small organisation like that of the *Telegraph*, he said, 'could learn his position in five minutes and the general set-up in twenty-four hours'. The chain of command at 135 Fleet Street, he considered, was 'perfectly simple, but the EIU inspectors, having no chart pressed into their hand, never made any attempt to elucidate it. The system was arranged for people, not the other way round'. As for budgets – he never believed in them, preferring to keep a close eye on costs at weekly meetings with his senior executives.

The only action which the *Telegraph* took as a result of the EIU report was to create a separate Marketing Department. This, however, was not a success, and after a trial period the post of Marketing Director was abolished and the function transferred back to the Advertising Department, whence it had come. The rest of the report's criticisms were ignored; but with hindsight it is clear that many of them were all too accurate.

Easily the most striking fact about the *Telegraph* in the 1960s was that it changed so little. The decade was one of sweeping social innovation. Just as, in Harold Macmillan's famous phrase, the wind of change was blowing through Africa, so a great gale of change swept through Britain. At the Old Bailey D. H. Lawrence's novel *Lady Chatterley's Lover* was declared not obscene – and sold at a phenomenal speed when it appeared in the shops. A group of four Liverpool boys calling themselves the Beatles began to send fans wild, and soon were acknowledged as a new force in the life of the nation by the award of the MBE. Pirate radio-stations broadcast pop music illegally from ships anchored off-shore. Women appeared in topless dresses at fashionable film premieres in London. Miniskirts climbed ever higher. Mrs Mary Whitehouse formed an association to combat sex and violence on television. James Bond made his screen debut. Gas – and later oil – were

---

* 'Abraham begat Isaac; and Isaac begat Jacob; and Jacob begat Judas and his brethren . . .' and so on for fifteen verses.

discovered under the North Sea. Carnaby Street – a decrepit alley behind Regent Street – became the centre of the young fashion world. Drugs and long hair swept in. Homosexual acts between adult men were made legal, as was abortion – both measures passionately opposed. Police introduced the breathalyser, and the death penalty was abolished.

Elsewhere, South African police massacred fifty-six black people at Sharpeville. The Soviet Union put Yuri Gagarin into space. The Communist Wall sprang up in Berlin, severing East from West. The United States became bogged down in an unwinnable war in Vietnam. The world went to the brink of nuclear catastrophe over the Cuban missile crisis. Rhodesia unilaterally declared itself independent of Britain. Israel smashed Egypt and other Arab states in the Six-Day War. Dr Martin Luther King, champion of racial equality, was assassinated in Memphis, Tennessee. France was shaken by student riots. Man first set foot on the moon. Denmark abolished all censorship, held a week-long Sex Fair in Copenhagen, and so ushered in the Permissive Society.

The *Telegraph* reported every one of these events or trends, of course; and usually its coverage was better than that of any rival. Yet the character of the newspaper remained astonishingly constant: grey, restrained, respectable. In most areas of the paper intellectual ideas and fine writing were firmly discouraged, and viewed with grave suspicion if attempted. The sub-editors cut out jokes and flourishes with the precision of surgeons – defending their destructiveness, if challenged, with the irrefutable observation that everybody was short of space. For the livelier members of the staff, the restrictions imposed by devotion to the formula were extraordinarily irksome. In the words of Peregrine Worsthorne:

> There was a dead hand on everything. Foreign and political correspondents were discouraged from writing anything fresh or challenging. It was a *boring* paper: those nightmare leader-page articles about the future of the gas industry! But the great thing was, it seemed to be what people wanted. It never shocked or upset readers with views they didn't like. If it had contained a lot that was exciting and original, they might have resented the feeling that they ought to plough through it all. As it stood, the fact that so much of it was unreadable worked in its favour and was one of its strengths.

One area in which both Daily and Sunday papers did change during the 1960s was that of business and City news. From the late 1950s financial journalism expanded rapidly, as editors belatedly realised that takeover bids and battles were not simply dry business matters but affected the lives of ordinary people. Thus City affairs became human matters, and generated widespread interest. The first City Editor of *The Sunday Telegraph*, Nigel Lawson, took full advantage of the trend, building a strong reputation for his section of the paper and attracting a wealth of advertising. As he later admitted to Hartwell, he got his job partly by subterfuge: when he came for interview from the *Financial Times*, he was still only twenty-nine, but thought he would stand a better chance if he said he was thirty – so he gave himself an extra year. When he left to go into politics less than three years later, everyone thought him crazy, not least McLachlan, who felt certain he had ruined his career. His successor, Kenneth Fleet, was another professional City man, who had worked on the *Sunday Times*, the *Birmingham Post* and the *Guardian*, and built strongly on Lawson's foundations before moving in 1966 to the Daily, whose financial pages he proceeded to revitalise. He, in turn, was succeeded on the Sunday paper in 1966 by Patrick Hutber, a man of high intelligence but erratic judgement, who had been financial adviser to the entrepreneur John Bloom. During his thirteen years on the *Telegraph* Hutber pulled off many City scoops, and his lively articles on the state of the economy won him a wide following. So well did he develop his own style of provocative comment and analysis that he was read with great pleasure even by people who knew nothing about City affairs, and his column became one of the strongest features in the paper. Among his colleagues he was chiefly renowned for the violence of his driving: unable to bear being overtaken, he would compete furiously with other motorists, and it was this recklessness that brought his career to an untimely end, when he died after a crash on the way home one evening at the age of fifty-eight. So violent was the impact of the collision that the engine of his sports car was found lying sixty yards from the rest of the vehicle.

Kenneth Fleet much enjoyed working for Hartwell, whom he found an ideal proprietor – interested, sympathetic and always ready with support if a complaint came in from one of the rich or titled people about whom the City staff had written. Besides, the City sections of both papers, which covered a specialised field, achieved a degree of independence. Yet in the main the character of both Daily and Sunday derived directly from the Editor-in-Chief. If an outside critic said that the papers were at their best (or worst) under one editor or another, the remark betrayed a lack of understanding. The prime weapon of the Daily – it cannot be too often repeated – was news, and in the coverage and presentation of the news, the Editor played no part: a fact which led one member of the staff to describe Hartwell as an emperor with a harem. 'He liked his editors to be castrated. He saw the *Telegraph* as his beloved bride, and wanted her attended by a lot of eunuchs, who would not be able to violate her.'

Even if that image was high-flown, it contained a large kernel of truth. For thirty-two years, from 1954 to 1986, the *Telegraph* was not so much under various editors as under Hartwell, whose devotion to duty was by any standards extraordinary. No proprietor can ever have taken a closer interest in his papers or worked longer hours. No Editor-in-Chief can have read his journals so minutely or striven so hard for their improvement.

Unlike his father, Michael Hartwell was not grand in any way. He hated any form of ostentation. He rarely broke into print, and when he did, his writing was simple and direct, very like his speech in its jerkiness. He certainly never sought to promote himself in either of the papers. He had natural authority and good judgement, but he was never bombastic: his decisiveness sprang from conviction, from knowing what he wanted. His personal habits were equally straightforward. His suits were expensive but not showy. The food and drink which he provided at staff lunches were adequate but never extravagant. Spurning a chauffeur, he always drove himself, usually in a small, cheap car.* At home in Cowley Street, his bedroom was in the basement. He had, it is true, the villa in the South of France, where he would usually spend a month in the summer, and perhaps ten days at Easter; but apart from this, his only real extravagance was the series of election-night parties, which he continued to give on a lordly scale in the tradition established by his father.

Nothing could have been more significant than the fact that, in his choice of a title, Hartwell styled himself 'of Peterborough Court'. That was where his heart lay, in the office. Cynics remarked

---

* Earlier, he had owned some powerful models, including several Rovers and a Cortina Savage, which had a huge, three-litre engine on a normal Cortina chassis. When George Ailles once said to him, 'Doesn't that thing take off?', he replied, 'Yes, it does from time to time.' In the year of Suez he bought a three-wheeled Messerschmitt bubble-car, in which he was often seen to cross Fleet Street in a couple of convulsive leaps. In 1973–74, when petrol rationing threatened, 'in a rush of patriotism' he bought a Mini, and stuck to the breed because it was so good in traffic. Finally in 1985 he switched to a 1.3 Metro – an eloquent contrast with the ostentatious Jaguars and Fords favoured by his senior managers. Lady Hartwell also drove a Mini, for their London garage would not accommodate two cars of larger dimensions.

that his motive in spending so much time there was to escape his wife's parties; the real reason was that he had inherited from his father an immensely strong sense of duty. He saw himself not as the owner of two newspapers, but as the trustee of a national institution, which had been given to him for safekeeping during his lifetime. This was why he always insisted that news must be impartial. The papers, in his view, existed to give a service to readers, and it was the readers who came first: better, therefore, that readers should be accurately informed than that journalists should gratify their own egos by showing off in print.

Even after more than fifteen years at the helm, Hartwell was known to scarcely any of his staff, and an inflexible routine guarded him against chance meetings with strangers or any need for fraternisation. Having worked at home during the morning, he would arrive in the office about twelve-thirty, with every syllable of editorial matter in the day's paper stored in his head, ascend straight to the fifth floor, and ring down for the Managing Editor. Having dealt with him, he might have a guest to a working lunch in his own dining-room – at least once a week, the Managing Director, H. M. Stephen, with whom he would discuss managerial problems. Before the meal he would have a couple of stiff martinis, made with vodka, but no wine with his food. He would work through the afternoon, seeing one or two senior executives on the management side, sending out suggestions for editorial follow-ups, or brief notes of criticism, often scribbled on bits torn from the pages of the paper, with a ring drawn round some offending passage, which reflected his obsessional concern with accuracy: 'Couldn't have been '52 as Attlee was ousted in '51', or, after Latin had been used in a leader, 'What on earth does this mean? Will our leader-writers please stop showing off.' On certain days he also had to fit in visits from the Editor and Managing Editor of the Sunday paper, which he controlled in exactly the same way.

At six the Editor of the Daily would come up to discuss the night's leaders, as he and his predecessor had done for the last twenty-five years, and sometimes, at about seven o'clock, Berry would go down to the Editor's office on the first floor, for an informal talk with the leader-writers. They, by then, might be having a drink, but he himself would touch nothing except soda-water, saying in jest that he never drank alcohol until eight in the evening, after which he never stopped. Then, if no exceptional news story was running, he would go home about eight.

He did make efforts to meet lesser members of the staff, mainly by holding lunches on Tuesdays, but for most people these occasions proved so formal and intimidating that no worthwhile conversation could develop. The meals always followed the same pattern precisely. After drinks, Hartwell sat in the middle of one side of a rectangular table, with seven other people ranged around him, two of them usually there for the first time. Nervousness made the talk stilted and banal, especially before alcohol got to work, for, as a conversation-stopper, Hartwell was in a class of his own. His manner was so abrupt, his responses so jerky, that he had a disastrously unsettling effect on most people talking to him: unnerved by the lack of response, they would chatter more and more wildly, working themselves into extreme positions, aware that he thought them very odd, yet quite unable to stop. As Peregrine Worsthorne put it, 'His long and chilly silences tempt the unwary ... further and further into the wilderness of error ... Being incapable of argument himself, he gives others enough rope to hang themselves with their own contradictions ... Thus he has transformed his own inarticulateness into a dialectical skill.'

To members of the staff, it seemed that there were not many subjects in which Hartwell was interested. He would talk about the City, of course, and politics, and any news story that showed signs of life; but music, the arts, books and sport appeared to evoke little enthusiasm.* Besides, his cast of mind was puritanical, and only someone very foolish or very drunk would have ventured to tell a dirty story in his presence. In general, he gave the impression of being cut off from ordinary life, and at the same time of longing to know what went on in circles less rarefied than his own. Often he seemed like a man who had just returned from a long absence abroad – as one day, after some desultory exchanges about commuting, he asked, 'What are the railway stations like these days? Are they very crowded?' He made it sound as if he had not travelled on a train for years.

On Saturday mornings, for the production of the Sunday paper, a general post took place. The editorial staff moved down from the second to the first floor, to use the large Daily Newsroom, and Hartwell came down to read proofs in the Sunday Editor's office

* The impression was misleading, and at least partly the product of shyness and deafness. Hartwell agrees that music means nothing to him, but vigorously defends his interest in sport, books and the arts, pointing out for example that it was he who chose the first (and most successful) theatre critic of *The Sunday Telegraph*, Alan Brien. Even so, when Kenneth Rose's life of George V won three major prizes – the Whitbread award for biography, the Wolfson prize for history, and the *Yorkshire Post* award for Book of the Year – Hartwell never so much as mentioned the book to its author.

thus vacated. To make him feel one of the team, McLachlan instituted the custom of a working lunch for senior staff, at which Hartwell would join them, in one of the offices. This was a much less awkward occasion than the formal meals on the fifth floor, for people came and went as their workload allowed, and conversation generally centred on the news of the day. Occasionally, however, the temperature fell sharply – as when once, with the Social Democrats surging ahead in the opinion polls, Peregrine Worsthorne raised the question of whether the papers should shift their age-old allegiance from the Conservatives. Hartwell gave him a withering look and said, 'You mean, get aboard the bandwagon?'

This was the only time when – so far as anyone could remember – the question of political allegiance was ever raised or challenged. Hartwell's method of setting the political tone was essentially negative. Having appointed middle-of-the-road editors, he made sure they did not deviate too far – not with heavy-handed directives, but with a hint here, a suggestion there, and mild criticism of any excess committed. The whole company was so permeated by the ethos which his father and he had created that their ideals became self-sustaining: someone had only to murmur, 'I don't think the fifth floor would like that', for the subject to be dropped.

Just occasionally a staff man would meet the proprietor outside the office and see his other side. One such was Fred Whitsey, the distinguished Gardening Correspondent of the Sunday paper since its inception, who was startled, on a Friday evening in the late 1960s, to find Lady Pamela at the end of his telephone. She had a problem: the family had bought a plot of land at St Tropez on which they were building a new villa, but the local people who were supposed to be designing the garden had produced a plan which she thought 'absolutely frightful'. Remedial action was urgent, for work had already started. Did Whitsey know anybody who could go out immediately and produce a better scheme?

With the weekend coming up, the only thing for it, he thought, was to volunteer his own services – so he did, travelling out on Sunday and staying in Nice with Hartwell, whom he found not only companionable but impressively well informed about gardens, and trees in particular. At the site, Whitsey proposed radical changes – not least that they should extend the area of north-facing patio so as to catch more sun. When the local contractors arrived, Hartwell introduced Whitsey as his adviser, and went off to sit on a rock while discussion proceeded. His own main requirement for the garden was that it should have the broadest possible lawn, and this entailed a lot of terracing on the steep hillside; but he accepted

Whitsey's suggestions with enthusiasm, and altogether the excursion was most successful.

Few members of the staff came as close to Hartwell as this. And yet, even though he did not know them, and was manifestly out of touch with the kind of lives they led, he commanded immense loyalty from all ranks. In part this was due to the feudal atmosphere which still pervaded the building, and which caused exchanges like this:

From: the Editor, Sunday Telegraph   24 December 1969
To: All Heads of Departments
I have received the following greetings telegram from Lord Hartwell. 'Christmas greetings and all good wishes to you and your staff.' I have replied: 'Staff Sunday Telegraph warmly reciprocate all good wishes to you and yours Christmas and after.'

To many people in the building, this kind of thing was both lamentable and ridiculous. Yet even those who mocked, referring to their Editor-in-Chief as Lord Copper, and enjoying it when *Private Eye* spoke of his wife as Screaming Lady Pamela, or worse, were eager to do their best for the shy but well-meaning man who controlled their immediate destinies. They knew that he was honest, decent, fair and self-effacing – and about how many other Fleet Street proprietors could that be said?

9 THE GROWING THREAT, 1970–80

For *The Sunday Telegraph*, the year 1970 began with a bang: a summons against the paper and its Editor, Brian Roberts, for contravening the Official Secrets Act. The charge was that on 9 January they had received a confidential report about the military situation in Nigeria, where a civil war had been raging, and on 11 January had 'communicated it to persons to whom they were not authorised to do so' – in other words, had published it. The case was eventually heard at the Old Bailey more than a year later, and the whole episode gave Roberts a new purpose in life: to campaign for the repeal of the Act, which he – like almost everybody in Fleet Street – regarded as hopelessly outdated.

Friday 9 January was as exciting a day at 135 Fleet Street as anyone could remember. The report, entitled 'An Appreciation of the Nigerian Conflict', arrived on the desk of the Features Editor Ralph Thackeray, sent in by Graham Watson of the literary agents Curtis Brown. Clearly it was of high interest and immediate importance, for it exposed, from an obviously inside source, the incompetence and corruption prevailing in the Nigerian army, which the British Government had been supplying with weapons for the past three years in its fight against rebels in Biafra – the eastern region of the country. By then the tribal struggle had reduced Biafra to a critical state, with starvation widespread. *The Sunday Telegraph* had been backing the rebel cause; and now this report, revealing that British aid had been grossly misused, and that the Prime Minister (Harold Wilson) and the Foreign Secretary (Michael Stewart) had misled the House of Commons on the issue, seemed God-given ammunition.

Rapid inquiries made by Gordon Brook-Shepherd (now an Assistant Editor) through the Foreign and Commonwealth Office confirmed that the document was genuine, and had been compiled by Colonel Robert Scott, Defence Adviser to the British High Commission in Lagos. For the moment nobody on the paper knew how it had reached England, but that hardly seemed important. Clearly there was a risk in publishing it, for it was marked 'Confidential', and, although it in no way threatened British national security, it was embarrassing to the Government. Yet as soon as Roberts took it up to the fifth floor that Friday afternoon, Hartwell decided to offer £750 for the right to print it, and to run it across a page-and-a-half.

In purely journalistic terms, there is no doubt that the initial decision to publish was right. To have secured the report was a scoop. Yet at the last moment the entire exercise was rendered worthless by the news that the Biafran resistance had collapsed. This sudden change left Roberts in an acute dilemma – which he sought to solve by giving minimal display to news of the Biafran surrender, and by running the Scott report as planned. That weekend the *Sunday Times* led the paper with a first-class story from Richard Hall in Sâo Tomé, under the headline BIAFRA DIES AS STARVING SOLDIERS FLEE, which revealed that the Federal breakthrough had come on Thursday, and that the Nigerian army was advancing into the heart of the breakaway state. *The Sunday Telegraph* also led on Nigeria, but from a very different angle, flaunting its own scoop with the headline SECRET BRITISH REPORT ON BIAFRA LEAKED, and relegating the real news to a short, single-column piece from Alex Macmillan in Paris, which said that, according to reports reaching the French capital, Biafra was on the point of collapse. Even this sketchy statement was contradicted by another, below it, in which a Biafran spokesman in Geneva dismissed the reports as 'absolute rubbish'.

To Colin Welch, this was 'the worst thing *The Sunday Telegraph* ever did'. Coming in on Sunday to edit the Daily, on Maurice Green's day off, he was completely misled about the state of affairs in Nigeria, having read only *The Sunday Telegraph*'s 'ludicrous feature, which was designed to prove that what had happened that very day could not happen'. Roberts, in Welch's view, should have offered his resignation – even though Hartwell, with his admirable habit of backing his executives, would certainly have refused to accept it.*

Sitting tight, Roberts soon received a visit from officers of the Special Branch, and after some unpleasant exchanges with the police found himself charged, on 17 March 1970, with breaking Section 2 of the Official Secrets Act, 1911. Two days later Hartwell

---

* This was a harsh judgement, for the news had come through at the most awkward moment of the night – after the second edition, when a large number of copies had already been printed – and it would have been extremely difficult, if not impossible, to pull out the feature and replace it with something else.

wrote to the Attorney-General, Sir Elwyn Jones, seeking to implicate himself by taking full responsibility for the receipt and publication of the article, and forwarding a copy of his letter to the Prime Minister, 'in his capacity as Head of the Security Services'. In his reply, the Attorney-General said that he had passed the letter to the Director of Public Prosecutions, but Hartwell was never charged.

In due course Roberts learnt that he and the paper might escape with a nominal fine of £10 if they pleaded guilty, but they did not want to take this option as it would have made life difficult for Colonel Douglas Cairns, another defendant in the case. It was Cairns, the former Military Attaché in Lagos, who had set the report on its way towards Fleet Street by passing it to a senior officer; but since then he had retired and joined Barclays Bank, where any conviction, even if only formal, would have led to his dismissal. So Roberts and the *Telegraph* came up for trial at the Old Bailey in June 1971. The case lasted four weeks and ended – thanks not least to the skilful advocacy of Jeremy Hutchinson, QC – in the acquittal of all the defendants – but not before Roberts himself had suffered the humiliation of being taken down from the dock to the cells every lunch-hour, and then released through a side-door.

Outside the court, Roberts told reporters that the remarks made by the judge in his summing-up had 'lifted the case to an historic level', and that they were bound to lead to a 'greatly strengthened movement to reform this stupid and ambiguous Act'. Later, in an article in his own paper, he wrote: 'It has not been funny for *The Sunday Telegraph* to incur very great expense . . . in fighting for four weeks charges which had been hanging over it for a year, or for its sixty-four-year-old editor to sit for nearly a month in the dock at the Central Criminal Court on a kitchen chair once occupied by one of the Kray brothers.'* The Act, he wrote, must be amended 'so that it can never again be used as a back-door method of attempting to impose Press censorship'.

At one point, in the dock, he provoked laughter by saying, 'The role of martyr is not congenial to me.' Afterwards, however, he made the most of the experience, becoming the hero and champion of those who wished to see the Act reformed, and quietly burying the fact that his triumph in court had derived from a dubious journalistic exercise.

---

* To ease his ordeal, the *Telegraph* management lent Roberts a cushion – and never saw it again.

On his own ground, Roberts was not tremendously impressive – and an incident which took place one Saturday morning in many ways epitomised his regime. At about nine-thirty word spread that somebody had died in one of the cubicles in the men's lavatory on the second floor (a cleaner, getting no response to his bang on the door, had looked over and seen a figure slumped on the seat). This news caused Roberts to lose his head. He ran up and down the corridors shouting, 'There's a shtiff in the gentsh! Get the poleesh!' and telling everyone to keep away. When the law arrived, and moved in on the scene, they found the cubicle empty: it transpired that the supposed corpse had been a tramp, who had come in during the night for a comfortable sleep, and then, when he found things getting rather noisy, had chosen his moment to slip away.

Roberts lived in terror that the *Sunday Times* would pinch all his best news stories – and indeed for years he was convinced that they had a spy in the building. This meant that the lists of stories made out in the Newsroom on Saturday mornings had to be vague enough to confuse a secret agent: as Hartwell remarked, 'You could tell who the author was, and whether he was writing about boxing or geology, but not much more.' Roberts was also a great holder-back of good stories. The first edition of the paper, going out at 6.30 pm, was immediately seen by all rivals, and the most effective way to stop them lifting stories was to withhold them until the second edition, at about 8.00 pm.

For subordinates trying to deal with Roberts, the most annoying fact was that he could be thoroughly agreeable – if he chose to be. His mind was very quick, and he had a waspish sense of humour. Whenever he made the effort to concentrate, his company was rewarding. Yet for most of the time his mind seemed to be either on his farm in Sussex or on the troubles of the North London Polytechnic, of whose governing body he was Chairman; and the need to make journalistic decisions seemed a great chore and provocation. He did, however, make one important change, in that he brought the two halves of the Sunday paper together under his own control, thus ending the traditional split between Editor and Managing Editor. Thereafter, the division between news and features was nothing like so sharp on Sundays as it was during the week.

Perhaps the high-point of his career came in February 1976, when the Queen and the Duke of Edinburgh visited 135 Fleet Street. By then the building, like many of its inmates, was showing its age, and frantic efforts were made to spruce it up, principally by washing down the white marble on the stairs and in the entrance hall – a process which did get rid of some of the grime, but still left the walls looking a dingy yellow. For Len Piddington, the Works Manager, the day was a fearful ordeal, his worst nightmares being caused by the lifts. Wonderful though they had seemed when brand-new in 1929, they were now at the end of their lives; and to make sure that the royal party was neither sent plunging to the depths nor stranded between floors, he had one man riding shotgun in the lift all day, and another stationed in the wheelhouse on the roof. As a central part of the Queen's entertainment, Roberts staged the *Sunday Telegraph*'s main feature conference in his office – an agonisingly artificial affair, for which everyone wore his best suit, tried to look intelligent, and spoke with adrenalin-boosted articulation.

By now the next generation of the Berry family was well established. Both Michael's sons – Adrian, born in 1937, and Nicholas, born in 1942 – had followed their father's example by going into journalism; yet neither, for different reasons, seemed tailor-made to take over from him if ever he decided to retire.

Friends who knew them as children could not help noticing how powerfully their mother dominated them. David Pryce-Jones, a contemporary of Adrian, who was then about twelve, squirmed during a voyage on the *Virginia* in the Mediterranean when Pamela kept saying loudly, to the whole company, 'Why can't Adrian swim like David? Is there something *wrong* with him?' In fact he could swim perfectly well; but other friends experienced the same sort of thing. Other friends experienced the same sort of thing with equal embarrassment – and the result of it was to drive the children in on themselves.

After Eton, Adrian followed his father to Christ Church, Oxford, where he established a reputation for eccentricity. Having missed National Service, he was two years younger than most of his fellow-undergraduates, who found him immensely enthusiastic about everything, and almost equally naïve, a curious mixture of ebullience and shyness. He was mad keen, for instance, to join the Drag Hunt, and made his first – and only – appearance immaculately turned-out; but, since he could scarcely ride, he caused an immediate disaster by losing his nerve as he approached the first fence and pulling his horse off to the left – a manoeuvre which brought down six others.

He was never quite in the smart set of people like Paul Channon, Jacob Rothschild and Edward Cazalet who frequented the Bullingdon Club; yet he established a claim to fame by launching and running the magazine *Parsons' Pleasure*, which Richard Ingrams, founder of *Private Eye* , later acknowledged as one of his models, and a pioneer in the field of satirical journalism. The title itself was faintly salacious – Parsons' Pleasure being the place on the river where nude male bathing was permitted – and Adrian looked back on the magazine from middle age as 'utterly juvenile'. On the desk in his office he kept a telephone which was connected to nothing except a switch with which he could make the instrument ring whenever he wanted to impress or divert a visitor. 'Oh, yes, Mr Vice-Chancellor,' he would say. 'I think we can accommodate you on that.' The device was about as subtle as the magazine, which invented, among other characters, a Russian professor called Fuckoff. But through his contacts Adrian was able to get articles from John Betjeman and his uncle Freddie Birkenhead, and George Gardiner (later a Member of Parliament) wrote an amusing account of how he had rigged the Oxford University Conservative Association's elections, in which his rival for President was the budding Cabinet Minister Kenneth Baker.

Parsons' Pleasure gained a certain notoriety, partly for the way it sent up pompous dons, partly for its condemnation of left-wing students who had taken over the undergraduate newspaper *Cherwell*. Some friends found Adrian 'quite potty', while others thought him very bright. Several times his magazine got into trouble: at one stage the proctors suggested, in the most urbane terms, that it should stop printing scurrilous rhymes about senior members of the university, and at another it was almost sunk by a libel action, brought on by a suggestion that homosexuality was a serious problem in the offices of *Cherwell*; yet it survived its founder, and continued to appear for some time after he had taken his degree.

Going to the provinces in traditional fashion, Adrian learnt all aspects of journalism on the *Walsall Observer* and the *Birmingham Post* before moving to the *Investors' Chronicle*. Then he spent a year writing the script of a film called *Caprice*, about industrial espionage, starring Doris Day and Richard Harris: he described the plot (which was handed to him) as 'brilliant', but reckoned that the film was ruined in the making. After that he spent three years in America – one on the old *New York Herald Tribune* and two on *Time* magazine. He also wrote two spy-thrillers, but grew more and more interested in science fiction and science writing generally, and in 1977 became Science Correspondent of *The Daily Telegraph*. His regular science columns were so lively that three collections of them came out as books. Other books also enjoyed widespread success, particularly *The Next Ten Thousand Years*, which sold 500,000 copies world-wide, and *The Iron Sun*, about black holes, which sold 300,000 copies, both effusively praised by Isaac Asimov, Arthur C. Clarke and other leading authors. Adrian also wrote four computer software packages, including one entitled *The Kings and Queens of England*.

All this was good training for editorial journalism, but not for newspaper management. In his father's words, 'Adrian turns green if he sees a balance sheet', and although he did work for short periods in various management departments of the *Telegraph*, his heart was never in them. As one manager put it, 'he wanted Star Wars, and that was it'. The remark may have been unfair, in that he was by no means obsessed by space weapons, having far wider scientific horizons; but it did sum up his lack of enthusiasm for the business side of the *Telegraph*.

A better bet, as a possible successor, seemed to be the younger son, Nicholas – a sharper, less easy-going version of Adrian, also an able journalist, but much more of a businessman, with a strong entrepreneurial sense. Outsiders thought – and urged – that he should be brought into the *Telegraph* management at an early stage: Nicholas, however, knew better than anyone how independent his father was – a man who liked to run his own show, and rarely accepted interference from anybody, inside or outside the family. As he said, 'The last person with whom he would willingly have shared power would have been one of his sons'.

Joining the firm, but at a comfortable distance from the fifth floor in 135 Fleet Street, Nicholas went to work in *The Daily Telegraph*'s City Office, in Queen Victoria Street, first under Kenneth Fleet, then under Andreas Whittam Smith – a period which he described as one of the most enjoyable experiences of his life. He started in the spring of 1967, and at the beginning wrote under his own name. Among his assignments was a trip to the United States in October 1968, when he reported the election campaign that returned Richard Nixon as President, and covered Governor George Wallace's campaign in Connecticut, in despatches which were lively and well informed.

In January 1969 he began a regular weekly column called 'Market Miscellany' which (in the words of Kenneth Fleet's introductory paragraph) looked at 'the personalities who make finance live and at the situations which make City life profitable'. Because his father did not want him to use his own name, he signed the column with his Christian names, Nicholas William, 'by way of showing him that I also could think up an idea', and over the next two-and-a-half years attracted a wide following, besides learning about finance.

In Nicholas, Fleet discerned many of his father's characteristics. He seemed shy and diffident, and appeared troubled by the fact that his mother had very little time for him. He was acute on detail, and a very astute reader of a balance-sheet. There was no question of his being a passenger on the City Pages: his column was excellent, by any standards. Yet whenever Fleet tried to talk to him about the possibility of moving into the main stream of the paper, he would sheer off and say that he wanted to build up a business of his own.

This he did, with marked success. It was, in his own words, 'the experience I got as a financial journalist that enabled me to strike out on my own'. First he bought into and ran a fairly small company in the City. In 1971 he sold out of that and invested in a smaller private company which ended up owning Harraps, the publishers specialising in French–English dictionaries. Over the next fifteen years he built this firm up into a flourishing business. The advantage of making his own way, he felt, was that whatever he had achieved was more or less due to his own efforts, 'and not to having been catapulted into the family firm'. It also had the secondary advantage of 'not having fouled up' his relationship with his father, which had always been very good.

The same could not be said of relations with his mother. Colleagues gained the impression that he could not get on with her, and the effect of this antipathy was profound, if incalculable: some reckoned that in the end it cost the family their business.

With neither son in direct line of business succession, it surprised friends that Hartwell never brought his nephew Robin Furneaux (later third Earl of Birkenhead) on to the board of the paper. Furneaux was a year older than Adrian, red-headed, shy, rather lazy, but a meticulous worker, a highly intelligent, sensible and likeable man, who enjoyed the world of money and had good financial judgement. Besides, he was without personal ambition, and had a strong loyalty to the family. As it was, Hartwell did give him advice on how to get a job in the City, and he worked in an investment trust and then for Kleinwort Benson, before withdrawing to write books, puzzled that no call from the family had come, and worried that he had done something to offend his uncle. (He died, aged only forty-seven, in February 1985.)

*   *   *

Meanwhile, *The Daily Telegraph* was still going strong, even if, on the editorial side, life was not easy. The main irritant was Peter Eastwood, who in 1970 had become Managing Editor, in charge of the news side, and so gained a pinnacle of power to which he clung for fifteen years. That he was a supreme newspaper technician, nobody denies; but whether the good he did by keeping the news team up to the mark was outweighed by the aggravation and despair which his machinations caused, is open to question. There were four main complaints against him: first, that he was constantly seeking to defend or extend his own territory; second, that, to this end, he kept picking rows with other people; third, that he moved people around arbitrarily, for his own purposes rather than for their own good or that of the business; and fourth, that he resisted every attempt at innovation. He himself believed that he was acting in the best interests of the paper, and his loyalty to both the *Telegraph* and its proprietor was unswerving; yet the fact remains that any number of people testify to the very great dislike in which he was held.

According to Colin Welch, who in all his time as Deputy Editor must have done about four years actually in the chair, while Maurice Green or his successor Bill Deedes were away, 'being Editor of *The Daily Telegraph* in the 1970s was largely a matter of keeping your end up against Eastwood. There was continuous grinding of icebergs – over such matters as who should appoint the specialist correspondents'. Green, for all his mild appearance, stood up to Eastwood better than anyone: a man of great attritional skills, he would win back by stealth ground that seemed to have been lost irretrievably, and at home in the evenings he would joke with his wife about any victories he had scored that day.

Few journalists had a clearer view of the struggle – or felt more vulnerable to its cut-and-thrust – than Frank Johnson, a sharp and witty writer who joined the paper in 1972 as author of the Parliamentary Sketch. Coming from the *Sun*, he saw the *Telegraph* through fresh eyes:

> The *Telegraph* had a dual nature. There was column after column of grey 'news' and seemingly endless 'sport' . . . But dotted around were a few oases: the Peter Simple column; some of the more inventive editorials; [Nicholas] Garland's cartoons; the occasional main feature when not written by a Conservative MP; some of the book reviews. Though the constitution was hazy and unwritten, the oases came under the authority of the

Editor: the surrounding desert under that of a Managing Editor called Mr Eastwood.

Johnson was warned by his predecessor Andrew Alexander that the Parliamentary Sketch was in a 'perilous position'. The writer was appointed by, and answerable to, the Editor; but the piece always appeared on one of the pages controlled by the Managing Editor:

Eastwood . . . was out to control the sketch, I knew it. He would like to have authority over what went in it, or whether it went in at all. Ideally, he would like his own man to write it, not the Editor's. The sketch was the warm-water port, control of which had been the historic aim of his foreign policy.

For eight years the battle flared up intermittently. Johnson's strategy was to enlist the support of the Editor or his Deputy, and get them to complain whenever his piece was left out; and although this would work for a while, 'there would always come a night when Eastwood or his men would move against the sketch once more'. Not till 1979 was the conflict settled. Then, during the General Election campaign, on a day when Johnson had not expected to write a piece, he heard that Mrs Thatcher was to visit a chocolate factory in the Midlands. The theme was too good to miss. Waiting until Eastwood would have gone home, he telephoned through a piece, which appeared on the front page.

Eastwood's displeasure was never made manifest in shouting or abuse. On the contrary, he was at his most dangerous when very quiet. Next day he sent for Johnson. There appeared to have been some failure of communication . . . He had not known that there was to be a sketch . . . Perhaps in future Johnson could let him know when he intended to write . . .

By then Johnson had been recruited to work for *Now!*, the magazine which Sir James Goldsmith was about to launch, and his days at 135 Fleet Street were in any case numbered. But in his next sketch, all ribald references to Tories were removed without his knowledge. He withdrew his services during the last three weeks of the election campaign, his only consolation being that, at the very end, the Editor allowed him to write one article for a page which he alone controlled:

So, after nearly eight years, Eastwood had won. True, I took care to put into my election-morning piece all the phrases which had been taken out of the earlier piece. But Eastwood was the victor.

Johnson found such office politics invigorating. Not so the staff of the Manchester office, with whom Eastwood fought a dogged, long-term battle. From the moment he took over as Managing Editor, he seemed determined to cut Manchester down to size. His ostensible aim was always to reduce the cost of the operation in the north, but his conduct was such as to convince subordinates that he was motivated largely by jealousy: it seemed that he could not bear having an outpost not fully under his control. (The editorial staff there was fifty-strong, and the Northern Editor had wide executive power over the content of the local edition. The leader- and City pages came up from London ready-made, but he supplemented news, sport and the arts with local stories.

Amateur psychologists, seeking to identify the origins of Eastwood's obsession, pointed to the fact that, although brought up in Yorkshire, he had been born in Manchester. This minor misfortune, however, scarcely seemed grave enough to warrant such hostility. More significant – they thought – was an incident which had taken place in 1954, soon after Michael Berry had assumed control of the *Telegraph*. After a blazing row in the Fleet Street Newsroom, one of the senior sub-editors had been dismissed, and, instead of replacing him with a London man, Berry had suddenly brought down Frank Walker, Chief Sub-Editor in Manchester, to fill his place. Eastwood (people said) was furious that his own upward progress should have been blocked by a man from the north – and took it out on Manchester ever after. There followed fifteen years of more or less open warfare, much of it directed against the Northern Editor, Michael Kennedy.

Kennedy first worked for the paper in Manchester as an office-boy in 1941, soon after he had left school and when he was only fifteen. After the war, and service in the Royal Navy, he returned and rose through the ranks to become Northern Editor in 1960. Not only did he show exceptional ability as a general journalist: he became – as he remains – an outstanding music critic, knowledgeable, enthusiastic and stylish, and a musical historian of distinction. To him Manchester was home, and he never had any ambition to work in London.

To the staff of the Newsroom in Fleet Street – and particularly to Andrew Hutchinson, who was Night Editor in the 1970s – it seemed that Eastwood was consumed with jealousy of Kennedy, partly because he wrote well, partly because he had intellectual interests outside the office. Again and again Eastwood let fall snide remarks about how the staff in Manchester were bone idle, how none of them was good enough to hold down a job in London, how they seemed to spend more time at concerts than at work. Sooner or later these shafts would strike home into the people at whom they were directed, if only by a roundabout route – for that was the way in which Eastwood operated: by oblique, indirect disparagement. Even his colleagues in London did not escape. Over lunch he would say things like, 'Maurice Green! You're more likely to find him at Covent Garden than at the leader-writers' conference.'

No sooner had Eastwood become Managing Editor than he appropriated three of the best reporters in Manchester – Kenneth Clarke, Roland Gribben and Chris Munnion – and moved them down to London. Thereafter he seemed to take every opportunity of emasculating the northern office, not merely by refusing to allow Kennedy to recruit new staff, but often by intervening to take Manchester reporters off major news stories while they were developing, and replacing them with London men, to the embarrassment and chagrin of Trevor Bates, the Manchester News Editor.

Hostilities reached a pitch in 1976, when a heavyweight delegation consisting of Eastwood, Bill Deedes, H. M. Stephen and John Evans, the General Manager, came north to let off a bombshell of an announcement. Having taken a room in the Piccadilly Hotel, they summoned the northern staff and told them that the introduction of new printing technology was going to render most of the Manchester operation obsolete. In the end their prediction proved correct; but because they said that the change would come within two years, rather than the ten which it actually took to bring about, 'their dramatic gesture' – in Kennedy's words – 'put the fear of God into everybody and made the NUJ chapel terminally suspicious of Eastwood'.

Thereafter Eastwood was utterly distrusted in Manchester, not only by the staff of the *Telegraph*, but also by members of the Thomson Organisation, in whose building the Manchester office was housed, and who printed the northern edition. As Kennedy put it, 'Getting the paper out became a nightmare, because the whole place was a cauldron of unrest.'

In the south, Kenneth Fleet, City Editor of the Daily, grew so exasperated with Eastwood that in 1976 he took the drastic step of sending a letter of complaint about him to Hartwell. The immediate cause of his outburst was a news story about a decision by the Stock Exchange to appoint a committee of inquiry into the share dealings of Sir Hugh Fraser and other directors of the House of Fraser. This news, Fleet thought, was so important that it ought to appear prominently in the main part of the paper rather than on the City pages. He therefore surrendered it to Eastwood – only to find, in the morning, that it had been suppressed.*

Writing to Hartwell on 22 September, he said that after thirteen years as City Editor of both the Sunday and Daily papers, he was distressed by the way in which 'the large fund of goodwill that formerly existed among the editorial staff' had largely been dissipated, and replaced either by low morale or by outright hostility. 'There are several important reasons for these regrettable developments,' he wrote, 'but undoubtedly one of them is the character, motives and methods of the Managing Editor, Peter Eastwood.' Claiming that Eastwood appeared to 'have a destructive urge', Fleet went on to say that his own professional standing had been undermined by the fact that the paper had missed an important City story. The incident had strengthened his belief 'that we are working for rival newspapers within *The Daily Telegraph*'. If his own knowledge and judgement of subjects within his own field were to be 'capriciously (and maliciously?) ignored or overruled', he did not know how he could carry on.

This blast had little effect. As Fleet knew, Hartwell hated dissension in the ranks, and lectured him sternly on maintaining good relations with his colleagues. But Eastwood, meanwhile, was causing dismay in the Newsroom, where reporters seemed to spend half their time chasing 'wanted' stories that reflected his own obsessions, whether or not they were of general interest. One inescapable subject was sailing, and in particular the Burnham-on-Crouch Yacht Club, whose affairs received an inordinate amount of publicity in the *Telegraph* because Eastwood by then lived close by. Another was trains, and another health, about which he had extraordinary theories. He once deeply embarrassed David Loshak, the paper's Health Correspondent, by asking him to arrange a lunch at the Stafford Hotel with two senior representatives of the National Health Service, with whom the *Telegraph* had been having a row. Hardly had the men settled down to the meal before Eastwood astonished them by telling them that the NHS was a Communist stronghold. 'That's why you're in such a mess,' he insisted. 'You've got to root the Communists out.' His

---

* Fleet was not wholly blameless, as he habitually shirked the news conferences, which he or a deputy was supposed to attend.

Into the computer age: *above*, the new building at South Quay, with the *Celtic Surveyor*, now a restaurant, moored alongside. *Centre*, the new print works at West Ferry Road. *Below right*, a robot handles paper reels in the new factory. *Below left*, inside South Quay.

Right, Directors of the *Telegraph*, 1988.
Back row, left to right: Adrian Berry, H. M. Stephen, David Radler, David Montagu, Lord Camrose, Lord Hartwell, Lord Rawlinson, Daniel Colson, Rupert Hambro.
Front row: Alan Rawcliffe, Joe Cooke, Sir Frank Rogers, Conrad Black, Andrew Knight, Tony Hughes, Anthony Rentoul.

Left: Lord Hartwell presides over a board meeting, December 1985.

New blood: *top*, Conrad Black, and *below*, Andrew Knight.

guests, according to Loshak, were bemused, and did not know what to say.

There was never a moment when Eastwood was not engaged in a battle with somebody; most of his campaigns he won, but one which he lost, spectacularly, was that against the News Editor, Bill Tadd. The saga dragged on for far too long, and was far too complicated, to be recounted here; suffice it to say that, after he had been sacked by Eastwood, Tadd sued him and the paper for libel and in the end, after a battle lasting seven years, was awarded costs, which he believed amounted to £200,000. The incident seemed finally to bring home to Hartwell some inkling of Eastwood's unpopularity.

If the daily paper was a desert dotted with a few oases, the Sunday was not much less dreary. One bright spark was Peregrine Worsthorne, who had established himself in his leader-page articles as a consistently provocative and entertaining commentator on matters political and social. Another was Albany, refined by Kenneth Rose into an astringent, upper-class version of Peterborough: the distinction of the column was confirmed one Christmas when the Literary Editor invited readers to parody their favourite section of the paper, and takeoffs of Albany far outnumbered all other entries.* A third was the Mandrake column, a miscellany run for years by the wonderfully etiolated and charming Lionel Birch (always called Bobby), who had been a founding father of *Picture Post*. Constantly pursued by creditors and former wives – five of them – and repeatedly let down by slow horses, he managed always to appear both helpless and full of merriment: a beguiling combination. Yet in general the Sunday was dull, the main constraint – apart from a desire to conform – being lack of editorial space. In their attempts to make the paper break even, the management kept it tightly packed with advertising, with the result that there was little room in which the writers might spread themselves. Every article had to be kept short, and most had to be cut, often savagely, to the chagrin of the authors, particularly the art, music and drama critics, who felt with some justification that the Sunday paper should have a more leisurely air than the Daily, and that all feeling of relaxation was consistently eliminated.

The principal scourge of the critics was Ralph Thackeray, the Features Editor, who kept his own wry sense of humour well

* The winning entry contained the sentence: 'Few other junior Liberals, I imagine, ride a dromedary before breakfast.'

hidden behind his mask of Lancastrian dourness. With Roberts taking little interest, Thackeray bore an enormous burden, and his one serious fault was that he would not delegate: whenever someone offered to help him, he would respond with a characteristic gesture of drawing together the mass of paper on his desk and folding his arms on top of the heap. He also had a singular method of conducting an argument: instead of raising his voice – as most people do – he spoke more and more quietly, and he had some memorable rows with a colleague who practised much the same technique: to the delight of onlookers, and to their own mutual infuriation, they would finish up in opposite corners of the room, both whispering.

Thack was a master-craftsman, a brilliant cutter and sprucer of slovenly articles, a genius at making things fit into his congested pages. Yet so imbued was he with the ethos of *The Daily Telegraph* that his instinct was to pare everything down to essentials. 'What's it *about*?' he would demand cantankerously of a piece that had become too elaborate – and in the unending drive to cut, it was inevitably the jokes and stylistic flourishes that went first. Young writers on the staff, desperate at the leaden form in which their articles appeared, used to say that if anything funny were printed in the paper, it would have to appear upside-down, or preceded by warning asterisks, with '*Joke' at the bottom of the column, in case retired admirals in Hove or colonels in Dorking should rupture themselves with indignation at finding their legs had been pulled.

Few jokes blew back more unkindly on their makers than the one which Peregrine Worsthorne hatched with his friend George Gale as they drove in a taxi to the BBC Television studios on the afternoon of 23 May 1973. That morning another splendid scandal had hit the headlines: Antony Lambton, Conservative MP for Berwick-on-Tweed and Defence Under-Secretary for the RAF, had announced that 'for personal and health reasons' he wished to tender his resignation. Rumours had been let loose a few days earlier by a report in a German news magazine to the effect that a member of the British aristocracy, with access to government secrets, was a regular client of brothels. Now it came out that Lambton had been photographed in bed with two call-girls, and that the police had taken out summonses against him, alleging possession of cannabis and amphetamines. Worsthorne had been invited by the BBC to discuss the affair with Anthony Howard, Editor of the *New Statesman*, on the tea-time programme 'Nationwide'; and on the way to the studios, he bet Gale that, if somebody asked him what the public thought about politicians going with call-girls, he would reply that he thought people didn't give a fuck.

In the event, this was exactly what he said – and the effect was electrifying. The BBC switchboard was swamped by protest-calls, and at the end of the programme the presenter Michael Barratt apologised for what had happened. Later the BBC put out a statement saying that they deplored the use of the word, but that, as the programme had been live, they had not been able to edit it out: 'It was over so quickly there was nothing we could do about it.'

That evening, the Night News Editor on duty at the *Telegraph* was Adrian Lighter. As the evening wore on, more and more telephone calls came in about the incident, and the Press Association news agency put out a story on how Peregrine Worsthorne, Deputy Editor of *The Sunday Telegraph*, had uttered a four-letter word on television. Clearly, the Night News Editor needed guidance on so delicate an issue. Hartwell had already gone, so Lighter tried to ring him at home, only to be told by one of his daughters that he was out. Insisting that he must speak to him, Lighter extracted another number and dialled that. This time he got the home of Adrian Berry, who came to the telephone but said that his father was in the middle of dinner. Again Lighter apologised and said that he needed Hartwell's instructions immediately.

Eventually Hartwell himself came on the line – whereupon Lighter, in some embarrassment, read him the Press Association story and asked what he should do. Having listened in silence, Hartwell instantly said: 'Three paragraphs, middle page, below the fold, but no fucking in the paper, please.' With which he hung up and went back to dinner – but, typically, sat down without a word of explanation. The rest of the family, rigid with curiosity but not feeling able to show it, were sure that a small war or at least a revolution must have started. Next morning the papers were full of the Lambton affair, which had broken in earnest. With its usual pose of absolute propriety, the *Telegraph* made the most of the scandal, running five stories about it on the front page alone. But when Adrian Berry rushed into the office saying, 'What on earth was all that about?' Lighter pointed to the right-hand centre page (the second main news page), where, exactly as prescribed, there appeared a short, inoffensive piece headed TV VIEWERS PROTEST AT FOUR-LETTER WORD.

Brian Roberts, greatly shocked, suspended Worsthorne immediately, and told Hartwell that he should be fired, or at the very least banned from appearing on television for six months. Maurice

Green was also shocked when he heard that the remark had been planned in advance; even so, he told Hartwell that dismissal would be too harsh a punishment. In the end Worsthorne was forbidden to appear on television for six months, but after a gap of only one week his column reappeared. As far as readers knew, everything had settled down. Yet the long-term effects of his gaffe were profound. Many colleagues believed that this one incautious utterance cost him the editorship of the Sunday paper when Roberts retired in 1976, and when he – the obvious successor – was passed over in favour of John Thompson.

Worsthorne himself was sure that this incident contributed to his downfall. There had, it is true, been one or two other indiscretions – as when he and Nigel Lawson's first wife Vanessa had exchanged shirts in a Brighton restaurant during the Tory Party conference. Hartwell had not found that at all amusing. But now Worsthorne received a ferocious letter from Lady Pamela, saying that his behaviour on television had been outrageous, inexcusable in a senior member of the *Telegraph*, and that he had let Michael down. Worsthorne was amazed that she took the whole thing so seriously; yet from that moment she turned against him.

Hartwell later gave a different account of his own reaction. He was certainly annoyed, mainly because the crucial word had not escaped Worsthorne in the heat of the television lights, but had been premeditated. Yet in his view there were two other considerations which put Worsthorne out of the running for the editorship. One was the fact that, 'come rain or shine', his weekly column was the best thing in *The Sunday Telegraph*, and Hartwell did not think that he would be able to combine the writing of it, which usually took him two whole days, with effective editing. The other reason was Worsthorne's general attitude to the paper, which had been exemplified by an incident when one of the journalists' unions called a strike on a Saturday afternoon. Bill Aitken, the Chief Sub-editor, not only downed tools himself, but tried to stop colleagues sending copy to the composing-room, whereupon George Evans (the Managing Editor) suspended him. Roberts then assembled the four Assistant Editors (Worsthorne among them), gave each of them a sheaf of copy, and told them to sort it out. 'They all,' Hartwell remembered, 'worked frightfully hard, except for Perry, who refused to do a thing, and confirmed me in my belief that he really wasn't interested in any part of the paper except his own column. It was clear to me that he wasn't a team man. It *was* a bit rough that he swore on television, but that had nothing to do with it.'

* * *

At 135 Fleet Street, it sometimes seemed that the main effort of the sub-editors, armed with that formidable weapon, the Style Book, was directed towards suppressing innovation. A new enlarged edition, brought out in 1971, made few concessions to modernity. 'The object of the Style Book is to protect the paper's literary standards,' began the introduction, 'to purge it of solecisms and slang . . . The underlying principle is that *The Daily Telegraph* is printed in English, a language sufficiently rich to render unnecessary the use of Americanisms or most foreign phrases.'

Even to die-hards, the use of slang presented problems: 'The expression "disc jockey" is now accepted as common usage and commonly understood. Accordingly, where necessary the phrase may be used, but always in quotes.' Similarly, '"Phone" or "'phone" are barred in the text of stories. Where "telephone" will not fit in headlines, "'phone" is permitted.'

Sometimes the hand of Eastwood was clearly evident:

A ship is 'secured' and never in any circumstances 'tied up'. Whenever we use the expression 'tied up', we are always bombarded with letters from seafarers. Similarly, a ship is never 'anchored to a buoy' or 'anchored alongside'. It either anchors in open water or is 'secured' to a buoy or alongside a quay.

It was, of course, still forbidden to give rivals any but bad publicity: 'No British newspaper and no newspaper proprietor anywhere are mentioned without special instruction.' Field sports were still a tricky area: 'Among other gaffes we have had "marksmen" (the word is "guns"). Marksmen are first-class rifle shots . . . Among sportsmen there is no such verb as "to bag". It is, however, properly used as a noun . . . Shoots "led" by Prince Philip. Shoots are not "led" by anybody. Prince Philip or anybody else "participates" or "organises" . . .'

Occasional touches of humanity crept in, as in one instruction to sub-editors. Paragraphs must still average five or six lines, but

When subbing music, film and other culture notices, allow the author more latitude as to length of sentences and paragraphs. *Les Sylphides* is not quite so fast as Spurs v. Wolves.

Yet often the impression given was of the paper knowing better than anyone else, of wanting to put the world in its place: 'Jesuits are "religious" and live in "houses" . . . All nuns, and only nuns, live in convents' . . . 'ELECTRONIC NOTEBOOK has been registered as a trade mark and should always be given capital E and N' . . . 'The word "plastic" as an adjective is incorrect. The plural form "plastics" should be used in every instance when referring to products of the plastics industry.' Doubtless it was a great comfort to sub-editors to know that 'it is no longer correct to describe Peterborough as "Northants"; Peterborough alone is sufficient'.

As on all newspapers, the tensions of life at 135 Fleet Street found release most easily in alcohol, and a good deal of imbibing took place, mainly in three nearby establishments. Of these the most highbrow was El Vino's – by no means the exclusive preserve of the *Telegraph*, but the resort of journalists from all the papers – where certain Editors sat ostentatiously at special tables, with bottles of champagne before them, and argument raged for years about whether women should or should not be allowed to stand at the bar. The next smartest watering-hole was the Cheshire Cheese, an ancient pub in Wine Office Court, a few yards away from No. 135, where, for the benefit of tourists, the landlord fostered a Dickensian atmosphere by scattering the floors with sawdust. Here, buffeted by Americans in summer, some of the *Telegraph*'s middle and senior executives would drink. But the refuge of most of the men from No. 135 was the King and Keys, a sleazy, troglodytic pub next door to Peterborough Court. Squashed into a single bar, long and narrow, in no mean discomfort from poor ventilation and people pushing past, the rank-and-file from the *Telegraph* sought to drown their sorrows. Almost always there would be a group of printers at the front, where the saloon was wider, and usually a knot of junior managers. Often Peter Utley was to be seen sitting in a corner, with a beautiful blonde on one hand and a glass in the other. Many an altercation broke out, but none was fiercer than those between Brian Harvey, one-time Features Editor of the Daily, and Michael Hilton, the paper's Diplomatic Correspondent, whose voice, when sufficiently lubricated, would fly up into a strangulated, fortissimo tenor and remain on that level indefinitely. The Harvey–Hilton show became the longest-running entertainment in the Keys, always ready to flare up at any provocation, always likely to end up on the floor, always liable to be banned by the landlord for the duration. Not that Hilton reserved his fire for Harvey: as a trader of gratuitous insults, he gave ground to nobody, and one evening after Peregrine Worsthorne's gaffe on television he shouted out: 'I suppose you're very proud of yourself. All I can say is, you're a *tinsel king* on a *cardboard throne!*'

Another day, two young men from the Sunday paper were having a quiet half-pint at about 2.45 pm in the Falstaff, right opposite the King and Keys. As they gazed out of the window, the bead curtain over the door of the Keys suddenly parted, and out stumbled a scarecrow figure, one of the leader-writers on the Daily. But he was not upright for long. Hitting the cool air, he pitched headlong to the pavement.

A companion emerged just after him. With a double-take that would have looked highly exaggerated on the stage, he found that his friend was not in sight. Then he looked down, spotted him in a heap on the pavement, dragged him upright by the collar, and held him in a standing position against the wall, with one hand clutching the lapels of his coat beneath the chin. The man's head lolled. His arms flapped at his sides. Still holding him, his friend began hailing taxis with extravagant gestures. Every time he half-turned to the street, his colleague slumped to the ground, only to be hoisted up again and repinned to the wall. At last an empty cab appeared and stopped. The friend shovelled in the gangling figure, and away he went.

It was a distressing scene; and, as the young men in the Falstaff remarked to each other, there were two possible explanations of it. Either, that was the state to which writing leaders for *The Daily Telegraph* reduced you; or, that was the state in which you had to be to contemplate so fearful an activity.

Of the old hands who kept up standards, none could claim longer service than H. J. C. Stevens, the Company Secretary, who had taken up the post in 1927, and now, though well past seventy, was still hectoring all who came to him for money. 'Ten thousand pounds!' he bellowed when Colin Welch once approached him for a loan to buy a house. 'You must be MAD! *You* can't afford that kind of a palace on *your* salary.' He exploded again when Welch sought to secure better pay for Peter Utley. 'I know that Utley,' Stevens stormed. 'There he sits in the King and Keys, drinking large scotches in rapid succession. I know – I've got my spies.'

'Well, then,' said Welch equably. 'You should sack your spies, because at the moment, on medical grounds, he's only drinking beer.'

'LIAR!' roared Stevens – whereupon Welch walked out, resolving never to speak to him again.

In December 1974 Maurice Green retired, aged sixty-eight, after ten entirely honourable years in the editorial chair, his donnish stoop a little more pronounced, his face whiter than ever. 'A wise, humane and cultured man,' said Hartwell at his farewell lunch: he was presented with a drawing by Augustus John and a piece of porcelain.

The atmosphere at 135 Fleet Street in Green's last year had not been easy – as an article by Bill Grundy in the *Spectator* pointed out. The *Telegraph*, he said, had reached a plateau and was on its way down. Eastwood was even less popular than usual, 'which is saying something', and the 'lunatic policy' of giving the Editor no say in the layout of the front page had had a disastrous effect, resulting in a complete lack of any sense of direction:

> Morale is so low that you have to go down to the basement to find it . . . The young Turks, some not so young, who write the leader columns, have been going their own wild way without very much control at all. Their Powellite leanings are not to the liking of *Daily Telegraph* readers, and they aren't to the liking of Lord Hartwell, and they're not even to the liking of the retiring Editor, Maurice Green.

Grundy might have added that Green himself had not always seen eye-to-eye with his proprietor, especially in the matter of economic policy. The paper had supported Edward Heath as Prime Minister for as long as they thought he was on the right track – and Lady Pamela became a great fan of his – but after he had done his economic U-turn in November 1972, suddenly imposing a compulsory freeze on prices and wages, the *Telegraph* began to criticise him strongly, and he accused the paper in bitter terms of having let him down. Colin Welch and Peter Utley saw things the other way round, and Green usually agreed with them, so that their leaders often brought what Welch called 'rumbles of Keynesian disapproval from the fifth floor'. Green, who was much tougher than he looked, and would always stand up for what he or his men had written, once asked Hartwell, 'Are you asking for my resignation?' Hartwell, much startled, stammered, 'Oh – er, yes . . . I mean, NO!'

Two men keenly hoped to succeed Green. One was Welch, who had beavered away as number two with exceptional good nature and tenacity; but Hartwell's reservations about him had, if anything, increased with the passage of time, and Welch had been driven almost to despair by the way in which every attempt at innovation was frustrated. Once he nerved himself to ask Hartwell if he had ever put a notional black-ball against his name – where-upon Hartwell 'became incredibly embarrassed, even more incoherent than usual, and muttered something about "lacking gravitas"'. Now, in 1974, Welch was passed over for the editorship.

So was Kenneth Fleet, whose 'dearest ambition' it was to become Editor. As City Editor of both papers he had been first-class, and he had got on particularly well with Hartwell, who had always encouraged and supported him; but now, he felt, the Daily had lost its way editorially, and urgently needed modernising, not least in the matter of its appearance. He did not apply to succeed Green. As he says, 'One doesn't put in for the editorship of *The Daily Telegraph*: one hopes for a summons.' When none came, he was severely disappointed.

The man Hartwell chose was Bill Deedes, then sixty-one, an old *Telegraph* hand who had successfully branched off into politics in mid-career and later returned to the fold. He came to the paper – it will be remembered – in 1937, with the *Morning Post*, and after war service with the Queen's Westminsters (during which he won the Military Cross), returned to work on Peterborough under Hugo Wortham. Then in 1950 he was elected Conservative MP for the Ashford division of Kent. Although he held the seat until September 1974, he reached the peak of his political career as Minister without Portfolio from 1962–4, in the Cabinets of Macmillan and Sir Alec Douglas-Home. When Labour returned to power, he began contributing to the *Telegraph* again, and so had been with the paper, in a fashion, for the ten years before he became Editor.

Presuming that Deedes had been appointed as a stop-gap, Fleet hung on for three more years; but when it became apparent that Deedes was going to stay, he left, moving to the *Sunday Times* but still hoping that one day Hartwell might recall him. In fact Hartwell took his defection very hard: once Fleet had announced that he was leaving, Hartwell scarcely spoke to him, and Deedes had the greatest difficulty in persuading him to join the party when he gave Fleet a farewell drink. Fleet left the *Telegraph* feeling sad and hurt, for after fifteen years in his service he regarded Hartwell as easily the best proprietor he had known, in that 'he was always 100 per cent behind his journalists'.

No nicer or more amusing man than Deedes can ever have sat in the Editor's chair: no one more urbane or self-deprecatory, no one with a wittier or more polished turn of phrase in post-prandial speeches. A slim, dapper man, with engagingly arched eyebrows, Deedes was in many ways the archetypal *Daily Telegraph* editor:

intelligent, civilised, amusing, with an intimate knowledge of politics, and innumerable contacts in high places. Yet he was never a very *strong* editor – and he himself was the first to acknowledge the peculiar nature of the hierarchy at 135 Fleet Street. 'Does the head of a family, the head of a family business, instinctively appoint immensely able people to work under him?' he asked, with characteristic self-effacement. 'I rather doubt it.' Deedes's personal slogan was, 'If you go on to a court to play tennis, you go on to play tennis, not to see if the lines are straight.' Knowing Hartwell's attitude, he simply said, 'Right, here we are playing tennis. Let's get on with it.'

Deedes was a delight to work for. 'I never issue an order in this office,' he would say – and it was true. Usually, when a colleague handed in an article, he would thank him or her profusely, and end the meeting with the remark: 'I'm infinitely grateful to you. Your reward will not be in this life.' It was his faintly Churchillian habit of shushing his 's's that gave rise to *Private Eye*'s catch-phrase 'Shome mishtake, shurely – Ed.'; and from his close friendship with Denis Thatcher, with whom he constantly played golf, sprang the immortal – though sadly one-sided – 'Dear Bill' correspondence.

No sooner had Deedes become Editor than Colin Welch told him that someone was 'going to have to have an almighty row with Eastwood'; but Deedes, perceiving that Hartwell did not want two of his editors at each others' throats, took care to avoid any direct confrontation, and tried to circumvent the problems by working closely with Andrew Hutchinson, the Night Editor, and David Ruddock, his deputy. By this means, he reckoned, he achieved 'a good deal of damage-limitation'.

Over the next twelve years, Deedes got as clear a view of Hartwell as anybody in the organisation. Every day at 6.30 pm he would ring up to the fifth floor on the intercom and say, 'Are you free if I come up now?', and by the end of his editorial stint, he reckoned he must have said that 3,500 times. If Hartwell were free, he would say, 'Oh, thank you,' and up Deedes would go. The Editor found his boss extraordinarily considerate, but so shy that it was hard to tell what he was feeling. He gave the impression of always being on a very tight rein of self-discipline – never animated, and never, even when angry, shouting or cursing, but giving vent at most to a cross mutter of 'It's too bad!' Sometimes, in a good mood, he could be very funny, his slightly sly sense of humour coming out in quickly made, cryptic jokes; but, as Deedes remarked, 'the pity was that so few people could share a joke with him'. The central fact of his life was that he worked immensely hard and carried a huge load, since he directed both the managerial and editorial functions of the two papers. Like his father, he was an editor rather than a businessman, naturally more interested in news and its presentation than in accounts. In general, his method was to manage and to mould policy by inches, by detail, rather than in grand sweeps. He would give a hint here, a hint there, rather than lay down the law.

The closeness of Deedes's relationship with Hartwell stood revealed in some of the memoranda which he sent up to the fifth floor. At one stage the Daily attracted the enmity of Sir James Goldsmith, who conceived that the paper was running a campaign against him. The *Telegraph* had criticised him four times in a row, but all over disconnected incidents, and according to Hartwell, the idea of a vendetta was nonsense: as he pointed out, he did not tell his City Editor what to write. But after space had been given to a review of Richard Ingrams's critical book *Goldenballs* on the leader-page, Goldsmith came in to complain to Hartwell and tell him that Deedes should be fired. Since Hartwell could not stand Goldsmith, he merely passed the information on with a grin; and later, when Goldsmith again made contact, Deedes wrote:

> Sir James Goldsmith rang me at 4.45 pm. He wanted me to know that he had won his case. I said that, as we were in the newspaper business, we had caught up with that.
>
> He went on to say that he wished me to know that he had been tackling a 'cancer' in the British Press [journalists leaking information to *Private Eye*, among them the former *Telegraph* man Maurice Barnfather]. This cancer was a menace to the free Press . . . I said I took serious note. He said he would jolly well hope so.
>
> Goldsmith said he regarded the DT as clean, since Barnfather had left the staff. I said I took serious note, and at that moment he was, providentially, cut off.

Deedes did what he could to modernise the paper. For a decade he tried to persuade Hartwell that they should carry a strip-cartoon, probably on one of the classified advertisement pages, and over the years presented him with several designs, only to be told that none was sophisticated enough, and that they must not take the paper down-market. He also pressed in vain for a proper index on the front page. All too aware of the fact that the make-up of the whole paper was amateurish, he paid people extra to redesign particular pages – only to have the results rejected. One problem was that Hartwell was so unfailingly civil, his manners and general attitude so mild: with such a gentlemanly proprietor, it was difficult to be tough. As Deedes remarked, 'In a family company of that kind, the boss is always right.'

Yet there was another constraint which stopped him pressing harder for reforms: his own feeling 'that *The Daily Telegraph* was an unchanging certainty, and that there was quite some virtue in it remaining unchanged in a disturbed world'. Once, when asked if he minded the paper being so grey, he replied, 'Grey? Grey? Well, I'd rather be grey than red or too blue. People find it something to hang on to . . . I sometimes think we're giving people a bit of a raft to carry them on the wild seas of events.'

The Sunday Telegraph was another such raft, and when the time came for a change of editors there, Hartwell's concern, once again, was not to rock it. Roberts retired in 1976 at the age of seventy, after thirty-seven years on the paper. He was described by Hartwell as 'the professional of professionals' in his unremitting drive for accuracy, and as having a touch of genius 'in the Victorian sense, of having the infinite capacity for taking pains'. Under his irascible guidance the paper had performed creditably in terms of sales, usually just behind the *Observer*, sometimes just ahead; but never had it been able to make any impression on the huge lead gained by the *Sunday Times*. The central irony of the position – not lost on Hartwell – was that in the matter of Sunday papers his endeavours had been undermined by the brilliance of his own father. In setting his stamp on the *Sunday Times* fifty years earlier, the first Lord Camrose had in fact created the natural weekend partner of *The Daily Telegraph*, and by the time *The Sunday Telegraph* came along, its place in the scheme of things was already occupied by a paper so successful that it could not be challenged.

Roberts's successor was neither the flamboyant, controversial Peregrine Worsthorne, nor yet any bright outsider, but a steady and serious-looking man from inside the house, John Thompson. After only six years on the Sunday paper, Thompson could hardly be described as one of the *Telegraph* family. Yet he was exactly suited to the role of a Hartwell editor, in that he was able without being aggressive, highly intelligent, of the correct political orientation, and above all civilised. He had what Bill Deedes called 'a safe pair of hands'. His previous career had been modest: he had held staff jobs on the *Yorkshire Evening News* and the London *Evening Standard*, and had been Acting Editor of the *Spectator* before joining *The Sunday Telegraph* as a political writer and assistant editor in 1970. Hartwell told Thompson that he hoped he would be a 'writing editor', but in the event Thompson found himself too busy to contribute many articles.

The new Editor was dismayed when he discovered how the destructive power of the print unions had invaded every sphere of activity. On the Saturday before he took over, his predecessor, Brian Roberts, invited him to observe routine from a spare desk in his office; but when he asked the messenger who carried in bundles of proofs to bring two sets instead of one, the man refused. Thompson watched incredulously as the Father of the relevant chapel, flanked by two unappetising subordinates, told the retiring Editor that they would not do as he had asked unless they received extra money. As neither Roberts nor Thompson was prepared to yield to such petty blackmail, the union simply disobeyed the order.

Over the next few weeks, in an attempt to improve the news pages, Thompson began to devise a more flexible system of lay out. Things seemed to be going well, and even Hartwell, for all his conservatism, approved of the proposed changes. Then suddenly Thompson received a pressing invitation to lunch from H. M. Stephen and John Evans. As they ate in the Savoy Grill, the two senior managers explained that if he went ahead with his plan, it would be the end of the paper: the unions would demand so much extra money for making only modest innovations that the firm would go bankrupt. When Thompson said he could hardly believe it, they assured him with the utmost gravity that they were right.

In due course, by stealth and patience, Thompson managed to create the effect he wanted without any union personnel noticing – and over the years he introduced some lively new writers to the paper, among them Auberon Waugh, Arthur Marshall, Alexander Chancellor, Stephen Pile, Mary Kenny and Oliver Pritchett. Yet he remained oppressed by the way in which the unions were bleeding the paper dry. They – as almost everyone knew – were siphoning off millions of pounds in fiddles and rackets. He, in ten years as Editor, was continually inhibited by shortage of funds, and was never able (for instance) to deploy a single resident foreign correspondent of his own – a frustrating contrast with the free hand enjoyed by his competitors.

In spite of his mild appearance, Thompson had – at any rate to begin with – a strong combative streak, and was quite willing (for instance) to sanction a spoiling operation against the *Sunday Times* in 1977. With much trumpeting, and for £76,000, the *Sunday Times* had bought the serial rights in Arianna Stassinopoulos's forthcoming biography of Maria Callas. The *Telegraph* heard that there existed a diary of Callas's last concert tour, kept by her accompanist, Robert Sutherland, which contained vivid glimpses of the great singer fighting to regain her confidence and technique. For less than a third of what the *Sunday Times* had paid, the *Telegraph* bought the rights in the diary, and so were able to advertise a serial of their own, mentioning all the magic ingredients – Callas, Onassis, yachts, Greek islands – a couple of weeks before the *Sunday Times* was due to launch its series, thus causing the opposition a gratifying amount of confusion and chagrin.

A far less satisfactory enterprise – a disaster, in fact – was the Sunday paper's attempt to serialise a book by Peter Bessell, the one-time Liberal Member of Parliament who in 1978 became chief prosecution witness in the trial of Jeremy Thorpe. Along with three others, Thorpe, the former Liberal leader, was accused – and finally acquitted – of conspiring to murder the male model Norman Scott. The defendants were charged in August 1978, and in October that year *The Sunday Telegraph* signed a contract with Bessell whereby he would receive £50,000 for up to six extracts from his forthcoming book on the Thorpe affair. In due course the Press Council severely censured the paper for making so provocative an agreement, and described the contract, drawn up while criminal proceedings were pending, as a 'flagrant breach' of its guidance to newspapers on payments to witnesses. Yet it was a subsidiary clause in the contract which particularly evoked official condemnation: this specified that if, on legal advice, the paper was not able to publish the book-extracts, the author would receive £25,000 for a series of six special articles, to appear after the trial had finished.

In the event, Bessell received two instalments, totalling £25,000, of his £50,000 fee, before his own disastrous performance in the witness-box at the Old Bailey brought the agreement down in ruins, and the paper terminated his contract with the trial still in progress. The *Telegraph*'s involvement provoked furious controversy, not least because Bessell stood to gain substantially from a conviction. If Thorpe and his co-defendants had been acquitted with the agreement still in force, the author would have received only the £25,000 paid so far; but if they had been convicted, he would have doubled his money. In the House of Lords, Hartwell argued that the paper was buying not Bessell's evidence but the rights in his autobiography as a whole, and the company narrowly escaped being charged with contempt of court; yet this let-off did not conceal the fact that the operation had been a fiasco.

*   *   *

In the mid-seventies, Lady Hartwell found a new outlet for her energies when she became Chairman of the British Museum Society, whose role was (and is) to support the museum and all its causes. Colleagues found her bossiness tiresome, but agreed that she was admirable at getting things done. In her own view, her main achievement at the museum was the transformation of its monthly bulletin from 'a sort of school mag done in his spare time by any young man who had a minute' into a glossy, good-looking publication packed with paid advertising and articles wrung out of the museum staff. The sale of advertisements made it possible to employ a professional sub-editor to produce the magazine. Under her brisk direction, the Society raised handsome amounts for museum funds. She worked at the job most assiduously, and by her own efforts extorted some £30,000 from City institutions. (So highly did the Society value her efforts that, after her death, it refurbished and renamed a room in her memory. Today the Pamela Hartwell room is used for small dinner-parties and the entertainment of VIPs.)

Her entertaining was still handsome, too; but in 1979 she shifted the venue of the traditional election party from the Savoy to Cowley Street, where, on the night of 3 May, excitement ran high as the Conservatives swept back to power. 'Noted turncoats like Lord Vaizey, Sir Richard Marsh and Paul Johnson were present to see their conversions reflected in the country,' reported the *Evening Standard*. 'It was said that when Joan Lestor held Eton & Slough, Lady Hartwell declared, "It's that awful school that makes them vote Labour."'

At first her own feelings towards the new Prime Minister, Margaret Thatcher, were not charitable. 'I do wish you would tell that Prime Minister of yours . . .' she would say to Bill Deedes, irked by the knowledge that he was much closer than she would ever be to the family in No. 10 Downing Street. At one of her evening parties she came bouncing up to him and cried, 'That Prime Minister of yours – *I asked her to come here*. And what do you think she said? She had an engagement with a school somewhere. Well, really!' Another time, at lunch in Cowley Street, she said to Deedes, 'I do think it's a bit much. Michael has never been invited so much as to set foot in No. 10 . . .' Back in the office, Deedes rang Richard Ryder, a former member of the *Telegraph* staff, and now in Mrs. Thatcher's Private Office, and said, 'Repair the damage. Let's get this right.' Ryder said, 'Absolutely', and went to work. Three months later, again in Cowley Street, the name of the Prime Minister came up. Deedes said that he hoped Michael had had a chance to meet her. 'Chance to meet!' exclaimed Lady Pamela. 'D'you know what happened? We were asked down to a lunch at Chequers. Rather an odd lot of people, I must say. And as far as I know they only exchanged two words, when the PM said, "Would you care to wash your hands before lunch?"'

There still persisted an undercurrent of suggestion that Pamela tried to interfere with the papers, and that Michael would not allow it. In Deedes's experience, she was no more interfering than any other newspaper proprietor's wife, and even though she sometimes rang him to ask a small favour – a mention for an author, perhaps – it was 'absolutely never anything that Michael would not have wished to have done'. Sometimes, however, she did unburden herself and reveal how bitterly she resented the way Michael immolated himself with the *Telegraph*: she felt that he worked far harder than he ought, and blamed the staff for constantly bothering him – although in truth (as she must have known perfectly well) it was the demands not of other people but of his own conscience that drove him on.

When the great crash came, in 1985, many critics claimed that, until the eleventh hour, the management of the paper had done nothing to plan for the future. This was far from true, and grossly unfair to H. M. Stephen, the Managing Director, who had been trying for more than ten years to re-equip with new forms of typesetting and new presses. As early as 1974 he had begun to urge Hartwell to invest in new machinery. His case was strong. For one thing, the presses installed in 1929 were growing less and less reliable, and would have to be replaced some time; for another, to increase the earning-power of the company, Stephen needed bigger papers – forty-page Dailies and forty-eight page Sundays, which the old presses could not turn out.*

He began the search for a new printworks on his own initiative, when he formed a two-man planning team. Over the next five years Hartwell twice told him to disband the unit, as the firm was not going to be in a position to finance a new building in the foreseeable future; but each time Stephen changed the men's job-titles, told them to keep their heads down, to pretend (if anyone asked) that planning had been suspended, and carry on as before.

The earliest of the planners was Jeff Spry, an inventive engineer who had been Chief Engineer on the *Times* at the age of twenty-six.

---

* Only four of the old machines could print forty-eight page papers. Trials proved that the rest were not up to it.

At the *Telegraph* he had been Deputy Chief Engineer, but after a heart attack, he felt that although he had made a good recovery, he ought not to return to night duties. His *curriculum vitae* included the fact that he was a draughtsman, and, noticing this, John Evans, the General Manager, sent him on a four-month course at Lancaster University, to develop that side of his talent. Back in Fleet Street, he was first given the task of making what improvements he could to the existing machinery, and he soon became so expert that he could talk in the most knowledgeable manner to manufacturers of new presses. Officially the machine-room draughtsman, he became a key man in the planning team.

The other man was Alan Rawcliffe, an electronics specialist who had joined the firm as Communications Manager, but who in 1974 was made Head of Planning and Development. The structure of the firm was so loose that to begin with he was none too sure what the job entailed. His first task was to find out how many men there were on the books; and this, as he later recalled, proved 'one hell of an exercise. There were three-day men, two-day men, one-day men, casuals, casual casuals – everything. We really didn't know how many men we had. The unions ran the departments, and called in whatever men they wanted'.

One of the firm's early ideas was to re-equip with letterpress – that is, to use a modern version of the old technology, with the type set out of molten metal on Linotype machines, and the curved printing plates also manufactured out of metal in the foundry. The initial aim was to remain on the Fleet Street site, replacing old presses with new ones – a difficult exercise that would have taken ten years to complete, but would have been physically possible. What ruled it out was the almost-certain knowledge that the unions would create dire problems while the new machinery was being installed, and that in the long term they would never accept – on that site – the low levels of manning essential to make the paper viable. Already, by demanding outrageous terms, they had made it impossible to use three new presses, Nos 18, 19 and 20, which had been installed in 1968 with the hope of producing larger papers. No. 18 never ran, and for years the other two never ran in earnest, merely being turned over now and then to prevent the bearings going flat.

To research the latest developments in typesetting and printing, the planners travelled many thousand miles, mainly in North America, but also in Europe (and they later pointed out to Hartwell's critics that he never grudged them money for travel). Rawcliffe, for instance, led a party consisting of Hartwell, John

Evans and Peter Eastwood on a week's tour of four plants in Canada and North-East America. In due course they decided that typesetting by computer photocomposition and web-offset printing were the technology of the future, and what the *Telegraph* must have. They also reached the conclusion that the only way to come to terms with the unions was to make a completely fresh start: to build a new plant, away from Fleet Street, and there dictate the terms on which they would hire labour.

Seeing where the future lay was one thing: persuading the unions – principally the NGA and SOGAT – to accept it, quite another. One night, at an early stage, Rawcliffe asked the Father of the *Sunday Telegraph* Imperial Chapel, a big, fat man called Eric Gregory, into his office for a drink, along with a few others, and outlined to them the need for new technology. Gregory was an intelligent and progressive union leader, but now his response was forthright. 'What you're asking us to do,' he said, 'is to walk to the edge of Beachy Head, link arms, let you blindfold us, and all jump off into the unknown. And you're guaranteeing to me that we won't get hurt.'

'That's a flowery way of putting it,' Rawcliffe agreed, 'but, basically, yes.'

'Right!' said Gregory. 'I'm getting f——g out NOW.'

That was the attitude of the unions, not merely at the *Telegraph* but in the newspaper industry as a whole, and as the 1970s wore on, it became increasingly extreme. Few men were more frustrated by it than Len Piddington, the *Telegraph*'s Works Manager, in charge of production, who described his life as 'a continuous battle with the unions', to which he was obliged to devote about eighty per cent of his time. Having come up through the machine-room himself, having worked on the *Radio Times* and the *Daily Mirror*, and having been at 135 Fleet Street since 1964, Piddington knew exactly what was going on: he knew that of the 2,000-odd production staff, fewer than half were necessary, and that 'we could immediately have knocked fifty per cent off the cost of the paper if we'd only been paying the number of men we needed'. There were thirty-six separate chapels in the building, and one or more was always going slow and causing trouble. Night after night Piddington was left 'hanging on a precipice', not knowing whether the paper would go to press on time, or, when the run had started, whether he would be able to finish it. As he remarked, 'Journalists rise or fall on their performance. If the same standards had applied in the machine-room, I wouldn't have had anyone at all.'

The most galling knowledge was that the paper could not afford to take the unions on in an all-out confrontation. The cost of losing a single issue – in sales revenue and advertising – was already £250,000, and rising fast. An all-out strike, lasting several weeks, would quickly make the company bankrupt. Some of the union leaders did not believe this: they thought the Berrys had countless millions, and would keep going anyway. Others thought that the family might go under – but so what? *The Daily Telegraph* was such a marvellous property that some other tycoon would soon snap it up, and their jobs would still be there.

The journalists' unions – the NUJ and the IOJ – had also started to show more muscle, and the first-ever strike by members of the *Telegraph*'s editorial staff was staged in support of a wage-claim during June 1974. The dispute was quickly settled, but it caused great alarm among senior ranks of the Conservative Party, who feared that one of the pillars of their world was crumbling. Such was their concern that Lord Chelwood (the former Sir Tufton Beamish, MP, and a pillar of the Party) approached Kenneth Fleet and asked if he should get together a consortium of wealthy individuals to buy the paper and secure its future. Fleet reassured him, and said that there was no reason for panic; but he got the feeling that if ever financial support was needed, it would be there.

On the industrial front, a trial of strength came in October 1978. At the beginning of the month members of the NGA working in the telecommunications and electronics section of the composing-room refused to handle telephoto equipment (which they had been operating for years) without a pay-increase. On Monday the second the management gave notice that, unless they worked properly in all areas, they would not be paid at all; but they refused to adopt the procedure approved for handling disputes, and on 5 October they went on strike, thereby bringing the London edition of the paper to a halt.

In spite of intensive negotiations, they stayed out for over two weeks. On 16 October, in desperation, Hartwell sent out a letter to every member of the staff, warning that the company was 'in danger of bleeding to death', and that if the stoppage continued, 'the ship itself will sink. Bankruptcy will ensue. The time is not very long.' Having summarised the main moves in the dispute, he finished:

The paper is stopped. No revenue is being earned, creditors' bills are becoming due, all salaries and wages . . . are pouring out – some £750,000 a week. Alone in Fleet Street we are not part of a great conglomerate. Oil, shipping, paper manufacturing will not come to our aid. We spend all our energy and all our resources on our newspapers. This used to be taken for a virtue. Now, if you do not all rally to us, it will be our downfall . . .

Do get it into the heads of those on strike that there is nothing to be gained from heroic gestures, nor is there money for ransom. On the *Telegraph*, Us and Them are the same people.

Yours sincerely, Hartwell, Chairman and Editor-in-Chief.

Only the author and one or two senior managers knew that the aim of the letter, parts of which were published in the paper of October 17, was to 'draw the badger' – for Bill Keys, the General Secretary of SOGAT, had gone to ground for the past week, answering neither written messages nor telephone calls. The device flushed him out. That morning he rang Hartwell and said, 'I see things are getting serious.' Hartwell agreed, and found himself invited to a meeting at the TUC, where, in a marathon session lasting from 5.00 pm to 1.30 am, a formula for ending the dispute was thrashed out. The strike ended on 19 October, when work restarted at 4.45 pm, enabling the London edition of the paper to appear next morning. In it Hartwell addressed a message 'to the readers of *The Daily Telegraph* who are still with us', lamenting the fact that, except for the shut-down of the entire London Press for four weeks in 1955, the stoppage had been the longest ever suffered by a national newspaper, and had cost the firm £1,500,000. During this 'nightmare fortnight', he added, 'we have not been able to write to you, but a great many have written to us. It is not an exaggeration to say that I have been moved by ninety-five per cent of the letters.' Most readers had said that there was no substitute for the *Telegraph*; some offered to take out a year's subscription, to provide some immediate cash; others asked if they could buy shares in the business 'with no thought of a return', and somebody suggested a whip-round of £10 per reader.

This demonstration of goodwill was heartening, and it hinted at one of the paper's main strengths: the immense loyalty of its readers. Yet in saying of the printers 'Us and Them are the same people', Hartwell was profoundly mistaken. It was one of his most cherished illusions that, by his own modest behaviour, his unfailing civility, his lack of airs, his evident commitment to the papers, he had made the printers feel part of the family. This was very far from the truth. As individuals, a great many of the printing staff were perfectly likeable men; but in the body of a union they became infected with unreasoning rapacity and behaved like selfish children. As individuals, they liked what they knew of Hartwell:

even though they hardly ever saw him, they had the image of a real gent – a toff, of course, but a man who was straight and fair and worked longer hours than anybody; yet *en masse* they were out to screw him for every penny they could get. In the end, it was the remorseless greed of the printers, as much as any other factor, that cost him his business. It is certainly true that the management team which he employed were not strong enough or tough enough to staunch the haemorrhage of money caused by over-manning, malpractice and industrial action; yet it is scarcely fair to blame them, for no other management in Fleet Street was any more successful in its battle with the unions during the 1970s.

It came as a shock to many people that the *Telegraph* – of all national institutions – could be strike-bound; at the end of October a rumour spread that the paper was for sale, and that Sir Charles Forte, the catering millionaire, was going to buy it for £14 million. The story was without foundation – and it soon became clear that other managements were in even worse trouble. Only six weeks after the *Telegraph* strike had been settled, a major dispute broke out in Gray's Inn Road, and publication of the *Times* and *Sunday Times* was suspended indefinitely.

Now, if ever, was the moment for the *Telegraph* to make hay. Fate – or a miracle – had temporarily removed its most serious competitor from the scene: and what did it do? Nothing.

When the *Times* strike was but a few days old, everyone in Fleet Street could see that the dispute was going to last for months. One afternoon at the *Telegraph*, when Bill Deedes took the main editorial conference at 3.30 pm, Andreas Whittam Smith made a startling proposal. Prefacing his suggestion with the disclaimer 'I know this isn't cricket, but . . .', he pointed out that it was extremely unusual in commercial life for one's chief rival to be disabled for a lengthy period. There was one task, surely, to which they should all set their minds: that of making certain that the *Times* never recovered its former position. Readers deprived of the *Times* were more likely to try the *Telegraph* than the *Guardian*. Therefore the *Telegraph* should systematically build up and improve all those areas in which the *Times* excelled, especially the letters and the obituaries, in both of which, until then, the *Telegraph* had been comparatively weak.

Deedes looked startled and not a little shocked. As editor, he did, on the whole, reckon he was playing cricket (or at any rate tennis), and this suggestion was certainly neither. But he agreed that Whittam Smith's proposal was important, and said he would mention it to the proprietor. Two days later, again at the afternoon conference, he himself brought the subject up. He had consulted the proprietor, he said, and together they had come to the conclusion that it would be quite wrong to make major innovations. 'You see,' he said, 'we're not sure that our own printers would allow us to make changes of that kind. We're terrified that they might go out on strike as well. We feel it would be very dangerous to change the product in any way.'

Whittam Smith was dismayed by this pusillanimous approach. Like several of the younger people present, he felt certain that much could have been achieved by stealth, and that the talk about the printers not accepting changes was merely an excuse for keeping everything cosily as it always had been. There was, of course, a strong argument in favour of doing nothing: the traditional formula *worked* – so why meddle with it? Hartwell himself was strongly opposed to changing the essential character of the paper for temporary gain; and in any case he did not regard obituaries as a particularly important ingredient.

For a while the conservatives seemed to be vindicated: sales of the Daily rose to an all-time record of more than 1,500,000, and those of the Sunday passed 1,000,000. This was as far as they could go: the old presses were at their limit, and advertisements were being turned away in sheaves, for the machines could not print papers large enough to accommodate them all. Yet what might have been achieved if aggressive innovation had been launched during the twelve months of the opposition's paralysis? Nobody can say; but at the time Whittam Smith was sadly disillusioned by the paper's failure to adapt.

So, to some extent, was Deedes. He too saw that this was a critical period for the *Telegraph*, and did what he could to suggest new initiatives – for instance, to run features, rather than news, on what was known as the Facing Page, opposite the leaders. Everyone, as always, was short of space, and a compromise was arranged: that the Facing Page should carry features of a special kind, in the form of background foreign news. Yet somehow this change was never implemented. Looking back with hindsight, ten years later, Deedes acknowledged that the paper 'ought to have taken a thorough re-stock. But it was a dangerous period because, with no opposition, everything seemed too easy. The truth was that the first Lord Camrose had devised a formula which worked. No one was quite sure why, but by God, it did, and people were reluctant to tamper with it.'

Circulation Figures

	The Daily Telegraph	Selling price	The Times	Selling price
1976 Jan–June	1,315,473		312,379	
July–Dec	1,300,567		306,741	
1977 Jan–June	1,310,011		306,115	
July–Dec	1,326,236		290,770	
1978 Jan–June	1,344,968	9p	293,989	15p
July–Dec	1,372,782		297,738	
1979 Jan–June	1,476,887		On strike	
July–Dec	1,510,766		On strike	
1980 Jan–June	1,445,883	12p March	315,724	20p March
July–Dec	1,433,077		279,059	
1981 Jan–June	1,400,935		282,186	
July–Dec	1,342,007	18p Sept	297,787	
1982 Jan–June	1,305,575		300,700	
July–Dec	1,302,404	20p Oct	305,774	
1983 Jan–June	1,266,069		336,189	
July–Dec	1,245,026		369,419	
1984 Jan–June	1,259,519		381,075	
July–Dec	1,235,489		456,557	
1985 Jan–June	1,221,092	23p Feb	479,640	23p Feb
July–Dec	1,202,290	25p Oct	478,174	25p Dec

So a golden chance was missed – the last, as it turned out, that Hartwell ever had to make a significant advance. From the high-point of 1979, when the circulation of the Daily averaged 1,510,000 in the six months from July to December, sales of both the papers gradually went down. For two years, it is true, they remained above the level which they had reached before the artificial boost of the *Times* strike, but thereafter they steadily declined. Hartwell and his brother had, however, made one important change in the structure of the company: in March 1978, 'to secure the long-term security of *The Daily Telegraph* publications', they had set up a newspaper trust, under the provisions of the Finance Act, 1975. As the Directors' Report for the financial year explained:

Of the ordinary shares of The Daily Telegraph Ltd, 3.1 million of the total 3.2 million were in March transferred from Berry family interests into a newspaper trust, to be known as the Telegraph Newspaper Trust. Control of *The Daily Telegraph*

* Influenced by the introduction of the Portfolio competition. In the same period the *Guardian*'s circulation increased from 308,700 copies to 487,080.

263

will continue in the hands of the Berry family as trustees. The balance of 100,000 shares will remain in Lord Hartwell's Charitable Trust. The [new] trust is set up so that the profits of The Daily Telegraph Ltd can be used to build up the necessary reserves for development, and to ensure the long-term security of our publications, not subject to penal rules of taxation.

The report went on to say that income from the trust could be used only for the general benefit of the papers, or for charitable purposes within the printing and publishing industry. The financial transaction itself was somewhat circular:

For legal reasons it was not possible to transfer the shares in the family trusts direct to the newspaper trust free of payment. It was therefore decided that the newspaper trust should purchase from all holders their shares at the price agreed with the Inland Revenue for capital gains tax and capital transfer tax purposes.

After negotiation, a price of fifty pence per share was fixed, and the family made arrangements to finance the cost – £1,550,000 – by means of a long-term loan, to be repaid out of dividends received from the company. At the same time, there was established The 140 Trustee Company – a management company, with nominal capital of £4, whose function was purely to get things done. (Its name came from part of the Fleet Street property, which extended from No. 135 to No. 140.)

The idea was admirable, but far too late. Funds for redevelopment were urgently needed, and here at last was a means of consolidating profits. Years of market domination, however, had been wasted. For decades the company had led the field by a distance, yet the proprietors' policy had always been not to make too much profit, since most of it would disappear in tax, and for years they held their cover price so far below that of the *Times* that they often came under pressure to raise it from provincial newspaper owners, who felt that the *Telegraph* was artificially holding the whole market back. Now, when the paper needed all the money it could get, its chance of big profits – except during the halcyon days of the *Times*' strike – had gone.

Another obvious deficiency was the lack of any pension fund. For thirty years at least suggestions had been put to the management, and by them to the proprietors, that the firm should establish a fund to which both the company and employees would contribute. Jack Cooper, then a chapel official, had made just such a proposal in the early 1950s, when enthusiasm for a pension scheme was so great that a union delegation offered to forego their next pay-rise, and put that amount into a fund, in lieu of the first company contribution. The idea was rejected, with derision, by H. J. C. Stevens, the Company Secretary, who said that Lord Camrose would never entertain such a proposal. Sure enough, word came down that the present arrangement, whereby the company paid grace-and-favour pensions out of current revenue, was perfectly adequate. So it may have seemed, in 1952; but if a pension fund had been established then, and if the company had contributed to it every year, instead of paying that amount in income tax, there would have built up, by 1980, a very considerable sum.

In an attempt to mobilise funds, the management had resorted to the expedient of selling their freehold in Fleet Street to Rothesay Developments Ltd., a property company, and leasing the premises back. The deal, first mooted in 1977 and signed in 1984, won the *Telegraph* an immediate payment of £10.6 million, another of 'not more than £3 million upon the satisfaction of certain conditions relating to planning permissions', a third of £2 million when the paper gave up vacant possession of its printing works, and two further amounts dependent on the development value of the site. And yet, although the scheme may have looked promising at the outset, it turned out to be a disaster, for one of Rothesay's requirements was that the *Telegraph* should pay for the modernisation of No. 135, including the installation of air-conditioning and ducting for computer networks, and this cost £9 million, on top of the rent of £1,040,000 a year. Fortunately the paper did better with another investment – the shares in Reuters presciently bought by the first Lord Camrose, who, as one of the news agency's trustees, had played a leading part in its reconstruction during 1947. When Reuters went public, the value of the shares held by the *Telegraph* rocketed, and by 1985 they were worth some £29 million. Yet even this amount seemed small when set against the tremendous expenditure that was looming.

10 SLIPPERY SLOPE, 1980–85

Hartwell never knew whether his meeting with Sir James Goldsmith had settled their differences. Early in 1980 the Editor of Goldsmith's new magazine *Now!*, Tony Shrimsley, commissioned Alan Brien to write a piece demolishing the old man of 135 Fleet Street; but Brien, who had been *The Sunday Telegraph*'s first theatre critic, and knew the Berrys of old, came round to see Hartwell and told him what was happening. He then reported to his Editor that he could not dig up enough dirt for the task in hand; whereupon the attack was switched to Lady Pamela, and Antony (formerly Lord) Lambton assigned to write the piece.

Lambton's article in *Now!* appeared in the issue of 11 April 1980, while Hartwell was on holiday at his villa in the South of France. In Fleet Street Peter Eastwood read it with a mixture of incredulity and horror. It was cast in the form of an obituary, as if the subject were dead: headed LADY HARTWELL – BEYOND THE REINS OF POWER, it asked whether she had been 'an *éminence grise*, the Madame de Maintenon of Fleet Street – a female Alberoni – the power behind the only great success in the second generation?'

Eastwood was appalled. Normally, when Hartwell was on holiday, he did not bother him unless some urgent managerial problem arose; but now he thought he must tell him what had happened, so at 11.00 am he put through a call to France. He found that Hartwell had already heard about the article, but did not know any details, so Eastwood had the embarrassing task of reading it out to him over the telephone.

After he had gone some way Hartwell stopped him and asked, 'What's he *on* about?'

'You have to realise he's made the awful assumption that your wife's not with us any more,' Eastwood replied. 'It's an obituary, and a pretty nasty one too.'

Hartwell, by his own account, was 'terribly hurt' and lost his temper. At once he sat down to write a reply, which took him 'three hours and about 40 cigarettes'. He then dictated the letter to his secretary, Eileen Fuller, in London, and asked Eastwood to get it straight round to the *Now!* offices. Eastwood tried to speak to Shrimsley, but found that both the Editor and Goldsmith were away. The man in charge was Michael Crouch, the Managing Editor, who normally dealt with production. Eastwood told him he would like to see Hartwell's reply in the next issue: it would be a bit of a scoop for Crouch, and no doubt he would like to lead the magazine with it. Crouch said he dared not touch it, and tried to take refuge in the fact that the letter was libellous. 'What do you think the *article* was?' Eastwood demanded. Crouch said there was nothing he could do. This news was relayed to Hartwell, who immediately said, 'All right – I'll give them an indemnity against libel.' This – as he found out later – was impossible, but Crouch did not know that, and agreed to publish.

Hartwell's counterblast was printed on 25 April, its effect not spoilt by the fact that it was given minimal display. He began by revealing that Lambton had asked for his name to be omitted from the list of birthdays published in the *Telegraph* because 'many members of the public, reminded of his publicised sexual excesses while Under-Secretary for Defence (RAF), wrote him letters of abuse. This distressed him. I complied.' Later (Hartwell went on) 'your publisher Sir James Goldsmith came to see me. He wanted to know whether *The Daily Telegraph* was running a campaign against him . . .'

So, back to the oldest and dirtiest trick of all – befoul the wife. No straight blows, of course, no statements obliging conviction, nothing like that. Take half a dozen innuendoes, sprinkle generously with malice and let simmer for 2,000 words . . .

Who was chosen as cook of this nauseous concoction? Why, Mr Tony Lambton, who is so sensitive to abuse! The man who let down his Service, his Government, his Party and his wife. The man who has made no amends. The man who idles on his vast estates and amuses himself by occasional spiteful attacks on erstwhile political friends. The man whose only explanation, when surprised by the *News of the World* photographers, was: 'I think that people sometimes like variety.'

Hartwell, Fleet Street

It was clear to senior members of Hartwell's staff that the incident had upset him badly. When he rang Bill Deedes from the South of France, he sounded 'really riled' – and suddenly Deedes realised how close to each other Michael and Pamela were, in spite of the difference in their characters. Yet neither Deedes nor anyone else in Fleet Street could appreciate how exceptionally cruel Lambton had been to cast his article in the form of an obituary: they did not know that Lady Pamela had already been stricken by cancer, which was to kill her less than two years later.

She fought the disease with characteristic courage, telling nobody – not even close friends – that she was ill; and when the end came, it was so sudden that even the *Telegraph* was taken by surprise. Just after noon on 6 January 1982 Kenneth Rose's telephone rang. On the line was Hartwell, who blurted out, 'Pamela's dying.' He did not like the obituary which the Daily had in stock, he said. 'Could you do another? I leave it in your hands.' There was a tiny pause, and then he added, 'Half a column will do.' The great professional, he knew exactly what everybody was worth, even his own wife.

Rose was shocked by the news. After a period of coolness, he and Pamela had become friendly again, and recently he had written a speech for her to welcome the Queen of Denmark, who came over to address the Friends of the British Museum. Now he set to work, and wrote a warm tribute; he also alerted Bill Deedes, who secretly had been to see George Weidenfeld to ask him for an appreciation. Pamela died next morning, and Rose's piece appeared in the daily paper, Weidenfeld's on Sunday. Hartwell astonished his staff by coming into the office on the evening of his wife's death, as if everything were normal; but they realised that he was using the edifice of his routine as a bulwark against shock and grief. He did the same on the evening of her memorial service, held in St Margaret's, Westminster – and when Deedes said how much he had enjoyed something in the service, he replied, 'Oh, no – the organist was much too slow.' Obituarists mourned her immense vitality, her wry wit, her genius for friendship. Elizabeth Longford remarked that she would have made a splendid Minister for the Arts 'if she had been absorbed *into* politics instead of *by* them'. Lord Weidenfeld recalled how far-flung and high-powered her contacts had been:

I had the privilege of seeing her in action, poring with Dr Adenauer over his collection of political cartoons (mainly of himself), inspecting the Biblical battlefields with Moshe Dayan, probing Albert Speer about his complex relations with the Nazi leaders, eliciting from Guy Mollet some of the untold secrets of the tripartite Suez collusion . . .

Peregrine Worsthorne recalled the excitement and sense of danger that her company induced. After a meeting, he wrote, 'there was always a glow of achievement, not unlike that of a soldier who has proved his courage in battle. Life may be safer now that she is gone. But infinitely less dramatic.'

Her death hit Michael very hard. Those in the office who knew him felt that he was never the same again. While Pamela was alive, malicious tongues said that he had stayed so late at work in order to avoid her parties; now he stayed just as long, but the reason was clear: it was pure devotion to duty that made him stick to his last. Yet now his manner was even more subdued than earlier, and a touch of melancholy had crept into it.

Even without the blow of Pamela's death, Michael was growing old, and problems of age were taxing his strength. For many years he had used a special chair to combat pain from what he thought was a bad back; then the trouble was diagnosed as being in his hips, and operations to renew both joints brought only partial relief, so that he was inclined to move in a stiff-looking shuffle. He was also rather deaf in one ear – a disability which reinforced his natural shyness, to make him still more staccato in conversation. Another physical oddity was that he liked to live in a high temperature: though he always wore a heavy, old-fashioned suit, with a waistcoat, he kept his room at a stifling heat, and he was much disconcerted when, one Saturday, he moved down to the Daily Editor's room to supervise production of the Sunday paper, only to find that engineers had installed air-conditioning. From units along the wall a stream of cold air poured forth. Hartwell was horrified, and on Tuesday said to Bill Deedes, 'Look here – you and I have got to get HM [Stephen] to alter this.' The Managing Director in turn was very put out, and said that it would cost £10,000 to isolate the room from the main system. Hartwell's answer was to send for extra telephone directories, which he laid over the hissing air-ducts, thereby sending the thermostats into paroxysms. Still not content, he imported an electric heater, to produce the tropical conditions which he liked.

Right to the end of his working life he retained one of his most admirable characteristics: generosity. On his papers in general rates of pay had always been low compared with those on national rivals, but whenever a member of the staff did exceptional work, or retired or fell ill, Hartwell was outstandingly open-handed. When Deedes or Eastwood discussed with him what pension a man should receive, he would always round up the figure they suggested to the next highest. If somebody had a serious operation, he would pay the hospital fees and send the patient on a cruise to help him convalesce. Even if someone needed treatment for alcoholism – not unknown in Fleet Street – he would help out. Perhaps the most admirable feature of his largesse was the discreet, unostentatious manner in which it was bestowed.

As he reached three score years and ten, in 1981, he still maintained a work-schedule that would have taxed men half his age; but the sad fact was that the formula which his father had invented, which he himself had nurtured with such devotion, and which had sustained the paper for more than half a century – this magic formula was at last starting to fail. As the table of circulation figures shows (see page 263), the balance of power among the serious daily papers shifted radically in the early 1980s. The *Times*, emerging with new vigour after its year on strike, forged strongly ahead, as did the *Guardian*; but *The Daily Telegraph* sank away from its peak in the second half of 1979, losing much of its age-old advantage.

Of various reasons for the decline, one, undoubtedly, was the poor standard of production. The 1930 presses were coming to the end of their lives, and the paper looked a mess. Besides, their frequent breakdowns meant that editions were often late or copies were lost when a run was interrupted. But mechanical difficulties were only part of the problem; another factor was the dreariness of the layout, and the fossilisation of the paper in an out-of-date format. Yet still Hartwell, backed up by Eastwood, resisted change.

Trouble was threatening from other directions also. From 1979, when unemployment started to rise, there was a sharp fall in display advertising for jobs – a field in which the Daily had for long led the market. At the same time, the cost of newsprint was rising – a factor which hit the *Telegraph* harder than its rivals, as it usually carried more pages. The combination of these two pressures forced the management to increase the price four times in the space of two years – from 12p to 15p, to 18p, to 20p: in the past the price of the *Telegraph* had always been comfortably below that of the *Times*, but by the autumn of 1982, it had caught up, for the first time since 1931, and for a few weeks even went ahead.

Taken together, these changes were insidiously damaging. Income was falling, expenses rising. In the three-year period ending March 1983 the company made a cumulative loss of £7.5 million. The truth – which everybody knew – was that the paper was being bled to death by the increasingly truculent attitude of the print unions; and this made it imperative for the firm to break out of the shackles of traditional Fleet Street malpractice by building a new printing plant which could be realistically manned.

The first site that Alan Rawcliffe and his planning team had in mind was a five-and-a-half acre plot in Wapping Lane, in the East End of London, on the north bank of the Thames just downstream from Tower Bridge; and when Hartwell wrote his usual Christmas message for *Peterborough Court*, the house journal, at the end of 1980, it was there that he predicted the new factory would be:

> The cost [of the new plant] will be daunting. That means we must earn large profits all the years it is a-building. In addition, a very high level of borrowing will be needed, and that, too, however skilfully arranged, must be serviced out of profits.

If wishful thinking could have wrought miracles, those remarks might have done the trick. In reality, Rawcliffe decided that the Wapping site was too small; and one day in July 1981, when he read in the Daily about the formation of a body called the London Docklands Development Corporation, which offered large tax advantages, he threw the paper across the desk to H. M. Stephen and said, 'Why don't we go *there* – to Dockland?' Soon, making his first visit to the area, two miles further east than Wapping, he found a wilderness of tumbledown buildings, disused quays and derelict dock-basins, with nettles, grass and trees sprouting from the ruins of an industrial wasteland. As he said later, 'I could have had any site I wanted – twelve acres, seventeen acres, twenty acres: I only had to name it.' The one he chose was a twelve-acre patch of broken-down warehouses on the side of the old outer Milwall Dock, just off West Ferry Road, on the circular peninsula almost cut off by a loop of the Thames and known as the Isle of Dogs. After negotiation with the LDDC, the *Telegraph* took a lease at an initial annual rent of £100,000 for a term of 200 years, beginning on 25 July 1983.

The West Ferry Committee, formed to design and build the new plant, was run by H. M. Stephen. Like his colleagues, Alan Rawcliffe was worried about where the money would come from – but, extraordinary as it seemed, there were no financial constraints. The message from the top was always the same: get a good deal on whatever you buy, of course, but go for the best equipment, regardless of expense.

Another of the committee, Jack Cooper, had been a *Telegraph* man for most of his working life: he had joined the firm in 1947, and had risen through the Circulation Department to become the paper's Manager in Manchester. Then, in 1976, he had moved to the Thomson Organisation (also in Manchester), before coming south again in 1981, now as Deputy General Manager. There were, he found, great differences between the two firms. At Thomsons everyone was 'very alert financially', and managers received some basic commercial training. At the *Telegraph*, they were given no commercial training, and no financial information, and were much hampered by never knowing whether or not the paper was in profit. Even so, coming back with his new-found expertise, Cooper could see at once that figures being put out by the *Telegraph* 'just couldn't make sense, and that nothing was being done to put the paper on a footing that would at some time produce the necessary finance'.

After their extensive research into new printing technology, Stephen and his committee were well placed to select the best equipment available. Their first choice of presses, in fact, had been Swedish, but the firm which made them was too small to complete an order worth nearly £30 million in the time available, and the contract went instead to Goss of Preston – an offshoot of Rockwell Graphic Systems of Chicago. The order was for forty Headliner units, which the manufacturers specially adapted to include refinements suggested by the *Telegraph* planning team. Some relatively small orders went abroad (including one of £4 million to Sweden for the robots which would move the paper-reels around the printing plant), but seventy-five per cent of the equipment chosen was British-made.

As Hartwell himself wrote, the sums involved were daunting. The budget for the new plant at West Ferry Road alone came to £74.5 million – and then, at the end of December 1983, the company found itself faced with another large and unexpected outlay. On 22 December a letter from the Head Office of the Thomson Organisation was delivered by hand to H. M. Stephen at 135 Fleet Street. It gave twenty-four months' notice to the firms whose papers were then being produced at the Withy Grove works in Manchester, where the northern edition of the *Telegraph* had been printed since October 1940. Thomsons' motive, apparently, was to push the various companies (which included the *Daily Mirror*) into buying the plant for themselves.

Stephen had no intention of doing any such thing, but he moved with lightning speed and sent round a letter accepting the two years' notice within an hour. What he knew, and Thomsons had forgotten, was that according to the Withy Grove contract, whoever gave notice was bound to find the redundancy payments for any workers dismissed. Since the amount involved looked likely to be £5 million, Stephen's swift riposte was extremely lucrative. As he said later, 'Thomsons had their answer so fast that they began to wonder why. But it stuck.'

Stephen moved fast in another direction also. Deciding at once that the paper must have its own printing plant in Manchester, precisely to be free from harassments of this kind, he took the initiative and, without consulting Hartwell, ordered new presses for the north as well as for the south. The move was a triumph of quick thinking and persuasion, for when Stephen telephoned Goss in Preston on 10 January 1983, he learnt that the Managing Director, Ron Stevenson-Smith, had that day gone to Glasgow in the hope of winning an order for new presses from the *Daily Record*. Stephen knew that Goss would be stretched to the limit to turn out the three six-unit lines that he needed for Manchester within the next twenty-four months; it was therefore imperative to forestall any further orders, so he rang Glasgow and with difficulty got Stevenson-Smith extracted from the *Record* board-room in Hope Street.

His call put Stevenson-Smith on the spot, for at that moment he was in the middle of selling the presses to the *Record*. Stephen leant heavily on him, reminding him that the *Telegraph* already had a £28-million deal with Goss, and threatening that he would go straight to the headquarters of the company in Chicago if Preston could not produce what he wanted. Under pressure from an old friend, Stevenson-Smith said he would do it if the *Telegraph* put up a cancellation fee of £500,000, which would be forfeit if the order were not taken up by 28 February. Stephen held out for half that amount, and in the end they settled on £400,000.

For the moment he told no one except Rawcliffe what he had done, but he was greatly relieved when, at a meeting in Fleet Street on 22 February 1983, Hartwell approved the idea of setting up a new plant in Manchester. Having made the decision, Hartwell turned to Rawcliffe and said, 'Well: all that remains – can we get the presses in time?' – at which Stephen had to confess that he had ordered them five weeks earlier.

At once a search began for a site, and in March one was found at Trafford Park, in Old Trafford, some two-and-a-half miles west of the city centre, in the traditional commercial and industrial heart of the Greater Manchester conurbation, and now another Development Area with tax advantages. Here the *Telegraph* took a 125-year lease on a 6.7-acre site, at a starting rent of £46,000 a year. The capital cost of the new plant was estimated at £28.1

million, for a building that would house new editorial offices, besides the printing presses, with sprinkler fire-systems throughout and air-conditioning in the press hall.

Several people tried to stop the company digging itself into this huge pit of debt. One was the Daily leader-writer Matthew Symonds, an economist by training, who took Adrian Berry out to lunch and urged on him the merits of contract printing: it would be far cheaper (Symonds said) to have the paper printed by an outside firm, particularly in the north. With the sophisticated equipment now available, there was no need to spend immense amounts on new plant. Adrian's response was that there was no point in even putting the idea to his father, 'as he never listens to anything I say'.

Another alternative was canvassed by Alan Rawcliffe. One day – before the Manchester plans had been completed – the Managing Director of the Liverpool *Daily Post* arrived at 135 Fleet Street offering to sell the *Telegraph* his modern plant in Liverpool, which had spare printing capacity, for £8 million. His hope was that the *Telegraph* and the *Mirror* would combine to share the new facility. To Rawcliffe the offer was the 'bargain of the year', and when Hartwell rejected it, on the grounds that labour relations were even worse in Liverpool than in London, he asked his visitor to wait for him downstairs. Then, with the man out of the way, he said jokingly to Hartwell, 'You lend me the money, and *I'll* buy the bloody thing!' Afterwards, he could not forbear to point out that, if the firm had taken up the offer, they would have saved £20 million, and probably the Berrys' necks.

As it was, by early 1983 the *Telegraph* had committed itself to the expenditure of £105 million on two new printing plants and ancillary equipment such as the Atex computer system for typesetting and making up the paper which would be installed in Fleet Street. Yet this was by no means all. The company was also faced with finding a very large sum for redundancy payments and buy-outs of restrictive practices, for it was determined to use the switch to new technology as the occasion for ending, once and for all, the gross over-manning which was threatening to bring not only the *Telegraph*, but the whole London newspaper industry, to its knees. The amount needed for this purpose was estimated at £37 million – which put the total cost of regeneration at more than £140 million. Outsiders were amazed, after the event, to find that Hartwell had launched into these immensely ambitious projects without making any arrangements for raising the necessary finance. He simply assumed that banks would lend him the money, when he needed it: as one of his senior executives remarked, 'He and his brother thought they were financially impregnable'.

So did John Holland, the Finance Director, who for thirty years had been the Berry family's investment adviser. Jack Cooper, who had often heard the *Telegraph*'s financial fragility openly discussed at Thomson Board meetings, assumed, as a matter of course, that the company was planning to go public, and that it would raise £100 million or so in equity, even if the Berry family retained over fifty per cent of the shares. But when he suggested this to Holland, he found he was entirely wrong. Holland told him that there was no problem: all sorts of people were offering to lend the firm money. 'I could get £100 million tomorrow,' Holland told him. 'I could get £300 million if I wanted it.'

To raise money was one problem. Another was to persuade the work-force that change must come. Faced with the threat of major innovation, the printers became ever more determined to cling to their privileges for as long as was humanly possible. By now the *Telegraph* had become notorious, even among its competitors, for the number and variety of fiddles practised in its composing- and machine-rooms; and of these none was more flagrant or scandalous than the reading-room sick-pay scheme. This one racket perfectly symbolised the difficulties that management was up against.

The reading-room was the department in which proofs of articles newly set in type were read and checked for mistakes; in it worked forty-eight readers, forty-eight copy-readers, nineteen revisers and runners – a total of 115 men, some of them members of the NGA, some of SOGAT. Over the years the department perfected a scheme whereby it claimed money for men who were off work, allegedly sick.

Most of the men worked in pairs, one reading the original copy, one checking the proof. Unlike other departments, into which the unions brought as many men as possible, the reading-room operated with the smallest staff that could do the job (and often the job was barely done, a good deal of copy never being read for the first edition). The rest of the men were always off sick – and the NGA chapel negotiated the right to charge for the work which those who did come in were having to do for those absent. Then, claiming that they could not tell how long the sick men would be away, they won the right to raise a charge for six shifts for every four that a man missed. Next, SOGAT came in on the act and also claimed six shifts, on the grounds that some of their own men, whose partners were absent, had nobody to work with, and so had to be sent home (also on full pay, of course). Then the revisers and runners demanded their share of the pickings, on equally specious grounds. Finally, in some inexplicable way, the management conceded everybody *ten* extra shifts, rather than six.

Fiddles of this kind were supposed to have been eliminated by a comprehensive new pay agreement negotiated in 1981. Somehow the readers' scheme had slipped through, and management gradually became aware that they were working a sickness rota. But when Jack Cooper instigated inquiries, he could not believe what he was hearing, the figures of extra earnings were so immense. Such was the smokescreen of intrigue and bogus agreements that it took him months to find out what was really happening, but in the end he discovered that eight or ten out of the forty-eight readers were alleged to be sick at any one time, and that the scheme was costing the firm at least £20,000 a week, or £1 million a year. When he challenged the Head Reader to produce a full account, the man went sick, never to return – even though he himself had done nothing wrong. That was by no means the end of it. In exasperation, Cooper took the matter through the official disputes procedure at the Newspaper Publishers' Association – only to have them rule against the *Telegraph* management, on the grounds that no written evidence existed to show that the 1981 agreement had bought out all the old SOGAT practices.

That was the official verdict. The unofficial one, among union members, was that the scheme was a disgrace, and the payments should be stopped. 'You can say that,' Cooper retorted, 'but what if the readers walk out?' Reporting back to his superiors, he warned that if management did not kill the scheme promptly, it might spill over into the rest of the composing-room, and start costing the company £3 million rather than £1 million a year. 'Well,' came the answer, 'at the moment, it's only losing us £20,000 a week, and the loss of one night's production in an all-out strike costs £250,000 – so perhaps we'd better leave it alone.'

This episode starkly reveals the dangers of Hartwell's command structure. At the time, Cooper was given to understand that the instruction to take no action had come down from the proprietor himself. In fact, the matter had never been taken up to Hartwell at all. He knew nothing about it, and was afterwards both astonished and outraged to learn what had been going on. Such a scandal would have been 'a red rag to a bull', and he would have 'fought it tooth and nail'. But, in the matter of the reading-room – as in many others – someone had either shirked facing him with something unpleasant, or had misguidedly tried to shield him from it.

The composing-room proper was riddled with malpractices of

its own. Once upon a time, payments had been based on the London Scale of Prices, established in the nineteenth century – a system which, when used honestly, had proved very fair. In those days each typesetter would place a slug bearing his name at the top of every 'take' or section of copy that he set; but as papers grew larger, and the pace hotter, such individual recording went to the winds, and a general scramble for money ensued.

The most obvious absurdity was that the Linotype operators were paid extra for correcting mistakes – so naturally it was in their interest to make as many as possible. Another bare-faced fiddle was that of 'fat', the generic name applied to any job for which money could be claimed but for which no work was needed. The most obvious example was whole-page advertisements, which came in already made up, except for the date at the top. Having set this one short line, the operators would charge for having set the whole page, and in the smallest possible type. So well was the system of rackets established that there was an 'A' pool of irregular fiddles, and a 'B' pool of regular ones. In the Black Book were kept details of jobs done on busy days but held back so that claims for slack days could be higher. As a result of all this, by the mid-1980s some operators at the *Telegraph* were earning over £700 a week – not quite up to their counterparts at News International, where a man could earn £1,000 a week by setting a few takes at one keyboard for the *Sun*, and then swivelling round to another to set a few for the *News of the World* – but all the same a hefty wage.

Down in the machine-room, the main racket was the numbers game. Each press needed only ten men to run it, but the unions had negotiated an establishment of twenty-two. Here, too, the haphazard development of malpractices had distorted a once-straightforward system. At first, because of the over-manning, each pair of workers would alternate: Charlie, having done a couple of hours, would go off to the pub (or across Shoe Lane, to put in a shift at the *Express*) while Bert took over, and vice-versa. Then, after disagreements among the men, the chapel moved in and organised the rotas. Next came the idea of staggered shifts: one man to do the first four hours of the night, his partner the later ones. The next stage was whole-night shifts: one man on, one off. In the end, though working a nominal four-night week, most men were doing two nights only, for a wage of £300.

These were only some of the frauds with which 135 Fleet Street was rotten.* In trying to curb them, the management was crippled

---

* It should be emphasised that *all* the national newspapers were then in a similar state, and that the *Telegraph* was by no means the worst.

not merely by fear of an all-out strike, but also by the fact that it lacked the basic strength to find out what was going on. The simple truth was that it had not got enough men to burrow down through the layers of deception woven by the unions: as Jack Cooper found when trying to investigate the reading-room, it took months to sort out the real state of affairs in one department – and the firm simply lacked the manpower to do it. (The unions, by contrast, had plenty of chapel officials who did nothing but scheme for the greater wealth of their men.)

In the summer of 1982 a sinister new trend emerged, when the unions twice blackmailed the editorial staff into giving them space in which to air their views on the National Health workers' dispute. On the night of 22 June, 78,000 copies of the paper were lost in Manchester, and in London, faced with unofficial strike action, the Night Editor eventually allowed the NGA a small space in the news columns. After another similar incident, Deedes wrote to Hartwell:

These events can only encourage the militant element in all our print unions to push their luck . . . on a new line of country. That is, demanding the use of columns of the newspaper, on one pretext or another and on terms no one else could get, for purposes of propaganda. If this trend is allowed to continue, we shall be on a perilous slope, which will undermine the independence of this newspaper and its editorial integrity.

In November 1982 the *Telegraph*'s very life was threatened by a dispute in the machine-room, from which the management wanted to remove one of the presses, put on to increase circulation when the *Times* had been on strike, as a means of saving money. The attempt brought 450 members of SOGAT out on strike and cost the company £1.5 million in lost copies. Another crisis threatened in March 1983, when the management put out a call for a fifteen per cent cut in manning (that is, 500 jobs), and a move from hot-metal typesetting to photocomposition. Their hope, in fact, was to achieve a ten per cent cut, in labour or wages: they took enormous trouble explaining their proposals to every one of the thirty-six union chapels in the building, and they made a certain amount of progress. Jack Cooper felt that they could have achieved ten per cent quite easily. But then, as soon as rumblings of discontent were heard, 'the whole scheme was killed from above. Word filtered down that advertising was starting to come back, so that perhaps there would be no need to force the issue. "We don't want to land ourselves in trouble while there's a chance of getting three or four thirty-six-page papers in a week."' Once more, prevarication won the day. Long-term reform, as usual, was sacrificed to short-term expediency.

Meanwhile, with the industrial storm clouds gathering, and tremendous decisions about the future hanging over him, Hartwell continued to act as Editor-in-Chief of both papers, with absolutely no falling-off in interest. He still saw Eastwood at noon, Deedes at 6.30 pm, the Editor and Managing Editor of the Sunday as necessary. 'Can't understand how this letter got into the paper like this,' he scribbled in a typical memo to Deedes. 'Starts with an obvious howler which makes us and the writer look ridiculous.' Another day: 'I don't know why we suddenly took it into our heads to print the Court Circular . . . with such extravagant display. Our Court Circular took over half a column more than the *Times*. Could you please have the style re-examined so that we do not suffer so much space-loss in future.' As ever, he paid the closest attention to detail. 'Warning!' wrote Peter Utley to Deedes one day in the summer of 1983. 'Lord H. thought Charles [Moore]'s leader on hereditary peers "perfectly frightful".' As always, the Parliamentary Sketch was close to the proprietor's heart. 'I think that Godfrey Barker in his sketches is rather too much entering into the fray himself,' he wrote to Deedes on 7 June 1984. 'He seems always to be among howling back-benchers, first on one side and then on the other . . . In the last two days he has attributed the following words to speakers: raved, rhubarbed, droned, shouted, stormed, rambled, thundered, bellowed, bleated, yelled. The result, I find, is confusing.'

Nothing displayed Hartwell's absorption with newspapers better than a letter he sent to young Mark Pooley and his fellow-pupils at a school in Devon, where pupils had been doing a project on *The Daily Telegraph*, and had written to the Editor complaining that the paper carried too much advertising. On 16 March 1984, Hartwell wrote,

Dear Mark,
The Editor has given me your letter because I am the one who wants so many advertisements put in. He would rather have no advertisements at all. Then you and your friends would not ignore all those leading articles he spends so much time on, telling everybody how to make the world better. He is rather hurt that you have put some of them down as 'news' and some as 'entertainment'.

The reason I want so many advertisements is that without them the paper would have to be terribly expensive – something like the price of a dictionary every day. Then nobody would buy it. Actually advertisements aren't a Bad Thing. An awful lot of ours are for jobs going, the sort of jobs people can get if they have done well at school . . .

Your research team says that sixty-seven per cent of all our space is spent on advertisements. I can't think which copy you chose, but if you must quote percentages, I must give you averages. Last week we printed 200 pages in six days, with 49.62 per cent of advertisements. That's 100 pages of editorial. We have eight columns on (almost) each page. That's 800 columns. We reckon 800 words per column without headings. That's 640,000 words per week. That's about eight novels. And you ask, is it a NEWSpaper!

Yours sincerely, Hartwell.

Still, after thirty years as Editor-in-Chief, such detail was bread and butter to Hartwell, and his amazing consistency showed itself in the fact that the editorial content of the papers had scarcely changed. Lord Bruce-Gardyne, the journalist and former politician, still reckoned that 'if you write an article in the *Telegraph*, you can guarantee that the vast majority of Tory MPs will read it. They perceive it as being a newspaper that has great influence with their grass roots.' He went on to say that, although Bill Deedes was 'accessible to the Prime Minister, and she has taken great trouble to get on net with the staff of the *Telegraph*, it would be a mistake to think that the paper was "editorially in the Prime Minister's pocket"'. This view was confirmed by Peter Utley, who pointed out that although the paper had been 'a little bit responsible for the choice of Margaret Thatcher as leader of the party', it had also been extremely critical of a lot of what she had done, 'and nowhere more so' than in its writing about Northern Ireland. 'I don't think,' said Utley, 'that any Ulster Secretary of State would regard the *Telegraph* as his natural friend.'

On the news side, Eastwood was as combative and prejudiced as ever, amazing a new generation. Peter Birkett, who had succeeded Bill Tadd as News Editor at the unprecedentedly tender age of thirty-three, found him a mass of contradictions: on one level immensely kind and avuncular, especially if someone he liked was in personal difficulties, but on another cruel, cold, scheming, and always liable to assert himself pointlessly if he thought his authority had been flouted. Once when Birkett heard of a good story in Belfast, he sent a reporter, Terry Shaw, there in the evening. The moment Eastwood heard that he had left, he said, 'What's he doing there? Get him back' – and Shaw came straight home, an hour after landing at Aldergrove. The same happened to Ken Clarke, another reporter, who was summoned back ten minutes after reaching Dublin.

By now Eastwood's prejudices were rampant. At least they were not political, but social and economic – yet this was bad enough, for he declined to acknowledge that a major recession had set in, and forbade the Newsroom to run stories about it. As everything went plunging, and the paper was losing advertising right and left, he kept exhorting Andreas Whittam Smith to write cheerful stories about how well the economy was doing. Again, just as the boom in property started, Eastwood declared that it was over, and tried to suppress all mention of soaring house-prices. The bottom drawer of Birkett's desk was stuffed with 'wanted' stories – pieces of little general interest which Eastwood had ordered to be written, and which the younger men on the staff tried to keep out of the paper for as long as possible.

Not much of all this reached Hartwell. Some people, among them Hugh Lawson (who by now was General Manager), felt that there was a certain merit in having on the staff one man so unpopular that he drew off everybody's animosity on to his own head, like a lightning conductor. But when Peter Birkett once took Adrian Berry to the canteen for a cup of coffee and said, 'Do you realise what Eastwood is doing to this paper?' Adrian merely replied, 'Oh no – he's by far the best Managing Editor we've ever had.'

The truth was that by then Hartwell had grown set in his ways, and deliberately surrounded himself with other ancients. Had he adapted Julius Caesar's appeal and called out, 'Let me have men about me who are old', everybody would have said, 'Hear, hear.' His own appearance was deceptive, for, unlike his father's, his hair never thinned or even turned grey, but retained its raven black. Even so, by 1984 he was seventy-three; his brother Camrose was seventy-five, Deedes seventy-one, Eastwood seventy-two, Stephen sixty-eight, Holland the same. (Stephen, in fact, had twice suggested that he should step down as Managing Director, but his requests had been brushed aside. Holland, the Finance Director, was also longing to retire.*) The result was a feeling of fossilisation, both

---

* In spite of their requests, Hartwell had persuaded himself that both wanted to stay on.

among the staff and in the building. Young recruits were amazed and depressed by the antiquity of the offices' inhabitants. Penny Jackson, joining in her twenties as a features sub-editor, found her arrival at the *Telegraph* 'a bit like ageing twenty years overnight. Suddenly you were surrounded by a lot of older people, older men; and because they are working in small offices on their own, no one really knows what they're doing, or how long they've been there.' In eight years on the paper she saw Hartwell only twice, both times in the lift, and the only words he spoke to her were, 'Which floor do you want?'

This intense shyness was another handicap with which the management had to contend. As one of them put it, 'It was no use trying to have a reasoned discussion with him about anything. You couldn't just walk in and ask, "Can we talk about so-and-so?" All you could do was say what you had to say, and that was it. Either you'd get an answer then, or he'd give it later.' In effect the managers were all but powerless, as it was Hartwell who invariably took important decisions – provided he was given the necessary information.

Even so, their loyalty to him was fierce – as was that of all the staff: a fact strikingly demonstrated in May 1983, when Peregrine Worsthorne contributed a profile of Hartwell to the *Times*. This, though in general laudatory, contained a telling passage about his daily arrival in Peterborough Court, and described how the commissionaires, 'following a ritual established by his father, all leap to attention before rushing to hold the lifts for the great man, brushing lesser mortals aside like flies in paroxysms of deference that visibly cause their reluctant recipient agonies of embarrassment'.

The truth of this passage was evident to anyone who had witnessed the scene; but it infuriated the commissionaires, who sought to relieve their feelings by drafting a letter to the Editor of the *Times*, in which they referred to Worsthorne as 'the illustrious Ass.[ociate] Editor':

> He has very little knowledge of the workings of the *Telegraph* as such, seeing that his total working hours must be all of six hours. As for his criticism regarding the Commissionaires more to his credit if he attended the man who pays his fabulous salary as the said Ex-Service men do. The Commissionaires who are on duty 365 days a year are not afraid of criticism but we do object to so-called Ass. Editors using the media of type to ridicule us.

As mentioned we are here 365 days a year and he could always spend ½ hour of his valuable time in telling us to our faces where we are going wrong. In fact if he cares to pay our salaries we would open his car door and get the lift on the very few occasions he is here . . .

The proprietor was at his least inhibited during the Saturday working lunches, which continued to be held in one of the offices while the Sunday paper was being put together. On these occasions Ivan Fallon, by now City Editor, found him not in the least shy, but eager for the latest gossip from the City, particularly if it were slightly malicious and to the discomfiture of people he did not care for, like Robert Maxwell, Sir James Goldsmith and Tiny Rowland. Here, on his own ground, Hartwell often became quite expansive; yet he would rarely venture forth to accept lunch invitations outside. Fallon, like his predecessor Patrick Hutber, repeatedly asked him to lunch in the City Office at the back of Bracken House, where they entertained distinguished politicians, economists and businessmen, but he would hardly ever go. Once when Fallon had secured two former Prime Ministers on the same day – Harold Wilson and Edward Heath – he very nearly accepted, but at the last minute refused. As Fallon later remarked, it was hard to imagine any other newspaper proprietor passing up such a chance.*

Many people shared John Holland's view that Hartwell, with his City contacts, would have no trouble raising money from banks. Yet the task proved harder than expected, and when, in 1984, with many contracts for new buildings and equipment already signed, the management found themselves in difficulties, they enlisted the help of the merchant bank N. M. Rothschild. Afterwards, some parties fiercely criticised Rothschilds for the part they played in the events that followed, but Michael Richardson, the senior partner who led the fund-raising, and a man of enormous experience, insisted that from the start his firm did everything possible to make the best of the position in which the paper had landed itself. It was, in his view, an extraordinary state of affairs. 'To us, as simple merchant bankers, it was barely conceivable that any family could have entered into an agreement with the Docklands Corporation and committed themselves so far if they hadn't got the money to

---

* Hartwell later explained that he did not like going to *Telegraph* functions unless he played the principal role. To have met former Prime Ministers at lunch in the City Office would (he felt) have made him look foolish.

pay. It's rather like you going out and agreeing to buy Blenheim without having any funds. What we were asked to do was to unravel the muddle into which Lord Hartwell had got himself.'

The first attempt was the circulation of a Supplementary Memorandum (supplementing the earlier 'Blue Brochure' on West Ferry Road) about the financing of the new printing facilities. The aim of this document was to raise loan finance from selected lending banks, but its main effect was to create uncertainty. Marked 'Private – Confidential', it was dated 19 August 1984, and its blue jacket was embossed with the name N. M. Rothschild & Sons Ltd; yet it began with a clearly stated disclaimer saying that although the merchant bank was distributing the document at the request of the *Telegraph*, it had not independently checked the information and projections contained in it. These had been supplied by the newspaper, and no warranty was given as to their accuracy or completeness. The views expressed in the memorandum were not put forward 'as representations upon which recipients should rely as the basis for making financial commitments'.

The memorandum itself briefly summarised the company's history, explained that in the past its true earning potential had never been realised, outlined the programme of reconstruction to which the firm had committed itself, gave details of the new plants at West Ferry Road and Trafford Park, and summarised plans for reducing the work-force to a realistic level. Appendix I projected trading figures over the next six years, forecasting profit and loss over that period.

The trouble with the whole document, as the banks to which it was sent soon saw, was that its projections were hopelessly optimistic. Sales of the Daily, for instance, were shown as rising from the present 1,230,000 to 1,342,000 in five years' time, and those of the Sunday from 735,000 to 835,000 over the same period – mainly as a result of the increased paging and improved appearance that web-offset printing would give.* Advertising revenue would increase because more pages could be printed on the new presses; business would no longer have to be turned away, and advertisers would gain confidence from the fact that the *Telegraph* was no longer losing thousands of copies through mechanical breakdown or industrial action. The potential for colour advertising would be a further incentive. Profits were forecast to rise from £2.4 million

---

* In fact, even after a brilliantly executed rescue operation, and a remarkable return to profitability, the respective circulations stood at only 1,150,000 and 640,000 in 1989.

in the latest financial year to £19 million in 1984–85, and to £34 million by 1988–89.

Given the past performance of the company, the banks found this forecast incredible – and indeed, as it later transpired, it was based at least in part upon false premises. What had happened was that John Holland had come to Hugh Lawson and Angus Clark (the Joint General Manager) and asked them for some figures about manning levels in the new plant in Manchester. Since he had needed the information within half an hour, they had jotted the figures down on the back of an envelope, and in their haste had omitted the whole of the overseeing staff from their calculations. The next thing they knew – to their horror – was that the figures appeared unchecked in the Supplementary Memorandum.

The *Telegraph* took its first steps to secure the necessary finance at the beginning of 1984, when the company approached its bank, National Westminster. After some discussion, NatWest replied that, before it would consider loan-finance, the firm must enlarge its capital base. John Holland took this to mean the issue of Preference Capital, which would have cost some sixteen or seventeen per cent, immediately payable. NatWest (he contended) had overlooked the fact that both *Telegraph* projects lay in Development Zones, which permitted 100 per cent capital allowances. Loan money could therefore be raised on lease at about half the current base-rate – in effect, five or six per cent – rolled over (that is, not payable until the plants were running) and still giving a decent profit to the bank.

When NatWest rejected his proposal, the new London branch of the San Diego bank Security Pacific, who were anxious to establish themselves in the London lease market, offered to lead a syndicate and arrange the whole leasing without the creation of more capital. In August they began getting a group together. In October they seemed confident, but a month later they began to report snags, because potential entrants were puzzled that the *Telegraph*'s own bankers would not play. Finally, in December, they admitted defeat, and said that the firm would have to raise more equity after all. So it was that a consortium led by Security Pacific, and including the National Westminster County Bank, the Hong Kong and Shanghai Bank and Wardley London, agreed to put up £75 million on condition that the *Telegraph* raised £29 million from the sale of shares. This, then, was the task which Rothschilds were called upon to carry out – the finding of the £29 million.

Their plan was to raise the money by a private placing of shares with leading institutions in the City (a private placing is one in which no general offer is made to the public). The proposal was that they should offer 21,500,000 Preferred Ordinary Shares at a price of 140p per share, which would convert into Ordinary Shares on a one-for-one basis by 1989. Net of expenses, the placing would raise a total of £29.1 million.

To strengthen the company's general credibility, Rothschilds suggested that two new, non-executive directors should be appointed, and in the spring of 1985 they approached two men of appropriate stature: Lord Rawlinson, the former Attorney-General, and David Montagu, a financial expert who held many City directorships and had worked with Hartwell on the Board of London Weekend Television. Both agreed to serve, but only on condition that the private placing was successfully carried through and the company adequately capitalised. The *Telegraph* also appointed Hartwell's sons Adrian and Nicholas as non-executive directors, and reinforced the main Board by promoting to it Tony Broke-Smith, the Advertisement Director, and Alan Rawcliffe.

For the launch of the share offer, Rothschilds prepared a new document, covering much the same ground as the Supplementary Memorandum, but going into the company's finances and plans in greater depth. The existence of the misleading Supplementary Memorandum was a nuisance. Now, in the words of Michael Richardson, Rothschilds 'were in the glue-pot of having to write a document which was absolutely correct – which would send everyone to prison if it was wrong'. To produce it, they carried out the exercise known as 'due diligence', examining every facet of the *Telegraph*'s business, both with executives in 135 Fleet Street, and with the company's auditors, the chartered accountants Saffery Champness. According to Richardson, 'The due diligence documentation was done in the most minute detail'.

By March 1985, the atmosphere inside 135 Fleet Street had become highly fraught. The most mundane irritation was that the building itself was in the throes of remodelling: the refurbishments demanded by Rothesay Developments, the firm which had bought the premises, were being carried out. Air-conditioning was being installed, and ducts laid for computer wiring; whole floors were being gutted and refitted. The staffs of the two papers moved round like droves of sheep in advance of the builders, cursing the dust and noise, as each department was rehoused. The general effect of the reconstruction was to increase the size of the rooms by removing many of the internal walls: the Daily and Sunday Newsrooms both became very large, open-plan areas. But the once-grand entrance hall was cut in half, horizontally, by the introduction of a mezzanine floor: when scaffolding appeared above the commissionaires' desk, less reverent members of the staff predicted that this must herald the construction of some special apparatus which would enable Lord Copper to make sudden, impromptu appearances, a *deus ex machina*, to startle the assembled multitude by addressing them from on high. The idea was enhanced, rather than spoilt, by the news that the management had forgotten the status of their grandiose entrance hall: its 1930s style was now regarded as worth preserving, and conservation bodies intervened to modify the reconstruction. In another phase of the alterations, a door leading off the stairs to the mezzanine floor at the back was blocked in: around this minor change Ronnie Payne and Michael Wharton wove a macabre fantasy, telling themselves and others that behind the doorway there had been walled up old H. J. C. Stevens, the former Company Secretary, now deceased. One day, they predicted, when some future owner of the building opened it again, a spring-gun would kill the first man in, and then a skeleton would come rattling out, with the *Telegraph* accounts still clutched in its bony fingers.

As building work went on, the management was locked in epoch-making negotiations with the print unions, to arrange the buy-out of restrictive practices and new pay scales for composing-room staff. The firm's aim was that, with the introduction of new technology, all compositors would start off at the same wage of £500 a week – but in order to achieve this, the management had to promise men who chose buy-out and redundancy up to £45,000 in compensation. Until every detail was agreed, the unions would not allow the new typesetting machines into the building; nor would they allow compositors to train outside for the new equipment. The result was that six months were lost and the training period had to be truncated, with disastrous results. In the machine-room the initial aim was to negotiate a fifty per cent cut in manning levels. By March or April the printers were at last beginning to realise that the firm meant business, and had started to accept compromises which would have seemed impossible a few months earlier.

Even though no information was officially forthcoming, members of the editorial staff could see that the paper was in deep financial trouble. Then, on 25 February 1985, Eddie Shah, owner of a chain of free newspapers, made the momentous announcement that he was going to start up a new national daily, *Today*, produced and printed outside London, without union labour. Immediately there popped into the head of Andreas Whittam Smith, City Editor of the Daily, the thought that 'this was the moment everyone had been waiting for', and that he should move to do something about it by starting a serious paper of his own. He felt torn between the excitement of his new idea and loyalty to the old firm. On the one hand, he hated the chip-on-the-shoulder attitude which many of the staff at 135 Fleet Street felt towards the *Times* – the idea that the *Telegraph* was a second-class citizen, which could never come to terms with the effortless superiority of its old rival. He also believed that, with more positive direction, the *Telegraph* could dig itself out of the hole into which it had sunk and gain a position of absolute supremacy. On the other hand, he saw that the new printing technology now available meant that it must be possible to launch a high-quality daily on a low budget – and on 25 March 1985 he wrote himself a brief memorandum headed *The Independent*, which outlined his first ideas on how to raise money, how to structure a new organisation, where he would have the paper printed, and what its aims might be.

At that moment, ironically enough, *The Daily Telegraph* was looking its worst. The combination of decaying presses and deliberate slovenliness on the part of the printers served to render its appearance disastrous: poorly printed, and full of mistakes, it had begun to tax the patience of even the most loyal readers. In April letters of protest were arriving at the rate of ten a day. Yet when Bill Deedes said that he thought it essential to remodel the paper before the new presses got going, Hartwell merely expressed alarm and said that in his view there was no need for a revolutionary approach.

No one, at this stage, had any idea that the *Telegraph* would change hands within a few months. As the private placing document remarked, 'It is hoped that the eventual successor to Lord Hartwell will be a member of the Berry family', and odd paragraphs in other newspapers narrowed the field by predicting that the man would be Nicholas. When the private placing was announced on 24 April 1985, the *Guardian* suggested that 'although ownership may be diluted by the issue [of shares], the family flavour at the centre will hardly be affected', and the *Times* echoed this conclusion: 'The City institutions are being left in no doubt that Lord Hartwell, now seventy-three, wishes to be succeeded by a member of the Berry family.' Hartwell himself was not worried: he left things to Holland and the Rothschild men, 'and tried to get on with the running of the papers'.

For a few days all seemed to be going well. On 27 April the

Guardian reported that the initial response to the placing had been good, and that 'funds are expected to be raised easily within two weeks'. Soon, however, it turned out that optimism was premature. With hindsight, it can be seen that most of the placing document's projections were reasonable and accurate – not least the comment that 'the combination of enhanced revenues and the rationalisation of working practices expected by the Directors leads them to the view that the *Telegraph* will achieve substantial profitability from 1988–89 onwards'.* Yet confidence in the whole project was undermined by the company's poor performance in the recent past: in the year ending 31 March 1985, on a turnover of £145 million, the directors estimated that they had made a net loss of £900,000 – a disastrous contrast with the record profit of £7 million made the year before. It seemed impossible that a firm with such a record could turn itself round in the manner projected.

Even with the help of the leading stockbrokers, Cazenove, Rothschilds found themselves in difficulties, and able to raise only £19 million, or sixty per cent, of what they needed. When the offer had run for two weeks, Cazenove advised Hartwell that they could not keep it open for much longer. Some of the people approached thought that, with the unions still rampant, the chances of the paper achieving the savings and profits for which it hoped were small. Others felt that if they did come in they would be very much in the hands of the Berry family. The institutions were deterred by the fact that outside investors were being offered the equivalent of only forty per cent of the company, and that even if all the available shares were taken up, the Berry family would still have fifty-seven per cent, and so remain firmly in control. In other words, if things went wrong, new shareholders would have no power to put them right. Several institutions told Cazenove that the terms of the placing should be amended so that, if various performance targets were not reached at given times, they (the new investors) would move up to a majority position. What they wanted was an agreement which set prearranged levels of profit, advertising, circulation and manning, and which speci-fied that failure to meet these targets could lead to a change in control.

As word leaked out that the private placing was in trouble, Whittam Smith found his loyalty under severe strain. Even though the embryo of his own paper was growing in his mind, he also saw that the *Telegraph* could raise the money it needed by means

---

* In the year ending 31 March 1989 the firm returned a profit of £29 million.

of the Business Expansion Scheme then being promoted by the Government. His idea, in a phrase, was that the Berrys should sell part of the paper to their readers. He realised that there would be no hope of persuading the family to reduce their stake below fifty per cent if they were selling 'to an ogre like Robert Maxwell or Rupert Murdoch'; but to sell shares to readers, he thought, would be 'a perfectly reasonable, civilised thing to do'.

He outlined the scheme in a memorandum to Hartwell dated 14 May 1985, putting the plan forward as 'a means of buttressing our financial position', and pointing out that it would be easy to launch, as a draft prospectus was already in existence. 'Securing extra capital in this way,' he wrote, 'would, I believe, increase the attraction of our current offer of Preferred Ordinary Shares to the City institutions and reduce the amount of lease- and debt-finance that we require ... Apart from extra capital, a successful BES offer would bring us the additional advantage of substantially strengthening our *rapport* with our readers.'

Whittam Smith explained the advantages of his proposal over four typed pages, and offered some ideas about how the plan could be put across. He suggested that the paper should publish a letter to readers from the proprietor explaining the background, and admitting that more capital was needed than had at first been envisaged. At the same time, he said, an employee share-ownership scheme should be established, and also a share option-scheme for senior executives. 'In this way,' he concluded, 'a unity of purpose would be established between readers, City institutions, staff and management. We should then be entitled to feel every confidence in the future of *The Daily Telegraph*.'

Before he sent the memorandum, Whittam Smith consulted directors of the company and friends in the City to make sure that every detail of it was feasible. He then took the paper up to Hartwell and went through it with him. The proprietor's reaction, Whittam Smith later reported, was 'very polite. He immediately showed his own acute financial sense by asking key questions, straight off the bat, and said he would consider it in detail.' But then, a few days later, down came a note saying that Hartwell had consulted the recently appointed non-executive director David Montagu, who had advised against it, saying that it was too late to get readers involved with the running of the paper.

For Whittam Smith, that was the end. He was, and is, convinced that his plan could have saved the Berry family. He felt certain that the paper would have been overwhelmed by the response – and, to judge by the public reaction to Hartwell's message of October

1978, he may well have been right. As it was, rejected, he decided to strike out on his own.

Perhaps if he had put up his proposal at a less tense moment, it might have had a more sympathetic hearing. With the private placing already launched, it had no chance. Yet the company was in dire straits. If the equity money could not be found, the Syndicate of banks would not put up their loan, and the *Telegraph* would be bankrupt. Contracts for the new plant and equipment had been signed; very large bills were becoming due. If Hartwell could not find the equity cash, he would have only two alternatives – either to put the *Telegraph* into liquidation, or to seek bids for the entire business. It was hardly surprising that when, at almost the last moment, Rothschilds found an investor prepared to put in the whole of the £10 million needed, representatives of the *Telegraph* headed in his direction at twice the speed of sound.

11 GIVING IT AWAY, MAY 1985

The series of events which culminated in the paper changing hands began between 10 and 12 May 1985 at Arrowwood, just outside New York. There, at the annual Bilderberg international meeting, Andrew Knight, Editor of the *Economist*, who had flown in from London, ran into the Canadian financier and entrepreneur Conrad Black, down from Toronto. The two men were much the same age – Knight forty-five, Black forty-one – and had known each other for seven or eight years. Once when Black came to London they had been out to supper and the theatre with their wives, and they had kept up an intermittent friendship, united by their interest in newspapers and international affairs, and (not least) by personal ambition.

Both were high-flyers. Black's career so far had been the more spectacular, but Knight was already much respected for his ability as both journalist and businessman. He had edited the *Economist* with distinction for the past ten years: a neat, trimly-dressed man of medium stature, he had a cool, steady look, and sometimes gave the impression of being a cold fish. Some newspaper people were disconcerted by the fact that he had interests in so many fields: he was Chairman of the Ballet Rambert, a governor of the Imperial College of Science and Technology, a governor of the Ditchley Foundation, a member of the Council of Chatham House, and on the Advisory Board of the Center for Economic Policy Research at Stanford University, California. He was also a member of the Steering Committee for the Bilderberg Meetings – international conferences on political, economic and strategic matters, so-called because the first had taken place in the Dutch town of that name.

The meeting at Arrowwood lasted two-and-a-half days. One evening Black and Knight stayed up late discussing a subject of consuming interest to the Canadian: the possibility that he might buy a stake in some British newspaper. They had talked before about opportunities which might arise in the United Kingdom, and now Knight gave an outline of the position at *The Daily Telegraph*.

292

By some extraordinary fluke he was not aware that Rothschilds had launched their private placing of shares: as he himself later agreed, it seemed scarcely possible that somebody so centrally placed in London journalism had not by then picked up this vital fact – yet it was true. He had gone to New York with no knowledge of the *Telegraph*'s fund-raising efforts. Yet even in ignorance of these, he instinctively sketched an organisation which seemed, by its very nature, to be ripe for change. The paper, he told Black, looked unstable. It was losing circulation and position. The two senior Berry brothers, Seymour and Michael, were both in their seventies. Seymour had no children. Of Michael's two sons, Adrian, the elder, was at heart a journalist and author, who loved the paper but had no desire to run it. Nicholas had gone off on his own to rebuild Harrap, the book publishers, and there was no sign of his becoming involved with the *Telegraph*. The long-term future of the paper looked uncertain.

Black was interested. It so happened that in the past few months he had liquidated some assets successfully, and, as he himself put it, 'flushed some money up'. He knew nothing about how the *Telegraph* was run, but said that it was the only English paper he read: he found it excellent, although rather grey. If a chance came to take a financial stake in it, he would very much like to know about it.

The conversation was no more specific than that. But only a few days later, on Saturday 18 May, when Knight landed back at Heathrow and bought a copy of the *Times* to read on the way home, there on the first page of the City section was a leader by Kenneth Fleet, the Executive Editor, saying that the private placing had received 'a gruff response' from the institutions, whom Rothschilds and Cazenove had hoped would put in at least £1 million each, and mentioning the Australian publishing company John Fairfax as a potential investor.

Knowing that Fleet made few mistakes, Knight quickly rang Evelyn de Rothschild, Chairman of the firm (and Chairman also of the *Economist*), to find out if what he had read was correct. The answer, in short, was Yes. Knight then said that he had one or two North American possibilities in mind (this was true: Black was one of several). Would they be precluded because they were outside the United Kingdom? Rothschild replied, 'No, not at all. We really want to raise the money, wherever it comes from.' Knight then asked him to forget the conversation unless he himself reopened it; but he felt fairly sure that the matter would go further, for he himself had introduced Rothschild to Black some years earlier, so that Evelyn already knew the man who now seemed likely to rescue his faltering operation.

Having got hold of a copy of the private placing document, Knight soon saw what it was that had undermined the confidence of other investors. Once an investment analyst himself, he had no difficulty spotting the weaknesses of the *Telegraph*'s position: with its circulation declining, and its cost-per-thousand advantage over rivals dwindling, the paper had committed itself to colossal expenditure – as was confirmed by the long list of legal agreements into which the company had entered. It took him only a short time to see that, with the new printing plants already under construction, and the clock ticking, the company was in terminal danger.

On Monday, at lunchtime in England, Knight tried to call Black at home in Toronto, but found that, since most of their previous communications had been made through their offices, he did not have his ex-directory telephone number. This he managed to discover from another Canadian friend, Don Macdonald (who later became High Commissioner in London). Eventually reaching Black's house, he got a cool reception. For one thing, he had miscalculated the transatlantic time-lag, which at that stage of the summer was six hours, rather than five, so that his call went through at 7.00 am Eastern Canada time. For another, he had not realised that 20 May was Victoria Day, the traditional Monday holiday in honour of Queen Victoria, who (as Black puts it) 'has some antiquarian status as the supposed founder of the country, although history shows that she wasn't much concerned about the Confederation Act'. At seven that holiday morning Black was fast asleep: he could not face the call, and asked Knight to ring back in a couple of hours.

When he did, the Canadian was fully awake. Knight told him the news: that he had spoken to Evelyn de Rothschild, that the position was wide open, that for £10 million he, Black, might be able to acquire twelve or fourteen per cent of the *Telegraph*. At once Black was keen; but he also perceived the snags that had put off the institutions: what use would fourteen per cent of the company be to him? With a stake as small as that, he would be a passenger. What would happen if he could not get on with Lord Hartwell, or if control passed to some other member of the Berry family with whom he turned out to have no *rapport*? Even if his shareholding went up after a while, he might still find himself locked into an unsatisfactory position. Worse, what would happen if the whole operation went 'down the tubes'? He was not, after all, 'in the business of making completely imprudent consecrations of money'.

Knight's answer was simple. The Berrys needed the £10 million badly. 'In fact, they need it *so* badly that if you went in now, you might be able to set your own terms.' At once Black saw that he might be able to negotiate a position in which, in return for putting in a substantial amount, he would get first call on any other shares which might be created in a rights issue, and pre-emptive rights on the shares already held by the family. In other words, if in due course the *Telegraph* found it needed to generate further funds to pay for its modernisation, he would automatically have a chance to increase his stake, or even to take control of the firm by obtaining a majority shareholding.

Black asked Knight to tell Rothschilds that he was interested, and to send a copy of the private placing document to Toronto by courier. This went off post-haste, and in the days that followed numerous transatlantic telephone conversations pushed the matter forward.

By Saturday 25 May, Black's determination had strengthened. At midday he rang another old friend in England, Rupert Hambro, then forty-two and Chairman of Hambros Bank. Tall, good-looking, smoothly cosmopolitan, and a millionaire in his own right, Hambro had first met Black when he went to live and work in Toronto twenty years earlier, and since then had seen him on countless occasions, often sitting up late, drinking a good deal of wine, and (in Hambro's phrase) 'setting the world in order'. Black would impress – and slightly annoy – Hambro with his phenomenal memory, always recalling every word he had said at their last meeting, even when they had both drunk quite a bit. Apart from their other connections, the two men owned holiday homes along-side each other in Florida.

Now, after lunch on Bank Holiday Saturday, Hambro was sitting in the garden of his farmhouse at Kidmore End, near Reading – oddly enough, within a few hundred yards of where Michael Hartwell once lived – when a call from Black came through. What did Rupert know about the *Telegraph* business? His answer was 'Not much', as he had not been following events in Fleet Street with any special interest. But he said he would take immediate soundings and ring back.

He telephoned Michael Richardson, who agreed that things were not going well, and explained the position at length. Richardson then put together a set of papers and sent them to Kidmore End by motorcycle. Hambro, having read them and made some independent checks, rang Black with a positive reaction, and then called Richardson again on Saturday evening, suggesting he should tell Hartwell that a potential investor had been found. This Richardson did. Hartwell's immediate reaction was, 'It's not Goldsmith, is it?' When Richardson told him it was Conrad Black, the name meant nothing, for Hartwell had never heard of him.

Black also asked Hambro to make another contact on his behalf – with Daniel Colson, an outstanding Canadian lawyer whom Black had met at university, and who was now running the London branch of the firm Stikeman, Elliott. A straightforward, humorous man, friendly yet tough, he had – and has – an exceptional knack of conducting complicated negotiations. His dogged honesty and intellectual strength, enhanced by a true Irish gift of the gab (his mother was Irish), made him a formidable agent for any deal to be done in London.

The *Telegraph* management reacted – by their own standards – like lightning, and immediately set up a meeting. Because other commitments made it impossible for Black to come to London, it was arranged that a party should fly to meet him in New York as soon as possible. He could not manage Monday, so it was agreed that they would take Concorde to New York on Tuesday morning.

Wiser executives might have waited one more day, so that they could have found out something about the man upon whose financial mercy they were proposing to cast themselves: on Monday – the Spring Bank Holiday – most sources of information were closed. It was typical of the *Telegraph* regime – and indicative of their desperation – that they flew off with only the sketchiest idea of who Black was, and without making any serious effort to find out more about him. None of them knew anything beyond what Rothschilds had chosen to tell them.

It is true that very little had been published in British newspapers at that stage; yet there existed *The Establishment Man*, a comprehensive biography of Black by Peter C. Newman, which had first appeared in 1982 and had been available in paperback since the autumn of 1983. Even a brief perusal would have warned the men from Fleet Street that their appointment was with no passive investor, but with a predator of exceptional power and appetite.

Describing Black as 'the heavy-set Toronto millionaire who has turned himself into a Roman candle among the wet firecrackers littering Canada's business landscape', the author, who had interviewed his subject at length, called him 'an Inheritor by upbringing, an Acquisitor by temperament', and declared that he had 'come to symbolise Canadian capitalism on the hoof'.

The book revealed that Black had begun to show entrepreneurial flair while still at school. In 1959, as a fifteen-year-old pupil at Upper Canada College, he had taken advantage of the confusion caused by major structural repairs to get hold of the key of the principal's office. There he found the papers to be set in that year's final examinations, which were imminent, and sold photocopies to fellow-students – an enterprise that made nearly $5,000 for him and his syndicate before they were discovered and expelled.

In adult business, easily his most spectacular success had been his victory in the fight for control of the Argus Corporation, one of Canada's largest business conglomerates. According to Peter C. Newman, 'Using an inherited seven million dollars as the trigger, Black and his personal search-and-destroy squad grabbed control of companies with assets worth about four billion dollars in four months of frantic manoeuvring.' As a result of this astonishing takeover, 'his name had passed into the language as a generic term signifying either wealth and influence youthfully gained, or corporate manoeuvres too clever by half'.

Of still greater significance, from the *Telegraph*'s point of view, was the fact that Black's most enduring interest lay in newspapers. From 1969, when with two partners he had bought the ailing daily *Sherbrooke Record* for $20,000, he had built up the Sterling Newspaper chain until it included twenty-one publishing properties and by 1981 was making a profit of $5 million a year. Over the years he shed many other businesses but always retained his interest in newspapers – with which, as he himself says, he feels at home. In 1979 he had bid up to $125 million for F.P. Publications, the second-largest newspaper chain in Canada, only to see the group bought by the Thomson Organisation for $165 million; and earlier in 1985 he had made himself 'conspicuously available as a white knight' to another large newspaper group, Southams, who gave him 'a gentlemanly doffing of the cap, but rushed past into the arms of someone else'. So, when the *Telegraph* opportunity came up, it arrived at the best possible moment for him.

The *Telegraph* men knew none of this. They did not know that Black was a big, hefty, bear-like man, six feet tall, with such a memory that he could quote whole speeches by Ronald Reagan (whom he greatly admired) verbatim or tell you instantly who had been the English Chancellor of the Exchequer in 1837. They did not know that he was a dedicated amateur historian, who had written a 740-page biography of Maurice Duplessis, five times the autocratic premier of Quebec. They did not know that his heroes included de Gaulle, Roosevelt, Lincoln and Napoleon, or that his new house in Toronto had cost more than three million dollars, or that among its amenities were a Grinling Gibbons fireplace and a copper cupola modelled on the dome of St Peter's in Rome. All this lay outside their ken. And yet, ignorant as they were of their man, they literally flew into his arms.

The delegation which foregathered at Heathrow on the morning of Tuesday, 28 May 1985, for Concorde flight BA 193 to New York, consisted of Hartwell, H. M. Stephen and Hugh Lawson from the *Telegraph*, Rupert Hambro, coming to advise Black, and Patrick Docherty, a junior executive from Rothschilds who was much liked and respected. John Holland could not accompany his colleagues, for he had no American visa, and could not obtain one on Bank Holiday Monday. The price of each return ticket was £2,678, so that the day's journey cost the all-but-bankrupt *Telegraph*, which paid for four of the seats, nearly £11,000. It was Hartwell who insisted on using Concorde, as he did not want to be away from his office longer than he could help.

Hambro, proceeding independently to the VIP departure lounge, sat down next to an elderly man whom he had never seen before but who, he soon realised, must be the proprietor of *The Daily Telegraph*. Hartwell, for his part, became extremely suspicious, for he noticed that the stranger beside him was equipped with two sets of figures relating to the newspaper, one of which even he had never seen. When Hambro introduced himself, and said he was representing a potential investor, Hartwell said, 'Really, you shouldn't have that set of figures. They're meant for the banks, not for investors', but Hambro went on studying them regardless.

Concorde took off at 10.30 am. The noise at supersonic speed made conversation difficult, and through most of the three-and-a-half hour flight Hartwell read *The Daily Telegraph* from first word to last, with minute attention to detail. He had brought a small overnight case with him, in case he was forced to stay, but was determined to return to England the same day if possible.

The flight landed at New York on schedule. During a brief wait at the airport, Hartwell noticed that Hugh Lawson was doing the *Times* crossword, and asked why he did not do the *Telegraph* puzzle instead – to which Lawson honestly but tactlessly replied, 'Because it's so terrible!' Soon after 9.00 am local time the party was installed in the sitting-room of a brassy, modern suite on the second floor of the Kennedy Hilton, whose double-glazed windows looked out over the airport and buzzed with vibration every time a jet took off. Black, however, was late: he flew down from Toronto in his own company jet, a Challenger, but the flight was held up, and he did not arrive until 9.45. The English delegation, expecting him to be accompanied by a posse of lawyers and accountants, were surprised when he walked in alone, and Hambro introduced him to the others.

The meeting which followed was informal, relaxed and friendly. No papers were handed round. Nobody kept an official record of what was said. The participants did not even use a table, but sat in armchairs and had a conversation, sounding each other out. If anyone led the proceedings, it was Black, who kept things going by asking questions: for instance, when Hartwell mentioned that his Board had recently been strengthened by the appointment of new directors, including David Montagu and Lord Rawlinson, Black immediately asked if the latter was any relation of that legendary soldier the first Baron Rawlinson, hero of – among lesser campaigns – the Boer War and the First World War (the answer was No).

To Hartwell, Black seemed 'magnificently relaxed'. Stephen thought him 'a quietly strong person, without much time for the Left wing or the popular press'. At first Hugh Lawson did most of the talking, giving a general account of the business and its problems. He did not impress Black, who quickly formed the impression that this portly fellow, with his luxuriant moustache and his monocle, was by no means on top of his job. To the Canadian, 'there was a slight atmosphere of buffoonery about him. It was abundantly obvious that he did not hold out a believable prospect of being able to deal with the kind of problems which were confronting the company.'

Next, Hartwell spoke about the difficulty which his firm had experienced in raising funds to pay for modernisation. His own men thought him unusually articulate and loquacious. With a hint of apology, he explained that his family had not been able to finance the introduction of new technology, and said that it had proved hard to find new money, because Fleet Street was not an attractive proposition except to a few people who understood it.

As he talked, Black gained the impression that here was a man of absolute, old-fashioned honesty and integrity, charming and intelligent, a figure of some authority, greatly respected by his entourage, who had the air of a survivor, and a certain rather faded elegance besides. For Hartwell, as a man, Black felt sympathy and respect. Yet at the same time he perceived what he called a 'credibility gap' between this old English gentleman and the immensity of the task which he had set himself. Having read the private placing document, Black reckoned (but did not now say) that the *Telegraph* management had 'projected themselves forward in an extremely imprudent manner. They had committed themselves to vast expenditure without arranging the finance, and without any assurance from their work-force that they would achieve the de-manning which alone could make the whole exercise economic.' In short, it seemed very odd to Black that Hartwell, who had operated for so long in a highly conservative way, should suddenly have lashed out in this extravagant fashion.

Next H. M. Stephen spoke – at just the right length – about the new printing plants in Manchester and the Isle of Dogs. He outlined their size, capacity and the timing of their completion. Black, armed with detailed technical knowledge, briefly compared the merits of the Goss presses which the *Telegraph* was buying with those of various rivals.

Then he himself held forth, telling Hartwell of the loyalty which he felt towards Britain, of the great interest he had in the country, of how impressed he was by what Mrs Thatcher had been doing to revive industry and individual initiative. It seemed to him that she had turned the corner in her efforts to get people back to work, although he still felt that the English did not work hard by North American standards – and this, he thought, was particularly true of the newspaper industry. None of his listeners could know that, although these remarks were genuine enough, they had been cooked up by him and Knight, who had agreed that some such sentiments might seem appropriate at that moment.

Quickly, however, Black passed from the general to the particular. He told Hartwell that he had read the Rothschild prospectus and thought that after a little more investigation (which could be done quite quickly) he would be able to put in the £10 million needed to complete the private placing. But – and any prudent person in his position would make the same condition – he would have to insist on being granted pre-emptive rights in any issue of new shares, or any sale of existing shares, should the company need to raise further funds.

At once, and without hesitation, Hartwell said clearly, 'I don't think we can resist that.'

At that momentous point, Black asked for a brief adjournment. He said he would like a private talk with Hambro, and went out with him for a stroll. It was a sultry day, humid and overcast, more conducive to lethargy than to decision-making. As the two men talked, they ambled round the perimeter fence of the hotel grounds, their voices intermittently drowned out by the roar of aircraft taking off.

Black had been impressed by the speed with which Hartwell agreed to the one serious condition which he wanted to impose. He had expected a lecture on the historical importance of *The Daily Telegraph*, on the great opportunity now facing him. He would not have been surprised if Hartwell had attacked him for 'trying to Shylock him'. Yet none of this had happened. As Black pointed out, Hartwell's phrase 'I don't think we can resist that' was the *mot juste*: he had recognised that there was no alternative.

Again Black and Hambro evaluated the opportunity and the snags. Asked for his recommendations, Hambro said that, although the figures they had seen looked bad, and terrible problems loomed, he felt that Black should go ahead. *The Daily Telegraph*, in his view, was the greatest serious newspaper title in the world outside Japan. Its masthead alone was worth an enormous – if so far unspecified – amount. In spite of its recent decline, circulation and readership were solid as rocks. If Black could give it the necessary time and money, the worst that could happen – the bottom line – was that the value of his investment might fall by half. On the other hand, if things went well, the topside would be that he would see his stake multiply by at least five times. Hambro recommended that he should put in the £10 million – provided he did not mind the idea of remaining a passive investor for some time.

Still pacing the wire, the two men then discussed the possibility that Black one day might gain control. Hambro, making his only mistake, said that although he might manage this in the end, it could hardly happen in less than two or three years. After twenty minutes or so, Black said he wanted to proceed, and went back up to the suite on the second floor of the hotel.

In his business dealings, Black takes care to show very little emotion. Close friends say that the only sign of his adrenalin rising is a tendency for his conversation to become more polysyllabic, for the length of his sentences to increase. Now, in New York, the *Telegraph* team noticed no difference in this big, heavy man, who seemed very methodical and deliberate. He confirmed that he would go ahead, although it might take him a few days to decide 'which pocket the money would come from'. Hartwell beamed. 'I'm flattered by your interest in our newspaper,' he said, 'and delighted to have you as a shareholder. I *welcome* you.' When Black repeated that he regarded the investment as a speculation, and said that as a safeguard he must have the option of the rights on the family shares, in the event of more funds being needed, Hartwell nodded and muttered, 'That's all right.'

In that moment, without realising it, he gave his birthright away.

Later, he said that he had agreed 'on the spur of the moment', and, when asked why he had given in so readily, said that he simply could not conceive that the company would need more money, or that a rights issue would become necessary. Besides, it was clear that if he had not agreed to Black's condition, the Canadian would not have come in, 'the whole deal would have flopped, our name would have been tarnished, and we would have had frightful trouble raising the £10 million anywhere else'.

Neither of Hartwell's henchmen was shocked by the suddenness of his decision. Indeed, neither realised what a cataclysmic step it might prove to be. Lawson felt vaguely disturbed, but no worse than that. Stephen, though he had been Managing Director for twenty-two years, knew nothing of the company's financial structure, and now did not understand what Black had proposed. As he later remarked, 'At no time had I known whether Hartwell and his brother owned ninety or ninety-five per cent of the equity. It was their money, their business.'

Here was the clearest possible indication of the old-fashioned methods which prevailed at 135 Fleet Street: senior managers could not imagine that the firm would ever have to raise more equity than the £29 million now secured. To professional outsiders – Knight, Hambro and Black among them – it was immediately obvious, from a study of the private placing document, that further finance would be essential, and probably quite soon.

After a few more questions from Black about recent falls in circulation, the age of *Telegraph* readers, and so on, the meeting ended in smiles, handshakes and an atmosphere of goodwill. No papers were drawn up, no documents signed. The agreement was entirely verbal; but – as Black had already sensed – Hartwell was in such a tight corner that there could be no question of him going back on it.

At 1.00 pm the English party drove back to the terminal building in a car which Black had standing by, and boarded the 1.45 Concorde flight BA 194 to London. By one of the quirks of supersonic flight across the Atlantic, they had both lunch and dinner in the same arc of sky, above Nantucket. Hartwell read the *Economist*, in which he found a note comparing the *Telegraph*'s readership favourably with those of the *Times* and the *Guardian*; and when Lawson, goaded by his earlier conversation with Hartwell, had a go at the *Telegraph* crossword, he found it every bit as bad as he had claimed.

12 DECLINE AND FALL, MAY 1985–FEBRUARY 1986

In London the lawyers got down to the job of turning the verbal agreement made in New York into a written contract. For Dan Colson, the Canadian lawyer representing Conrad Black, it was an exciting and unusual project: he found himself working 'not just on a straightforward business transaction, but on the salvation of what was clearly a national institution in the United Kingdom'. He had handled other deals much bigger than this one, but none which generated such emotion.

During the crucial six months which followed the meeting in New York, Black made only two brief visits to London. The fact that he came so rarely was thought by some to show Macchiavellian cunning: by lying low in Toronto, it was said, he avoided mention in the British Press, and so kept gossip and possible opposition to a minimum. In fact he felt confident of his representatives' ability to handle negotiations, and in any case he was constantly on the telephone. (Later, there was another reason why he kept in the background: this was Andrew Knight's conviction that in hammering out new working agreements the print unions must learn to deal with negotiators nominated by the proprietor of the paper, rather than with the Managing Director or even with the proprietor himself. Knight felt that in the past Hartwell and Stephen had made themselves too available, and from the start it was part of his strategy that Black should not be so accessible.)

At the start, whenever the going became rough, it was Colson who took a lot of opprobrium really meant for the entrepreneur in the background. To Colson, the building at 135 Fleet Street, and in particular its fifth floor, seemed a stunning anachronism. From his office in Gresham Street it was a six-minute walk to Hartwell's headquarters, and every time he went there, Colson felt he was stepping back about a century. 'You call the fifth floor thirtyish?' he said. 'You're being generous! It was built in the thirties to look like the 1880s – this wood-panelled office with hardly any lighting, this figure of his Lordship, surrounded by old newspaper bills, this butler at the door. You look out of the window, and there's a garden, the only one I've ever seen seventy-five feet up in the air. The whole thing was like a movie – but a *bad* movie.'

At first everything seemed fairly straightforward. After the private placing, the disposition of the *Telegraph*'s share capital was as follows:

	per cent
The Telegraph Newspaper Trust	
31,000,000 Ordinary Shares	57.9
The Cowley Charitable Trust	
1,000,000 Ordinary Shares	1.9
New Shareholders	
The Daily Telegraph Pension Fund	
1,250,000 Preferred Ordinary Shares	2.4
The Ravelston Corporation	
(one of Conrad Black's companies)	
7,500,000 Preferred Ordinary Shares	14.0
Other institutions	
12,750,000 Preferred Ordinary Shares	23.8
	100.00

Black, in the form of Ravelston, thus had fourteen per cent of the company, and Clause 9 of Appendix III in the private placing document spelled out details of the arrangement outlined in New York:

In return for Ravelston agreeing to subscribe for 7,500,000 Preferred Ordinary Shares under the placing, The 140 Trustee Company has granted Ravelston two principal rights. The first is, for a period of ten years, to match any third-party offer to buy Ordinary Shares from The 140 Trustee Company to the extent that, upon disposal, The 140 Trustee Company would be left with less than fifty-one per cent of The Telegraph's issued share capital. The second right is for Ravelston, until listing on The Stock Exchange of The Telegraph's Ordinary Share capital, to take up The 140 Trustee Company's entitlement to shares on a rights issue, so far as the relevant terms of the issue allow, or, if the terms of the issue prevent this, for Ravelston to require

The 140 Trustee Company to take up its rights and sell the relevant shares on to Ravelston at the issue price.

These crucial clauses were enshrined in a Memorandum of Agreement drawn up by the lawyers and signed on 14 June 1985. Colson had done everything he could to make the document legally binding – and once, during the months of tense manoeuvring that followed, he got Lord Rawlinson to double-check it for possible loopholes. The former Attorney-General took a copy of it home with him one night, and rang in the morning to confirm that it was bomb-proof. In effect, Black, through his representatives in London, was in command of the *Telegraph*'s financial future from the moment that agreement was signed: he did not yet have an overall majority of shares, but he did have the power to prevent any other investor coming in on such a scale as to gain control, and, if there was any major redistribution of shares, to gain control himself.

Black thought he had made 'a reasonably good deal'. He knew he was taking a bit of a gamble: if the worst occurred, and the company went bankrupt, he might lose his £10 million investment, or part of it; but he was confident that if the *Telegraph* could be kept going, he would get a chance to increase his stake in the business at some stage in the future. Yet neither he nor Colson foresaw that the picture would change anything like as quickly as it did. It seemed that if the papers did as well as predicted, and were in profit over the six months ending 30 September 1985, the Syndicate of banks would make funds available, as arranged, and everything would settle down, at any rate for the time being, with Hartwell and his family still in control, while the new printing plants were completed and came into operation, the excess men were paid off, and costs tumbled with realistic manning.

As a new financial structure was being hammered out, the conversion from hot-metal typesetting to photocomposition had begun. The first of the Linotype operators were being trained to use the Atex computer system, and for a while the old and new technologies ran in parallel. As soon as enough men were proficient, one page at a time, starting with that carrying radio and television programmes, was switched to the new method of production. This naturally put immense extra pressure on the composing-room, and the standard of printing fell to an all-time low, the paper being spattered with words misspelt, lines misplaced and stories ending in mid-sentence. Worse, setting was so slow that on some nights the paper appeared thirty columns short of what it should have contained, and editions were missed, making the supply of copies erratic and further reducing sales.

Things became so bad that in July Hartwell himself came out with a 'Letter to readers (and future readers)' cast in the form of a leader-page article. 'Dear Reader (and Friend)', it began, 'This newspaper, you may have noticed, is not very well printed . . . If any one person is responsible, I am. I have been Chairman of *The Daily Telegraph* for thirty years . . .'

He went on to sketch past attempts at upgrading the presses and to outline the present plan for comprehensive modernisation. He contrasted the 'Dickensian basements' in which Fleet Street production still took place with the modern factories, built on greenfield sites, to which the *Telegraph* was about to move. 'But we shall be the first, by a long way the first, to provide the technology . . . to constitute the most modern plant in Europe.' Having explained that seven new directors had recently joined the Board, among them his two sons, he concluded:

> I and my family remain in charge of the traditions and conduct of our two newspapers. In sum, I believe we have taken the right steps to give our newspapers a good future, and a far better appearance, well into the next century. For the moment, and I am sorry about this, our readers will have to share some of our difficulties with us. It is our firm intention that before very long they will also share the rewards.

The article was signalled by a trailer on the front page, quoting from the text, part of which appeared as, 'I believe we have taken the right steps to give our newspapers a godo future'. This drew a hail of abusive letters, many of them sarcastically misspelt. 'I am sending you up a batch of letters about your article,' wrote Deedes. 'The nice ones are marked A, the not-so-nice ones B.' Of three published in the paper, the first began: 'Please desist immediately from the new typesetting and production arrangements described. Do you not appreciate that over the last few years the number of spelling errors, misplaced lines and other errata has grown to such proportions that the daily interpretation of your newspaper is now a far greater intellectual challenge than your crossword?'

For Hartwell the position was anything but amusing: plunged as he was in a financial crisis, he was also beset by adverse commercial trends outside his control. The unluckiest was the fact that in the Budget the Chancellor of the Exchequer had imposed Value Added Tax on some forms of advertising – a move which depressed the volume of financial and government advertising generally available. At the same moment, the *Times* was offering artificially low advertising rates, which attracted business away from the *Telegraph*. On the *Telegraph* itself the management belatedly found that the cost of conversion from hot-metal setting to photocomposition would be nearer £4.5 million, in training and buy-outs, than the £1 million estimated. Worst of all, in Manchester, where the new printing plant at Trafford Park was rapidly taking shape, it emerged that the number of men demanded by the unions to run it was going to be much higher than originally calculated, so that the savings achieved there would fall below expectations. The hope had been that the low level of manning would yield enormous economies, but suddenly these had disappeared. In Hartwell's view, this was the blow that did the greatest damage and most unsettled the lending banks. The agreement with the Syndicate had stipulated that savings from the new manning scales would finance the interest on the loan. It was now clear that they would not, and the *Telegraph* was technically in default. The calculations made on the back of an envelope had already done serious damage.

Yet it was in 135 Fleet Street itself that the most alarming defects came to light. David Montagu had been appointed to head the Audit Committee, which would sort out the company's tangled affairs; but before this body began to sit, he held an informal meeting in May with John Holland and the *Telegraph*'s auditors, Saffery Champness. He was appalled by what he found, being especially astonished to discover that the company had never had a budget, and had no real idea of its financial position. Looking at the figures, several of the outside advisers immediately came to the conclusion that Rothschilds had been 'grossly negligent' in putting out the private placing document, which gave the impression that, once the £29 million of equity had been raised, the company would be adequately capitalised. In Montagu's view, Rothschilds had 'handed the Berry family's balls to Conrad Black on a silver salver'.

Montagu was almost equally dismayed by the *Telegraph* management, whom he described afterwards as 'hopeless, geriatric, and like small boys being brought one after another into the headmaster's study'. At no stage did he suggest that there had been any dishonesty or deliberate deceit. It was simply that nobody had the faintest idea of what was going on. This state of affairs, he could see, had built up over many years, with the managers crippled not so much by their own incompetence as by the antiquated command structure, which had outlasted its useful life.

Rothschilds' answer to criticism was that they had made every effort to establish the company's true financial position, and that they had only been able to work on the figures which the *Telegraph* had given them. Behind the scenes, doing everything he could to salvage a difficult position, was the Chairman of the firm, Evelyn de Rothschild. He had known Hartwell all his life, and felt strong sympathy for him. Besides, as a director of the *Daily Express* in the 1970s, he had seen that newspaper beset by similar problems, and now had a strong sense of *déjà vu*. His policy, as always, was to keep in the background and let the account executive in charge – Michael Richardson – lead negotiations; but it was essential to him both that the *Telegraph* should survive, and that Rothschilds, having been initially misled, should bring the affair to a satisfactory conclusion. He therefore kept a close eye on what was happening, and several times visited Hartwell at 135 Fleet Street to offer advice.

In his view, Rothschilds did not let the Berrys down at all. It was a fact (he said later) that the *Telegraph* management 'was in a pretty serious state. Their accounting procedures and general systems were not up to the standard of any normal business. The whole place was archaic. Far from failing to look into their procedures closely enough, we saw that the quill-pen attitude of the company had to be altered. The difficulty was to persuade Lord Hartwell that he needed a complete change of management.'

As a start, in place of Safferys David Montagu appointed Coopers & Lybrand the *Telegraph*'s new auditors; but his own disquiet spread to the Syndicate of banks, and over the next few weeks he devoted much time to the task of 'trying to keep them onside'. This was not easy, and when Conrad Black flew into London for a three-day visit in September, he met the banks as a group – at their insistence – in an attempt to impress on them the seriousness of his commitment to the project. This proved a crucial meeting: the moment at which the banks accepted 'the guy with the blank chequebook from Toronto' as their only means of salvation. Then, over lunch in Rupert Hambro's office, together with Montagu and Rawlinson, he agreed that, to gain credibility in the eyes of the banks, the Board of the *Telegraph* should appoint a new Chief Executive as soon as possible. He already had in mind Andrew Knight, but another possibility was Ian Irvine, a brilliant accountant who was then battling to save the Express Newspapers from the clutches of the much-larger United Newspapers. That same evening, after the monthly Board meeting at the *Telegraph*,

Black dined at Cowley Street, and had what he called 'a very nice evening', at which Hartwell entertained many of the people concerned with the refinancing of the paper. At dinner Black sat next to Nicholas Berry, whom he found 'perfectly affable'. The banks were not yet seriously perturbed.

By the terms of his agreement with The 140 Trust Company, Black was entitled to have two directors on the Board. One was himself (and Rupert Hambro sometimes stood in for him). As the other, Andrew Knight suggested Frank Rogers, a tough and wise veteran, then sixty-five, with immense experience of journalism behind him. *Daily Mirror* reporter for twelve years, Editor of the Nigerian *Daily Times*, Managing Director of the *Mirror* in the 1960s – Rogers had seen it all. He had known Hartwell on and off for twenty years, and several times, when a Director of the Newspaper Publishers' Association, had called on him at 135 Fleet Street, out of sheer friendliness, trying to warn him that the time would come when the *Telegraph* would have to re-plant, and that he should be making some provision for that day. Yet, although he had always been able to talk straight to his own Chairman, Cecil King, he found it almost impossible to conduct a conversation with Hartwell, who had grown so used to hearing only what his executives thought he wanted to hear that 'he became completely isolated from anything that might be going wrong'.

Now, in September 1985, Rogers found himself one evening invited to dinner by Knight at the top of the *Economist* building in St James's. There he met Conrad Black, and at once the two got on famously. Black found Rogers 'so likeable and sound' that he very soon asked if he would fill the vacant place on the Board. Then, as Black recalled the conversation,

> In his inimitable fashion Frank started to ask some questions. In the event that it fell to me to nominate the next Managing Director of the *Telegraph*, did I have any candidate in mind? I said, 'Yes, as a matter of fact, I do. The candidate I have in mind is none other than our genial host, Andrew Knight.' Frank said, 'As I understand things, this most agreeable occasion brings together a potential director of *The Daily Telegraph*, a potential Managing Director of *The Daily Telegraph*, and a potential proprietor of *The Daily Telegraph*. Let us therefore delete the word "potential" and discuss what we are going to do with our newspaper.'

Next month Black was back in London, for only twenty-four hours, flying in on Concorde at the special request of Montagu, who wanted him to be present at the October Board meeting. On the morning of the meeting he went to see Hartwell and urged on him the merits of appointing Andrew Knight as Managing Director. As he later recalled, he had 'to walk the wire' between remaining loyal to Hartwell, who was still Chairman of the company, and protecting his own investment. His line was that Hartwell simply must convey to the banks 'the believable impression that he was addressing the company's problems and making progress', and that the best way to do this would be to appoint a top-flight chief executive from outside, whose recruitment would impress the financial community. As it turned out, Black had no difficulty getting his way: in the morning Hartwell was perfectly amenable, and in the afternoon the Board (on which Rogers took his seat for the first time) agreed that Hartwell should ring Knight and offer him the post of Chief Executive. To catch his flight home, Black had to hurry straight from Fleet Street to London airport; but in the Concorde departure lounge at Heathrow he had time to ring Knight and say, 'Your hour of destiny has struck.'*

Seeing Hartwell again, Rogers found it extraordinary that he 'had such loyalty to the people round him, because, quite frankly, they were utterly useless, and had let him down completely on the business side'. There was a stark contrast, in his view, between Hartwell the Editor-in-Chief, with his high ethics and talent, who conducted his papers with great shrewdness, and Hartwell the out-of-date Chief Executive whose old-fashioned methods had run his business into the ground.

By now the Audit Committee had begun to meet, and such were the anomalies which it encountered that on 16 October, with the weekly figures growing rapidly worse, Montagu directed Coopers & Lybrand to make an urgent financial review of the company's position. So poor was the cash-flow, and such was the pressure being exerted by the banks, that the new auditors launched an emergency investigation. During the five days from 17 to 21 October they worked day and night, Sunday included, to find out what was happening. The old guard at the *Telegraph* felt that this was no mere accounting exercise: so high-powered was the team

---

* It so happened that in 1984 Knight had travelled to Oxford with Evelyn de Rothschild, the *Economist*'s Chairman, to tell the magazine's senior trustee, Lord Franks, that after ten years as Editor he felt he should leave some time in the next three years, and that the trustees should therefore be looking for a replacement. He was thus, fortunately, free to move when the offer came.

of investigators that it seemed more like an evaluation of management. The doubts were not misplaced. According to Montagu, the *Blitzkrieg* search 'exposed all the false hopes, the ridiculously optimistic projections, the ludicrously understated redundancy charges. Everyone, from John Holland, the Financial Director, down, had put down what the headmaster wanted to hear. Everyone was tainted with sycophancy.'

Coopers & Lybrand's verdict was devastating. Their analysis revealed that in the six months ending 30 September 1985, for which management had predicted an operating profit of £0.2 million, the company had in fact made a loss of £6.5 million. Further, for the whole financial year, ending 31 March 1986, Coopers forecast a loss of £8.1 million – in damaging contrast to the company's own original prediction of a £5 million profit. A report prepared by Coopers for the Board, though cast in restrained language, made it clear that the *Telegraph*'s accounting procedures were totally inadequate, and recommended the immediate introduction of new methods of control, not least budgets.

Now Evelyn de Rothschild rang Black in Toronto, saying that the option clauses in his agreement suddenly looked highly relevant. Almost certainly the *Telegraph* was going to need a further injection of cash. A rights issue was in prospect, and with it a chance for Black to increase his stake. In London, the report put Montagu in an embarrassing position. On the one hand he wanted to give maximum support to Hartwell, who had brought him on to the Board, but on the other he now had to tell the banks that there were serious inconsistencies in the figures which they had been given. Not surprisingly, they became more and more nervous, and over the next six weeks a series of highly fraught meetings took place.

Life was made no easier by the fact that Nicholas Berry now mounted a last-minute counter-attack. In May – characteristically enough – his father had not told him that he was flying to New York to meet Black: the first Nicholas knew of the Canadian's involvement was when he read about it in the *Wall Street Journal*. Yet what really dismayed him was the discovery that his father had not merely let in a hungry outsider, but had also promised away the family's rights.

In the autumn, as it became clear that control might pass from his family, Nicholas began a desperate rearguard action, trying to find other sources of finance, other people who might buy into the business. To most of those involved – Black and Colson for two – he seemed unable to grasp the fact that his father had signed a binding agreement. In fact he knew this perfectly well, but he also saw that anyone with enough money could in theory buy the entire firm, Black's share included, provided the Canadian was prepared to get out with a quick profit on his investment to date.

Now that he scented danger, he fiercely resented the way Rothschilds had handled the private placing. In his view, they had done his father a very grave disservice, first by not analysing the business thoroughly or pointing out its managerial weaknesses, and second by recommending Black as an investor. 'It wasn't my father's job to know who Conrad Black was,' he said afterwards. 'It was Rothschilds' job to point that out. A glance at his record would have shown into which category he fell. I don't criticise the man for being what he is – a predator. I just notice.'

That did not seem so at the time. Nicholas appeared bitterly to resent the fact that Black had gained such a strong position. A scatter of articles which appeared in the British Press, attacking the Canadian, were widely but wrongly ascribed to his influence – Nicholas himself denies having had any connection with them.

Every time somebody did have his appetite whetted, he inevitably found that Black's agreement with Hartwell was watertight. One hopeful inquirer was Lord Hanson, the financier and businessman; but as soon as he saw the Memorandum of Agreement, he agreed that there was nothing to talk about.

Another possible source of funds, in Nicholas's view, was the Fairfax family, the millionaire Australian newspaper-publishers. As it happened, two senior members of the firm – Greg Gardner, the Managing Director, and Fred Brenchley, who was in charge of printing operations – were in London at the height of the crisis, and Nicholas had no doubt that their firm would have made ideal partners in the *Telegraph*'s reconstruction. As he said, 'What we needed was expertise in handling an enormously ambitious printing project, and money to finance it, in the form of equity – and they had both.' His main concern was to make it possible for the Fairfaxes to buy a substantial stake in the *Telegraph*, but still to keep the firm under his own family's control. Failing this, he thought, his family's best bet would have been to sell the whole firm for a reasonable price on the open market.

Black's option left him in command, but many outsiders did not realise this. In Colson's view 'The banks didn't know what the hell was going on. There were people beating the bushes all over town.' One day two Fairfax representatives walked into Colson's office and announced that they were ready to do a deal. They were very aggressive, and claimed that Black's agreement was not binding.

Colson found it hard to take their approach seriously. 'I wanted to throw these guys out on their ass. I said, "Who are you going to do a deal *with*? We control this thing. Go to hell."'

What Colson did not know was that Hartwell, together with Tony Hughes, his finance director designate, had seen Gardner at Fairfax's London office and put it to him that his firm should buy out Black and the outside shareholders at, say, 160 pence a share, and put £20 million into the *Telegraph* in return for providing the management and a fifty per cent share of the equity. Gardner swiftly referred the proposal back to his board, but the idea of giving Black such a large profit stuck in their gullet.

At 135 Fleet Street, meetings dragged on at all hours of the day and night as the Board feverishly tried to decide where to turn next. Money was running out at an awful speed, and the banks, alarmed by the figures they were seeing, kept refusing to release any more. Again and again the company was on the verge of bankruptcy, and twice, in September and October, Hartwell of his own accord produced a cheque for £1 million, from family funds, to keep within the overdraft limit. Then, at seven o'clock one evening, during a meeting at which all the bankers and directors were present, the Syndicate said that if another £1.3 million were not found by close of business – which meant 3.00 pm next day – they would put the company into liquidation. When they asked Michael Richardson whether Rothschilds could find the money, he replied that he was not briefed to answer the question. They therefore turned to Hartwell, who, again borrowing from family funds, guaranteed them a cheque. (Richardson's lack of support at this critical moment did not prevent him coming up to Hartwell after the meeting and asking that Rothschilds be used for any further share issue.)

These meetings with the bankers seemed interminable. Hartwell was oppressed by the sheer numbers of people involved: his deafness made it hard for him to hear when several voices were raised at once, and he found the marathon document-signing sessions tiresome. Board meetings were similarly long and tense – and at one Hartwell gravely alarmed his colleagues by collapsing. One minute he seemed all right; the next, he began giving terrible, inarticulate roars and groans, turned dark purple in the face, and fell sideways from his chair. Montagu and Rawlinson thought he was dead. So did Colson, who felt guilty at having given him cardiac arrest. Hugh Lawson rushed out of the room and sent for an ambulance. Adrian ran to help, but he was less worried than the rest, for he had seen this happen before, and knew that his father had a capacity for fainting spectacularly. Sure enough, when they had carried him out into the corridor, and loosened his collar and tie, he soon came round. He vigorously resisted the idea of going to hospital, and afterwards seemed little the worse, although he could not go on with the meeting. Frank Rogers was amazed to see him stand up and walk away: he too had thought Hartwell was dying, and would never walk anywhere again. For several minutes confusion reigned. Eileen Fuller, Hartwell's faithful secretary, summoned the house nurse, who appeared promptly; but to Dan Colson it seemed that she was determined not to let this 'paramedic' touch her employer: if anyone laid hands on Lord Hartwell (he thought she said), it would have to be a proper doctor.

In general it was felt that the representatives of the Syndicate behaved atrociously: obviously they had cause to be worried, but the boorishness with which they treated Hartwell seemed inexcusable – unless its underlying purpose was to accelerate a transfer of ownership. (Some of those involved suspected that the banks, seeing how the papers were being run into the ground, secretly wanted Hartwell and the old management out as soon as possible.) Hartwell himself formed the lowest possible opinion of the National Westminster, who had been the *Telegraph*'s clearing bank for more than a hundred years, and who now, in his view, showed uncommon pusillanimity. They were, in the view of one leading participant, 'singularly unimaginative, and seemed unable to acknowledge the fact that they had a substantial new share-holder, with large funds available, who was behind the papers and wanted them to succeed'. At one point, of his own accord, Montagu went to see Lord Boardman, the NatWest Chairman, and asked for a further loan of £5 million. Boardman refused, saying that the bank would immediately have to write the money off. Looking back, Hartwell reckoned it might have been better to approach the Chief General Manager, from whom he himself had raised a temporary loan of £4 million a few years before.

Montagu – in Hartwell's view – played a difficult role with outstanding skill. At the countless financial meetings the banks always seemed totally negative, and at one, when it looked as though their attitude was actually going to bring about the demise of the *Telegraph*, Montagu, in a final attempt to make them more constructive, sought to enlist the help of the Governor of the Bank of England. On the telephone he got through to a private secretary, only to learn that the Governor was not available; but he continued to talk, in front of all the bankers, as though he were addressing the Governor himself: 'Surely, Governor, you agree it would be very bad for the City if it attracted the full odium of having a national institution brought down by a few banks? Quite. Thank you.' The ruse worked, and the immediate crisis was averted.

Throughout this period, though under severe strain, Hartwell kept up his normal routine, seeing his editors, going through the papers minutely, staying late in the evening, driving himself to and from Fleet Street in his brown Mini. He said little or nothing about what was going on to members of the editorial staff. When Bill Deedes or John Thompson went up to the fifth floor, Hartwell would occasionally mutter something about the latest financial crisis; but on Saturdays, when he had a working lunch with the senior editorial staff of the Sunday paper, he never once brought the subject up. Peregrine Worsthorne, who by then had known him for thirty years, wrote later that he felt 'a shade hurt at not being informed, let alone consulted' about the future of the business. 'Throughout this troubled period conversation ranged over many subjects, including, as always, the latest City goings-on, but not a word was ever said about our own affairs.'

Hartwell could perhaps derive a little cold comfort from the reflection that his newspapers were by no means the only ones in trouble. On 20 October 1985 came the announcement that after a long battle United Newspapers had won control of the old Beaverbrook empire with a takeover bid of £317 million. The prime mover was David Stevens, Chairman of Montagu Investment Management, described in one press report as a 'dapper merchant banker with Napoleonic physique and ambitions', who now spoke boldly of breaking the print unions' stranglehold by moving national newspapers out of Fleet Street, and of reducing the *Express*'s 6,500-strong work-force by more than twenty per cent. Another newspaper tycoon, Rupert Murdoch, was also running out of patience with the unions, and had just told chapel officials at News International that all national newspaper production departments were over-manned by 50 to 300 per cent, with working practices that were 'a continuing disgrace to us all'. He said he had strained himself and his senior colleagues 'physically, emotionally and financially' to build up the business, and that he had met 'nothing but cynicism, broken promises and total opposition'. Yet another heavyweight – Robert Maxwell, owner of the Mirror Group – predicted that, with the 'cold wind of competition' catching up on Fleet Street, everything was 'about to break loose'.

For Hartwell, November turned out to be the cruellest month. The pressures on him mounted inexorably, and speculation raged. On 9 November the *Times* suggested that he and his family would soon be forced to yield control, and that 'City investors who participated in last year's [sic] fund-raising are said to be furious about the turn of events'. For as long as it could, the *Telegraph* held back the disastrous results for the six months ending 30 September, and gave as its reason the fact that Coopers & Lybrand, the new auditors, were 'reviewing accounting practices'. On 17 November, in a last-ditch attempt to staunch the outflow of money, the Managing Director H. M. Stephen issued a general appeal to the staff, calling for 'substantial economies', freezing all wages, eliminating 'all unjustified payments' and introducing 'stringent controls and economies in all expenditure and expense areas'. Journalists on both papers responded, on 21 November, with a unanimous vote of no confidence in the ability of the management to save the company from bankruptcy. Nothing more clearly demonstrated the total lack of communication between one side of the business and the other than the fact that an NUJ chapel meeting could now, at the fifty-ninth minute of the eleventh hour, pass a resolution urging the directors to 'revitalise the moribund and elderly policies which have contributed to the crisis'. For months a large number of able people had been struggling to do just that, but nobody had given the journalists any information about what was going on. Among the staff, rumours of impending collapse became so strong that Matthew Symonds, one of the leader-writers on the Daily, drew $2,000 advance expenses for some hypothetical trip abroad, and for weeks kept the money salted away, against the evil day when his monthly pay-cheque should fail to come through.

In the second half of the month, persistent rumours claimed that Hartwell was about to resign. On 20 November, in an attempt to calm speculation, and counter what they described as 'considerable knocking propaganda' from Rupert Murdoch's News International, the Board issued a statement listing some of their achievements. Chief among these were the two new printing plants, one of which was on schedule, the other six weeks ahead. In London, at West Ferry Road, the building begun in February 1984 was two-thirds complete, and would be finished in time for the first press to be commissioned in September 1986. In Manchester, where the company had not been able to obtain access to the Trafford Park site until 14 June 1984, the plant, machinery and office accommodation were almost finished after less than eighteen months' work: one press was already set up, and would be ready to run six weeks ahead of schedule, if a full-scale stoppage at Withy Grove made it necessary. The estimates for both projects had proved extremely accurate, the cost in each case coming out less than two per cent different from the figures originally budgeted. The transfer from hot metal to photocomposition was proceeding according to plan, and relationships with the unions were 'at an unprecedentedly good level'.

This statement, though perfectly truthful, highlighted the fundamental difference of opinion which had developed between Hartwell and his management on the one side, and the new directors on the other. The old guard felt that, with only a little more luck, they could have saved the paper and kept control: that if advertising revenue had not fallen at such a critical moment, and if the Manchester costs had been kept down, they could have held on until the point of breakthrough, when clean, well-printed copies of the papers began to roll off the new presses, and costs went tumbling because of the realistic levels of manning, thus putting the whole enterprise strongly back into profit. The new guard considered this an impossible dream: in their view, the old management was so far out of its depth, and so chaotic, that it had no chance of escaping from the morass into which its own lack of control had sunk it.

Meanwhile, in the background, Hartwell had been manoeuvring hard to maintain his position. An approach had been made – as the whispers maintained – to Ian Irvine, to see if he would come in as Chief Executive; but after his battle at the *Express*, Irvine did not want to take on another national newspaper. At the start of November Hartwell therefore wrote to Andrew Knight, who twice came to see him at home in Cowley Street, where he had been a guest at Pamela's parties. After some discussion, Knight said that he was fascinated by the idea of taking on the *Telegraph*, but that he had one serious reservation: he feared that reconstruction of the company would be difficult, if not impossible, with Hartwell still the major shareholder. Where would a Chief Executive's authority to change things come from? In spite of his doubts, he agreed to hold himself ready to come in, but said that if any rumour of his involvement escaped, he would have to deny it and give up the chance of getting the job.

After the second meeting he sent Hartwell a handwritten letter confirming his interest, but concluding that he did not think that the sort of arrangement proposed would work. In effect, he rejected Hartwell's overtures, and for a fortnight the matter drifted. Then, towards the end of the month, as the *Telegraph*'s weekly figures grew worse, the banks intensified their pressure, and it became clear that a rights issue was inevitable, so that control of the company was going to have to pass to Black, Knight re-entered the lists. Twice more, avoiding 135 Fleet Street, he saw Hartwell at home. From his point of view, the meetings went well; but although he came to discuss details of his own appointment, he found Hartwell 'desperate to stop Conrad Black', if possible by bringing in the Fairfaxes. 'What have you got against Conrad?' Knight asked, and Hartwell answered, 'Oh, I like him a lot. He's very helpful, very constructive. But – the Fairfaxes are newspaper people, *our* sort of people.'

In Fleet Street, spurred on by the feeling that great events were imminent, Bill Deedes had begun to keep a diary, typing or dictating snatches whenever he had a moment:

12 November 1985 Called Hartwell at 6.15 pm. Tied up. 6.45 pm calls to say still tied up and we won't bother tonight. Courtesy under stress.

13 November 1985 By some strange finger of fate, find myself at No. 10's lunch for Emir of Qatar, sitting between the Swiss Ambassador and Rupert Hambro. After dealing with H.E. through sole, turn to Hambro for duck, pudding and coffee . . . He says, 'I find myself involved in your affairs.' We discuss Michael Hartwell with mutual sympathy. Agree it is end of feudal dynasty. He supposes I have seen Conrad Black. I disabuse him. Hambro seems genuinely puzzled by what Berry family want to carry into future . . . Hambro says, Hartwell has had a horrid time. No argument about the status of the DT, only about the feckless way they've gone about their company business. Hambro doubts if Hartwell has been given all the facts all the time. Too many courtiers! I have to admit, true.

For the period 22–29 November, Deedes noted: 'Fraught week. Talk about make-up. Appoint a professional. Hartwell says we need to know where we're going.' With his habitual diplomacy and good manners, Deedes unobtrusively did whatever he could to help. On 29 November he sent up to the fifth floor a memorandum suggesting that the staff should pay for at least one seasonal extravagance: 'Some of us think it would be fitting if we, your annual guests at the Christmas lunch, gave you and Lord Camrose the usual lunch (by your leave in the usual place and style), and shared the cost among ourselves'. By then, however, Hartwell was Chairman only by courtesy, and felt he could not act as host to the paper's top brass at a party that would almost certainly have turned out more a wake than a festivity. Had the lunch taken place at all, he would have insisted on paying for it himself.

Other people were trying to help as well. In a note marked 'Strictly Personal' Deedes told Hartwell:

> During the weekend Eddie Shah, whom I have never met and do not know personally, sent me a message as a lifelong reader of the DT and admirer of yourself . . . He wishes you to know privately he is willing to do all in his power to help . . . He claims he could win bankers over. Anything he did would remain totally private. The whole gesture relates to you.

This gesture evoked no response. Hartwell, pummelled into submission by a succession of blows, had run out of ideas, and at last accepted that another infusion of capital was essential. At a meeting on Thursday, 28 November, he told the Board that he had effectively lost control. Nicholas walked out, looking distressed, and shortly afterwards resigned as a Director.

In Fleet Street journalists had formed a dim view of their potential saviour. 'Black the prospect', noted Deedes in his diary. Yet still the paralysing uncertainty dragged on – and further doubt, at least in the public mind – was created by the front-page story run on 4 December by the *Daily Mail*, that the Al-Fayed brothers, Egyptian owners of Harrods, were bidding to take over the *Telegraph*.

This was a red herring: in fact 4 December was a crucial day of meetings on which Hartwell moved nearer to surrender. 'At it since dawn,' Deedes noted:

> Broke-Smith takes view Black will now get control. £20 million guarantee essential. Only Black can provide. Nicholas proved difficult. Late into the act. Very anti-Black . . . So Hartwell caught between obdurate bankers, need for £20 million guarantee, Black, and son who does not want Black.

The final act came next day, Thursday 5 December, when the Board agreed terms for the rights issue, in which Hollinger, another of Black's companies, would acquire 39,907,125 Ordinary Shares at 50p apiece, giving Black a total holding of 50.1 per cent of the company. A draft official statement said that Hartwell would remain Chairman and Editor-in-Chief, but that H. M. Stephen would retire as Managing Director in the New Year. The name of the new Chief Executive was not given, although by then everyone involved knew it would be Andrew Knight.

When Deedes saw Hartwell that evening, he found him 'looking unexpectedly relaxed', as if his predominant emotion was relief that the uncertainty was over. He began by saying, 'I seem to have lost out. I shall be a minority share-holder.' Then he went back over the whole financial saga before saying, 'It's a rather embarrassing question – but do the staff want me to stay on?' Deedes replied that although there was some feeling against the management for the way they had reneged on the pay-increase originally promised to the journalists when they converted to the new technology, there was none whatever against him personally:

> If he were to go, I say, change too sudden. Both staff and readership, which counts also, would be reassured by his continuing. I hope he will lighten management load, since business and editorial for both papers is too much for one man. No comment – only a smile . . . [I] reiterate that Berry family seen as part of paper's ethos.

Other journals hastened to print their versions of the settlement, but the *Telegraph* waited until Mr Leon Brittan, the Secretary of State for Trade and Industry, had ruled that, since Conrad Black had no other newspapers in this country, the deal need not be referred to the Monopolies and Mergers Commission. Then, on the following Thursday, 12 December, Hartwell himself published a small article in the Daily saying that extra finance was 'having to be arranged'. Details would be disclosed next day, he promised, and he very much regretted that

> readers and staff have so far had to rely on incomplete reports in other papers. The new arrangements are complex and are dependent on consents from a number of outside parties. The Company will have to be restructured . . . By agreement I shall remain Chairman and Editor-in-Chief of the *Daily* and *Sunday Telegraph*.

This official confirmation of what everybody knew led to emotional scenes in several of Fleet Street's hostelries, and in none was the drinking deeper than at the King and Keys. In Saturday's tightly controlled leader, the hand of Bill Deedes was clearly discernible. 'We owe to our readers a few words about ourselves and about our future,' it began:

> We also owe them an apology. The apology is due because,

while arranging our financing for a better newspaper in the years ahead, we have not been as free as our contemporaries to speculate about the arrangements. Our readers, and indeed our own staff, are entitled to feel that they have been left too much in the dark. But company law is restrictive. Today we can at last tell the facts . . .

Over the years our character has not changed much. A newspaper's traditions are more enduring than the movements of capital . . . For more than half a century we have stood on foundations built by the late VISCOUNT CAMROSE, who transformed the paper. With two new plants in the offing, there is to be another leap forward.

And, since LORD HARTWELL does not interfere with the editorial policies of his newspapers, we are free to add these few words more. For fifty-eight years we have been in the hands of a family who have thought it more important to run a newspaper honourably than profitably. We salute that.

In his diary for 20 December Deedes wrote:

Andrew Knight brought to conference room, 2.33 pm. After the event participants seemed pleased. Optimists will say, Thank God, we have a journalist who will be more sympathetic to journalists' feelings as Chief Executive than most. A pessimist will say (as Hartwell inclines to say), He'll be drawn into interfering with the editorial side of the paper.

Within the building, at every level, discussion raged about possible new editors. Those fancied for the Daily included Ian Ball, the paper's Chief of Bureau in Washington, and Charles Moore, Editor of the *Spectator*, who had worked on the paper from 1979 to 1983, but was still only twenty-nine. Deedes minuted his own discussion with Hartwell:

Ian Ball too much involved in America. Hartwell asks, Andreas Whittam Smith? I reply cautiously. Pressed as to my choice, plump for Charles Moore. Stress age against him. Also stress experience under Algy Cluff, then Fairfax [owners of the *Spectator*]. Stress character, which is important. Deliver little homily on unity of paper, saying no personal problems with Peter Eastwood, but that is not the way to run a ship. Runs a tight ship, but possessive and predatory. Can't go on like that. He agrees. Presses on point that Andrew Knight and Andreas

Whittam Smith would not hit it off. Reveal we have had exchanges . . .* Jock Bruce-Gardyne too much with Lords now, and too abrasive. Colin Webb of *Times* not suitable. 40 mins.

On 21 December Peregrine Worsthorne amazed even friends who knew his capacity for self-destructive revelation by publishing some less-than-flattering remarks about Andrew Knight in the *Spectator*. Having described how once, after a night's drinking with Claud Cockburn in Ireland, Knight had remarked that journalists must be the best company in the world, Worsthorne went on:

> I recalled these words when reading that he had been appointed to manage, rather than edit, the *Telegraphs*. For if Fleet Street journalists are some of the best company in the world, Fleet Street managers (with notable exceptions) must be among the worst. So is it really conceivable that Andrew Knight will be content to spend the years ahead simply managing? I don't believe it for a moment.

As Hartwell was still Editor-in-Chief, he supposed that he still had the right to appoint, or at least to approve the appointment of, new editors – but he soon found out that he was wrong. Before that discovery, however, he got a different kind of shock. On 27 December the *Financial Times* broke the news that Andreas Whittam Smith, City Editor on the Daily, was about to resign and start up a paper of his own, along with two of the *Telegraph* leader-writers, Matthew Symonds and Stephen Glover. This mass defection hit Hartwell particularly hard. He saw it as a lack of loyalty, and could not understand it. When Whittam Smith went to see him and was asked what he thought his position was after the leak of news, he replied simply, 'Untenable.' But he did not add that one important factor which had rendered it so was Hartwell's rejection of his own plan for saving the *Telegraph*. Nevertheless, Hartwell wished him good luck.

The first few weeks of 1986 were an extraordinarily difficult time. Knight was not due to take up his appointment until 3 February, and the rights issue, though approved by the Board, would not go through until the end of that month. There was thus

---

* These remarks came as a surprise to Knight, who thought highly of Whittam Smith, and considered that he had a major role to play at the *Telegraph*. He had said as much to Hartwell, but when he suggested Whittam Smith (who was in his forties) as a possible Editor, Hartwell had replied, 'Much too young.'

an interregnum in which the future was uncertain and funds extremely short: the new government, so to speak, was in waiting, but did not yet have access to the real levers of power.

Even so, in the opening days of the year many key decisions were taken. Knight found this one of the most awkward periods of his life, for he already knew that Rupert Murdoch was about to break the print unions' monopoly by the drastic expedient of moving operations to his heavily-fortified plant at Wapping, yet he could not make this knowledge public. Before formally taking up office, he held two weekend meetings with the *Telegraph* managers who were negotiating manning levels for the new plant at West Ferry Road, and on various pretexts stopped them taking their talks any further until he saw what happened when Murdoch made his move.

According to Dan Colson, who was working at 135 Fleet Street as a stopgap, the period was one of 'absolute pandemonium. Hartwell was sitting on the fifth floor, still firing off memos and getting people on the intercom. But he wasn't in financial control any more, and people were wandering around with quizzical looks on their faces, wondering who to take orders from. Soon they began coming in and saying, "Hartwell asked me to do so-and-so. Is that all right?" But if we didn't like it, we told them to stop.'

Then came the fundamental breakthrough. In the fourth week of January Murdoch finally called the unions' bluff and shifted News International's publishing operations to the factory at Wapping which had stood idle – since the unions had refused to man it – for the past seven years. There, on 26 January, he showed that it was possible to bring out the *Sunday Times* with no union labour at all. His move proved historic – the beginning of the end of Fleet Street as it had been for the past hundred years; and although his demolition of union power came too late to save Hartwell, it did ease things slightly at the *Telegraph*, as it hit chapel officials like a blow in the solar plexus and reduced their appetite for obstruction.

When Knight took over at 135 Fleet Street on 3 February 1986, almost his first action, at 9.15 that Monday morning, was to fire Hugh Lawson. Hartwell had warned Lawson, the week before, that Knight was after his blood; but it was Conrad Black, as much as anyone, who had decided that the man with the monocle must go. Ever since their first meeting in New York, he had felt that Lawson was 'simply not plausible as a senior executive'. Lawson was stunned to be thus sent packing, after the management had come so close to achieving its new plants, its demanning, its new deal. He felt he was being used as a fall-guy, a scapegoat. Yet he was not dismissed immediately: for two weeks Knight kept him on as a kind of personal assistant, using him to make introductions both within the building and at the NPA. Lawson's wife Hilary took a robust view. 'Thank God,' she said. 'Now you can come skiing' – and off the family went to Verbier.

In the hot seat, Knight at first found that senior managers still felt obliged to report to Hartwell as a matter of course. He let them carry on for a couple of weeks, but then issued an order that nobody was to talk to Hartwell about company business without telling him, and certainly no one was to take any instructions from the former proprietor. This, he knew, was very painful for Hartwell, but it was also, in his view, inescapable.

In general, both he and Black did everything they could to cause Hartwell as little offence as possible, and Knight detailed Jack Cooper, the Deputy General Manager, to see that within the building irritation was kept to a minimum. Yet soon there came a development which inevitably caused distress to the Berry family: the invasion of their sanctuary on the fifth floor. For years the paper's City staff had been based at the back of Bracken House, just beyond St Paul's; but now the lease of their offices had expired, and accommodation had to be found for them elsewhere. At that point, with the paper still in the hands of the banks and the management unable to sign cheques of any size, Knight found that it was proposed to take on two new suites of offices to accommodate the City staff. Hartwell had refused to sign the lease, aware that he must not bind the hands of the new management; and Knight, knowing that the fifth floor was uninhabited except by Hartwell, Camrose and the Finance Director, insisted that for the time being the Sunday City office should be housed there, while he himself moved into the directors' dining-room. It was, he acknowledges, 'a terribly hurtful thing to do', but at a time of critical difficulty it saved £300,000.

Before the City staff arrived, Cooper organised the removal of the family's private possessions, including all the silver and the valuable Sèvres porcelain collected by the first Lady Camrose. One morning, together with the butler, he supervised the packing of these effects, which were taken to a bonded store in outer London. Hardly had they gone, however, when the second Lord Camrose's companion, Princess Joan Aly Khan (whom he later married), telephoned to suggest that they would be better off at Hackwood where there was ample storage space in the cellars. Cooper demurred: some of the things, he said, belonged to Lord Hartwell personally. Hartwell – who showed astonishingly little regard for possessions – agreed that the things should be sorted out, and had his own share brought back to Fleet Street.

One of Knight's most urgent tasks was to appoint new editors. Months earlier, during a reception at No. 10 Downing Street, Hartwell had complained to him that Conrad Black was in too much of a hurry. 'He keeps talking about getting new editors,' Hartwell had muttered. 'Bill Deedes has got many years in him yet.' So he had – as later events proved. But when control of the company changed hands, Deedes was the first to suggest to Knight that, at the age of seventy-two and after twelve years in the chair, he had been Editor long enough. John Thompson, who was sixty-five, had already said that he would like to retire, but, characteristically, Hartwell had persuaded him to stay on. When the paper changed hands, Thompson again said that he wanted to go. Again Hartwell tried to dissuade him, but this time he was adamant, feeling certain that the new owner would want fresh blood. Even then one of the old hands on the paper wrote a note chiding him for going before he had reached seventy – 'the usual *Telegraph* age'.

At first Knight had planned to leave both men in place until the summer. But then, as he saw circulations plunging still further, he concluded that new editors must be found in time to make a real impact before Andreas Whittam Smith's *Independent* came on the scene in the autumn. His own recommendation to Black was that the new men should be Max Hastings for the Daily and Perry Worsthorne for the Sunday. In total secrecy he despatched both of them, separately, to meet the new proprietor at his home in Toronto. Somehow Worsthorne could not gain access through the gates of the house, and was found by Black himself floundering through snowdrifts in the garden; but in spite of this mishap the Canadian was impressed by both his visitors.

Both names caused a good deal of surprise when they became known. Worsthorne, passed over ten years earlier, was already sixty-two – and in any case had apparently ruined his chances with his remarks about Knight in the *Spectator*. Hastings, at only forty, had not occurred to many people as a possible candidate. An outstanding journalist, and author of several admirable books, he had made his name as a military historian, principally with *Bomber Command*, his study of RAF operations during the Second World War, published in 1979. Then, in 1982, his brilliant reporting of the Falklands War had confirmed his reputation as a leading practitioner and authority in the field. But, apart from a stint on the *Evening Standard*'s Londoner's Diary, he had never worked in a newspaper office, and had no experience of editing.

Yet it was with these two already chosen – and with both of them standing by breathlessly for news of their appointments to be released – that Knight came to the *Telegraph* boardroom on 25 February. His tactics were to give Hartwell no warning, and so bounce him into acceptance of the nominees. The meeting was carefully timed: the new share issue had gone through the day before, and Hartwell no longer had the power to block innovations.

The result was an explosion, or rather several. In a preliminary meeting, held at 2.00 pm, Hartwell 'blew his top' (his own words) at Frank Rogers and Andrew Knight, for trying to fling a *fait accompli* in his face. 'Surely, if I'm still Editor-in-Chief, I control these appointments?' he cried. 'Why didn't you tell me what you were doing?'

'Well,' replied Knight coolly, 'I didn't think you'd agree.'

At the main meeting, which began at 2.30, Hartwell let fly again. Not wanting to discuss the matter in front of the executive directors, he sent them away, and then had 'an up-and-down for half an hour' with the remainder of the Board. For the first time in the experience of those present, he quite lost his self-control. Far from muttering, as he usually did, he remonstrated loudly and passionately. In Knight's phrase, his reaction was 'very violent'. Hastings he did not know: he would have liked to meet him before a decision was taken. The choice he could not swallow was that of Worsthorne. 'He couldn't edit his school magazine, let alone a national newspaper!' Hartwell cried. 'He's a brilliant writer, but terrible with people. It would be a disaster. You're mad!' He brought up the famous television gaffe, citing it as evidence that the man was unfit to take charge. So angry did he become that David Montagu feared he was going to pass out on them again, and to reduce the tension he took Hartwell off to another room for a recess, together with Lord Rawlinson, hoping to talk him round. 'You don't know anything about these people, David,' said Hartwell bitterly. 'How can you sit there and accept them?' Montagu replied that the papers now belonged to Conrad Black, and that if he wanted to appoint editors who turned out to be useless, that was his lookout.

When the meeting reconvened, Stephen sought a delay: he suggested that, as Hartwell had already flown the Atlantic once in the course of this deal, he should do so again, to confer with Black himself on so crucial a matter. Knight, however, insisted that they must reach a decision there and then, for he knew that news of the appointments could not be contained for much longer, and that if word leaked out prematurely, chaos would ensue. Worsthorne was at that moment in the building, and had somehow (for once) managed to keep the news to himself. Hastings was in his club, Brooks's, whence, as the afternoon wore on, he bombarded Knight's secretary with increasingly frequent telephone calls.

In the boardroom Adrian, loyal as he was, spoke out with honesty and courage. He was, he said, the only person present with personal experience of Worsthorne in action. He had often been at editorial conferences when, with John Thompson away, Perry had taken the chair. The meetings had always been most stimulating, for Perry encouraged debate and the development of ideas. He would, Adrian thought, make an excellent editor.

Eventually, as a last throw, Hartwell asked if they could put the matter to a vote. The first man round the table was H. M. Stephen, who said, 'Of course, I vote with the Chairman.' But when it came to Adrian he said, 'Well, Father, I will not vote against you, but I will abstain.' No full count was taken, and Hartwell accepted defeat with great dignity.

The management were amazed – and extremely impressed – that something which they regarded as inconceivable had happened so quickly. Yet even they scarcely appreciated the true import of that meeting. It was the moment at which Hartwell finally lost control. Already he had yielded financial supremacy to Black; but now, although still nominally Editor-in-Chief, he effectively handed over what had always been closest to his heart – the editorial direction of the two papers. The regime founded by his father in 1928, and run with such flair and tenacity by father and son for more than half a century, had come to a sudden end.

Epilogue

After months more of dire financial uncertainty, which led in the end to yet another rights issue, the new management led by Andrew Knight achieved a phenomenally successful financial recovery. In the year ending 31 March 1989 the company made a profit of £29 million, and forecast one of £40 million for the year that followed – a transformation so startling that one participant suggested that it should be written up as a case history for study in business schools.

As Knight grappled with the task of releasing the company from the stranglehold which the banks had on it, many heads rolled, both editorial and managerial. For the staff who remained, the most traumatic event was the company's departure from 135 Fleet Street, which took place in the summer of 1987. For a combination of reasons, financial and technical, the new management decided that they must vacate the 1930 premises, and after a frustrating search for a more central alternative, during which they were twice gazumped, their choice fell on a brand-new, six-storey building at South Quay Plaza on the Isle of Dogs, only a few hundred yards from the new printing works at West Ferry Road. The design of the new building was certainly distinguished: its steeply-angled pediments gave a hint of classical Greece, and the predominantly dark-grey-blue of its glass and granite walls lent it monolithic solidity, as if it were one huge lump of rock. The past lived on in the name of the new building – Peterborough Court at South Quay.

When members of the staff first saw it, they were amazed. Having vacated a white marble palace, grandiose in its day, they found they had come to a black marble palace, with a lowering, pretentious entrance hall, immense, partition-less floors, air-conditioning throughout, and no window that could be opened. One of the first buildings to be finished in that area, it rose from a wilderness of ruins and a maze of construction projects less far advanced. Behind it lay old dock basins, giving a pleasant outlook over water, and a pensioned-off ferry, the 165-foot *Celtic Surveyor*, which in due course became the staff canteen and, on the top deck, a restaurant. To the great annoyance of the *Telegraph* management, the caterers rechristened the vessel *Le Boat*, until threats of a boycott by the paper's staff forced them to remove the name from the canteen area and use it for the restaurant only.

In front and on either side of the building a swarm of bulldozers, diggers and heavy trucks roared and grunted, while the ground vibrated day and night with the remorseless, thudding clank of pile-drivers. In the early months there were no shops, no houses, no restaurants, no grass, no trees, and only (at a distance) a scattering of pubs which had somehow survived from the old days of the docks.

The shock of the move was intensified by the fact that it came when the journalists were in the middle of learning to use the Atex computer system, on which they themselves typed and edited their own articles. During this rapid conversion to 'direct in-putting' – the final break from the old hot-metal typesetting – Adrian Berry proved an exceptionally able teacher, but the crash transition put everyone under strain. Yet by far the deadliest drawback of the new office was its location. Five miles east of Fleet Street, three miles beyond the Tower, two miles further from civilisation even than Murdoch's Fortress Wapping – itself regarded as the back of beyond – South Quay seemed like the world's end.

Going to the Dogs was (and is) an ordeal. To ease it, the management arranged river taxis, in the form (at first) of two boats, the *Max* and the *Perry*, which plied up and down the Thames. The idea was attractive, but the service, like any other, was liable to interruption from breakdowns and rough weather, and even on good days the best it could do was to decant or pick up passengers at a point seven minutes' fast walk from the office. An alternative means of transport was the much-vaunted Dock-lands Light Railway – a system of two-coach trains, alleged to be fully automatic and decked out in saucy blue-and-red livery, which ran on overhead tracks from the Tower eastwards, with one station right outside the front door of the building at South Quay. Once again, this sounded admirable but fell short in practice, being often reduced to a standstill by technical troubles, or blown out of action by high winds. A third means of travel was the minibus service which the company maintained, with vehicles running continu-ously between South Quay and Fleet Street or Blackfriars; and a fourth was private cars. But all road transport was liable to bog down in the traffic, which was far greater than the out-of-date roads could carry. How, from this outpost of high technology, could a reporter on Peterborough slip out for a chat with a contact, or for a quick drink with a Member of Parliament who had some useful piece of information to impart? Suddenly Westminster was an hour's journey away, instead of ten minutes.

The old building in Fleet Street died a sudden death. With the humans gone from it, life departed too. To anyone who walked through it even a few days later, the change seemed extraordinarily abrupt. Somehow the spirit of the *Telegraph* did not linger in those deserted rooms: moving with the people who embodied it, it had gone elsewhere. On the fifth floor balcony, the flowers wilted and the grass of the lawn grew long. Soon extraordinary sights were to be seen in Peterborough Court, as wrecker-gangs went in to demolish the ancient presses: up from the bowels of the earth came an amazing assortment of rollers, gear-wheels, cables and vast lumps of metal, all shining black with the ink and oil of ages.

Effective, imaginative direction was obviously one key element in the dramatic turn-round of the business; but another was the end of over-manning and union malpractice which the previous management had planned and almost carried through and which now produced enormous savings, even greater than those hoped for. In Fleet Street, there had been 2,200 men in the production departments. At West Ferry Road, by the end of 1988, there were 507. In the old plant, the composing-room and its satellites alone had employed 413; now the equivalent number was twenty-seven. The old foundry had needed eighty-three people every night: the new operation used nine. The crew on each press, once twenty-two strong, was down to five.

Both new printing-plants came into operation on schedule, with a startling improvement in the appearance of the papers, in south and north alike. The contrast between the airy, space-age premises at West Ferry Road and the black, subterranean dungeons of Fleet Street could not have been sharper; and nothing symbolised the difference between old and new more perfectly than the self-propelled, computer-guided robots which carried the paper-reels round the modern factory. Not only did these do their job without constantly breaking off to hold tea-breaks and unofficial union meetings: whenever one of them finished a task, it obediently went back to base and waited for the next command.

The new technology immediately put life into both Daily and Sunday papers. Not only was the quality of print and photographs immensely improved: just as in 1930, the advent of fresh money and more pages enabled designers to let air into their layouts. No longer did every story have to be cut to the bone, every illustration pared right down. Spectacularly improved looks helped *The Daily Telegraph* fight off the challenge of the *Independent*, which was successfully launched in October 1986. Within two years the new paper established a circulation of 400,000 copies a day, but it made more impact on the *Guardian* and the *Times* than on the *Telegraph*, which retained a sale of 1,150,000. *The Sunday Telegraph* also did well at first.

The two new editors both proved conspicuously successful choices. Max Hastings, a tough but inspiring leader, gave the Daily new purpose and direction. Many readers, of course, found fault with any innovation; but the majority remained loyal, and if some were disappointed that the politics of the former Torygraph became diluted, many more were delighted to find that news coverage was imaginatively expanded, sports reporting greatly improved, features made more lively, and that for the first time in its history the paper gave knowledgeable coverage to field sports and country matters. On the Sunday paper, Perry Worsthorne confounded Hartwell's predictions of disaster and emerged as an editor of distinction: besides continuing to write his own column, he gave the paper style and character, and made it, in the opinion of the veteran commentator Paul Johnson, 'the best and liveliest of all the national qualities'. For a few months sales rose above 750,000. Hartwell himself was big enough to admit his mistake: a few weeks after the change-over, he called Worsthorne into his office one Saturday and said, 'I just wanted you to know that I think I was wrong.' Considering how painful it was for him to make any personal statement, this was a handsome apology.

Later, however, both he and the management began to have doubts. Sales of the Sunday paper fell sharply when the colour magazine was transferred to Saturday, in September 1988. Then, in the summer of 1989, the Daily and Sunday papers were merged into a single unit – the seven-day *Telegraph* – under the editorship of Max Hastings, with Worsthorne relegated to control of Sunday's opinion and arts pages: a move which reduced morale among his staff to rock bottom. Yet another earthquake shook the Sunday paper in October 1989, when it suddenly acquired an Editor of its own once more, in the form of Trevor Grove, who had done excellent work in rebuilding the features on the Daily.

After the takeover in 1986, Conrad Black confounded fears that he would prove a meddlesome proprietor and interfere with editorial matters. Far from it: he came to England rarely, and let his executives get on with rebuilding the shattered company. As he saw it, there were two shoals of which it was important that he should steer clear. One was the risk that he might look like 'just another publicity-seeking, self-promoting Commonwealth person, who came rushing over trailing his coat tails in search of a peerage'. On the other hand, he was anxious not to appear 'as a materialistic caricature of a North American businessman with no respect for British institutions'. Not being either of these types, he found no difficulty in keeping his distance. Only in the autumn of 1989, when the business was back on a secure footing, did he announce that he would take over day-to-day control as Chief Executive from Andrew Knight.

Michael Hartwell never made the move to South Quay. For eighteen months he hung on at 135 Fleet Street as Chairman and Editor-in-Chief, but at last retired on 1 September 1987, aged seventy-six. Although retaining a seat on the Board as a non-executive director, he moved his office to an anonymous modern building in the shadow of New Scotland Yard, near Parliament Square, where his family had difficulty persuading him to furnish his spartan room with a carpet, for which he said there was no need. To the end he maintained that there had been no takeover, only a buy-in, and that given a little more luck – for instance if Murdoch had made his move to Wapping earlier, or if the Manchester manning figures had been better – he himself 'might have got away with it'.

In purely financial terms, his family had done extraordinarily well. They remained, as they had always been, millionaires.* Neither he nor Camrose had held any shares in the *Telegraph* since they had established the Newspaper Trust in 1978, but when Hartwell retired the Newspaper Trust was transferred into a family trust, with the shares held in the names of the grandchildren and great-grandchildren of the first Lord Camrose. The family trust's holding in *The Daily Telegraph* had been reduced to eleven per cent; but by the autumn of 1989 the company was conservatively valued at £420 million, and in private Rupert Murdoch reckoned that the title would cost £1 billion to buy. As plenty of observers remarked, it was surely better to own eleven per cent of a business worth that amount than ninety-seven per cent of a bankrupt firm worth nothing. Ivan Fallon – once City Editor of *The Sunday Telegraph*, and now Deputy Editor of the *Sunday Times* – found the deal the most astonishing he had witnessed in twenty-five years of financial journalism: 'Conrad Black in a sense paid himself – he bought into a firm which ended up under his own control. Hartwell's

---

* A word long banned by the Style Book.

share fell from ninety-seven per cent to eleven per cent without him getting anything for it. To give away nearly £900 million, and what he had lived for, is one of the great financial as well as personal tragedies of the age.'*

Hartwell himself looked back on what had happened with exemplary lack of bitterness. Yet to many people who knew him there was something tragic about the fact that a man who had laboured devotedly to preserve his family inheritance should have lost it after such Trojan efforts. As he himself put it, he had 'always stuck to the last'. His creed had been very simple. 'I worked on the papers because they fascinated me,' he said. 'I was always terribly shocked when other people ran their newspapers like biscuit factories, just to make money. Whether or not we made money out of ours was immaterial to us. My whole endeavour was to think first of the staff, and then of the papers, and of myself a good deal last. What I was trying to do was to make the *Telegraph* a national institution, without the awful connotations that the expression normally carries – that's to say, an institution which is respected and admired, and which would leave the world poorer if it were not there. It sounds awfully boring, but I regarded it as my life's work – that's all.'

* He had in fact received one payment of £10 million direct from Black.

ACKNOWLEDGEMENTS

My greatest debt is to Lord Hartwell, formerly Michael Berry, who gave unstinting help. Even though I approached him at an inauspicious time – soon after he had been through the traumatic experience of losing financial and editorial control of his family business – he talked freely about the *Telegraph* and his own career. His response was especially generous, considering that he was already working on a life of his father, the first Viscount Camrose, so that we were, up to a point, rival authors. Because of this, I did not feel that I could decently ask to see the Camrose archive: my loss. Lord Hartwell also read a draft of my typescript, eliminated many errors and suggested useful additions.

I am grateful also to the present Viscount Camrose, who responded to a request for help by inviting me to lunch at Hackwood Park, his splendid home near Basingstoke. Much light was shed on the Berry family by Alistair Forbes, Selina Hastings, Alan and David Pryce-Jones, Paul Johnson and the Hon. Jacob Rothschild.

For information about the moves which led to the takeover, I am indebted to Conrad Black, Daniel Colson, Rupert Hambro, the Hon. David Montagu, Michael Richardson, Sir Frank Rogers and Sir Evelyn de Rothschild.

I am especially grateful to Andrew Knight, Chief Executive of the *Telegraph* from 1986 to 1989, not only for his insights into the takeover, but also for permission to quote extensively from back numbers of the paper, and from company documents.

Many former colleagues on the *Daily* and *Sunday Telegraph* made valuable contributions. I should like particularly to thank the following:

The late George Ailles, Desmond Albrow, Nicholas Bagnall, Trevor Bates, the Hon. Adrian Berry, the Hon. Nicholas Berry, Peter Birkett, Gordon Brook-Shepherd, Jack Cooper, Jeremy Deedes, Lord Deedes, Christopher Dobson, John Dudman, Peter Eastwood, George Evans, John Evans, Ivan Fallon, Kenneth Fleet, Eileen Fuller, Peter Gill, Max Hastings, Selina Hastings, Peter Heath, Clare Hollingworth, David Holloway, Winefride Jackson, Frank Johnson, Michael Kennedy, the Hon. Hugh Lawson, Adrian Lighter, David Loshak, Mrs Donald McLachlan, E. H. Marsh,

Ronald Payne, Len Piddington, Anthony Powell, Alan Rawcliffe, Kenneth Rose, Ivan Rowan, Rivers Scott, Adrian Secker, H. M. Stephen, Matthew Symonds, Bill Tadd, J. W. M. Thompson, Colin Welch, Fred Whitsey, Andreas Whittam Smith, Malcolm Williams and Peregrine Worsthorne.

I am grateful to Curtis Brown for their permission, on behalf of the Estate of Winston Churchill, to quote the passages by Churchill on pages 67 and 147.

I am much indebted to Robert Smyly, a grandson of Lord Buckland, for permission to quote from his private memoir of the Berry family; to David Cole for his expert introduction to the family's haunts in Merthyr Tydfil; to Graham Jones, Editor of the *Merthyr Express*, for digging out details from back numbers; to Lucia Whitehead, custodian of the Lawson family archive, for information about the first and second Lords Burnham; and to J. C. Trewin for reconstructing the final hours of the *Morning Post*; and to Douglas Matthews, librarian of the London Library, for compiling the index with such skill and despatch.

The hoard of papers and objects which George Newkey-Burden, former Classified Advertising Manager of *The Daily Telegraph*, rescued from 135 Fleet Street when the paper moved to Docklands yielded many extra details, and the help which he gave in finding illustrations was invaluable. Finally, I must record that I could never have completed my research without the inexhaustible patience and good nature of Joyce Meachem, the *Telegraph* Librarian, and her staff.

References

DT = Daily Telegraph   ST = Sunday Telegraph

1   The Berrys of Merthyr Tydfil

page

11   Beyond their control — *Merthyr Tydfil* (Merthyr Teachers' Centre Group, 1981), p. 233.

12   His sons proved to be — Much of the family detail is taken from an unpublished memoir, 'The Berry Brothers', compiled by Robert Smyly, grandson of Seymour, Lord Buckland, and printed for private circulation in 1982.

13   His neighbour W. J. Cole — Verbatim David Cole.

14   This is Labour policy — Smyly, *op. cit.*

15   A recherché breakfast — *Merthyr Express*, 7 September 1907.

18   Plate-glass window — Verbatim Cole.

21   A jovial, red-faced villain — Leonard Russell, *The Pearl of Days*, p. 67.

22   Somewhat rough exterior — *Manchester Guardian*, 16 June 1954.

23   He looked the man . . . — DT, 16 June 1954.
Nicholas Berry — Verbatim to author.
Newspaper ambitions — Stephen Koss, *The Rise and Fall of the Political Press in Britain*, Vol. 2, p. 364.

24   Further . . . in no case — Camrose, *British Newspapers and their Controllers*, p. 66.
Come into the open — *Ibid*, p. 35.

2   The Burnham Era, 1855–1928

29   Far-sighted memorandum — *Peterborough Court*, p. 8.

31	In the early years	*Ibid*, p. 16.
32	Ran a tight ship	DT archive.
33	I fear you and I	*Peterborough Court*, pp. 20–1.
	Lord Burnham's words	*Ibid*, pp. 25–6.
34	Skull-and-crossbones	Hugh Lawson's papers.
35	I asked him	Unpublished DT typescript, p. 42.
36	Ugly old man	*Peterborough Court*, p. 43.
37	Tastefully decorated	*Illustrated London News*, 8 July 1882.
39	Overdone it a bit	John Gore, *King George V*, p. 230.
	I watched the King	*Ibid*.
40	Nearly 6,000 birds	Burnham family archive.
	We, the undersigned	DT typescript, pp. 289–90.
41	It created havoc	*Ibid*, p. 252.
44	To the great anger	Verbatim Hugh Lawson.

3 THE BERRYS TAKE OVER, 1928–30

45	Went to see Berry	*Peterborough Court*, p. 189.
46	In the billiard-room	DT, 13 June 1939.
	Green baize aprons	*The Pearl of Days*, pp. 183–4.
	Some secret recess	*Ibid*, p. 185.
	You bladdy Jew	*Ibid*, p. 186.
	Emotions ran high	*British Newspapers*, p. 30.
48	A glass-fronted cubicle	Gander, *After These Many Quests*, pp. 104–5.
49	Lakin's flamboyance	*The Pearl of Days*, p. 189.
52	Extremely conscious	*Peterborough Court*, p. 190.
	An immense improvement	Camrose papers, quoted in Koss, *op. cit.*, pp. 474–5.
53	Loved a great joke	Smyly memoir.
54	A cheer went up	David Cole verbatim. The story is echoed in Cecil King's memoirs, *Strictly Personal*, p. 122.
	First time	David Cole.
55	Anti-Lloyd George	Koss, *op. cit.*, p. 478.
	In thanking Baldwin	Camrose papers, quoted in Koss, *op. cit.*, p. 489.
56	Escaped from the terrace	*The Pearl of Days*, p. 184.
	On the first floor	*Ibid*, p. 185.
	Young George Ailles	Verbatim to author.
60	*World's Press News*	27 November 1930.

61	Tired of newspapers	*Ibid.*
63	Very extraordinary	*British Newspapers*, p. 18.
	Nearly every newspaper	*Ibid*, p. 18.
	Gradually going mad	Koss, *op. cit.*, p. 478.

4 TOWARDS THE MILLION, 1930–39

64	The random harvest	Gannon, *The British Press and Germany, 1936–39*, p. 1.
	As Watson remarked	*Peterborough Court*, p. 194.
65	Straight in the back	*Ibid*, p. 195.
66	A more inquiring mind	*Ibid*, p. 194.
67	Baldwin's request	Koss, *op. cit.*, p. 501.
	I am sorry to find	Churchill archive, Churchill College, Cambridge.
68	I am sorry	*Ibid.*
	My Dear Winston	*Ibid.*
	I was very pleased	*Ibid.*
70	Picture the hush	DT, 27 December 1932.
71	A joyous, epicurean don	*Victorian Eton and Cambridge*, pp. 5–6.
72	They wanted supreme	Verbatim Bill Deedes.
73	Ministry of Publicity	DT, April 1935.
74	Last night I watched	DT, February 1935.
	Camrose let it be known	*Fleet Street*, pp. 178–9.
75	I do my utmost	Gannon, *op. cit.*, p. 114.
	As he later recorded	DT archive.
76	Burking the truth	DT, 11 July 1934.
77	Another confidant	Nicolson, *Diaries and Letters*, 7 April 1936.
78	Faintly improbable story	Smyly, *op. cit.*
	In May 1935	*Merthyr Express*, 11 May 1935.
79	Has many advantages	*Evening Standard*, 23 June 1935.
81	Lady Longford	*Tatler*, June 1982.
	Death of her father	DT, 2 October 1930.
82	Pugnacious remarks	*Queen*, 20 April 1932.
	The day before	DT, 6 January 1936.
83	Unpunctual, untidy	Channon, *Chips*, 18 May 1937.
	Gay, dark, vivacious	*Ibid*, 12 September 1937.
	Handsomely rewarded	Koss, *op. cit.*, pp. 414–15.
	Emerged with most credit	*Edward VIII*, p. 269.
	Astors and Berrys	Channon, *Chips*, 7 December 1938.

84	Financial basis	*British Newspapers*, p. 34.
86	A desperate shock	J. C. Trewin, letter to author, 1989.
88	It is the custom	DT, 14 October 1937.
90	The first envelope	DT, 11 December 1937.
	I overdid it	DT, 1989.
	Given the sack	Churchill archive, Churchill College, Cambridge.
91	When the series ended	*Ibid.*
	A tough leader	Gannon, *op. cit.*, pp. 44–5.
93	Barack – the Duke	Gedye *Fallen Bastions*, pp. 337–8.
	There is still time	*Ibid*, Foreword.
	Violently worded commentary	*New Statesman and Nation*, 22 April 1939.
	Mr Watson writes	*Ibid*, 20 May 1939.
94	Posse of politicians	Koss, *op. cit.*, p. 587.
	Quite threatening	Channon, *Chips*, 3 July 1939.
	I am vexed	Koss, *op. cit.*, p. 588.
98	Controlled by Jews	*British Newspapers*, p. vii.
	The round million	DT, 13 June 1939.
99	I am not boasting	DT, *ibid.*

5 AT WAR, 1939–45

100	Clare Hollingworth	Verbatim to author.
102	Alarmed his subordinates	Verbatim Hartwell.
	In a sour note	Koss, *op. cit.*, p. 609.
103	Night Editor	Verbatim Hartwell.
	Unfaltering confidence	In Churchill's eulogy at St Paul's, 3 May 1956.
105	In contradistinction	DT, 14 March 1941.
111	Quite horrible	*Editorial*, p. 170.
	Reached a compromise	*Ibid*, p. 169.
	Far from golden	*Ibid*, p. 215.
	Camrose was bored	Verbatim Hartwell.
112	Under May skies	DT, 2 May 1944.
114	Philanthropic thoughts	Letter to author from Eton College Archivist, 15 June 1988.
	Wartime secrets	Gilbert, *Finest Hour*, p. 1,200.
117	It was a measure	Camrose papers, quoted in Gilbert, *Road to Victory*, pp. 1,347–9.
118	Hotel Metropole	DT archive.

6 NEW HEIGHTS, 1945–54

119	Today I began	Muggeridge, *Diaries*, 1 June 1945.
120	Great consternation	Muggeridge, *The Infernal Grove*, p. 261.
121	On that same day	Notes of conversation taken by Camrose and kept in his papers; quoted by Gilbert in *Never Despair*, p. 100.
122	He had been walking	Muggeridge, *Diaries*, 9 December 1945.
	Was it worth it?	*Ibid*, 17 January 1951.
123	His aspirations	Muggeridge, *The Infernal Grove*, p. 261.
	One facet of Camrose	Gilbert, *op. cit.*, pp. 255–6.
124	This meant, in those days	Muggeridge, *The Infernal Grove*, p. 260
	At the end of 1947	Verbatim Ronald Payne.
125	One man who got in	Verbatim Gordon Brook-Shepherd.
128	A young reporter	Verbatim George Evans.
129	At last, on 27 November	Gilbert, *op. cit.*, p. 273.
132	An Homeric bore	Verbatim Anthony Powell.
	Another colleague	Verbatim David Holloway.
	Curious episode	Muggeridge, *Diaries*, 9 and 17 February 1948.
	Thanking Churchill	Churchill archive, Churchill College, Cambridge.
133	To the Savoy	Muggeridge, *Diaries*, 23 February 1950.
	A family solicitor	Muggeridge, *The Infernal Grove*, p. 260.
134	If only I shared	Verbatim Colin Welch.
	I can't say my dislike	Lascelles archive, Churchill College, Cambridge.
	Discomfort became acute	Cooke, *Editorial*, pp. 164ff.
136	Come down in the world	Verbatim Peregrine Worsthorne.
137	Put it in Baldini!	Verbatim Nicholas Bagnall.
	Take it from me	Verbatim Kenneth Rose.
139	Some newspapers today	DT, 8 May 1947.
144	All Camrose residences	Muggeridge, *Diaries*, March 1954, p. 468.
	On one voyage	Verbatim David Pryce-Jones.
146	A telegram	Churchill archive, Churchill College, Cambridge.

	He was a staunch friend	Nicolson, *Diaries and Letters*, 15 June 1954.
147	My dear Lady Camrose	*Ibid.*
	Rose's journeys	Verbatim Rose.

7 SECOND GENERATION, 1954–60

151	He only understood	Verbatim Hartwell.
	Nobody plays cricket	*Ibid.*
	Father was not	*Ibid.*
153	Gospel of tyranny	*Party Choice*, p. 4.
	Masterly analysis	*Ibid*, p. 13.
154	Socialism is inferior	*Ibid*, p. 51.
	The job of Britain	*Ibid*, p. 98.
156	A new broom	Verbatim Hartwell.
158	Could not bear	Verbatim Kitty McLachlan.
	A most wonderful house	Crossman, *Backbench Diaries*, p. 995.
159	Hard-boiled, political journalistic	Crossman, *Diaries*, 4 February 1968.
	Aristocratic and corrupt	Evelyn Waugh, *Letters*, p. 429.
	I have just come back	*Ibid*, p. 233.
	I spent the weekend	*Ibid*, p. 257.
	Are you having	*Ibid*, p. 297.
	A sort of booster	*Ibid*, p. 349.
	Faded from my life	*Ibid*, p. 444.
	Impressed the locals	Verbatim David Pryce-Jones.
	In excellent form	Muggeridge, *Diaries*, 15 January 1954.
160	She never made any effort	*Tatler*, June 1982.
	Frank Giles	*Sunday Times*, p. 195.
161	The high voltage	*Tatler*, June 1982.
	The political commentator	Verbatim Paul Johnson.
162	It was widely believed	*Tatler*, ——.
	A brash young man	Crossman, *Diaries*, Vol. 2, 5 October 1967.
163	Called at Cowley Street	Verbatim Hartwell.
	Everyone goes wild	DT archive.
164	Lady Pamela Berry	*Daily Express*, 31 May 1957.
165	Bitchily described	Ann Fleming, *Letters*, p. 201.
166	Those of us who wished	*Ibid*, p. 203.
	You don't want a lot	Verbatim Hartwell.

168	He mentioned that	Wharton, *The Missing Will*, p. 215.
169	A selection of pieces	*Way of the World*, first series, Foreword.
	His first choice	Verbatim Hartwell.
170	Smack of Firm Government	DHMcL archive; verbatim Rose; verbatim Hartwell. In his official life, *Anthony Eden* (Weidenfeld & Nicolson, 1986), Robert Rhodes James quotes Eden as writing in his journal: 'Nobody knows the personal vendetta that lies behind it' (p. 425). The headline of the article is wrongly given as 'The Firm Smack of Government'.
	She seemed piqued	DHMcL archive.
171	Lunch at Brooks's	Verbatim Rose.
	Dining out	*Ibid.*
	Told H. B. Boyne	DHMcL archive.
	Letter of apology	*Ibid.*
173	Here, one day	Verbatim Payne.
	I *do* hope	*Ibid.*
174	The great reconciliation	*Ibid.*
175	We wear bowlers	Verbatim Rivers Scott.
	The Aga Khan	Verbatim Rose.
176	This Armenian fellow	Verbatim Scott.
	Most famous moment	Verbatim Hartwell.
	Nicknamed Mad Stowell	Verbatim Payne.
177	The French Government	Verbatim Johnson, Worsthorne.
179	Camrose as 'greedy'	King, *Strictly Personal*, p. 124.

8 The Sunday Telegraph, 1961–70

181	As the younger man	Verbatim Hartwell.
181n	Only half in jest	*Ibid.*
182	Afterwards Thomson	Thomson, *After I Was Sixty*, pp. 77–81.
184	McLachlan's origins were modest	Verbatim Kitty McLachlan.
	M. R. D. Foot	DHMcL archive.
186	As an editor	Many of the details and stories in this section are from former colleagues.

188	Confidential memorandum	Kenneth Rose archive.
190	With two days to go	DHMcL archive.
	Its London Letter	*Guardian*, 6 February 1961.
191	He likes it very much	Hartwell archive.
	Where we went wrong	Verbatim Hartwell.
	Brash enough to ask	ST, 1 February 1981.
192	Stylish paradox	DHMcL archive.
193	A hard time	Verbatim Hartwell.
194ff	Denning Report	DHMcL archive.
196	Old Churchill	Verbatim Hartwell.
	A petulant message	Verbatim Kitty McLachlan.
197	On a second visit	*Ibid.*
	Threatened him	ST, 31 October 1982.
	As Kitty McLachlan	ST, 7 November 1982.
199	By the terms of his contract	Verbatim Hartwell.
	He points out that	Verbatim Martin Gilbert.
201	The London Hilton	Verbatim Kitty McLachlan.
	A serious accident	*Ibid.*
202	A curious episode	Knightley, *The Second Oldest Profession*, pp. 385–7.
	For years friends	Verbatim Douglas Botting.
203	I've spent seven years	Verbatim Rose.
	Introduced Stephen Ward	Coote, *Editorial*, pp. 284–8.
205	Maddened by this habit	Verbatim Hartwell.
206	Much put out	*Ibid.*
208	In those days	Verbatim Peter Eastwood.
211	One serious argument	Verbatim Hartwell.
212	Lady Pamela, for her part	*Ibid.*
	Since the two men	DHMcL archive.
	I find myself	Hartwell archive.
213	Enjoyed editing enormously	*Evening Standard*, 10 March 1968.
214	One of her parties	Verbatim Rose.
	Seized by the arm	Verbatim Welch.
215	Terrible people	Verbatim Rose.
216	Obsessed with 'plots'	Barbara Castle, *Diaries*, 29 September 1966.
	Rigorously Tory	Williams, *Inside No. 10*, pp. 231–2.
217	I tried to talk	Crossman, *Diaries*, Vol. 2, 5 October 1967.
	Strength of the *Telegraph*	Verbatim Cole.
218	As one manager admitted	Verbatim Jack Cooper.
	EIU report	Quotations from DT, 18 January 1967.
220	Then, as in 1967	Verbatim Hartwell.

221	There was a dead hand	Verbatim Worsthorne.
223	His beloved bride	*Ibid.*
224	Couldn't have been '52	Deedes archive.
225	Long and chilly silences	*Times*, 9 May 1983.
226	A staff man would meet	Verbatim Fred Whitsey.
227	Exchanges like this	Deedes archive.

9 THE GROWING THREAT, 1970–80

229	The worst thing	Verbatim Welch.
230	Lifted the case	DT, 4 February 1971
232	One man riding shotgun	Verbatim Len Piddington.
	During a voyage	Verbatim David Pryce-Jones.
	Could scarcely ride	Verbatim Adrian Berry.
233	Utterly juvenile	*Ibid.*
	Kept a telephone	*Ibid.*
234	Adrian turns green	Verbatim Hartwell.
235	He would sheer off	Verbatim Kenneth Fleet.
	The experience I got	Verbatim Nicholas Berry.
	It surprised friends	Verbatim Jacob Rothschild.
236	Being Editor	Verbatim Welch.
	A dual nature	Johnson, *Out of Order*, pp. 10 ff.
238	His conduct was such	Verbatim Michael Kennedy, Trevor Bates.
240	Large fund of goodwill	Deedes archive.
	To arrange a lunch	Verbatim David Loshak.
242ff	Few jokes blew back	Verbatim Worsthorne, Adrian Lighter, Hartwell.
247	Of the old hands	Verbatim, Welch.
248	Morale is so low	*Spectator*, 14 December 1974.
249	Incredibly embarrassed	Verbatim Welch.
	Dearest ambition	Verbatim Fleet.
250	Does the head of a family	Verbatim Deedes.
	Damage-limitation	*Ibid.*
251	Sir James Goldsmith	Deedes archive.
252	An unchanging certainty	Radio 4 programme, *Pillars of Society*, 5: 20 February 1986.
	Described by Hartwell	In a funeral oration, 1988.
253	The new Editor	Verbatim John Thompson.
255	Noted turncoats	*Evening Standard*, 4 May 1979.
	I do wish	Verbatim Deedes.
257	One hell of an exercise	Verbatim Alan Rawcliffe.
258	At an early stage	*Ibid.*

	A continuous battle	Verbatim Piddington.
259	Such was their concern	Verbatim Fleet.
260	Only the author	Verbatim, Hartwell.
261	A startling proposal	Verbatim Andreas Whittam Smith.
262	Ought to have taken	Verbatim Deedes.
264	Then a chapel official	Verbatim Cooper.

10   SLIPPERY SLOPE, 1980–85

266ff	In Fleet Street	Verbatim Eastwood.
268	On the line	Verbatim Rose.
	Who went secretly	Verbatim Deedes.
	I had the privilege	ST, 10 January 1982.
269	After a meeting	*Tatler*, June 1982.
	Hartwell was horrified	Verbatim Deedes.
271	He threw the paper	Verbatim Rawcliffe.
272	Just couldn't make sense	Verbatim Cooper.
	Delivered by hand	Verbatim H. M. Stephen.
273	Ordered new presses	*Ibid.*
274	Several people tried	Verbatim Matthew Symonds, Rawcliffe.
275	I could get £100 million	Verbatim Cooper.
276	'Well,' came the answer	*Ibid.*
278	After another similar incident	Deedes archive.
279	Can't understand how	*Ibid.*
	Dear Mark	*Ibid.*
280	Lord Bruce-Gardyne	Radio 4, *op. cit.*
	Confirmed by Peter Utley	*Ibid.*
	A good story in Belfast	Verbatim Peter Birkett.
282	Penny Jackson	Radio 4, *op. cit.*
	How the commissionaires	*Times*, 9 May 1983.
	Relieve their feelings	Deedes archive.
283	Simple merchant bankers	Verbatim Michael Richardson.
285	Asked them for some figures	Verbatim Hugh Lawson.
286	In the glue-pot	Verbatim Richardson.
288	This was the moment	Verbatim Whittam Smith.
290	To an ogre	*Ibid.*
	Securing extra capital	Whittam Smith archive.

11   GIVING IT AWAY, MAY 1985

292	Meeting at Arrowwood	Verbatim Andrew Knight, Conrad Black.

294 At lunchtime in England — *Ibid.*
295 Hambro had first met Black — Verbatim Rupert Hambro.
296 It's not Goldsmith — Verbatim Hartwell.
297 Conspicuously available — Verbatim Black.
298 That set of figures — Verbatim Hambro.
299 The meeting which followed — Details from the participants

12 DECLINE AND FALL, MAY 1985–FEBRUARY 1986

303 Exciting and unusual — Verbatim Dan Colson.
304 In return for Ravelston — Private placing document.
305 A reasonably good deal — Verbatim Black.
306 Letter to readers — DT, 19 July 1985.
    Of three published — DT, 25 July 1985.
307 He was appalled — Verbatim David Montagu.
308 He had known Hartwell — Verbatim Evelyn de Rothschild.
309 A very nice evening — Verbatim Black.
    He had known Hartwell — Verbatim Sir Frank Rogers.
    In his inimitable fashion — Verbatim Black.
310 Seeing Hartwell again — Verbatim Rogers.
311 All the false hopes — Verbatim Montagu.
    The first Nicholas knew — Verbatim Nicholas Berry.
312 A very grave disservice — *Ibid.*
    A scatter of articles — Especially one in the *Spectator* by John Ralston Saul, 23 November 1985.
    What we needed — Verbatim Nicholas Berry.
313 In Colson's view — Verbatim Colson.
315 Hartwell himself formed — Verbatim Hartwell.
    In a final attempt — Verbatim Montagu.
    A shade hurt — *Spectator*, 14 December 1985
317 Among the staff — Verbatim Symonds.
318 Twice came to see him — Verbatim Knight.
    Begun to keep a diary — Deedes archive.
319 Other people — *Ibid.*
320 I seem to have lost out — Deedes archive.
321 We owe to our readers — DT, 14 December 1985.
323 I recalled these words — *Spectator*, 21 December 1985.
    After the leak — Verbatim Whittam Smith.
324 Simply not plausible — Verbatim Black.
    Used as a fall-guy — Verbatim Hugh Lawson.
327 Blew his top — Verbatim Hartwell, Knight, Montagu, Stephen

EPILOGUE

SOURCES

PUBLISHED

The most fertile single source has been *The Daily Telegraph* itself. For most quotations I have given exact dates of publication, but a few have been impossible to pin down. This is because the version of each day's paper recorded in the archive is the final edition; some articles in the cuttings library were taken from earlier editions, did not survive in the final edition, and have now lost their precise dates.

Books consulted include the following:

Berry, Michael, *Party Choice*, Eyre & Spottiswoode, 1948.

Burnham, Lord, *Peterborough Court: the Story of the Daily Telegraph*, Cassell, 1955.

Camrose, Viscount, *British Newspapers and Their Controllers*, Cassell, 1947.

Castle, Barbara, *The Castle Diaries*, two vols, 1964–70 and 1976–80, Weidenfeld & Nicolson, 1984 and 1980.

Channon, Henry, *Chips: the Diaries of Sir Henry Channon*, edited by Robert Rhodes James, Weidenfeld & Nicolson, 1967.

Coote, Colin R., *Editorial*, Eyre & Spottiswoode, 1965.

—— *The Other Club*, Sidgwick & Jackson, 1971.

Crossman, Richard, *The Diaries of a Cabinet Minister*, three vols, Hamish Hamilton & Jonathan Cape, 1964–78.

—— *The Backbench Diaries of Richard Crossman*, ed. Janet Morgan, Hamish Hamilton & Jonathan Cape, 1981.

Faulkner, Alex, and Hartman, Tom (eds), *All the Best People*: The Pick of Peterborough, 1929–45, Allen & Unwin, 1981.

Fleet Street (Fourteen editors), Macdonald, 1966.

Fleming, Ann, *The Letters of Ann Fleming*, ed. Mark Amory, Collins Harvill, 1985.

Gander, Leonard Marsland, *After These Many Quests*, Macdonald, 1949.

Gannon, Franklin Reid, *The British Press and Germany*, 1936–39, Clarendon Press, 1971.

Gedye, G. E. R., *Fallen Bastions*, Gollancz, 1939.

Gilbert, Martin, *Winston S. Churchill*, Vol. VI: *Finest Hour* (1983), Vol.

VII: *Road to Victory* (1986), Vol. VIII: *Never Despair, 1945–65* (1988), Heinemann.

Giles, Frank, *Sundry Times*, John Murray, 1986.

Gore, John, *King George V.* John Murray, 1941.

Hamilton, Denis, *Editor-in-Chief*, Hamish Hamilton, 1989.

Hobson, Harold, Knightley, Phillip and Russell, Leonard, *The Pearl of Days*, Hamish Hamilton, 1960.

Johnson, Frank, *Out of Order*, Robson Books, 1982.

King, Cecil, *Strictly Personal*, Weidenfeld & Nicolson, 1969.

────── *The Cecil King Diary*, 1965–70, Jonathan Cape, 1972.

Knightley, Phillip, *The Second Oldest Profession*, André Deutsch, 1986.

Koss, Stephen, *The Rise and Fall of the Political Press in Britain*, Vol. 2, Hamish Hamilton, 1984.

Merthyr Tydfil, Merthyr Teachers' Centre Group, 1981.

Muggeridge, Malcolm, *Chronicles of Wasted Time*, Vol. 2: *The Infernal Grove*, Collins, 1973.

────── *Like It Was: the Diaries of Malcolm Muggeridge*, ed. John Bright-Holmes, Collins, 1981.

Newman, Peter C., *The Establishment Man*, McLelland & Stewart, Toronto, 1982.

Nicolson, Harold, *Diaries and Letters*, ed. Nigel Nicolson, three vols, Collins, 1966–68.

Thomson, Lord, *After I Was Sixty*, Hamish Hamilton, 1965.

Waugh, Evelyn, *The Letters of Evelyn Waugh*, ed. Mark Amory, Weidenfeld & Nicolson, 1980.

Way of the World, first series: 'The Best of Peter Simple', 1955–57, Daily Telegraph, 1957.

Wharton, Michael, *The Missing Will*, Chatto & Windus, 1984.

Williams, Marcia, *Inside No. 10*, Weidenfeld & Nicolson, 1972.

UNPUBLISHED

Three or four typed copies of an untitled, anonymous history of *The Daily Telegraph*, from its foundation until 1928, have survived.

Robert Smyly, grandson of Lord Buckland, quarried energetically in newspaper archives and works of reference to produce his admirable booklet *The Berry Brothers*, photocopied for circulation among the family in 1982.

The archive assembled by the late Donald McLachlan, first Editor of *The Sunday Telegraph*, and his widow Kitty, contains much illuminating material, including some fragments of autobiography.

The Lawson family archive contains useful material on the Burnhams' tenure of the *Telegraph*.

Lord Deedes, former Editor of *The Daily Telegraph*, generously put his collection of papers at my disposal.

Many members of the *Telegraph* staff past and present, from the Editor-in-Chief down, have contributed verbatim memories.

INDEX

NOTE: Ranks and titles are generally those applying at the time of mention in the text and may now have changed.